Leaves from an Autumn of Emergencies

Leaves from an Autumr

Samuel Hideo Yamashita

# of Emergencies

Selections from the Wartime Diaries of Ordinary Japanese

 The University of Hawai'i Press | Honolulu

© 2005 University of Hawai'i Press
All rights reserved
Printed in the United States of America
10 09 08 07 06   6 5 4 3 2

Library of Congress Cataloging-in-Publication Data
Leaves from an autumn of emergencies: selections
from the wartime diaries of ordinary Japanese /
Samuel Hideo Yamashita.
     p. cm.
Includes bibliographical references and index.
ISBN-10: 0-8248-2936-0 (hardcover : alk. paper)
ISBN-13: 978-0-8248-2936-0 (hardcover : alk. paper)
ISBN-10: 0-8248-2977-8 (pbk. : alk. paper)
ISBN-13: 978-0-8248-2977-3 (pbk. : alk. paper)
     1. World War, 1939–1945 — Personal narratives,
Japanese.   2. World War, 1939–1945 —Campaigns
— Japan.   I. Yamashita, Samuel Hideo.
D811.A2L37 2005
940.53'52'0922 — dc22   2005007999

Designed by April Leidig-Higgins
Printed by The Maple-Vail Book Manufacturing Group

To My Wife, Margaret

Contents

Acknowledgments

When I left Japan in 1975, after two and a half years of dissertation research on Itō Jinsai and Ogyū Sorai, a Japanese friend gave me a copy of *Kike wadatsumi no koe* (*Listen to the Voices from the Sea*), a famous collection of letters and diaries written by Japanese university students who perished in the Pacific War. It sat unread on my bookshelf for more than six years while I completed my dissertation. When I finally got around to reading this little classic, it inspired me to begin collecting and reading the wartime letters and diaries of ordinary Japanese.

In 1992 I began translating some of these letters and diaries, chiefly to use in my courses on modern Japan. Several years later, when I described what I was doing to Patricia Crosby, executive editor of the University of Hawai'i Press, and asked whether she would be interested in publishing a small collection of these translations, she responded positively, and she has enthusiastically supported the project from its inception. As I prepared the translations for publication, Frank Gibney and Hijino Shigeru convinced me to hire someone to help secure the permissions I would need to publish my translations. While I was searching for such a person, another old friend, William Steele, recommended his former student, historian Miyazawa Eriko, who, when I contacted her, graciously agreed to help. She has proved to be a superb literary agent, contacting authors, authors' families, and publishers on my behalf. This book would never have come to be without her hard work.

I would like to extend my deepest thanks and appreciation to those who gave me permission to publish my translations of the diaries in this volume: Itabashi Toshiko, Orihara Noboru, Sugita Keizō, Nomura Seiki, Kano Nobuhiro, Nagasaki Shōko, Kobayashi Keisuke, Aikawa Jindō, and Maki Mihōko. Without their cooperation, my translations could never have been published, and I can only hope that my rendering of the diaries does them justice.

Several colleagues read an early version of the introduction and made helpful suggestions: William Hauser, Lynne Miyake, Clyde Nishimoto, Lisa Tran, Helena Wall, and George Wilson. Eileen Cheng sent me a number of theoretical pieces that sharpened my interpretation of the diaries. And I am especially grateful to James Huffman and Stefan Tanaka, who read the manuscript for the press and offered both encouragement and thoughtful criticism. I have followed much of their good advice.

I could not have completed this project without the assistance of a number of librarians: Koide Izumi, formerly librarian at the International House of Japan and now director of the Resource Center for the History of Entrepreneurship, Shibusawa Memorial Museum, made a series of bibliographic searches that led me to the women's diaries; Higuchi Keiko, librarian at the International House of Japan, gave me valuable advice on copyright issues; Niki Kenji, curator of the Japanese collection, the Asia Library, at the University of Michigan, allowed me to copy a part of a 1946 edition of *Kuni no ayumi*. Miura Isamu, head of the Asian Studies collection at Honnold/Mudd Library at the Claremont Colleges, gathered biographical information about my diarists and identified obscure places and items mentioned in the diaries. Kaia Poorbaugh and Peggy Rhoades and their staff at the interlibrary loan service at Honnold/Mudd Library supplied the books and articles not available in our collection.

I also am indebted to many others as well: Liza Dalby offered informed advice on kimono terminology; Koike Masako explained a number of food items that appeared in the diaries; Koike Yoshiaki puzzled over some difficult Japanese surnames with me; Bill Nelson produced a fine and highly readable map; Mark Peattie and Tagaya Osamu checked my translations of naval aviation terminology; Takahashi Hisashi identified obscure military institutions; Takahashi Kazumi helped me make sense of many unclear passages; and Minh Huynh and Melanie Sisneros helped me prepare my illustrations. Yoshinami Sumiko, whom I met by chance on my one visit to Fukumitsu, generously shared her memories of the schoolgirls evacuated to her town, provided information about families mentioned in the Nakane diary, and explained words from the local dialect. My research assistant Malcolm McLean, the only person who can read my handwriting, typed up several of the diaries. Mieko Erber tracked down and confirmed the reading of some obscure place-names.

In addition to Patricia Crosby, I would like to acknowledge two other people at the University of Hawai'i Press: Masako Ikeda, who offered some early assistance with the permissions, and Cheri Dunn, the managing editor, who oversaw production of the book.

No one, however, has done more to see this book into print than my wife, Margaret Barrows Yamashita. I will never be able to repay her for the long hours she spent poring over the manuscript that became this book and for her wise and expert editorial recommendations.

Finally I would like to thank Dean Gary Kates and the research committee at Pomona College for their generous and unstinting support over the last four years. I received three grants for short research trips to Japan and a substantial

Sontag Research Fellowship, which funded still another trip to Japan, allowed me to hire someone to serve as my agent, and provided funding for usage fees.

Japanese names in this book follow the Japanese convention, with the surname preceding the given name. For example, Itabashi is the surname of the first diarist and Yasuo is his given name. The names of Japanese authors whose articles and books are written in a Western language are, however, listed in the Western order.

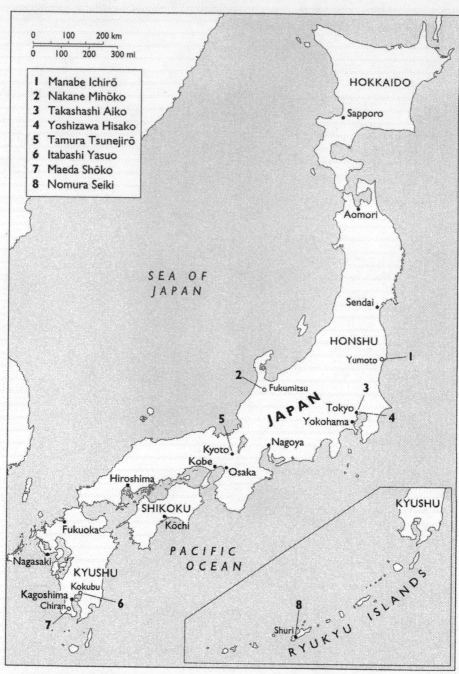

Locations of the eight diarists, 1945.

Introduction

ONE

In this autumn of emergencies,
when the life or death of the
state is at issue, the weak have
become food for the strong.
—Tamura Tsunejirō,
November 11, 1944

The Pacific War and Ordinary Japanese

The wartime diaries of ordinary Japanese are not well known outside Japan. The reason is simple: almost nothing written by ordinary Japanese during the war is available in English translation. Moreover, the few wartime diaries that have been translated into English are those written by journalists, intellectuals, and politicians. Examples are the journalist Ishikawa Tatsuzō's *Ikite iru heitai* (*Soldiers Alive*), a firsthand account of Japan's disastrous invasion of China, and the wartime diary of Kiyosawa Kiyoshi, a well-known liberal journalist. *Kike wadatsumi no koe* (*Listen to the Voices from the Sea*) is a translation of a collection of letters and excerpts from the wartime diaries of university students who died in the war.[1] Although *Soldiers Alive*, Kiyosawa's diary, and the university students' letters and diary excerpts are interesting, they are not very typical accounts. Far more typical are the wartime diaries kept by servicemen, male civilians who remained behind on the home front, women, teenagers, and children. But despite the thousands of these that have survived, only one has been translated into English.[2]

For many years, most Western historians either left World War II out of their histories of modern Japan or said little about it—because of the cold war. In 1947, Japan became an important ally of the United States, which required that the once hated enemy be recast as a friend.[3] This new, and more positive, postwar view of Japan engendered a narrative account of its modern history that highlighted its rapid transformation from an isolated feudal kingdom into a modern, Western-style state and offered Japan as a success story and a model for Third World countries. Obviously, World War II presented something of a problem for the writers of this new narrative of Japan's modernization, which they solved by describing the conflict as an aberration and downplaying its significance.[4] Most Western historians writing about modern Japan in the 1950s, 1960s, and 1970s embraced this Whiggish view of Japan.[5]

The first Westerners to write about the war and its impact on ordinary Japanese were American and British journalists. John Hersey's *Hiroshima*, which described the horror of the atomic bombing of Hiroshima, appeared in the *New Yorker* in 1946 and became a minor classic. Several years later, Frank Gibney wrote *Five Gentlemen of Japan*, one of the first attempts to humanize the erstwhile enemy. John Toland's *The Rising Sun: The Decline and Fall of the Japanese Empire, 1936–1945*, published in 1970, offered the first general account of the Pacific War and won a Pulitzer Prize in 1971. Toland described his book as "a factual saga of people caught up in the flood of the most overwhelming war of mankind, told as it happened — muddled, ennobling, disgraceful, frustrating, full of paradox."[6] Around the same time, two books on Emperor Hirohito appeared — Leonard Moseley's *Hirohito, Emperor of Japan* and David Bergamini's *Japan's Imperial Conspiracy* — both by journalists. That journalists gave us the first accounts of the war is not surprising, since as one literary critic pointed out, the "modernist" prose of midcentury American journalism was well suited to war writing, as the success of Ernest Hemingway, Ernie Pyle, and John Hersey — to cite the most popular examples — shows.[7]

These journalistic accounts of the war have both strengths and weaknesses. Generally, the best are highly readable and thus reached a large audience interested in the Pacific War. But most of the journalists writing about Japan — with the exception of Gibney and Bergamini — were not fluent enough in Japanese to read untranslated documents and thus necessarily relied on English-language materials, research assistants who could read Japanese, and interviews conducted with the help of interpreters. When Toland was doing the research for *The Rising Sun*, for example, he interviewed 365 people, ranging from notables involved in important decisions, battles, and campaigns to ordinary Japanese, Chinese, and Filipinos who offered their own firsthand accounts of the war. Although Toland's book won a Pulitzer Prize, one scholar criticized him for relying so heavily on interviews: "How reliable," the reviewer asked, "is anyone's memory after twenty-five years?"[8]

Bergamini's *Japan's Imperial Conspiracy* raised even more scholarly hackles. When Bergamini asserted that Emperor Hirohito was involved in the planning and execution of the war, scholarly reviewers took him to task for not providing sufficient documentary evidence for his bold claims and for misreading important documents or mistranslating key words. Richard Storry ended his review by observing that "the material that is presented does not support a foundation on which to build a theory of imperial conspiracy." Alvin Coox spoke of Bergamini's "misleading use of sources to buttress a tortured thesis." Shumpei Okamoto was even more dismissive. "Mr. Bergamini's *Japan's Imperial Conspiracy* is no history," he wrote. "The book may be accepted as a fiction, for a simple reason that it presents an imaginative plot."[9] Suffice it to say that much of the current journalistic writing on the Pacific War exhibits the same strengths and weaknesses as Bergamini's book does.[10]

In the 1970s, around the time the Toland, Moseley, and Bergamini books appeared, the first scholarly studies of the Pacific War were published.[11] The first of these, David Steinberg's *Philippine Collaboration in World War Two*, dealt with Japan's occupation of Southeast Asia. This was followed by two other works on the Japanese presence in Southeast Asia: Joyce Lebra's *Jungle Alliance: Japan and the Indian National Army* and *Japanese-Trained Armies in Southeast Asia: Independence and Volunteer Forces in World War II*. Thomas Havens' "Women and War in Japan, 1937–1945" and *Valley of Darkness: The Japanese People and World War Two* were the first works on the Japanese home front, and Paul Dull's *A Battle History of the Imperial Japanese Navy (1941–1945)* offered the first scholarly account of the Japanese navy in World War II.

In the next two decades, nearly two dozen new scholarly works were published, dealing with different facets of the Pacific War: diplomatic relations, military campaigns and engagements, life on the home front, censorship, wartime culture, and the imperial institution. The most notable of these are Akira Iriye's *Power and Culture: The Japanese American War, 1941–1945*, an innovative study of the political and cultural dimensions of U.S.–Japanese relations; Alvin Coox's *Nomonhan: Japan against Russia, 1939*, a prize-winning account of the battle of Nomonhan; and John Dower's *War without Mercy: Race and Power in the Pacific War*, an analysis of wartime propaganda that won several prizes and had wide influence. *Kaigun: Strategy, Tactics, and Technology in the Imperial Japanese Navy, 1887–1941*, by Mark Peattie and David Evans, set a new standard for studies of the Japanese military. Peter Duus, Mark Peattie, and Ramon Meyers also gave us several fine volumes on Japanese overseas expansion. The first book-length studies of Japanese war crimes and atrocities began appearing in the 1990s: Gavin Daws' *Prisoners of the Japanese: POWs of World War II in the Pacific*, and Sheldon Harris' *Factories of Death: Japanese Biological Warfare, 1932–1945*. Also noteworthy are Yuki Tanaka's *Hidden Horrors: Japanese War Crimes in World War II* and Yoshimi Yoshiaki's *Comfort Women: Sexual Slavery in the Japanese Military during World War II*, both of which are translations of works originally published in Japanese.

This growing attention to the Pacific War and its broad impact, although long overdue, might be seen as part of two larger developments in recent Western historical writing on war. Beginning in the 1970s, American and European military historians began to look beyond battles and generals and to correct the shortcomings of the conventional "bugle and trumpet" histories traditionally favored in their field. In 1984, Edward Coffman and Peter Karsten referred to a "new military history" that examined the whole array of ideas, practices, and institutions that made war possible. Inspired by the "new social history," Coffman, Karsten, and others turned away from war to the military institutions that recruited, trained, deployed, and provisioned troops; the societies that supported the war effort; and the cultures that affirmed military service and war. Many of the best examples of the "new military history" were written in the 1970s and 1980s and continued to be published in the 1990s.[12]

In the 1980s, German historians began to write what they called "histories of everyday life" (G. *Alltagsgeschichte*), the second important development in the contemporary study of war. Critical of institutional and comparative histories of Germany under Hitler that dealt with "big structures, large processes, huge comparisons," the historians of everyday life focused on the "little people" (G. *kleine Leute*), "those who have remained largely anonymous in history." They also noted that historical change at the level of everyday life is conspicuously "uneven" (G. *unegal*) and quite unlike the apparent smoothness and uniformity of historical change conceptualized from above, as, for example, in histories that highlight "modernization." Their studies revealed that ordinary people are never passive but always respond to historical change by interpreting what they are experiencing in their own terms and then sharing those experiences with their families, neighbors, friends, and coworkers and expressing their feelings about them in "*privatized arenas* of (self-) expression."[13] The most interesting examples of this new historical approach are the studies that explain why the great majority of Germans supported the Nazi regime.[14]

Both the "new military history" and the histories of everyday life offer new ways of looking at the Pacific War and encourage scholars to turn their attention from the political and military elites to the general population. Havens' "Women and War in Japan, 1937–1945" and *Valley of Darkness* anticipate *Alltagsgeschichte*'s interest in ordinary people, as does Dower's brilliant *Embracing Defeat: Japan in the Wake of World War Two*. Some of Edward Drea's work and the new studies of Japanese war crimes and atrocities signal the movement away from conventional "bugle and trumpet" military history. The small but growing body of scholarship on "comfort women" exhibits the "active identification and involvement" with their subjects that is the hallmark of the histories of everyday life in wartime Germany.[15]

These new perspectives also raise important questions. First, did the general population in the Japanese home islands, Okinawa, and the colonies condone their government's foreign and domestic policies and their military's strategies and tactics? Second, how successful was the wartime government in generating support for the war effort? Third, is there any evidence that ordinary people had misgivings about these policies, strategies, and tactics and opposed or resisted them? Finally, what responsibility, if any, do ordinary Japanese and Japanese colonial subjects have for the war and the way it was conducted?

The last question is a difficult one because in both Japan and the West, the prevailing official and popular accounts of the war have held the top wartime military and civilian leaders, excluding the emperor, responsible for planning and executing the war. As one of the first postwar Japanese textbooks put it in 1946, "the Japanese people suffered terribly from the long war. Military leaders suppressed the people, launched a stupid war, and caused this disaster."[16] When it concluded its proceedings on November 12, 1948, the International Military Tribunal of the Far East found all the surviving Class A war criminals guilty of at least one but usually several of the counts brought against them and thus also responsible for the war. Seven were executed, and the rest were given prison sentences ranging from shorter terms to life imprisonment. The Allies also tried six thousand servicemen and officials — Japanese nationals and colonial subjects — as Class B and C war criminals and executed 920. In addition, the Allied Occupation authorities purged 201,815 other politicians, military men, and business leaders for their contributions to the war effort.[17] No one, however, held the general population — the "Japanese people" — accountable for what they did during the war.

Japanese scholars were the first to look closely at the issue of culpability. Their research led them to ascribe responsibility for the war not only to military and civilian leaders but also to Emperor Hirohito and his advisers, bureaucrats, businessmen, intellectuals, writers, artists, and those who served in the wartime organizations that mobilized and controlled ordinary Japanese. In the 1980s and 1990s, even members of the Buddhist establishment recognized their community's contributions to the war effort. Since the 1990s, a number of Western scholars have followed the lead of their Japanese colleagues. Herbert Bix made a powerful case for holding the emperor responsible for the war. John Dower offered a detailed account of the concerted and calculated effort of Allied Occupation authorities to save the emperor from persecution. Brian Victoria documented the Zen establishment's support for the war, and James Heisig, John Moraldo, and others argued for the complicity of the famous Kyoto school of philosophers and the broader Buddhist community. But most Japanese historians who have looked into this issue do not hold ordinary Japanese responsible for the war, and many insist that they really were victims.[18] Historian Carol Gluck challenged this view:

The victims' history repeated in the post-Showa retrospectives omitted a painful lesson of World War II since learned around the world: that it is not possible to wage a total war with 28, 280, or even 28,000 people and that the responsibility for war lies far more broadly in society than was earlier believed, or hoped. Just as in Europe, where it is no longer possible to explain such things solely in terms of Hitler, Mussolini, or Pétain, the ways in which vast numbers of ordinary people were entwined in the complex mesh of war must be counted. Even those who did not actually march or collaborate are now judged as participants. It takes both states and societies—which is to say the individuals who comprise them—to make a total war.[19]

Gluck's challenge raises an important question that must be answered to complete our understanding of the Pacific War: were ordinary Japanese responsible for the war?

Wartime Japanese Diaries

For the Japanese, the war began on July 12, 1937, when their armies invaded China, and they had lost 185,647 men even before the December 7–8, 1941, attacks on the Allied possessions in the Pacific. By August 15, 1945, when Japan surrendered to the Allies, well over two million Japanese—both combatants and civilians—had perished. Indeed, when the broader Japanese population, Japan's colonial subjects, and those living in areas invaded or controlled by Japan are included, as many as twenty million people died.[20]

In gauging the impact of the Pacific War on ordinary Japanese and assessing their responsibility for the war, there is no better source than their wartime diaries. Diaries relate fairly directly their writers' experiences and have an immediacy and vividness that memoirs lack. Furthermore, unlike memoirs, the contents of diaries are not filtered through the selective haze of retrospection or shaped by the demands of ex post facto rationalization. Because it was dangerous for Japanese to express anything that could be construed as leftist, defeatist, or unpatriotic, the abundance of wartime diaries is striking and indicates that many Japanese felt strongly enough about what was happening to record their innermost thoughts and feelings.[21] Teenagers and children, however, kept diaries during the war for other reasons, as will be explained shortly.

Most of the wartime diaries that have been published were written by Japanese servicemen, and long excerpts from two of them are included here.[22] The first is from the diary of a navy pilot named Itabashi Yasuo, who saw action in the Pacific in 1944 as a member of the 503rd Air Wing.[23] Itabashi was even shot down at one point and survived, but it took him five months to get back to his unit. When he did, he discovered that it "had been decimated" and that he was one of only a handful of survivors. He volunteered for a special-attack unit—the official designation for what is known in the West as a *kamikaze* (divine wind) unit—but was ordered to train pilots for several months before flying off on his final mission at the very end of the war. The second diary is that of an ordinary soldier, Nomura Seiki, a private stationed on Okinawa when it was invaded by Allied forces in the spring of 1945.[24] Nomura survived the invasion and hid in bunkers and caves with other stragglers until he was persuaded to give up on September 14, 1945, almost exactly a month after Japan surrendered. His diary graphically documents the last months and weeks of the war as they were experienced by an ordinary soldier.

Some of the home-front diaries were written by men. One of the most interesting was kept by Tamura Tsunejirō, the seventy-five-year-old proprietor of a billiards parlor in Kyoto.[25] Fiercely independent and outspoken, Tamura appears to have recorded exactly what he was thinking and feeling. Moreover, he spent the war in Kyoto, one of the few Japanese cities to escape the systematic Allied bombing, which makes his diary all the more exceptional and valuable. A lengthy excerpt is included here.

Surprisingly few women's diaries have survived, and only six have been published. Although this might suggest that few women kept diaries, I suspect there were other reasons, including the burdens of daily life during the war and the women's reluctance to draw attention to themselves. Of the six published women's diaries, one had actually been discarded and was saved by an observant bookseller, and another was initially published under the name of the diarist's husband. All were written by women living in cities during the war. I have translated long selections from two of these diaries. The first is by Takahashi Aiko, a housewife and mother of two teenage children who lived in Hiroo in central Tokyo with her physician husband. The second was written by Yoshizawa Hisako, a young working woman who lived in the Asagaya area in western Tokyo.[26] Both women are surprisingly frank in their diaries and give us not only their own thoughts and feelings about the war as they experienced it but also their accounts of the dramatic changes occurring in Tokyo in the last year of the war. They offer, as well, a glimpse of the impact of the war on women and domestic life.

If women are underrepresented in the corpus of wartime Japanese diaries, teenagers and children are not. Their diaries are numerous, largely because the Japanese authorities required the teenagers who were mobilized for war work and the children who were evacuated from the big cities to keep diaries, which they periodically submitted to their superiors or teachers for what one teenage diarist called "diary checks" (J. *nikki kensa*). As we might expect, the evacuated children often were homesick, hungry, and unhappy, and their diaries allowed their teachers to monitor their morale. Besides being an invaluable source of information about how the war affected children, what makes these diaries doubly interesting to historians are their teachers' comments, which often survived as well.

After the war ended, many citizens' groups and organizations collected and published these diaries, thereby making them available to a broader readership. I chose three for this book. The first is a short diary kept by Maeda Shōko, a teenage girl mobilized to work at an army air base near her home in southern Kyushu, where she got to know the pilots who flew to their deaths on "special attacks." The other two were kept by children—one by an eleven-year-old boy, Manabe Ichirō, and the other by a nine-year-old girl, Nakane Mihōko—who had been evacuated in 1944/1945 from Tokyo to small towns in northern and central Japan.[27]

Despite the abundance of wartime diaries written by Japanese, most Western scholars have made little use of them. Although Paul Dull's history of the Japanese navy during World War II relies heavily on official war diaries and daily action reports, and Thomas Havens used personal diaries to add texture to his descriptions of wartime life in *Valley of Darkness*, they are the exception. Most historians have ignored the diaries kept by servicemen or the letters they wrote home from the front lines. In her *Kamikaze, Cherry Blossoms, and Nationalisms: The Militarization of Aesthetics in Japanese History*, anthropologist Emiko Ohnuki-Tierney analyzes four diaries kept by young men who were members of special-attack units, although only three contain entries written during the months and weeks before their deaths. Albert Axell and Hideaki Kase also used diaries in their *Kamikaze: Japan's Suicide Gods*, although they do not always identify their sources.

Several scholars, however, have recognized the value of firsthand postwar accounts, memoirs, and interviews. Alvin Coox's *Nomonhan: Japan against Russia* is, without a doubt, the best account of the Japanese military written by a Western scholar. Coox interviewed nearly four hundred survivors of the battle of Nomonhan and based his study on their accounts. In 1986, the *Asahi shinbun*, one of Japan's leading daily newspapers, invited its readers to write about "the war" (J. *sensō*), and more than four thousand responded. Frank Gibney and Beth Carey selected and translated three hundred of the eleven hundred letters that the *Asahi* printed in 1986/1987, which were published as *Sensō: The Japanese Remember the Pacific War*. Theodore and Haruko Cook interviewed nearly several dozen Japanese and Koreans about their experiences during the war and published parts of their interviews in *Japan at War: An Oral History*.

Even so, Western scholars who can read Japanese have missed an opportunity to use the small mountain of Japanese servicemen's diaries to study what military historian John Keegan termed the "soldier's view."[28] Keegan's insistence that historians look at "why ordinary soldiers fight" is typical of the new military history mentioned earlier, and his *The Face of Battle* is an exemplary study of the experience of war in three important battles—Agincourt, Waterloo, and the Somme. Clearly, the great number of Japanese servicemen's diaries would allow scholars to generalize with some certainty about the ordinary Japanese soldier and why he fought as he did.

Similarly, home-front diaries could be used to reconstruct what the historians of everyday life call the "material circumstances" and "inner world" of everyday life in wartime Japan. They would permit scholars to focus on the "lives and sufferings of those who are frequently labeled . . . the 'small people'" and to reconstruct "their work and nonwork . . . housing and homelessness; clothing and nakedness; eating and hunger, love and hate." No doubt these diaries would reveal what historian Geoff Eley described as "the ambiguities and contradictions of ordinary people's perceptions and behaviors as they actually live their lives."[29] Most important, the home-front diaries would reveal whether ordinary Japanese were truly victims of the war, as many have argued for so long, or patriotic supporters.

My collection of wartime Japanese diaries has a more modest aim: it offers a glimpse of how the war affected eight ordinary Japanese people and how each responded. A close reading of the diaries in this volume suggests tentative answers to questions about popular support for the wartime government's policies and the military's strategies and tactics, as well as opposition and resistance to them on both the home front and overseas.

Japan in Wartime

Japan's wartime diaries would be hard to understand without knowing who wrote them—their age, gender, education, social standing, and occupation—and without knowing the conditions prevailing where and when these people wrote their journals, whether on the home front or battlefield and at the start, middle, or end of the war. Diaries also are cultural artifacts, so we cannot overlook the cultures that their writers embrace and the discourses they invoke or allude to—whether civilian, military, religious, secular, urban, rural, male, or female. In short, diaries must be carefully historicized before they can be mined for information or interpreted. Accordingly, the readers of these diaries first need to have some grasp of the war itself, not only its major campaigns and battles, but also the changing situation in the Japanese home islands.

The first six months of the Pacific War — from December 7, 1941, through May 1942 — were an exhilarating time for Japan. At lightning speed, Japanese forces streamed into Hong Kong, the Philippines, Burma, Malaya, and the Dutch East Indies, either beating American and British forces into submission or driving them into retreat. Indeed, the impressive string of Japanese victories made it seem as though everything that had been said about the superiority of the vaunted Japanese military was true. By the spring of 1942, the Japanese controlled much of Asia: in addition to their colonies of Taiwan and Korea and their puppet regime in Manchuria, they held much of the Chinese littoral, most of Southeast Asia, the Philippines, and other formerly American-held islands in the South Pacific, holdings that comprised a formidable wartime empire.

Then in the spring of 1942, the tide began to turn, in two decisive battles in May and June. The first was the battle of the Coral Sea, which took place on May 7 and 8 and effectively stopped the Japanese advance toward New Guinea. The second was the battle of Midway in early June, which halted the Japanese advance toward Hawaii. Early in the following year the Allies began to take back the Japanese-held islands in the South Pacific. They took Guadalcanal in February 1943 and many more in 1944 — Kwajalein in February, Saipan in June, Guam in August, and the Palau Group and northern New Guinea in September. In March 1945, the Allies secured Iwo Jima, which gave them an airfield less than seven hundred miles from Tokyo. Although extremely costly in terms of men and matériel, the island-hopping campaign was important, since the anticipated Allied invasion of the Japanese home islands would be launched from the Pacific side. The crowning blow for the Japanese came in the Philippines in October 1944: the Allied victory in what is now known as the battle of Leyte Gulf established, once and for all, American naval superiority in the Pacific.

As Japan was losing the war in the Pacific, it was losing it at home as well. The Japanese had not expected the war to be a long one and thus had been slow to transform the domestic economy into a war economy. As a result, industrial production actually fell during the war, for several reasons. Allied submarines were sinking Japanese ships at will, so raw materials from Southeast Asia were not reaching Japan. There also were problems, "qualitative deficiencies," with the labor force and a poor program of distribution. At this point, even the vaunted "Japanese spirituality" was not adequate compensation.

One of the war's greatest impacts on ordinary Japanese and Japanese colonial subjects in the home islands and overseas possessions was the drafting of men and boys to fight in the war. Although the Japanese army had been drafting twenty-year-olds since 1873, less than a third of those eligible were actually inducted. Most failed the physical exams. But this changed in 1937 when the Japanese invaded China. Between 1937 and 1940, more than 300,000 men were conscripted each year, and nearly every family either sent sons, nephews, cousins, fathers, or uncles into the military or had relatives or friends who were drafted. By 1940 more than a million Japanese were serving overseas in some capacity. After the attack on Pearl Harbor, even more men and boys were conscripted. In 1943 the growing demand for new recruits led to the drafting of college students, and by the end of the war even middle-aged men were being taken.[30]

The public send-off of these recruits was one of the most important rituals of the war. In the cities, family members and others from the recruit's immediate and surrounding neighborhood participated in his send-off. First they went to the local Shintō shrine, where they prayed for his success on the battlefield, and then walked the recruit to the closest train station, where they put him on the train that carried him off to war.

Rural send-offs were even more elaborate, perhaps because they took place in smaller, more stable, and more intimate communities which supported the war more enthusiastically. One rural recruit described his send-off in March 1945:

> The house was crowded that evening with guests who gathered for the farewell party. This party was much like the others, with animated conversation and bursts of laughter. It was surprising that everyone had more than enough to eat and drink; the food shortage had become severe even in this farming community. The kinds of food suitable to serve at parties had long been unavailable, I thought.
>
> Early the next morning, I was ready to leave for Tokyo to report for duty but felt somewhat restless. Soon people would arrive to say their good-byes, deliver their good wishes and words of encouragement. Two women came to the door in the uniform of the Japan National Defense Women's League. . . . The relatives who had attended the party arrived. "Iwao, stay well. We know you'll be a strong and brave soldier," said an aunt. More neighbors and schoolchildren joined us and were served a cup of saké or tea with which to drink a farewell toast to me.
>
> Three men from the Veterans Association arrived in their khaki uniforms. This signified that it was time for everyone to line up behind them for a procession to the neighborhood shrine. The village people had gone through the ritual repeatedly in recent months and were accustomed to the practice.[31]

This recruit's party then marched to the village office, where the mayor and spokesmen for various patriotic organizations and other recruits waited. Speeches followed. The recruits were allowed to say a few words and then were marched to the village train station and sent on their way. This particular recruit was sent to Manchuria in August 1945. He never fired a shot and was captured by Soviet forces and held for nearly three years but returned alive.

Other recruits were not so lucky. As the Allies recovered from their earlier losses and began their island-hopping campaign in 1943, the number of Japanese combat deaths and casualties rose sharply. When their remains were brought home, the ritual of sending off recruits was simply reversed. Family members, local officials, and representatives of the same patriotic organizations that had sent off the men with rousing orations met the train carrying their ashes and, with their remains, marched solemnly back to the village, where the villagers and schoolchildren stood waiting "to greet the spirits of the war dead."[32] As the war continued, more and more "spirits" were welcomed home in this way. These rituals of sending off and welcoming back local men and boys brought home the war to every neighborhood and village in the Japanese empire.

The war touched the home front in several other ways as well. The rationing of food and other scarce commodities was universal and had a great impact. Like conscription, its effects began to be felt well before 1941, for the government had been controlling and rationing scarce commodities since 1938, when voluntary austerity was encouraged and college students were asked to give up one meal a week. Later that year, mandatory austerity campaigns resulted in the rationing of a growing list of commodities. Consumption of every imaginable resource of strategic value was restricted, including gasoline, coal, and telephones. In 1940 sugar, charcoal, and matches began to be rationed, and in February 1941 a system for rationing rice was created. As vital commodities became more and more scarce, substitutes were found. For example, when rice consumption was restricted late in 1940, saké was made not from rice but from sweet potatoes and acorns. Shark, salmon, and whale skin replaced leather. The result was, not surprisingly, a drop in the quality of everyday goods, as one Tokyo housewife discovered when she bought a "wooden bucket": "When I tried using it," she wrote, "the water just ran through it." In 1940 the government imposed controls on the production of cotton goods, and in 1941 it rationed clothing, with the result, observed the same housewife, that "our clothes are in tatters, and it's almost as though we've been defeated in battle."[33]

By 1943 the shortages of food became acute, and in 1944 the basic elements of a meal — rice, fish, soy sauce, miso, and sugar — began to disappear from Japanese tables. There was simply less and less food. The growing food shortages had a huge impact on the home-front population. Now many people were constantly hungry, and for good reason. In 1944, the average caloric intake was 17 percent lower than it was on December 8, 1941. On average, a Japanese person consumed 1,925 to 1,975 calories a day until 1944 but only 1,793 calories a day in 1945. In Kyoto, this caloric intake dropped to 1,677 in the summer of 1945, and by the end of the war, the official food ration provided just a meager 1,040 calories. Malnutrition and illness caused by the shortages became more common.[34]

Many people tried to find food on their own. Housewives watched for special offerings, and family members were sent to line up for scarce commodities and foods. Most city dwellers had no choice but to buy food on the black market, even though it was illegal and strongly discouraged. When the black market ran out of supplies, they went directly to the farmers living on the outskirts of the city or in neighboring prefectures, often traveling for several hours. On any given day beginning in the fall of 1943, several thousand Tokyoites, most of them children, would go to the outlying farms to buy fresh vegetables. One Tokyo housewife left the city at least once, and sometimes twice, a week during the summer, and one filial daughter spent entire days traveling by train from Kyoto to farms several hours away to buy sweet potatoes, and on one occasion, she even went as far as Tokyo.[35]

Equally as affecting as the drafting of local men and the shortages of food and other commodities was the government's attempt to mobilize the home-front population. In the spring of 1938, the Diet passed a national mobilization bill that called for the formation of "community councils" (J. chōnaikai or chōkai), and the Home Ministry, which had been creating these bodies since 1930, assumed responsibility for implementing the bill. In the cities each community council consisted of several hundred households, and in the countryside the "village council" (J. buraku-kai) was usually made up of a single village . These councils were designed to carry out savings-bond and cleanup campaigns, conduct air-raid drills, and collect taxes. By 1940, there were 197,458 community councils: 79,028 in the cities and towns and 118,430 in the countryside. Their members met between the twentieth and twenty-fifth of every month.[36]

Even more significant for ordinary Japanese was the formation of a second government-sponsored organization, the so-called neighborhood associations (J. tonari-gumi). These neighborhood groups usually consisted of nine contiguous households.[37] In September 1940 the government began creating these bodies, and by 1942 they numbered 1.3 million in Japan and its colonies. The neighborhood associations had seven official functions:

1. They met with the community councils.
2. They coordinated air and fire defense in each neighborhood.
3. They watched for spies.
4. They prevented crime.
5. They sold savings bonds.
6. They implemented government reforms.
7. They distributed food and other rationed goods.

The neighborhood association served as the channel through which the war reached each household in the Japanese empire: circulars were passed from house to house transmitting the latest government orders, news of distributions, and the schedule for one or another meeting or drill. Meetings were held on the eighth day of every month and whenever else they were necessary, and each household was expected to send a representative. Neighborhood association members served their small communities in other ways as well: they took turns distributing food and other rationed goods, patrolling their neighborhoods, standing watch, serving in bucket brigades, and spying on one another.[38]

The neighborhood associations had an interesting gender dimension. Although the captains of the associations usually were men, because they had jobs or businesses their wives ended up doing all or most of the work and spending their days toiling "for the sake of the neighborhood assocation."[39] Since most of the assistant captains also were women, women effectively ran many of the neighborhood associations and assumed such major responsibilities as picking up and distributing increasingly scarce commodities like food, soap, shoes, and paper. This meant that they were caring for not only their own families but also the rest of their immediate neighborhood. Women also were full participants in the air-defense drills and worked on the bucket brigades that went into action when the cities were bombed. As happened in the United States and Europe as well, women thus came out of their homes and joined the war effort on the home front.

Japan's community councils and neighborhood associations had another noteworthy dimension. In the cities, they brought together individuals and families who, owing to differences in wealth, occupation, social status, and education, normally did not interact much with one another. The authorities were well aware of the problems this might cause, as the government-issued *A Reader for Neighborhood Associations* explained to its readers:

> Up to now, the main purpose of neighborhood associations has been social, and there is nothing wrong with that. But as neighborhood associations are steadily solidified, they will be obliged to cooperate more for daily living

and have some connection with distributing commodities. . . . The associations that will be hardest to set up will be the ones in exclusive residential areas. The main reason for this is the great difference in the standard of living, both material and psychological, among their members. . . . Because they find that interaction is difficult, they don't want to associate with poor people. Thus if we can only eliminate this cause, we can set up meetings and expect to solidify the neighborhood associations.[40]

Nonetheless, the interclass tensions persisted, often surfacing in the wartime diaries.

These tensions notwithstanding, the community councils and neighborhood associations generally functioned as designed, and they served another important purpose as well: the government used them in its "spiritual mobilization" campaigns. For example, when the community councils met between the nineteenth and twenty-fifth of every month, the assembled representatives discussed not only the obvious topics — air defense, savings programs, and collection drives — but also war goals, imperial worship, and silent prayers for the dead. Much the same was true for the neighborhood associations, which met once a month, initially on the first of every month but then, starting in 1942, on the eighth. Besides the usual business of scheduling cleanups, night patrols, and food distributions, neighborhood association members spent their meetings listening to NHK broadcasts, reading *The Way of the Subjects*, and discussing war aims.[41]

The government made good use of another powerful weapon to maintain popular support for the war: censorship. Government censorship of the press had long been established in Japan, and it simply was intensified after the outbreak of the Sino-Japanese War in the summer of 1937. That September the cabinet formed its own press service, the Cabinet Information Office, which in December was renamed the Cabinet Information Bureau. With its staff of six hundred, the bureau controlled reporting on the war, overseeing what appeared in the press and how stories were presented to the public and deciding who would offer interpretations of the news. A year earlier, the government merged two private news services to form the Dōmei News Service, which functioned as a semiprivate news service and became the "only official service for out-of-town and international news." Together, the Cabinet Information Bureau and Dōmei attempted to control information about the war.[42]

Because the censors required that the relevant office clear articles before they were published, the press sections of the army and navy cleared any news stories dealing with military affairs; the Foreign Ministry and Ministry of Greater East Asia handled international stories; and the Censorship Department of the Home

Ministry's Police Bureau vetted everything else. The staggering volume of censored material suggests that the censors did their job well: in 1943, 90,000 news items were submitted for clearance; 77,000 (87%) were approved, and 13,000 (13%) were rejected. This practice, begun in 1937, worked surprisingly well. According to historian Ben-Ami Shillony, "there was seldom a need to admonish or punish a newspaper. Consequently no major newspaper was shut down during the war and no editor of a major daily newspaper was arrested or prosecuted."[43]

The government controlled the press in other ways, too, with its reduction of the number of newspapers and magazines being one of the most dramatic. This winnowing process began in September 1940 when the Tokyo and Osaka branches of the *Asahi shinbun* merged. Then in 1942 several newspapers joined to form the *Yomiuri hōchi*, the *Tōkyō shinbun*, and the *Nippon sangyō keizai*. In 1943 the *Tōkyō mainichi* and the *Osaka mainichi* became the *Mainichi shinbun*. The effect on the smaller newspapers was even more drastic. At the beginning of the war, there were several hundred small newspapers, but by the end of 1943, only fifty-four remained. Two other measures were equally as dramatic. The first was the reduction in the size of the newspapers, a process actually begun during the Sino-Japanese War (1937–1945). Morning editions were shortened from eight to fourteen pages to four to five, and evening editions from six to eight pages to two to four. Magazines got similar treatment. In 1936 there were 11,400 magazines, but by late 1939 only 7,700 had survived. The number of women's magazines dropped from eighty to seventeen by 1941, and that of arts magazines, from thirty-nine to eight.[44]

In addition, the government used professional organizations to control the press. In May 1941 the Japanese Newspaper League was founded, and although membership was voluntary, the league's control over newsprint encouraged newspapers to join. Indeed, the newspapers not only joined; they kept their writers in line. In July 1942 the league was renamed the Japan Newspaper Association. Finally, the Cabinet Information Bureau created the Patriotic Publicists Association in December 1942 and made it clear that it expected this body "to take the lead in the empire's internal and external ideological warfare."[45] The editors of newspapers or magazines that published articles of which the government censors disapproved usually were warned the first time and then were censured if they continued to publish such articles. Although most journalists toed the official line, to their credit many worked hard to tell the truth, or as much of the truth as they could slip by their censors. As a result, some got into trouble with the authorities, were blacklisted, or lost their jobs. But most cooperated with the government and became willing collaborators.[46]

Predictably, censorship affected the content of the print media, although how much it did so depended on when a particular article was published and what it was about. As a rule, the reporting on the European theater was more accurate and timely and remained so for the duration of the war. Breaking war news in Europe — especially news about Japan's Axis allies — was reported in Japanese newspapers within days. For example, one Tokyo housewife heard about Italy's surrender just one day after it took place and about the Soviet Army's breakthrough into Berlin as it was happening. Home-front news also was surprisingly accurate, perhaps because it had to be. As the Allied forces pushed closer and closer to Japan and the bombing of the home islands began, the Japanese people had to be kept abreast of the latest developments in order to prepare for the Allied attacks. Bomber sightings as well as air-raid warnings and alerts and damage and casualty reports were broadcast on the radio almost instantaneously. In fact, the reports of bomb damage were so accurate that commuters could use them to plot their route to work each day. One commuter listened to the latest damage reports every morning before she left for work, choosing a particular train or trolley on the basis of what she heard.[47]

The reporting on the war situation in Asia was different. Until events began to turn against Japan in June 1942 — when the Japanese suffered a huge defeat in the battle of Midway — the reporting was good and generally truthful. But after Midway, it always was inaccurate and full of misinformation. Desperate for any news about the fighting in the war zones, Japanese scoured the papers, carefully reading between the lines. Upon hearing of a cabinet reshuffle, one home-front civilian wondered, "What exactly is happening? It's like picking out colors in the dark." Another knew that the newspapers were "not reliable" but confessed that he still read them anyway, out of force of habit.[48]

By the fall of 1943, it was clear that the war was not going well for Japan. Deferments for college students over the age of nineteen who were not majoring in engineering or a science were ended, and 130,000 students were quickly inducted. In September, teenage girls over the age of fourteen were drafted into the "Girls' Volunteer Labor Corps," and 2,880,877 were mobilized over the next six months. Then in October the government decided to evacuate the big cities. The hope was that mothers, children, the elderly, the infirm, and those not involved in war work would leave the cities and move in with relatives in the countryside. The general response was less than enthusiastic, however. The government even released a documentary entitled *Evacuation* which showed Japanese cities in flames, obviously hoping that this would encourage more people to evacuate.[49]

The following year brought even more evidence that things were going poorly for Japan. In April 1944, the government mobilized all children over ten years of age for war work in factories and farms. Then on June 30, the government issued its "Outline for Encouraging the Evacuation of Schoolchildren," which ordered third through sixth graders to leave the major cities. Three hundred thousand children already had left the cities for the countryside, and in accordance with the latest government plan, the evacuation of those remaining began in August 1944. By the end of March 1945, 450,000 children had been evacuated.[50] They were sent to rural communities and housed in temples, shrines, schools, inns, or private homes. The children whose diaries are included here were part of this exodus from Tokyo: Manabe Ichirō left in August 1944 and Nakane Mihōko in April 1945.

Just how badly the war was going was revealed most clearly in the Allies' systematic bombing of cities and towns in the Japanese empire, which began in earnest in November 1944. On November 24, 111 B-29s attacked Tokyo, eighty-one on November 27, twenty-four on November 29, and nearly seventy on December 3.[51] Nagoya, Kobe, Osaka, and dozens of other small cities were bombed as well. Initially, the home-front population was not greatly affected because the first targets were military and industrial and the bombers attacked from an altitude of around thirty thousand feet, which meant that on a clear day they could be seen but not heard.

In January 1945, this changed when the Allies adopted new bombing tactics. First, American bombers began to attack residential areas. They also began to use incendiary bombs, M-69s, which had been created especially for Japanese cities. Finally, the Allies began to attack at night and to drop their bombs from an altitude of less than eight thousand feet, which meant that the B-29s could carry more bombs and drop them with deadlier accuracy.[52] The result was both devastating and horrible for those on the ground.

Everything came together on the evening of March 9–10, 1945. On March 9, 325 B-29s left their base on Tinian in the Mariana Islands, reaching Tokyo just before midnight. The planes approached the sleeping city at six thousand feet, and their target was a twelve-square mile area in central Tokyo that straddled the Sumida River, stretching from Asakusa in the northwest to Honjo in the northeast, Fukagawa in the southeast, and Nihonbashi in the southwest. The target area was home to dozens of small factories that made machine parts and also a large residential population of more than 1.5 million people. Since each bomber carried an average of six and a half tons of incendiary bombs, more than two thousand tons of incendiary bombs were dropped that night on the target area, with devastating results: 83,793 people were killed, 40,918 were injured, 1,008,000 lost their homes, and the resulting fires destroyed nearly sixteen square miles and burned for days.[53]

The devastating air raid of March 9–10 was only the first of many. Tokyo was bombed eight more times before the end of the war, with the biggest raids on the evening of April 12–13, when 272 B-29s attacked; on May 23, when 562 B-29s attacked; and on May 25–26, when 464 B-29s attacked.[54] The attacks flattened central Tokyo and, later, Osaka into what observers described as "burned-out fields."

Tokyo and Osaka were not the only cities the Allies bombed, however; nearly every major city and large town in the Japanese empire was hit at some time. The Shimonoseki Strait separating the main island of Honshu from the southernmost island of Kyushu was attacked thirty times during the war. Kyushu itself was struck twenty-seven times. Targets on the island of Shikoku were bombed sixteen times, and Nagoya, hit early, was attacked fifteen times. Although the destruction in the large cities was greater, the smaller cities suffered proportionately more damage. For example, the following percentages of the largest cities were destroyed: Yokohama (57.6%), Kobe (55.7%), Tokyo (50.8%), and Osaka (35.1%). In contrast, the smaller cities sustained comparatively more damage: Toyama (98%), Fukui (86%), Tokushima (85.2%), Kōfu (78%), and Hitachi (72%).[55] Although less of their total area was razed, the size of the big cities made the bomb damage even more impressive and unforgettable.

The Japanese military responded with "special-attack" tactics, sending wave after wave of special attackers against the growing numbers of Allied warships and transports in the battle areas. Although the general staffs of both the army and the navy had decided to use special-attack tactics as early as the summer of 1944, they were used successfully for the first time in the Philippines in late October 1944 and continued to be used against the Allied forces attacking Iwo Jima and Okinawa until the very day that Japan surrendered. These desperation tactics sank or damaged hundreds of Allied ships and killed many hundreds and injured several thousand Allied troops, but they did not stop the advance toward the Japanese home islands. More than five thousand Japanese navy and army pilots — career army and navy men as well as recruits — were expended in these special attacks. Itabashi Yasuo was a career navy man who could hardly wait to sortie on a special attack but was used instead to train younger pilots for their special attacks. In early April, he received his order to attack, but inexplicably it was postponed for several months and did not come until the closing days of the war.

By the summer of 1945, defeat seemed imminent. Japan's allies — Italy and Germany — had surrendered, and the Allies now were concentrating on Japan. Even though Japanese forces continued to fight hard and often to the death, they suffered one military setback after another. The Japanese lost control of the seas around the Philippines in the fall of 1944, then were driven out of southern Luzon in the early months of 1945, and finally abandoned Manila on March 4, 1945. Later that month they lost Iwo Jima, which was less than seven hundred miles and three hours' flying time from Tokyo, and the Allies invaded Okinawa on April 1, putting ashore 290,000 men. Although the battle for Okinawa was costly to both sides, the island was taken on June 27, with stragglers like Nomura Seiki holding out until early fall.

That summer, conditions on the home front reached their lowest point. Most Japanese were living at the poverty level, owing to the wartime annual inflation rate of 20 percent that over several years had effectively reduced their wages to slightly more than half what they had been ten years earlier. Ironically, though, this may not have mattered, since there was little that most Japanese could afford to buy. The food situation was desperate. In June the daily ration per person was one cup of rice with soybeans or corn mixed in, slightly more than one ounce of vegetables, and less than one-third ounce of dried sardines (J. *niboshi*) or fish preserves (J. *tsukudani*) delivered every six days. In July the government decided to reduce these allotments by 10 percent. In addition, the neighborhood associations made sure that everyone who was fit was mobilized. Three million children over the age of ten were doing war work, and with the suspension of high school and university classes, nearly three million older students were mobilized as well. All the remaining able-bodied men, women, and students were organized into "People's Volunteer Corps," which had them rising early to worship at the local shrine, training with bamboo staves, and digging defense works for the "decisive battle." Adding insult to injury, the relentless Allied bombing of cities and towns had so disrupted the transportation networks that often only 20 to 30 percent of workers ever made it to work. Others, tired of working long hours under hazardous conditions and at starvation wages, simply stayed home or fled.[56]

As the conditions on the home front deteriorated even further, the Allied leaders met at Potsdam in Germany to discuss postwar arrangements and Japan's surrender. They had received word that the emperor himself was willing to surrender, and so the conferees began working out the terms. They agreed on five main points: first, that the Japanese would free themselves from their "self-willed militaristic advisers" who had "deceived and misled the people of Japan into embarking on world conquest"; second, that Japan would be occupied by the Allied forces; third, that Japanese military forces would be disarmed and demilitarized; fourth, that Japan would lose all its territorial possessions; and fifth, that the Allies would "call upon the government of Japan to proclaim now the unconditional surrender of all Japanese armed forces and to provide proper and adequate assurances of their good faith in such action. The alternative for Japan is prompt and utter destruction." The Allies sent the Potsdam Declaration, as the document came to be called, to the Japanese leaders on July 26, 1945. Even though the emperor asked Prime Minister Suzuki Kantarō to accept it, the cabinet decided "to kill it by ignoring it" (J. *mokusatsu*). President Harry Truman interpreted the Japanese silence as a negative response and thereupon approved the dropping of an atomic bomb on Hiroshima on August 6.[57] Two days later, the Soviet Union declared war on Japan, and Soviet troops marched into Manchuria.

The dropping of the first atomic bomb and the Soviet Union's entry into the war prompted the Japanese leaders finally to act. Early on the morning of August 9, the emperor asked Kido Kōichi, lord keeper of the privy seal, to inform Prime Minister Suzuki that it was time to act. Suzuki convened the Supreme War Guidance Council that very morning, and as their meeting began, news of the dropping of a second atomic bomb, on Nagasaki, was brought in. They promptly decided on surrender. Suzuki assembled the cabinet to formalize the council's decision, and they deliberated for six and a half hours but could not reach a decision. When the emperor was told about the deadlock, he asked that another body, the Imperial Conference, be assembled. The Imperial Conference members presented arguments both for and against surrender, and then the emperor offered his own view. In no uncertain terms, he called for surrender. The cabinet reconvened to ratify the Imperial Conference's decision, which it did by 4:00 a.m. on August 10.

Later that day, the Japanese government communicated its acceptance of the Allies' surrender ultimatum. Two days later, the Allies radioed their acceptance of Japan's surrender. On August 14, the emperor had the Imperial Conference convene again, to confirm the decision to surrender. That evening, his surrender declaration, scheduled to be broadcast at noon on August 15, was taped, and copies were secretly carried out of the palace. An announcement about the emperor's speech was broadcast several times, but nothing was said about its content. Most Japanese feared the worst.[58]

At noon on August 15, Japanese throughout the home islands — in cities, towns, and villages — gathered around their radios to hear the emperor's announcement. Most had no idea what he would say. When the broadcast began, there was a lot of static, and many could barely hear the emperor's voice, much less understand everything he said. But the gist of his remarks was clear. Japan had surrendered, and the war, the terrible war, which had caused so much misery to so many, was over.

Reading the Diaries

There are many ways to read diaries like the ones in this book. They can be read as *historical documents* that offer information about the war, its impact on ordinary Japanese, and their responses. Historians favor this approach. Some critics prefer to see the diaries as a *form of subjectivity* and the record of a distinctive self representing itself in writing. Others, following the lead of the practitioners of the "new historicism," regard the very act of keeping a diary as a *practice* that allows their writers to shape their own life as they live it. Finally, some regard diaries as *literary texts* that, when read carefully, reveal the voices of the writers, their audience's expectations, and the particular language they use. Although obviously different, each of these ways of reading diaries has merit and reveals things that the others exclude, downplay, or ignore.[59] Using all four approaches, I consider what the diaries in this volume reveal about ordinary Japanese in the closing years of the war and identify ten themes that emerge.

Support for the war is the first theme. Even the most cursory reading reveals that all eight diarists supported the war. Predictably, the servicemen — the navy pilot Itabashi Yasuo and the army private Nomura Seiki — were the most ardent. Both were ready and willing to fight to the death. Itabashi died in a special attack at the end of the war, and Nomura held out beyond the end of the war. In contrast, the home-front adults supported the war more strongly at its outset than at its close, but even they dutifully sent off loved ones to do the government's bidding. Tamura Tsunejirō, the seventy-five-year-old Kyoto businessman, sent two family members into the military. The first was his grandson, Inao, who was drafted in the fall of 1944. Then in the spring of 1945, his forty-three-year-old son, Fujihira, was drafted, which made Tamura both pleased and proud. "That our son, an old soldier of forty-three, would leave behind a wife and children for the sake of the honorable country and eagerly serve was truly a happy affair." Tamura also sent off his teenage granddaughter, Sumiko, when she was mobilized for war work, at what they learned later was a munitions plant. "We'll truly miss her," he admitted, "but in wartime you have to work for the state, if even just a little, and because complaints are undemocratic and forbidden, I'll send her off with strict orders to work hard." Takahashi Aiko, a Tokyo housewife, also sent off her teenage son to do war work, and she and her husband did what any parent would do: they worried about him. A year later, her other child, a teenage daughter, was evacuated. Takahashi was sorry to see her go, but with the Allies' intensified bombing of the home islands, she recognized that her daughter would be safer away from Tokyo.[60]

The teenagers and children represented here enthusiastically accepted their government's order to do war work or to evacuate the cities. Like Tamura's grand-daughter and Takahashi's son and daughter, fifteen-year-old Maeda Shōko, who lived in Chiran in southern Kyushu, was mobilized for war work at a nearby army air base, where she cleaned the quarters of special-attack pilots, mended their clothing, did their laundry, and wrote letters to their families. She also spent quite a lot of time with the pilots and saw them off when they left on their final missions. Eleven-year-old Manabe Ichirō, who was the "man of his house," did everything the government asked of him: he handled the paperwork for his evacuation himself, got his preevacuation inoculations, helped move the luggage that would accompany the evacuated children, and even attended the Parents Association meetings held for the parents of children about to be evacuated. When she heard that her group's evacuation site had been chosen, nine-year-old Nakane Mihōko was ecstatic. "I am so happy," she wrote. "I can't bear it."[61] Without exception, the authors of all eight diaries supported the war effort until the very day of the surrender and, in one case, even beyond it, although several had misgivings about their government's policies.

At first, the home-front diarists accepted without complaint the changes the war caused in their daily lives. They made do, for example, with the shortages of food and other commodities, which is not surprising, since rationing had been a part of their lives since 1938. Tokyo housewife Takahashi Aiko and her family were constantly on the lookout for food. Her February 21, 1942, entry describes her excitement over finding freshly made fish tempura in a Shinjuku department store and her disappointment when the fish turned out to be spoiled. The Takahashi family even hulled its own rice in the way recommended by the government. "We hull rice using the beer bottle method," Takahashi wrote, "until blisters begin to form on our hands, our sleeves start to tear, and we get tired. We use the fine powder that the hulls leave in the bottle to make flour and then steamed bread, which everyone eats." And six months later, when Takahashi's son found sugarcane being sold in central Tokyo, he bought some and the family attempted, unsuccessfully, to make sugar.[62]

All the home-front adult diarists in this volume also were members of their neighborhood associations and community councils, and their journals show that they did as they were told. They saw off local boys and men leaving for the front. They sent a family member to the monthly meetings of the neighborhood association. They circulated the government orders sent to the community councils and neighborhood associations. They served their neighborhood associations in various ways, by distributing scarce commodities and food, preparing for the expected Allied attacks and participating in air-raid and blackout drills, serving in the neighborhood fire brigades, and taking their turn on the fire watch. They also subjected themselves to the scrutiny of the community council officials who were constantly checking one thing or another. Clearly, what made their new duties and obligations and the shortages of food and other commodities tolerable was the fact that their country was at war.

In 1943, however, the views of the adult home-front diarists started to change, and this is the second important theme. They began to fill their diaries with complaints about the community councils and neighborhood associations. They expressed resentment of the endless series of drills. "Each time there is an air-defense drill," grumbled Takahashi, "we are made to line up in single file, call out our names, and roll is taken, with lots of muttering about which houses are not represented, who was late, and which wife sent her maid in her place." They even got tired of sending off the neighborhood boys and men, even their own relatives. When Tamura Tsunejirō's grandson Inao was about to be sent to the front, no one wanted to see him off, and finally it was Toshie, Tamura's daughter, who represented the family.[63]

The adult diarists also resented being ordered about by the community council officials. In the summer of 1942 Takahashi Aiko began to complain about "these sorts of people," and by spring 1943 her feelings had intensified. Her description of the officials who inspected her neighborhood's air-defense preparations in March 1943 leaves little doubt that she despised them. "The community council big shots," she wrote, "put on their pompous clothes and their pompous faces and strutted about with a pompous number of people." Takahashi found their arrogance intolerable. In the same diary entry, she described a maddening incident involving an inebriated local official. Tamura, the Kyoto billiards parlor owner, had his own infuriating encounter with a local air-raid warden and shared Takahashi's low opinion of local officials.[64]

The attitudes of the home-front diarists changed for other reasons as well. The shortages of daily necessities became acute. Cigarettes began to be rationed, charcoal was in short supply, and there simply was not enough food. Families looked forward to the periodic distributions of meat, fish, fresh vegetables, and staples such as rice and miso. "Salmon was distributed at 9:00 a.m.," wrote Manabe Ichirō. "When we got our salted salmon, we were given one slice, the head, and two more pieces."[65] This amount was for three people: Manabe, his mother, and his older sister. As the food shortages grew worse in the last year of the war, people simply had less to eat, and they began to tire more easily and to experience what one diarist called "exhaustion." The food shortages were especially hard on the elderly or those who were fussy about what they ate. Tamura was convinced that he was starving to death. "The rice ration is three-quarters of a pint for people over sixty," he complained, "but I'm a big guy and that's not enough. I can't bear to have an empty stomach day after day, and it's only because of others' thoughtfulness . . . that I escape starvation."[66] Although food was available in Kyoto, it was being sold at prices that Tamura's family could not afford.

Political attitudes also changed in 1943/1944, a third important theme. At the start of the war, most Japanese accepted their government's policies even when they had misgivings. For example, writing on February 18, 1942, after Singapore fell to the Japanese, Takahashi observed that "the entire Japanese people gained self-confidence from their country's newfound power, and they were deliriously happy." She herself, however, felt uneasy and ambivalent about the growing exuberance of her fellow Japanese. Although her reservations about the war deepened in 1943, she kept them to herself. Both she and Tamura felt that they had no choice, as publicly criticizing the government or its policies was out of the question.[67] It would invite unfriendly gossip in the neighborhood and perhaps even a visit by the tokkō (special police) or the kenpeitai (military police).[68]

Leadership changes in the summer of 1944 brought more disappointment. "This morning when we opened the newspaper," Takahashi wrote, "there was an article reporting that Prime Minister Tōjō also will serve as chief of the general staff. Is there something going on again? Perhaps something big is about to happen." Her fears were realized when Tōjō resigned on July 18, 1944. Likewise, Tamura, as someone who had "believed" in Tōjō, was deeply disappointed. "The world is in desperate straits! How will things turn out? We'll probably die. We depended on Mr. Tōjō to the end, but I hear he just up and resigned. What a shame!" Tamura fumed for several weeks and called Tōjō a "weak-kneed" and "small-fry general." Even eleven-year-old Manabe criticized Tōjō and his cabinet for resigning, writing, "I think they are cowards."[69] Manabe may have had his own political opinions, but more likely, he overheard adults complaining about Tōjō.

These criticisms of Tōjō demonstrate that keeping a diary served several functions. First, it allowed its writer to vent freely and even to express "dangerous thoughts," something one could do only in personal correspondence and diaries. Confining one's criticisms of the government to a diary kept them from the prying eyes of neighbors and local officials and the stern gaze of the tokkō or the kenpeitai. These diarists may even have been carrying out what Samuel Hynes called small "acts of resistance." Apparently, many Japanese had similar feelings about the government and its policies. Some found it impossible to keep these feelings to themselves and simply said what they thought. Others sent antiwar letters to the prime minister, generals, and other officials. As a consequence, many were arrested, interrogated, tortured, and/or killed by the authorities.[70]

In the last year of the war, the home-front diarists began to lose confidence in their armed forces, which forms a fourth important theme. Early on, the Japanese military did well, scoring a string of "brilliant victories" and making the Japanese people proud of their country. These victories made it easy for them to do what the authorities recommended, namely, "to leave the war to the soldiers." Already in 1943, however, the increasing numbers of young and old men being conscripted into military service pointed to a worsening military situation. As Takahashi observed in her June 10, 1943, entry, the new conscripts were now being sent off with conspicuously less enthusiasm, and the processions of departing servicemen were "rather pathetic affairs" with fewer flags, less rousing war songs, and a handful of relatives and the neighborhood association folks who had to show up.[71]

Several months later, Takahashi commented on the growing number of conscripts: "All able-bodied males between the ages of eighteen and forty-five are being drafted, and it seems that the Japanese home islands are being emptied." As the mother of a teenage son, she had good reason to notice this. Although her son Nobukazu was too young to be drafted, he was participating in the send-offs of classmates and friends, which reminded his mother just how close he was to being taken. Other mothers felt exactly as Takahashi did. Hatano Isoko, herself the mother of a teenage son, cried when she saw recruits being sent off in late May 1944.[72] Clearly, their reactions, though seemingly insignificant, might be read as small "acts of resistance."

The appearance of a new word, *gyokusai*, confirmed that the military situation was deteriorating. Japanese newspapers first used the word in April 1943 to describe the fate of the Japanese defenders of Attu Island in the Aleutians, all of whom perished in an Allied attack. *Gyokusai*, which literally means the "shattering of the jewel," appears in an ancient Chinese classic but was used during the Pacific War to mean "total annihilation."[73] By 1944, the word appeared with some frequency in the popular press to describe the deaths of Japanese troops in the Pacific.

Later that same year, both Tamura and Takahashi noticed a change in the ages of the new recruits. "Yesterday I saw a soldier in his forties leaving with no one to send him off," Tamura noted. "He was saying good-bye to his parents, wife, and children, who watched forlornly as his train disappeared in the east." Writing three weeks later, Takahashi observed that second sons were now being taken and described the drafting of an acquaintance's son. It is telling that both Tamura and Takahashi saw the loss of Saipan in June 1944 as a turning point in the war and that both closed their August diary entries with the same observation, namely, that although in the past a human life lasted for fifty years, it now lasted for only twenty-five.[74] The understated irony of their calculations reveals their misgivings about the military's strategy and tactics.

The reporting on the war further undermined the people's confidence in the military leadership. Japanese had only their heavily censored and "not reliable" newspapers for war news, and they scrutinized every article, all the while reading between the lines. They did this, for example, when Italy surrendered in September 1943. Takahashi wrote: "The newspapers report that although Italy has surrendered, Mussolini is holed up in the north and has proclaimed the establishment of 'North Italy.' Thus nothing has changed in the secure three-country [Axis] alliance." Ever perceptive, she noted, "Recently all newspaper reports have been written in this style, and thus one has to use intuition and much more when reading the papers." The absence of war news was troubling as well. "Recently there haven't been any newspaper articles on the war in the South Pacific," she observed. "What in the world is happening?" In the fall of 1944, when the radio broadcasts were announcing the victory celebrations on Taiwan, Takahashi observed that Taiwan had actually been attacked, and there was no celebration. She closed her diary entry with an attack on the "authorities": "I couldn't help but feel contempt for the authorities who treat us as though we were stupid."[75] Had they not been private, Takahashi's comments could easily have gotten her into trouble. In any event, her misgivings only grew in the fall and early winter of 1944.

The military's increasing reliance on special-attack tactics was even more alarming. In the summer of 1944, the Japanese army and navy decided to adopt these tactics, and the first successful attack took place on October 25, 1944, in the Philippines. In his December 1, 1944, entry, Tamura noted that there were photographs of special-attack pilots in the newspaper "who were either students or teenagers who had just turned twenty and who once had had a future." News of the special attacks offered little comfort. In February 1945 Tamura wrote, "Our attacking squads, our attacking squads that go off like cattle — what are they doing? 'Body-crashing,' 'body-crashing' — what's that?"[76] His choice of words conveys well his growing skepticism about the strategy and tactics of the military. Clearly, he was no longer willing "to leave the war to the soldiers."

Tamura's distress points to the fifth theme, the unmistakable deterioration of home-front morale, which began in late 1944. Nothing did more to undermine Japanese morale than the Allied bombing of their country, which began in November 1944 and continued until the day the war ended. No other topic, with the possible exception of food, is mentioned more often in the diaries than the bombing. At first, the diarists responded calmly to Allied bombing raids, perhaps because they had been prepared for them but also because they still had no real conception of what it was like to be attacked from the air. Yoshizawa Hisako, for example, described the November 29 raid on Tokyo in the most matter-of-fact way: "Bombs have fallen on Kanda, Kōtō, and Shiba. Apparently incendiary bombs fell just thirty houses away from O's house. They say the bombs looked like falling wind chimes." When seventy B-29s returned to bomb Tokyo on December 3, Yoshizawa continued to distance herself from the attacks, writing, "The American planes were directly overhead, but nothing fell. I was entranced by their glittering, white, and beautiful bodies. All we could do was to watch the advancing American planes, which seemed to be pulling the moving patterns of the clouds. I wasn't worried at all. I just thought this was war." Yoshizawa seemed to regard these first attacks as nothing more than a distraction. In Kyoto, Tamura reacted similarly, describing the first air raids as an intrusion. "Yesterday Nagoya was hit by air raids, and half of Ginza Avenue in Tokyo was destroyed. The Tōkaidō Line is not running. Today enemy aircraft came to reconnoiter Osaka and Kobe."[77] These two diarists' detachment and calm may be surprising but suggest once again that writing in their diaries may have been therapeutic, allowing them to distance the bombing and contain their fears.

But as the bombing of the home islands moved systematically from city to city, this equanimity gave way to anxiety and fatigue. Each of the home-front adult diarists represented in this book responded to the bombing slightly differently. As the air-raid warnings and alerts were issued, called off, issued again, and called off again, sometimes several times in one night, fatigue began to take its toll. "The fatigue brought on by the sleep deprivation that the air raids are causing is leading to a sort of brittle self-interest that makes boarding and getting off trains frightening. Try as I might to remain calm, my nerves are on edge," Yoshizawa admitted in her January 6, 1945, entry. Two weeks later, she conceded that she "finds the current sort of exhaustion unbearable."[78]

As the bombing raids continued, anxiety and fatigue gave way to depression, outrage, and real terror. Yoshizawa wrote about being depressed. "From ten in the evening until dawn there were three air raids, and five from noon. I'm gradually getting depressed." What frightened Takahashi was the thought of her family's being "separated during an air raid." When Tamura realized that the bombers were dropping high-explosive and incendiary bombs on both industrial and residential areas, he got angry and described the bombing as "indiscriminate" and thus "intolerable."[79] He was right. On February 4, sixty-nine B-29s dropped incendiary bombs on residential areas in Kobe, and 172 B-29s did the same to Tokyo.[80] These three diarists' very different reactions to the bombing of Japanese cities is revealing: Tamura lashed out at the Allies; Yoshizawa internalized her feelings; and Takahashi worried about her family. Their responses may be a reflection of their family situation and ages and their gender as well: Tamura was a seventy-five-year-old grandfather; Takahashi was a fifty-one-year-old mother of two teenage children; and Yoshizawa was twenty-seven and a single working woman.

As the Allies continued to attack using these new tactics, shock turned into disbelief. On the night of March 9–10, 325 B-29s attacked central Tokyo with incendiary bombs; on March 11, 285 B-29s attacked residential areas in Nagoya; and on the evening of March 13–14, 275 B-29s dropped bombs on Osaka. In the last of these raids, eight square miles of central Osaka were leveled in three hours.[81] Afterward, Tamura, writing from the protection of the still-unbombed Kyoto, was incredulous. "By 9:30 a.m. Osaka had been burned up by the enemy attack that rained bombs on that city, and it was a burned-out field. It was a re-peat performance of what happened in Tokyo and Nagoya. I half believed and half doubted." Takahashi admitted to being afraid when she realized that her neighborhood would be bombed in the near future. Yoshizawa reported that the bombing had made people more skittish than normal. She related how, a day after the March 9–10 raid, people were mistaking clouds for aircraft and conceded that her depression was deepening.[82] The home-front diaries amply document the physical and psychological effects of the Allies' sustained bomb-ing of the Japanese home islands: it was simply wearing them down.

After the change in Allied bombing tactics and with the steady advance of Al-lied forces toward the Japanese home islands and the surrender of Germany, the home-front adult diarists' loss of faith in their leaders, both civilian and military, became obvious. Even the patriotic Tamura wrote that "the military's incom-petence in the south is the butt of jokes" and openly expressed his reservations about those in the government who "make war, resign, and feign ignorance." "I resent what they have done," he added. Even Yoshizawa was critical of the government and angry about its policies. Commenting on the Koiso cabinet's evacuation order in the summer and fall of 1944, she wrote, "The government's irresponsibility has given us much to be angry about." When she heard about Germany's surrender, she hoped that this would give Japan's leaders "a freer course of action," but she worried anyway. "Mentally, we Japanese have the narrowness of an island people and so although we're honest, our thinking is too limited. I sincerely hoped our diplomats would be broad-minded. No, more than that, it made me sad that there were no politicians willing to take real risks."[83]

Their freely recording such "dangerous thoughts" in their diaries suggests how strongly Tamura and Yoshizawa felt about what was happening and confirms the therapeutic function of keeping a diary. Interestingly, they wrote as though they were complaining to someone else. Of course, Yoshizawa was writing for her absent mentor, who had asked her to keep a diary and thus would be reading it when he returned. Tamura's audience is less obvious. Perhaps he was simply complaining to an alter ego that existed only in his diary.

As the Japanese lost faith in their leaders and their morale sagged, social conflict and tension — the sixth theme — surfaced in their diaries. Several diarists were troubled by the thought that others had unfair advantages and thus more income, food, and access to scarce commodities. They indicated that they believed the families of military men had special privileges not extended to others. On February 28, 1945, Yoshizawa recorded two rumors she heard at work.

The first was about a young lieutenant's family that moved into a new neighborhood. When neighbors mentioned that they had not eaten tofu for some time, the lieutenant's wife "made a call and a truck full of tofu arrived. Everyone in the neighborhood was furious." The second rumor was similar but involved heating oil. *"These rumors reveal the weakening of the people's trust in the military,"* Yoshizawa concluded. *"Most of the rumors I've heard recently are like these two, and soldiers appear in many of them"* [italics in original]. Barely two weeks later, Tamura, writing in Kyoto, related a strikingly similar story and drew the same conclusion.[84] That stories like these were circulating said much about morale on the home front.

In addition, Tamura had strong feelings about "upper-class leaders." In May 1945 he reported that his son Aeba, who worked as a bellhop at the Miyako, Kyoto's fanciest hotel, received a one-hundred-yen tip, an unheard-of extravagance. Tamura was shocked. It prompted him to wonder "whether the sort of extravagance we just witnessed would allow Japan to win the war against the American and British enemy and whether it was appropriate for upper-class leaders to do this sort of thing."[85] As becomes evident later, Tamura grew more and more disappointed with those leading the country.

The home-front diaries contain evidence also of urban–rural conflict. When food became scarce, urban dwellers had to turn to farmers, a move that they resented. Writing in January 1944, Takahashi commented on changing town–country relations: "In the past, the daily lives of farmers were not blessed in any sense, but now they suddenly hold the key to our lives — food — and sit in the kingly position of lords of production. By selling on the black market, they are enjoying extraordinary prosperity." Eleven-year-old Manabe Ichirō's description of a farmhouse that he and his mother visited on a vegetable-buying foray into the countryside epitomizes their feelings: "We went to a very big house with a tile roof that didn't look like a farmer's house." City dwellers felt superior to their rural cousins and did not like having to presume on the kindness of farmers. But the situation only got worse. When inflation made the wartime currency virtually worthless, the farmers would accept as payment only material objects such as kimono, clothes, and artworks. Consequently, "the contents of city dwellers' dressers are finding their way into country folk's dressers." In the last years of the war, some urban families even saw "establishing relationships with country folk — by taking a bride or groom from the country — as a necessary means of survival."[86]

Most telling of all is the seventh important theme, the Japanese beginning to contemplate defeat, their own defeat. Interestingly, it was the women — Takahashi and Yoshizawa — who first broached this subject. Takahashi mentioned "giving up the fight" in the summer of 1944. "No matter how favorably you look at the war situation," she wrote, "after the fall of Singapore, it has been impossible to imagine that Japan enjoys the advantage. Hearing about the *gyokusai* of our troops on Saipan makes us angry. We should have the courage, come hell or high water, to give up the fight." Three months later, in October 1944, she spoke of "the specter of Japan's imminent defeat." Not until late January 1945 did the word "defeat" appear in Yoshizawa's diary. After three nighttime air raids, she observed that *"most people no longer believe in victory."* After the devastating attacks on Tokyo in late February and early March, Yoshizawa's thoughts again turned to defeat. After the February 24 attack, she visited the areas that had been bombed and described what she saw: "Seeing figures trudging along in *tabi* on snow-covered roads and piling burned futon on carts, noticing people's blackened faces and hands, and witnessing the movement of troops, *somehow I can't feel that our country is winning the war"* [italics in original]. After the terrible fire raid of March 9–10, Yoshizawa reported that others seemed to agree with her. "I saw what remained of my friend's neighborhood after the bombing. The faces of the people moving out of the houses that had been destroyed revealed no certainty about victory," she wrote.[87] For Takahashi and Yoshizawa, by the spring of 1945 Japan's defeat was a foregone conclusion.

The prospect of defeat elicited a variety of responses from ordinary Japanese. Writing at the end of March 1945 about the situation at the company where she worked, Yoshizawa observed that "everyone tends to criticize others" and to act selfishly. A community council meeting she attended a week later became a verbal fistfight, and even the normally placid Yoshizawa admitted to getting "irritated at the stupidity of those bickering over details." Some Japanese took an "others-be-damned" attitude, with a few doing whatever was necessary to survive. At the beginning of August 1945, she confessed that she had "gotten used to not thinking about tomorrow," which was one way of dealing with the unsavory prospect of defeat and occupation.[88]

The home-front diarists found solace in unexpected places. Memory, for example, was a powerful salve. One night Yoshizawa overheard her brother and his friends reminiscing about life with their families before the evacuation and how they missed sitting with their wife, sipping *sake* and teasing the children. Others found solace in nature. Yoshizawa looked after the flowering plants in her garden — her azaleas sitting "proudly in their greenery," the spreading leaves of her hydrangeas, and the first leaves of her Indian redwood. Takahashi Aiko lamented the sparseness of cherry blossoms in the spring of 1945, and as she meditated on their evanescence, she began to cry "for no reason at all." Three months later, swallows returned to nest in the entryway of her house, offering a pleasant and needed distraction for Takahashi and her husband.[89]

Their spring 1945 diary entries give us a clear picture of Takahashi and Yoshizawa, as they reveal a distinctive "self." Takahashi is more self-centered, more intent on recording exactly what she thought and felt, whereas Yoshizawa is more controlled and vents less than Takahashi does. Did Takahashi's time in the United States and her Christian faith make her more self-assertive, more inclined to speak her mind? Although their personalities and experiences may account for these differences, their intended audiences may as well. After all, Takahashi was writing for herself and thus able to write whatever she wanted. In contrast, Yoshizawa was writing for her absent mentor and may have suppressed her real feelings because she knew he would expect her to *gaman*, "to persevere," no matter how difficult her circumstances were. Their diary entries from the spring of 1945 also reveal something more. The fact that both Takahashi and Yoshizawa turn to nature and find relief in the spring blossoms but Tamura never mentions such things may mean that the turn to nature is a gendered response.

Living in the shadow of defeat, Yoshizawa and Takahashi nonetheless managed to find reasons for hope. Yoshizawa simply insisted on living with a positive attitude. Late in April, she wrote, "No matter what happens, I'll try to live a life that has not lost any of its optimism. I'm ready to die tomorrow but will try to live today full of hope. I'll do this to ensure the brightness of my surroundings." On June 1, she added, "No matter what happens, I'll continue to exist with the same state of mind and the same face I have today." What gave her hope was the way her fellow Tokyoites bounced back after air raids, doing what they could in the burned-out areas, building makeshift huts with tin roofing, planting vegetable gardens, and finding new pleasures in little things. Takahashi was happy simply to be alive and counted her blessings. "Life in a city with no gas, electricity, or water is sad," she wrote. "From the point of view of the victims, however, we were kings."[90]

As Takahashi and Yoshizawa prepared for their country's defeat, Japanese children were being readied for the final battle that would decide the fate of the homeland, the eighth important theme. War had been a part of the children's lives since 1937, and the daily, weekly, and monthly rituals of war had them standing at attention and reading aloud the emperor's declaration of war, putting up with the food shortages and the rationing of scarce commodities, and drilling under the menacing gaze of local veterans. After they were evacuated to the countryside beginning in the fall of 1944 and throughout the spring and summer of 1945, the children's lives were focused completely on the war: they did calisthenics and competed with one another; they practiced marching and took long hikes; and during the summer months, when it was warm, they swam nearly every day. Much of their time also was spent doing war work of one kind or another. Once summer arrived, nine-year-old Nakane Mihōko and her classmates gathered "mountain vegetables" and edible insects at least once and sometimes twice a week. They also collected firewood and carried it from nearby forests back to the village. Some children were even sent to do day work at local factories. Eleven-year-old Manabe Ichirō and his classmates, for example, were sent to help at a sardine-processing factory.[91]

Predictably, the children's spiritual training also intensified during their evacuation. They studied national heroes like Yamato-Takeru-no-Mikoto or war heroes. They listened to martial music, such as "A Record of Victory," which brought back memories of the Pearl Harbor attack, watched war films like *The Consoling of Eight Evacuated Children*, and sang war songs. All these activities were meant to make them "good children." Nakane's diary entries are revealing in this regard because they show just how hard she was working at becoming a "good child" and how her efforts were being guided by her teachers.[92]

Indeed, the children's journals confirm the importance of diary writing as a wartime practice. First, their diaries offered a structure for their lives as evacuated children, and they also created a record of the children's thoughts, feelings, and activities for their supervisors. Nakane's teachers read her group's diaries once a week, usually after the children had gone to bed. Judging from her determination to become a "good child," the compulsory diary keeping gave Nakane and her classmates a way to police themselves as they were being transformed into willing subjects.[93] Nakane's August 10, 1945, entry, for example, shows just how effective the practice of keeping a diary writing was: she describes a dream she had in which a god appears and scolds her for telling lies. He warns her that if she tells a lie, she will fall into a "huge hole deep in the forest." Nakane concluded, "I thought about the dream I had just had, and from now on I must not tell lies. If I do, I thought, it'll turn out just like my dream."[94]

Keeping a diary, however, was only one of many discursive practices shaping the evacuated children's lives. That the children were actively encouraged to reproduce wartime rhetoric is clear from Nakane's frequent references to the "good child" discourse found in the prewar and wartime ethics textbooks. Consider her efforts to become a "good child" and her plaintive query, obviously addressed to her teachers, "Was I a good child?" Nakane also referred to another discourse found in the ethics textbooks, what might be called the "beautiful Japan" discourse. For example, when she wrote in her diary on May 8 and June 8: "Today is Imperial Rescript Observance Day. When I went to the school in the morning, the beautiful rising sun flags on each house were fluttering in the morning breeze," she was echoing passages like the following from "The Rising Sun Flag" chapter of her third-grade ethics textbook:

A clear blue sky.
Flying just at the eaves,
the rising-sun flag
is truly dignified.

Snowbound houses,
Flying just at the eaves,
the rising-sun flag
Somehow seems warm.[95]

Here Nakane was doing exactly what Ministry of Education officials hoped she would do. In the 1930s when government textbook writers revised the fourth edition of the ethics textbooks for the coming war, they decided "to work on developing the affective and volitional aspects of the youngsters' moral character . . . and to take special care to affect their feelings."[96] Nakane's diary demonstrates that their strategy worked. It also is not a coincidence that she wrote these entries on the eighth of May and June, the day that Japanese throughout the empire stood and read aloud the imperial rescript announcing the declaration of war against the Allies and the children wrote "comfort letters" to Japanese servicemen. The children's diaries confirm that they were rehearsing and reproducing the wartime discourses they studied in school.

Clearly, the children were being prepared for the decisive battle expected when the enemy invaded Japan. Veterans and servicemen showed up from time to time to regale the children with war stories and to show them the implements of war. Manabe Ichirō described the visit of the Toyama Army School Band, whose members not only played and sang for the children but also demonstrated sword unsheathing and matched warships. Nakane's group also was taken on long hikes to a glider base at Tatenogahara, deep in the mountains, where her teachers practiced flying gliders, perhaps in preparation for attacks on the Allied invasion force.[97]

THE PACIFIC WAR AND ORDINARY JAPANESE 37

The teachers had the children perform many other rituals of war. They played war games in which they learned how to throw a hand grenade, how to strike and kill with a sword, and how to thrust a spear at an enemy. One such clinic in hand-to-hand combat taught Nakane that "even one person can kill a lot of the enemy." Her observation rehearses the tactic, common among Japanese servicemen, of trying to kill the enemy even while being killed oneself. And just below Nakane's entry, one of her teachers added, "You really persevered, didn't you?"[98] Although Nakane did not realize it, this game was preparing her for a final, terrible battle.

The children often performed two other war rituals: the first was sending off local men and boys, including some of their own teachers. Nakane's description of the departure of one of her favorite teacher is especially moving. The second was greeting the "departed spirits," the ashes of deceased servicemen brought back to their villages.[99] Obviously, when they were performing these rituals of war, the children were rehearsing wartime practices, enunciating wartime discourses, and readying themselves for the decisive battle that would result, they were told, in a Japanese victory.[100]

Like the children, Japanese servicemen reacted to the worsening war news and the prospect of defeat by reaffirming their intention to die in battle. Their willingness to die is the ninth important theme and is found in nearly all Japanese servicemen's diaries. Navy pilot Itabashi Yasuo's response was the most predictable, perhaps because he was still part of an organized military unit and one being readied for a special attack. His diary reveals actually three distinct responses, each of which reproduced a particular wartime discourse.

Itabashi's first response was to avenge his deceased comrades. Hearing that the Allies had taken Iwo Jima and that the "Iwo Jima home guard unit committed gyokusai," Itabashi wrote in his diary, "I will avenge them. I definitely will avenge them. . . . We must not let the brave warriors who committed gyokusai die a dog's death."[101] This rhetoric of revenge was central to warrior discourse from early modern times, and the modern Japanese military appropriated it for its training manuals and wartime strategies and tactics.

Itabashi insisted that Japan was winning and had to win, which was his second response. Despite the setbacks at Attu, Kwajalein, Rota, Saipan, and Tinian, he remained convinced in January 1945 that Japan still was winning. "We are definitely winning this war," he declared. "At the moment, Japan will make a comeback with this last stand, break the enemy's nose, and push with irresistible force, push to the end." That Japan was really winning despite the many setbacks was, of course, the military's official line, fed not only to credulous servicemen but also to an increasingly skeptical public that had been told "to leave the war to the soldiers." "Whether right or wrong," Itabashi wrote on March 22, 1945, "Japan must win!" A day later, he put it even more strongly. "Japan absolutely cannot be defeated!"[102]

Itabashi also responded in a third way. To help Japan achieve victory, he wrote, he was willing to sacrifice himself and "to die brilliantly." In November 1944 he had pledged to go off on a special-attack sortie "to see many of my old war buddies" and to contribute to Japan's victory. "To help us prevail," he added two months later, "I'd happily see my little five-foot body smashed to pieces." In February 1945, Itabashi's memories of his old squadron, now decimated, strengthened his resolve to die: "I'll be satisfied if I'm able to destroy myself. It's probably survivor's guilt. But then again, I'm still alive and must fight. . . . When I catch up with my war buddies, I won't be late."[103] Itabashi's third response has several layers. "It's probably survivor's guilt" obviously reveals a psychological dimension and the personal angst that his surviving had caused him. "When I catch up with my buddies, I won't be late" exhibits the kind of intense unit loyalty that men in modern armies seem to feel, a loyalty that is universal.[104] Furthermore, Itabashi's feelings of guilt and unit loyalty are cast in the distinctive lexicon of the special-attack units, with its references to "my small five-foot frame," "being smashed to pieces," and "annihilating the enemy."[105]

Even after Itabashi was flown back to Japan in early March 1945, his determination to fly on a special-attack mission never wavered. Then on April 7, he got the long-awaited order to fly to Kokubu Air Base in southern Japan, which was closer to the battle then raging on Okinawa. He was ecstatic. "At long last, we received the order we've been waiting, and hoping, for," he wrote. "We'll go to Kokubu. The appointed day is the day after tomorrow. Banzai! I'll do it! This will be to avenge my several hundred war buddies from the 503rd! I'll do it! I'll be decisive!" His last diary entry, written a day later, is full of optimism. Itabashi closed his entry with "last letters" to his parents and surviving siblings.[106]

The fact that special-attack pilots like Itabashi wrote "last letters" tells us that their families were the readers of not only their letters but also their performance as special-attack pilots. Hence the recurrence of the phrases "I go off smiling," "Be proud of me!" "Please be assured that I am in good shape," and "Say I did well!" But the "last letters" were intended for relatives, friends, teachers, and local officials as well, as we know from the pilots' requests that greetings be sent to them, too. To the extent that the "last letters" were shared with others, they were public documents, and the pilots' final missions were public acts. Just as their communities sent them off, their "last letters" brought them home.

The Japanese thus were encouraged to participate in the war less as individuals than as members of families, neighborhood associations, schools, village or

THE PACIFIC WAR AND ORDINARY JAPANESE 39

community councils, and military units. Consequently, their diaries were one of the few places where Japanese adults could safely express themselves or simply be themselves. Consider the diary of an army private, Nomura Seiki. As a straggler, he was not part of an organized unit, and therefore his response to the worsening war situation and the prospect of defeat was quite different from Itabashi's. In August 1945, having survived the fierce Allied invasion of Okinawa, Nomura was awaiting orders for a counterattack. But he had been wounded and his wounds had not healed completely, and he wondered whether he would be able, physically, to join the counterattack or even to keep up with the retreating troops. Occasionally he thought about whether he even had the resolve to be part of the counterattack.[107]

Nomura even wondered whether Japan had done the right thing in going to war. "There are those who complain that 'Japan started a reckless war!'" he wrote on August 6. "Although we heard this occasionally in the midst of intense fighting, even more radical thoughts occur to a straggler."[108] That a member of the Imperial Japanese Army would entertain, much less write down, such "dangerous thoughts" reminds us how anomalous Nomura's position as a straggler was. Because he was not part of a command structure, he was under no pressure to use the authorized language of the army. No officers were looking over his shoulder as he wrote in his diary.

Even more surprising, however, are Nomura's feelings about the emperor in whose name so many Japanese servicemen had gone off to die. "The emperor was too distant, a presence that had nothing to do with me. Somehow I just couldn't get used to the idea of shouting 'banzai!' and dying for him. I have fought not for the emperor but for the homeland where [my] more familiar parents and siblings, relatives, and friends live and for the ancestral country. Even now, my thoughts about the emperor haven't changed."[109] Here Nomura was rejecting the emperor-centered ideology of both the military and the wartime educational system. He also was rejecting the emperor as the ultimate source of the serviceman's authority to fight and the monarch described as a "father" of the nation, the ruler to whom Japanese were to feel both loyalty and filial piety.[110] Nomura's reflections reveal how the psychology of the ordinary soldier in the Imperial Japanese Army changed when he was released from formal command structures and was solely on his own.

Nonetheless, Nomura was ready and willing to die. After hearing that many stragglers had surrendered, he resolved not to do this. "As someone who'd chosen the path of death for a time, I definitely did not want to become a prisoner," he wrote. He was encouraged by reports that "there were, as before, soldiers hiding out in the mountains and bunkers in the southern part of the island, including several named units." A few days later, he put it more bluntly, "I don't want to be called a coward."[111] Of course, choosing death over surrender was what every Japanese serviceman was taught and was the gist of the *Field Service Code* which they memorized in basic training. Thus, Nomura's resolve to die was expected: the death-before-surrender discourse of *The Field Service Code* was deeply inscribed in his consciousness and, as we shall see shortly, his body as well.

When the announcement that Japan had surrendered came on August 15, 1945, it was a complete surprise to only some Japanese. This is the tenth and final important theme. Relatives and friends of both Yoshizawa Hisako and Takahashi Aiko had told them that the emperor was about to announce the surrender of Japan. Although it was a secret, it was one that had been in wide circulation before August 15. Indeed, Takahashi had heard it five days earlier, on August 10, and Yoshizawa heard the same news on the evening of August 13.[112]

Yoshizawa and Takahashi were among the lucky ones, however, as most Japanese were not expecting their country to surrender. "The people around me know nothing about the surrender," Takahashi wrote, "and their faces are as they were yesterday, severe and pitiful. I feel so rejuvenated by my happiness that I worry that although I'm doing my best to conceal my secret thoughts, I may unwittingly relax the expression on my face." Then on August 14, a radio broadcast informed the nation that "there would be an important announcement at noon tomorrow."[113]

The wildest rumors circulated on the morning of the emperor's "important announcement," rumors about how banks would stop giving out money, about how the moment of the decisive battle had arrived, and so forth. Takahashi and her husband had their lunch early and then moved into their living room to await the broadcast. They were joined by a certain Mr. Iwase, who worked at the neighborhood bank and came over because he wanted to hear the broadcast on their radio. Yoshizawa decided to listen to the emperor's announcement outside, in the street. She remembered that "half the crowd seemed to understand what was about to happen, [and] half had puzzled looks on their faces, looks that said they expected the worst." At noon, a siren went off, a stillness descended on the waiting crowd, and the emperor began to speak. When the broadcast was over, Yoshizawa recalled that "people's faces had no particular expression. Perhaps they were exhausted. As to how they felt about the war ending, an unmistakable brightness in their faces told the story."[114]

Ten-year-old Nakane Mihōko didn't hear about the surrender until she and her classmates were having breakfast on August 16. They were told that "His Majesty said, 'We have endured hardships and sadness, but we have been defeated by that atomic bomb, and all Japanese could be injured and killed. It is too pitiful for even one of my dear subjects to be killed. I do not care what happens to me.' We heard that he then took off the white gloves he was wearing and began to cry out loud." Nakane reacted to the news of the surrender in the way that the whole array of wartime practices, rituals, and discourses had trained her to respond: she vowed revenge. Despite her rage and vengeful feelings, however, her life returned to normal the next day.[115] This was how the surrender was received on the home front.

At 2:14 p.m. on August 9, Itabashi took off on his special attack, finally joining his war buddies who had preceded him in death. Nomura did not learn that Japan had surrendered until September 12, when an American pacification team brought word of the surrender to the bunker where he and several other stragglers were hiding. He was absolutely incredulous when he first heard that Japan had surrendered, and he remained so through that evening and all the next day. Then, when the American pacification team brought incontrovertible proof of the surrender — copies of the Potsdam Declaration, the emperor's surrender rescript, and clippings from the major Japanese dailies — Nomura experiences what can only be described as a series of visceral reactions to the surrender that came one after another: first, he felt as though his "whole body had suddenly collapsed," then he was overcome by "a dark loneliness"; and finally he was "assailed by an inexpressible anger."[116] Given Nomura's training and his strong feelings about surrendering, his response is predictable, beginning with feelings of loneliness and then anger. But his writing "Who or what in the world was the object of my anger I couldn't say" is not clear. Was he referring to his immediate superiors? The commander of Japanese forces on Okinawa? The emperor? Nomura does not say. He remembered that rather than expressing his anger, he kept his feelings to himself, "left the group, and slowly walked to the back of the bunker." Whereas he had once suppressed his "dangerous thoughts" about the emperor and the war, he now suppressed his feelings about the "surrender" and simply stopped writing. He did not resume writing in his diary until long after he and the other members of his group surrendered to the Americans on September 14.

Notes

1. See Eugene Soviak and Kamiyama Tamie, trans., *Diary of Darkness: The Wartime Diary of Kiyosawa Kiyoshi* (Princeton, NJ: Princeton University Press, 1999); Tatsuzō Ishikawa, *Soldiers Alive*, translated by Zeljko Cipris (Honolulu: University of Hawai'i Press, 2003); and Midori Yamanouchi and Joseph L. Quinn, trans., *Listen to the Voices from the Sea: Kike Wadatsumi no Koe* (Scranton, PA: Scranton University Press, 2000).

2. The combat diary of Lieutenant Sugihara Kinryū was translated into English and

published in 1995 as "Diary of First Lieutenant Sugihara Kinryū: Iwo Jima, January–February 1945," *Journal of Military History* 59 (1995): 97–133.

3. John Dower, *War without Mercy: Race and Power in the Pacific War* (New York: Pantheon Books, 1986), 293–317.

4. See James William Morley, "Introduction: Choice and Consequence," and Edwin O. Reischauer, "What Went Wrong?" in *Dilemmas of Growth in Prewar Japan*, edited by James William Morley (Princeton, NJ: Princeton University Press, 1971), 3–30 and 489–510.

5. There were four notable exceptions. Robert Butow's *Tojo and the Coming of War* (Princeton, NJ: Princeton University Press, 1961), a study of the Japanese decision to go to war, was far ahead of its time. Thomas Havens' "Women and War in Japan, 1937–1945," *American Historical Review* 80(1975): 913–934, and *Valley of Darkness: The Japanese People and World War Two* (New York: Norton, 1978) are pioneering accounts of the impact of the war on ordinary Japanese. Alvin Coox was the first Western historian to devote his career to the study of the modern Japanese military and World War II. His best-known works are *Year of the Tiger* (Philadelphia: Orient/West, 1964); *The Anatomy of a Small War: The Soviet-Japan Struggle for Changkufeng/Khasa*, Contributions in Military History, no. 13 (Westport, CT: Greenwood Press, 1977); and *Nomonhan: Japan against Russia, 1939* (Stanford, CA: Stanford University Press, 1985). Gordon Daniels, a British historian, was one of the first to write about Japan's wartime experience in the 1970s. See his "The Great Tokyo Air Raid, 9–10 March 1945," in *Modern Japan: Aspects of History, Literature and Society*, edited by W. G. Beasley (Berkeley: University of California Press, 1975), 113–131.

6. John Toland, *The Rising Sun: The Decline and Fall of the Japanese Empire, 1936–1945* (New York: Random House, 1970), xxxv.

7. Margot Norris, ed., *Writing War in the Twentieth Century* (Charlottesville: University of Virginia Press, 2000), 21–22.

8. Hugh Borton, Review of *The Rising Sun: The Decline and Fall of the Japanese Empire, 1936–1945*, by John Toland, *American Historical Review* 77 (1972): 193.

9. Richard Storry, review of *Japan's Imperial Conspiracy*, by David Bergamini, *Pacific Affairs* 45 (1972): 276; Alvin Coox, review of *Japan's Imperial Conspiracy*, by David Bergamini, *American Historical Review* 77 (1972): 1169–1170; Shumpei Okamoto, review of *Japan's Imperial Conspiracy*, by David Bergamini, *Journal of Asian Studies* 31 (1972): 416.

10. Iris Chang's *The Rape of Nanking: The Forgotten Holocaust of World War II* (New York: Basic Books, 1997) is typical in this regard. A best-seller that brought the Nanjing massacre to the attention of an American reading public, *The Rape of Nanking* is riddled with historical errors, filled with the most tendentious and preposterous historical generalizations, and not at all well grounded in primary source material.

11. The first of these deal with Japan's occupation of Southeast Asia: David Steinberg's *Philippine Collaboration in World War Two* and Joyce Lebra's *Jungle Alliance: Japan and the Indian National Army* and *Japanese-Trained Armies in Southeast Asia: Independence and Volunteer Forces in World War II*. Thomas Havens' "Women and War in Japan, 1937–1945" and *Valley of Darkness* give us unforgettable images of the home front during the war, and Paul Dull's *A Battle History of the Imperial Japanese Navy (1941–1945)* offers the first scholarly account of the Japanese navy in World War II.

The 1980s brought much more: Akira Iriye's *Power and Culture: The Japanese Ameri-*

can War, 1941–1945, an innovative study of the political and cultural dimensions of U.S.–Japanese relations; Theodore Friend's *The Blue-Eyed Enemy: Japan against the West in Java and Luzon, 1942–1945,* a study of the Japanese occupation of two parts of Southeast Asia; Ben-Ami Shillony's *Politics and Culture in Wartime Japan,* a collection of essays on Japan's wartime leadership and culture; Alvin Coox's *Nomonhan: Japan against Russia, 1939,* a prize-winning account of the battle of Nomonhan; John Stephan's *Hawaii under the Rising Sun: Japan's Plans for Conquest after Pearl Harbor;* Shunsuke Tsurumi's *An Intellectual History of Wartime Japan, 1931–1945,* a translation of his *Senjiki Nihon no seishinshi;* Gregory Kasza's *The State and the Mass Media in Japan 1918–1945,* a study of the Japanese government's control of the mass media; Grant Goodman's article on Filipino students in wartime Japan; Mark Peattie's *Nanyō: The Rise and Fall of the Japanese in Micronesia, 1885–1945,* a groundbreaking examination of Japanese expansion in the South Pacific; and John Dower's *War without Mercy: Race and Power in the Pacific War,* an analysis of wartime propaganda which won several prizes and had a wide influence.

The 1990s produced an embarrassment of riches: Peter Duus', Ramon Myers', and Mark Peattie's books on Japan's colonial and wartime empires; Meiron Harries and Susie Harries' *Soldiers of the Sun: The Rise and Fall of the Imperial Japanese Army,* the first English-language history of the Japanese army; Ian Buruma's *Wages of Guilt: Memories of War in Germany and Japan;* Abe Mark Nornes and Yukio Fukushima's *The Japan–America Film Wars: WWII Propaganda and Its Cultural Contexts;* Roger Dingman's *The Sinking of the Awa Maru;* Mark Peattie and David Evans' *Kaigun: Strategy, Tactics, and Technology in the Imperial Japanese Navy, 1887–1941,* a new history of the Japanese navy which won the Samuel Eliot Morison Prize; Paul H. Kratoska's *The Japanese Occupation of Malaya, 1941–1945: A Social and Economic History;* Brian Victoria's *Zen at War,* which documents the compliance and resistance of the Zen establishment; Edward J. Drea's *In the Service of the Emperor: Essays on the Imperial Japanese Army;* Janice Matsumura's *More Than a Momentary Nightmare: The Yokohama Incident and Wartime Japan,* a study of the most famous case of wartime censorship; and Peter Wetzler's *Hirohito and War: Imperial Tradition and Military Decision Making in Prewar Japan,* a fresh examination of Emperor Hirohito's involvement in the decisions that led to war. Finally, although it deals with postwar Japan, John Dower's *Embracing Defeat: Japan in the Wake of World War II* is a brilliant study of how Japanese coped with defeat which won a Pulitzer Prize and ten other prizes.

The first scholarly work on Japanese war crimes and atrocities also appeared in the 1990s. In 1994, two important studies were published: Gavan Daws' *Prisoners of the Japanese: POWs of World War II in the Pacific,* the first systematic study of Japanese treatment of Allied prisoners of war; and Sheldon Harris' *Factories of Death: Japanese Biological Warfare, 1932–1945,* an examination of the Japanese biological warfare program. Tanaka Yuki's *Hidden Horrors: Japanese War Crimes in World War II,* originally published in Japanese, followed in 1998 and offered a careful analysis of Japanese atrocities in the South Pacific. Daqing Yang wrote two important accounts of the debates surrounding the Nanjing massacre: "A Sino-Japanese Controversy: The Nanjing Massacre in History" and "Convergence or Divergence? Recent Historical Writings on the Rape of Nanking."

Scholarly interest in the war shows every sign of continuing in this century. Herbert Bix's *Hirohito and the Making of Modern Japan;* Joshua Fogel's *The Nanjing Massacre in History and Historiography;* and Yoshiaki Yoshimi's *Comfort Women: Sexual Slavery in the*

Japanese Military during World War II, a translation of his *Jūgen ianfu*, were published in 2000. Mark Peattie's *Sunburst: The Rise of Japanese Naval Air Power, 1909–1941*, a study of Japanese naval aviation, appeared in 2001. Emiko Ohnuki-Tierney's *Kamikaze, Cherry Blossoms and Nationalisms: The Militarization of Aesthetics in Japanese History*, the first scholarly study of the kamikaze phenomenon; and Brian Daizen Victoria's *Zen War Stories*, a sequel to his earlier *Zen at War*, were released in 2003.

12. Edward M. Coffman, "The New American Military History," *Military Affairs* (January 1984): 1–5; Peter Karsten, "The 'New' American Military History: A Map of the Territory, Explored and Unexplored," *American Quarterly* 36 (1984): 389–418; Richard H. Kohn, "The Social History of the American Soldier: A Review and Prospectus for Research," *American Historical Review* 86 (June 1981): 553–567. Also see Gerald F. Linderman, *The Mirror of War: American Society and the Spanish-American War* (Ann Arbor: University of Michigan Press, 1974), *Embattled Courage: The Experience of Combat in the American Civil War* (New York: Free Press, 1989), and *The World within War: America's Combat Experience in World War II* (New York: Free Press, 1997).

13. Alf Lüdtke, ed., *The History of Everyday Life: Reconstructing Historical Experiences and Ways of Life*, translated by William Templer (Princeton, NJ: Princeton University Press, 1995), 3–4, 16, 18–19 (italics in the original).

14. One of the best of such studies is Detlev Peukert's *Inside Nazi Germany: Conformity, Opposition, and Racism in Everyday Life*, translated by Richard Deveson (New Haven, CT: Yale University Press, 1987).

15. See Edward J. Drea, "Trained in the Hardest School" and "A Signals Intercept Site" in *In the Service of the Emperor: Essays on the Imperial Japanese Army*, by Edward J. Drea (Lincoln: University of Nebraska Press, 1998), 75–90, 110–126; Gavin Daws, *Prisoners of the Japanese: POWs of World War II in the Pacific* (New York: Morrow, 1994); Sheldon H. Harris, *Factories of Death: Japanese Biological Warfare, 1932–1945*, rev. ed. (New York: Routledge, 1994); and Yuki Tanaka, *Hidden Horrors: Japanese War Crimes in World War II* (Boulder, CO: Westview Press, 1998). German novelist Christa Wolf coined the term "active identification and involvement"; see Lüdtke, *The History of Everyday Life*, 24. Also see Yoshiaki Yoshimi, *Comfort Women: Sexual Slavery in the Japanese Military during World War II*, translated by Suzanne O'Brien (New York: Columbia University Press, 2000); and Chungmoo Choi, ed., "women: colonization, war, and sex," a special issue of *positions* 5 (Spring 1997).

16. Monbushō, *Kuni no ayumi* (Tokyo: Monbushō, 1946), vol. 3, 51.

17. Hans H. Baerwald, *The Purge of Japanese Leaders under the Occupation*, University of California Publications in Political Science (Berkeley: University of California Press, 1959), vol. 8, 78.

18. See, for example, Rekishigaku kenkyūkai, comp., *Taiheiyō sensō-shi* (Tokyo: Aoki shoten, 1971), vols. 4 and 5.

19. Carol Gluck, "The Idea of Showa," *Daedalus* 119 (3): 13. Lisa Yoneyama raises similar issues in her analysis of the ways in which the atomic bombing of Hiroshima has been remembered. See her *Hiroshima Traces: Time, Space and the Dialectics of Memory* (Berkeley: University of California Press, 1999), 1–13, 208–210.

20. See Havens, *Valley of Darkness*, 34. Some scholars regard the Japanese invasion of Manchuria in September 1931 as the start of what they call the "Fifteen-Year War." See Ienaga Saburō, *The Pacific War: World War II and the Japanese*, translated by Frank Baldwin (New York: Pantheon Books, 1978), 3. Also see John Dower, *Embracing Defeat:*

Japan in the Wake of World War II (New York: Norton/New Press, 1999), 37, 294–301. Citing a 1956 report of Japan's Ministry of Health and Welfare, Ienaga Saburō stated that 2.3 million Japanese died between July 1937 and August 1945 from "combat, combat-related injuries, and war-related fatal illnesses" (*The Pacific War*, 152).

21. Samuel Hynes distinguishes diaries and journals from memoirs, observing that the former are typically written for oneself and have an immediacy lacking in memoirs, which are written well after the fact and include considerable reflection. See Samuel Hynes, "Personal Narratives and Commentaries," in *War and Remembrance in the Twentieth Century*, edited by Jay Winter and Emmanuel Sivan (Cambridge: Cambridge University Press, 1999), xx. Also see Ienaga, *The Pacific War*, 208.

22. I am referring to personal diaries and not the official war diaries and daily action reports that Japanese officers, like officers in all modern armies, were required to keep.

23. "Itabashi Yasuo nikki," in *Ware tokkō ni shisu: Yokaren no ikō*, compiled by Orihara Noboru (Tokyo: Keizai ōraisha, 1973), 358–399.

24. Nomura Seiki, *Okinawa haihei nikki: Gyokusaisen ittōhei no shuki* (Tokyo: Taihei shuppansha, 1974).

25. Tamura Tsunejirō, *Shinsan: Senchū sengo kyō no ichi shōmin nikki*, in *Sōsho-dōjidai ni ikiru*, compiled by Oka Mitsuo (Kyoto: Mineruva, 1980), vol. 4.

26. Takahashi Aiko, "Kaisen kara no nikki," and Yoshizawa Hisako, "Shūsen made," in *Shōwa sensō bungaku zenshū*, edited by Agawa Hiroyuki et al. (Tokyo: Shūeisha, 1972), 322–357 and 358–388.

27. Maeda Shōko, "Joshi kinrō hōshi taiin no kiroku," in *Chiran tokubetsu kōgekitai*, compiled by Muranaga Tsutomu (Kagoshima: Yugensha japurau, 1998), 76–89; Nakane Mihōko, *Sokai gakudō no nikki: Kyūsai no shojo ga toraeta shūsen zengo* (Tokyo: Chūō kōronsha, 1965); "Manabe Ichirō nikki," in *Shiryō de kataru gakudō sokai*, vol. 5 of *Gakudō sokai no kiroku*, compiled by Zenkoku sokai gakudō renraku kyōgikai (Tokyo: Ōzorasha, 1994), vol. 3, 276–314.

28. John Keegan, *The Face of Battle* (New York: Penguin Books, 1978), 45–46.

29. Geoffrey Eley, foreword to *The History of Everyday Life*, by Alf Lüdtke, viii–x.

30. Drea, *In the Service of the Emperor*, 78; Harries and Harries, *Soldiers of the Sun*, 259–260; Havens, *Valley of Darkness*, 140–141.

31. Peter Sano, *A Thousand Days in Siberia: The Odyssey of a Japanese-American POW* (Lincoln: University of Nebraska Press, 1997), 26–28.

32. See Nakane Mihōko nikki, 5/10/45, 7/9/45, and 7/23/45. The "greeting of the spirits of the war dead" is depicted beautifully in Kinoshita Keisuke's 1954 film, *Twenty-four Eyes* (*Nijūshi no hitomi*), which is based on Tsuboi Sakae's novel of the same title.

33. Rekishigaku kenkyūkai, *Taiheiyō sensō-shi*, 5, II, 97–98; Akimoto Ritsuo, *Sensō to minshū: Taiheiyō sensōka no toshi seikatsu* (Tokyo: Gakuyō shobō, 1974), 103–106; Takahashi Aiko nikki, 6/22/43.

34. Havens, *Valley of Darkness*, 119–123, 131–132; B. F. Johnson, with Mosaburo Hosoda and Yoshio Kusumi, *Japanese Food Management in World War II* (Stanford, CA: Stanford University Press, 1953), 151–164.

35. Rekishigaku kenkyūkai, *Taiheiyō sensō-shi*, 5, II, 109; Manabe Ichirō nikki, 7/26/44, 8/2/44, 8/4/44; Tamura Tsunejirō nikki, 11/30/44.

36. Havens, *Valley of Darkness*, 7, 10–14, 16–19, 25, 36–43.

37. Akimoto, *Sensō to minshū*, 48–49. Akimoto says the average number of households in a neighborhood association was ten, but his statistics suggest nine.

38. Havens, *Valley of Darkness*, 77; Rekishigaku kenkyūkai, *Taiheiyō sensō-shi*, 5, II, 117–118.

39. *Asahi shinbun*, 5/14/44, cited in Akimoto, *Sensō to minshū*, 65.

40. Havens, *Valley of Darkness*, 72–73.

41. Havens, *Valley of Darkness*, 84.

42. Gregory J. Kasza, *The State and the Mass Media in Japan 1918–1945* (Berkeley: University of California Press, 1988), 14–20, 200–206; Havens, *Valley of Darkness*, 21; Ben-Ami Shillony, *Politics and Culture in Wartime Japan* (New York: Oxford University Press, 1981), 94.

43. Shillony, *Politics and Culture in Wartime Japan*, 93–94.

44. Kasza, *The State and the Media*, 217–218, 223–225; Shillony, *Politics and Culture in Wartime Japan*, 92; Havens, *Valley of Darkness*, 62. Havens and Shillony differ slightly on this point: Havens believes that there were 454 newspapers at the outset; Shillony says 848; see Havens, *Valley of Darkness*, 22.

45. Havens, *Valley of Darkness*, 63.

46. Haruko Taya Cook and Theodore F. Cook, comps., *Japan at War: An Oral History* (New York: New Press, 1992), 208–220; Kasza, *The State and the Media in Modern Japan*, 225–231; Matsumura, *More Than a Momentary Nightmare*, 13–24; Frank Gibney, ed., and Beth Cary, trans., *Sensō: The Japanese Remember the Pacific War* (Armonk, NY: Sharpe, 1995), 106, 195, 197–198.

47. Takahashi Aiko nikki, 9/9/43, 4/25/45; Yoshizawa Hisako nikki, 3/10/45.

48. Shillony, *Politics and Culture in Wartime Japan*, 96; Takahashi Aiko nikki, 4/21/43; Tamura Tsunejirō nikki, 10/22/44.

49. Rekishigaku kenkyūkai, *Taiheiyō sensō-shi*, 5, II, 119–120; Havens, *Valley of Darkness*, 140, 161–162.

50. Havens, *Valley of Darkness*, 162–163.

51. Kit C. Carter and Robert Mueller, comps., *U.S. Army Air Forces in World War II: Combat Chronology, 1941–1945* (Washington, D.C.: Center for Air Force History, 1991), 505, 508–509, 513.

52. E. Bartlett Kerr, *Flames over Tokyo: The U.S. Army Air Forces' Incendiary Campaign against Japan, 1944–1945* (New York: Donald I. Fine, 1999), 21–54, 89–121, 148–149.

53. Carter and Mueller, *Combat Chronology*, 594; Kerr, *Flames over Tokyo*, 151–154, 207.

54. Carter and Mueller, *Combat Chronology*, 626, 654–655. The May 23 attack was the largest B-29 mission of the entire war.

55. Kerr, *Flames over Tokyo*, 324–335, 337–338.

56. Havens, *Valley of Darkness*, 124, 188–189; Rekishigaku kenkyūkai, *Taiheiyō sensō-shi*, 5, II, 111, 123–124, 127, 133, 136, 174.

57. See Harry S. Truman, *Memoirs*, vol. 1, *Years of Decisions* (Garden City, NY: Doubleday, 1955), 419.

58. Alvin Coox, "The Pacific War," in *The Twentieth Century*, 372–376, vol. 6 of *The Cambridge History of Japan*, edited by Peter Duus (Cambridge: Cambridge University Press, 1988).

59. Rachel Langford and Russell West, "Introduction: Diaries and Margins," in *Marginal Voices, Marginal Forms*, edited by Rachel Langford and Russell West (Atlanta: Rodopi B.V., 1999), 6, 12; Suzanne L. Bunkers, ed., *Diaries of Girls and Women: A Midwestern American Sampler* (Madison: University of Wisconsin Press, 2001) 14; Cathryn Carter, *Voix feminists, Feminist Voices: Diaries in English by Women in Canada, 1753–1995, an*

Annotated Bibliography (Ottawa: CRIAW/ICREF, 1997), 20; Margo Culley, ed., *A Day at a Time: The Diary Literature of American Women from 1764 to the Present* (New York: Feminist Press at CUNY, 1985), 10; Hynes, "Personal Narratives and Commentaries," 210; Hayden White, *Tropics of Discourse: Essays in Cultural Criticism* (Baltimore: Johns Hopkins University Press, 1978), 82–83, 121–134.

60. Tamura Tsunejirō nikki, 10/8/44, 11/5/44, 4/1/45; Takahashi Aiko nikki, 6/17/45.

61. Nakane Mihōko nikki, 4/9/45.

62. Takahashi Aiko nikki, 2/21/42, 4/21/43, 11/11/43.

63. Takahashi Aiko nikki, 3/27/43; Tamura Tsunejirō nikki, 10/8/44.

64. Tamura Tsunejirō nikki, 1/15/45.

65. Manabe Ichirō nikki, 7/21/44.

66. Yoshizawa Hisako nikki, 1/30/45; Tamura Tsunejirō nikki, 3/5/45.

67. Takahashi Aiko nikki, 2/18/42, 4/21/43; Tamura Tsunejirō nikki, 7/19/44.

68. During the war the *tokkō* (*tokubetsu kōtō keishisai* [special higher police]) and the *kenpeitai* (military police) monitored and suppressed the activity of any individuals, groups, or political movements that threatened the national security, *kokutai* (national polity), and/or the emperor.

69. Takahashi Aiko nikki, 2/22/44; Tamura Tsunejirō nikki, 7/21/44; Manabe Ichirō nikki, 7/21/44.

70. See the recollections in Gibney, *Sensō*, 177–179.

71. Takahashi Aiko nikki, 6/10/43.

72. Takahashi Aiko nikki, 10/21/43; Isoko Hatano, comp., *Mother and Son: The Wartime Correspondence of Isoko and Ichiro Hatano* (Boston: Houghton Mifflin, 1962), 11–12.

73. See Ōda Makoto's contemporary account of *gyokusai* in the English translation of his novel *The Breaking Jewel*, translated by Donald Keene (New York: Columbia University Press, 2003).

74. Tamura Tsunejirō nikki, 8/2/44; Takahashi Aiko nikki, 8/29/44.

75. Tamura Tsunejirō nikki, 10/22/44; Takahashi Aiko nikki, 9/9/43, 3/10/44, 10/19/44.

76. Tamura Tsunejirō nikki, 12/1/44, 2/20/45.

77. Yoshizawa Hisako nikki, 11/30/44; Tamura Tsunejirō nikki, 12/15/44. Actually, seventy or more B-29s bombed Nagoya on December 13. See Carter and Mueller, *Combat Chronology*, 520.

78. Yoshizawa Hisako nikki, 1/6/45, 1/30/45, 2/20/45.

79. Yoshizawa Hisako nikki, 1/28/45; Takahashi Aiko nikki, 2/25/45; Tamura Tsunejirō nikki, 1/16/45.

80. Carter and Mueller, *Combat Chronology*, 563, 582.

81. Carter and Mueller, *Combat Chronology*, 595, 597.

82. Tamura Tsunejirō nikki, 3/14/45; Takahashi Aiko nikki, 3/10/45 and 4/15/45; Yoshizawa Hisako nikki, 3/11/45.

83. Tamura Tsunejirō nikki, 3/10/45, 3/11/45; Yoshizawa Hisako nikki, 4/8/45, 5/10/45.

84. Yoshizawa Hisako nikki, 2/28/45; Tamura Tsunejirō nikki, 3/12/45.

85. Tamura Tsunejirō nikki, 5/3/45.

86. Takahashi Aiko nikki, 1/4/44; Manabe Ichirō nikki, 7/21/44.

87. Takahashi Aiko nikki, 7/18/44, 10/6/44; Yoshizawa Hisako nikki, 1/12/45, 2/26/45, 3/14/45.

88. Yoshizawa Hisako nikki, 3/30/45, 3/31/45, 7/1/45, 8/4/45.

89. Yoshizawa Hisako nikki, 6/4/45; Takahashi Aiko nikki, 4/10/45, 7/11/45.

90. Yoshizawa Hisako nikki, 4/30/45, 6/29/45; Takahashi Aiko nikki, 5/27/45.

91. Manabe Ichirō nikki, 11/25/44, 12/6/44, 12/9/44, 12/11/44, 12/17/44, 12/21/44, 12/24/44, 12/25/44; Nakane Mihōko nikki, 4/18/45, 4/21/45, 4/22/45, 4/23/45, 4/25/45, 5/1/45, 5/4/45, 5/6/45, 5/10/45, 5/11/45, 5/21/45, 5/24/45, 5/25/45, 5/27/45, 5/28/45, 6/1/45, 6/3/45, 6/4/45, 6/10/45, 6/12/45, 6/15/45, 6/18/45, 6/20/45, 6/26/45, 6/27/45, 7/5/45, 7/22/45, 7/29/45, 8/2/45, 8/3/45, 8/4/45, 8/6/45, 8/13/45.

92. Manabe Ichirō nikki, 12/2/44, 12/19/44; Nakane Mihōko nikki, 4/27/45, 5/1/45, 5/2/45, 5/14/45, 5/19/45, 6/9/45, 6/30/45, 7/14/45, 8/1/45, 8/10/45.

93. See Michel Foucault's discussion of the "subject" in modern states in his "The Subject and Power," *Critical Inquiry* 8 (Summer 1982): 777–795.

94. Nakane Mihōko nikki, 8/10/45.

95. Nakane Mihōko nikki, 5/8/45, 6/8/45; Kaigo Muneomi, ed., *Nihon kyōkasho taikei* (Tokyo: Kōdansha, 1962), vol. 3, 403–404.

96. Kaigo, *Nihon kyōkasho taikei*, III, 640.

97. Manabe Ichirō nikki, 11/26/44; Nakane Mihōko nikki, 4/18/45, 4/23/45, 5/7/45, 5/24/45, 5/28/45, 5/30/45, 6/10/45, 6/15/45.

98. Nakane Mihōko nikki, 6/17/45; the special-attack pilots that Maeda Shōko and her classmates befriended encouraged them "to kill at least one person before they die." See also Linderman, *The World within War*, 159–160.

99. Linderman, *The World within War*, 159–160.

100. Manabe Ichirō nikki, 11/29/44, 11/30/44, 12/12/44; Nakane Mihōko nikki, 4/13/45, 4/14/45, 5/9/45, 5/22/45, 7/7/45, 7/12/45, 7/17/45, 7/19/45, 7/21/45, 7/23/45. Judith Butler's conception of "performative acts" inspired this analysis. See Judith Butler, "Performative Acts and Gender Constitution: An Essay in Phenomenology and Feminist Theory," in *Performing Theory and Theater*, edited by Ellen Case (Baltimore: Johns Hopkins University Press, 1990), 270–273.

101. Itabashi Yasuo nikki, 3/22/45.

102. Itabashi Yasuo nikki, 1/3/45, 3/22/45, 3/23/45.

103. Itabashi Yasuo nikki, 11/15/44, 1/14/45, 2/22/45.

104. Linderman, *The World within War*, 263–299.

105. See the "last letters" collected in Mabuchi Fujio, comp., *Kaigun tokubetsu kōgekitai no isho* (Tokyo: KK Bestu serazu, 1971); Naemura Shichirō, comp., *Mansei tokkōtaiin no isho* (Tokyo: Gendai hyōronsha, 1976); and Hakuō izokukai, comp., *Kumo nagaruru hate ni* (Tokyo: Nihon shuppan kyōdō kabushiki kaisha, 1953).

106. Itabashi Yasuo nikki, 4/7/45, 4/8/45.

107. Nomura Seiki nikki, 8/5/45, 8/19/45.

108. Nomura Seiki nikki, 8/6/45.

109. Nomura Seiki nikki, 8/10/45.

110. See, for example, references to the emperor in the most widely distributed pieces of government propaganda: the Ministry of Education's *Way of the Subjects* and the Imperial Japanese Army's *Field Service Code*; both were issued in 1941.

111. Nomura Seiki nikki, 8/17/45, 8/18/45.

112. Takahashi Aiko nikki, 8/10/45; Yoshizawa Hisako nikki, 8/13/45.

113. Takahashi Aiko nikki, 8/10/45, 8/14/45.

114. Takahashi Aiko nikki, 8/15/45; Yoshizawa Hisako nikki, 8/15/45.

115. Nakane Mihōko nikki, 8/17/45.

116. Nomura Seiki nikki, 9/13/45.

Japanese Wartime Diaries

The Diary of a Navy Special-Attack Pilot

Itabashi Yasuo was born in Fukushima Prefecture in 1923. In April 1941, when he was eighteen, he enlisted in the navy and underwent basic training at Tsuchiura Naval Air Base in Ibaraki Prefecture. In October he began specialized pilot training at Yatabe, Usa, and several air bases in Kyushu, where he saw action for the first time. In October 1943, he was transferred to the 503rd Air Group, which was based at Kisarazu Air Base in Chiba Prefecture.

Itabashi moved with elements of the 503rd to the South Pacific in February 1944 and flew combat missions from air bases on Truk, New Guinea, Peleliu, and Yap. While attacking Allied shipping on June 8, Itabashi's aircraft was hit by antiaircraft fire, and he was forced to land on Biak Island, a Japanese-held island just off the northeast coast of New Guinea. Later, he left Biak for Manokwari in western New Guinea, where he was stranded for four months. In October 1944, he was ferried by flying boat to Macassar in the Celebes and spent the next four months in Java, the Philippines, Singapore, and former French Indochina. He was flown from Saigon to Japan on March 3–5, 1945.

Once back in Japan, Itabashi discovered that most of his comrades in the 503rd had been killed, and he made clear his wish to fly on a special-attack mission as soon as possible. Instead he was reassigned to the 601st Air Group, based at Katori Air Base in Ibaraki Prefecture, where he trained navy pilots to fly dive bombers. On August 9, Itabashi finally got his wish. At 2:14 p.m. that afternoon he flew from a naval air base on Kyushu as a member of the No. 4 Great Shield Special-Attack Squadron and was killed in action in Kingazan Bay off the island of Okinawa. At the time of his death he was twenty-one years old and a superior flight petty officer. He was also the second of his siblings to die in a special attack; his older brother Origasa was killed in an attack on an American carrier in the seas off the Philippines in November 1944.

Itabashi's diary is included in *Ware tokkō ni shisu* (*We Will Die in Special Attacks*), 358–399, edited by Orihara Noboru and published by Keizai ōraisha in 1973.

February 18, 1944

This is my final departure from the home islands. I have paid my respects to those who have helped me. I have no regrets.

February 22, 1944

We took off from Kisarazu Air Base, forty Comets advancing on a course to the site of the decisive battle.[1]

We arrived at Iwo Jima at 1:00 p.m., and our planes immediately were armed.[2]

We remained on Iwo Jima for about ten days. On February 7 Truk was bombed, and then on the thirteenth Saipan and Tinian were hit, too. Thus our standing by on Iwo Jima was unavoidable.

The advance group of aircraft that left at the beginning of February reached Truk just as it was being attacked, and they went into the drink. Everyone felt terrible about this.

I met Uesugi on Iwo Jima.[3]

Also enjoyed eating sugarcane.

And I had a good time flying patrols and the like.

March 1944

We finally moved on to Saipan in March.

We were to stay there for a while. We were housed at the official instructors' residence, which was in front of a primary school, and we were separated according to squadron.

Our stay on Saipan was interesting. I would buy sweet potatoes and have them for a late-night snack. If I were in my quarters on standby in the afternoon, I would "break out" of Charanka and Garapan and lay in a store of beef and green onions for a late-night snack.[4]

---

1. Kisarazu was the site of a naval air base in eastern Japan. The Yokosuka D4Y Suisei (Comet) was a carrier bomber developed to replace the Aichi D3A2 (Val). Comets began to be used in the fall of 1942 and saw action through the end of the war.

2. Iwo Jima, the center island of the three Volcano Islands, is about 660 nautical miles from Tokyo.

3. Itabashi does not identify Uesugi or explain their relationship.

4. It is not clear what "breaking out of Charanka and Garapan" refers to. Both are cities on Saipan.

Itabashi Yasuo (third from left in second row), July 27, 1943. Courtesy of Itabashi family.

We then left the easy life of Saipan and at long last moved on to Kaedejima Air Base — and the real war.[5]

What was most astonishing were the air raids. Consolidated B-24 strikes caused a ruckus.

I've forgotten what day it was, but there was an air raid at about midnight, and we cleared the air.

The attack resulted in six deaths — beginning with Sergeant Yoshimatsu, the First Squadron's senior noncommissioned officer, and including Yamazumi, Imai, Sei, Miyamoto, and Sawamura.[6] They were the 503rd Air Group's first war dead.

Once I got used to it, Kaedejima Air Base was interesting. Each squadron's quarters were situated on the side of a hill that looked like a small mountain. Since its formation, our unit, the Second Squadron, has not had any deaths, and our morale continues to rise. Whenever there's liquor, we stage variety shows and have a good time.

---

5. Kaedejima Air Base was on the island of Truk, then held by the Japanese, in the Caroline Island Group.

6. Itabashi uses "sacrificial victim" (J. *giseisha*), the conventional epithet for someone killed in action.

If there's an air raid during the day, air operations are suspended, and there's bomb damage.

Senior Warrant Officer Kunihara and Itakura from the Third Squadron shot down a B-24.[7]

Four aircraft (1/22, 1/12, 1/25, 1/33) went out searching for the enemy in a 1,200-nautical-mile area.

First Lieutenant Yano and Sergeant Yamazaki manned 1/12. Theirs was a reconnaissance mission behind enemy lines in Kabien, and after they sent a "fire" transmission, they disengaged.[8] It seems that enemy fighters got them, and they both died.

Second Lieutenant Nishimura and I, in 1/22, searched for the enemy for seven hours but found nothing and returned to Truk after sundown in the midst of a squall.

We got a report out of the blue that Palau and Yap were being bombed by aircraft from an enemy task force, and the 503rd's Comet Carrier Bomber Squadron was armed and flew to an air base on Guam.[9] When there were no reported sightings, we returned to Truk after three or four days.

As might have been expected, Guam had Yankee dwellings, which were extravagant.

When we took off for Guam, Yamamoto and Konō from the First Squadron stalled on takeoff and crashed, and the Third Squadron's Sergeants Kimura and Kasai, my flying school classmate, made an emergency landing somewhere between Truk and Guam and were lost. And on the return flight to Truk, the Second Squadron's Sergeant Hayasaka and Suzuki made a forced landing in the same area. All together, this mission produced six deaths.

April 1944

In mid-April, a surprise-attack unit was formed, and the Second Squadron became the No. 3 Surprise-Attack Unit, and we flew to the No. 2 base in Harujima and stood by. They weren't quite ready for us, and our living quarters, clothing, and food were inadequate, but it was an interesting time.

Hearing that an enemy fleet was in the vicinity of Greenwich Island, we sortied for an attack, but the enemy wasn't there.

Hatakeyama, Kugino, Okimoto, and Kujima were killed on this mission.

---

7. The Comet had a two-man crew: a pilot and a radio operator/gunner.
8. The word *hi* "fire" is in code, and its meaning is not clear.
9. Guam is an island in the Mariana Island Group, then held by Japan.

April 26, 1944

We finally got orders to go to New Guinea. We left for Truk early on the morning of April 25, passed Guam and Peleliu, and arrived at Baboo Air Base on New Guinea on the afternoon of the twenty-sixth.[10]

There was only one bomb cart, and it took a whole day to arm all the planes (sixteen aircraft).

April 27, 1944

We were bombed early this morning, and although our planes were not damaged, I felt more dead than alive. The bombing was extremely precise.

On the way, Yabu and Hamazaki made an emergency landing on Yap, and Third Squadron fliers Senior Warrant Officer Kunihara and Itakura made an emergency landing at Soron.[11] Both were unharmed.

April 30, 1944

On April 30 we received a report that an enemy task force was attacking Truk.

We also heard that the remaining four Comets and five Heavenly Mountains sortied but that none of them returned—I was furious and sorry.[12] The dead—Mukojima, Matsuura, Matsuda, Dogi, Hayakawa, and a brand-new first lieutenant.

If all of us had been at Truk, not one carrier would have returned (there were reports of ten enemy carriers in the area).

We were ordered to return to our home squadron and left Baboo Air Base.

At the base on Peleliu we passed the time guarding the fleet.

After four or five days we were ordered to move to an air base on Yap, which was the first time we had moved as a squadron to Yap. Here, too, we stood by and guarded the fleet.

May 31, 1944

"The 'A' Strategy Commenced."

Ten aircraft carriers advanced in a single line.

The 503rd Air Group was ordered to proceed to Soron. We left Yap on May 31 and headed to Peleliu.

---

10. Peleliu is a tiny coral atoll at the south end of the Palau Island Group.

11. Soron Air Base was on Peleliu.

12. The Nakajima B6N Tenzan (Heavenly Mountain) was developed as a carrier-based torpedo bomber.

June 1, 1944, clear

Early in the morning we took off from Peleliu, headed for Washire Air Base. Our flight consisted of fourteen planes. The fighter group had forty-five planes.

June 2, 1944, clear

Fourteen of our Comets took off from Washire and returned to Soron. Our planes were immediately armed and put on alert.

June 3, 1944, clear

Our first encampment. Early in the morning we left Soron Air Base to attack the enemy fleet south of Biak Island.[13]

We attacked despite bad weather.

Twenty P-40s stood guard in the air above the fleet, and they suddenly went into a daring dive from four thousand meters. We had nine Comets and thirty-two Zeros.

The results were one destroyer sunk, one cruiser heavily damaged, one transport damaged, and ground installations burned.

On our side, three Comets and six Zeros did not return (Kawasaki, Sasaki, Takahashi, Hara, Adachihara, Togashi).

June 4, 1944, clear

We made great military gains.

We were elated to get a report that an enemy task force consisting of two carriers had been sighted, and six dive bombers and thirty fighters sortied. Having flown yesterday, I couldn't go today.

The carriers turned out to be misidentified first-class heavy cruisers.

Our force consisted of nine Comets and nine Zeros.

The results were two heavy cruisers and one destroyer sunk.

We launched a night torpedo attack with a full complement of three planes.

One Comet did not return (Maruko and Matsui).

June 5, 1944, clear

Given what we've achieved with our unrelenting attacks, morale is steadily rising.

Today there were no good enemy targets and thus no attacks. In the afternoon, we were on standby in our quarters, which allowed us to do our laundry for the

---

13. Biak Island is located off the northeast coast of New Guinea.

first time in quite a while, swim in the ocean, and nap. The brave warriors did not spread their wings.[14]

Cool breezes blew through the coconut groves.

June 6, 1944, clear

Today, too, there were no decisive reports from the search planes. No sorties. I'm dying to use my skill as a pilot and am not happy about this situation. Empathize if you can with the feelings of the sea eagles. If a ship appears, I'll take care of it.

As dusk approached, I wondered whether the four planes that hadn't returned would eventually.

June 7, 1944, cloudy then rain

The days with no sorties continued. Second Lieutenant Amori received orders to attack a transport convoy east of Biak Island before dawn tomorrow, June 8.

Our spirits improved a hundredfold, and I went to bed looking forward to certain victory in battle tomorrow.

June 8, 1944, cloudy

We woke at 12:30 a.m., took off at 2:30 a.m., and proceeded to attack the enemy transport convoy.

Today I was in the lead plane. We found the enemy thirty nautical miles from Biak Island and went into a dive. I executed my first dive, then did it again. As I executed my second dive — from 2,500 meters — I dropped my bombs and pulled up. A huge explosion — each one hit! Full speed, full speed! When I looked at my left wing, there was a huge hole about thirty millimeters across in my auxiliary fuel tank, and weren't those flames blowing about? Flying at full speed, I was able to land at Biak's No. 1 Airfield. The moment I touched down, there was a huge conflagration. I was touched by the kindness of the army units. In the evening I went to the navy units' bunker. There was an incredible air raid and an equally incredible naval bombardment.

June 9, 1944

This was the first time I experienced intense ground combat. I was impressed by the pain the enemy aircraft caused. I'm not able to describe fully the courage and tragedy I witnessed.

---

14. The pilots referred to themselves as "sea eagles."

Every night the base is subject to attacks, and it recovers by the next day. It was horrible for those of us without aircraft, and we cried.

I sincerely take my hat off to my war buddies who labor with only *kanpan* to eat all day and with no sleep day or night.

June 10, 1944

I woke suddenly at about 12:30 a.m. I was surprised and happy to discover Adachihara standing in front of headquarters reporting for duty. Togashi was with him.[15] In the morning we got together and talked.

During the June 3 attack, they ditched their plane and then swam for two days and nights and walked for two days—I was surprised at their miraculous return. This should toughen them up, mentally.

At about eleven in the evening, we left the bunker and retreated from the front lines. Our destination was Korimu Bay, ten miles away. We walked silently and avoided the shells that fell on the road.

Lieutenant General Numata, the army chief of staff for the area, was with us, as was Okada, who is with the information team.[16]

At about ten in the morning, we arrived at the six-mile marker, and for a time we walked along the Wahōru River. It has been tough going without water, but from now on there will be rivers, which will be a great help. The evening cold was penetrating. We arrived at the seashore at 1:00 p.m.

At Korimu Bay, there was an army platoon and ten navy guard and communications men. I'm indebted to the navy units.

June 13, 1944

There's no tobacco, and provisions are running low. They say we'll run out in a day or two. I want to return to my base immediately, and although we can wait and survive for a time, there are no ships.

Today there's only the pain of waiting for tomorrow and the loneliness, and besides that, I'm coming down with a cold. Things are getting worse and worse. Sitting in the bunker, we wait impatiently for reinforcements to land. Did I think that? Or didn't I? The reinforcement units haven't come! When I think of the officers and enlisted men in the bunker with me, life at the other bases seems extravagant.

In any case, I'm a patient person. With nothing to do, I just sleep as a way of

---

15. See Itabashi's 6/3/44 entry.

16. Lieutenant General Numata Takazō was the commander of Imperial Japanese Army forces on Biak Island until July 15, 1944, when the island fell to Allied forces.

not getting hungry. There is a group that plays cards, which makes the boredom bearable.

June 16, 1944, clear

In the evening, two navy ships and four army ships arrived all at once. If the conditions are good, they'll set sail tomorrow evening.

June 20, 1944, clear

We arrived safely at Manokwari at 3:30 a.m.[17] The escape from Biak was over.

The guard unit had a surprising report. On the seventeenth, enemy army units landed on Saipan, and B-29s bombed the home islands.[18] Ninety enemy ships and ten enemy carriers are in the process of attacking Saipan.

I really regret not being able to participate in this battle that will decide our fate.

July 19, 1944, clear

At breakfast we heard that our forces on Saipan committed *gyokusai.*

A whole array of emotions suddenly welled up in my chest, and I didn't know what to say. It was as though the chests of those of us without aircraft were about to explode. Why do I have to suffer in this way? Damn![19]

The enemy aircraft were having a field day! Damn!

July 20, 1944, clear

As of today, it's been one month since I came to Manokwari. Lately, it's gotten really hard mentally, and I have loads of psychological problems. There were four enemy air raids, and I felt lousy. It was the piddling work of P-40s.

July 21, 1944, clear

We heard that the Tōjō cabinet resigned.[20] There was an air raid early in the morning, and we were bombed. We wired the commander. Because there's no air service, we are scheduled to go by land to Baboo on the twenty-fifth.

July 22, 1944, clear

Our orders arrived, telling us to go overland to Baboo, and we'll follow them.

---

17. Manokwari is located in western New Guinea.

18. Saipan is an island in the Mariana Island Group that at this time was home to large numbers of both Japanese civilians and servicemen.

19. *Chikushō* is the Japanese equivalent of "damn."

20. Prime Minister Tōjō Hideki resigned on July 18, 1944.

B-24s bombed us at 1:30 p.m., and two bombs fell next to our quarters, and they were a shambles. We managed, with some difficulty, to retrieve our belongings. I feel lousy.

July 23, 1944, cloudy

The enemy has come ashore at Ōmiyajima. The Koiso cabinet was formed.[21] We spent the day preparing for our overland trek, and our preparations were completed by sundown. Tomorrow will be the start of heavy bombing (according to enemy flyers).

July 24, 1944, light rain

We were bombed in the morning. Strafed by P-40s. Our machine-gun nest returned fire, and the men were really brave! One plane was shot down.

Our departure was scheduled for the day after tomorrow.

Yonai Mitsusada was appointed navy minister in the Koiso cabinet.[22]

July 25, 1944, rain

It rained hard in the morning but cleared up after about two o'clock. Our scheduled departure was canceled because of the weather. We slaughtered chickens for dinner — they were really delicious!

The enemy has a plan to come ashore at Tinian, and our forces will repulse them.[23]

July 26, 1944, cloudy

Early this morning we were strafed by four P-40s. The men showed real courage.

---

21. After the Tōjō cabinet collapsed, Koiso Kuniaki formed a new cabinet on July 22, 1944. Like Tōjō, Koiso was an army man, a graduate of the Army War College. He served in the General Staff Office and was head of the Military Affairs Bureau at the time of the March incident of 1931 and was sympathetic to the conspirators' plan. Koiso then served as the minister of colonial affairs in the Hiranuma and Yonai cabinets and as governor-general of Korea.

22. Yonai Mitsusada (1880–1948) was a career navy man who graduated from the Etajima Naval Academy in 1901 and rose quickly through the ranks. He served in Russia, China, and Korea and was something of a Russian specialist and could speak and read Russian. He held the highest command positions, including that of commander in chief of the combined fleet (1936–1937), and served as navy minister in three prewar cabinets before agreeing to fill the post of navy minister in the newly formed Koiso cabinet.

23. Tinian is an island in the Mariana Island Group, located just south of Saipan and north of Guam. American troops landed on Tinian on July 24 and, despite stiff Japanese resistance, secured the island by August 1.

July 27, 1944, clear

The weather gradually improved. There was no indication of when we'd make our overland trek. Lieutenant General Numata, the chief of staff, will go too, which I don't understand. I've lost hope and am no longer interested in living. The enemy has landed on Tinian.

July 29, 1944, clear

Happiness can't be gained without effort. I will make an effort. After all, I have to make the return trip.

At 9:30 a.m. we received a report that "nine warships followed by what look like transports had been spotted," and a general alert was called. We got dressed and waited.

In the afternoon we realized a mistake had been made: they were just PT boats. What a relief!

July 31, 1944, cloudy

There was a report that the enemy had landed at Soron and Manokwari. It appears that the convoy spotted the day before yesterday was the real thing. Will Palau be the next to be bombed? It seems that the enemy task force is coming our way. Will the next landing be at Palau? The situation is coming to a head, but I don't understand the Japanese army's movements at all. Even though the army units are struggling and kicking in places like this, they don't initiate anything. They just wait for a good opportunity.

If the enemy lands here, we'll just fight hard and die. If they come, I say let them come!

August 20, 1944, clear

I had a dream last night. It was about two of my older brothers, Origasa and N. N. has not given me one satisfying dream.

I really want to return quickly to my base, but I'm not the master of my own fate.

August 29, 1944, cloudy

We had a general cleaning of our quarters, both the inside and outside. In the afternoon, Togashi and I finally blew up at each other and came to blows. I was slightly injured. This will be one memory of "Manokwari."

September 6, 1944, cloudy

We did farmwork in the morning and field cooking in the afternoon. Most of the army guard units on Manokwari cook vegetables in a frenzied way.

September 9, 1944, cloudy

I had the day off. I have a feeling the men in the guard units here are colonial subjects.[24] They have had absolutely no training in deployment, but in a pinch, it's said, they can go to general quarters in five minutes.

September 10, 1944, cloudy

In the morning, the guard units had deployment drills, and I was impressed. Because they were away on these drills, we cooked breakfast for ourselves. In the afternoon, we worked in the fields and had *tonkatsu* for dinner.

October 1, 1944, clear

The looked-forward-to month of September ended without incident and became October. I came down with "three-day malaria" and went into the sick bay.

Today was the commemoration of the founding of the Eighteenth Guard Unit—for the main force. We drank heavily, which raised our spirits. Today and tomorrow, reconnaissance seaplanes will arrive from Ambonia.[25] They will take passengers—three officers from headquarters and me—and I'm scheduled for tomorrow. The pilots are, after all, my allies.

October 2, 1944, clear

I was deeply moved last night by Flight Sergeant Major Yonezawa's words: "We'll get you out come hell or high water!"

I left the sick bay. Army Sergeant Major Ōhara's warmth really touched me.

In the afternoon, I paid my respects to the commander and the executive officer, and we had dinner together. Murata came off guard duty at Towan, and I heard his beautiful voice for the last time.

October 3, 1944, clear

While I was fishing on the suspension bridge to kill time, the seaplanes arrived.

It's now 1:00 a.m. I'll finally escape from Manokwari. I felt sad about leaving

---

24. Itabashi may be referring to Korean and Taiwanese conscripts. The Japanese had colonized both Korea and Taiwan, and approximately 200,000 Taiwanese and 200,000 Koreans served in various capacities in the Japanese military during the war.

25. Ambonia is on the island of Ceram in the Molucca Islands.

behind Ashidachihara and Togashi, and when the plane left the water, I was quite overcome with emotion.

The Ambonia-based seaplanes had a crew of twelve men, twelve men for two aircraft.

The base was bombed all day beginning early in the morning, which completely surprised me. We received all sorts of military supplies. Yesterday and the day before I didn't sleep for two nights and am suffering from the lack of sleep.

October 4, 1944, clear

The bombing was intense. I got to sleep last night at about 2:00 a.m.

According to the division commander's story, it appears that our squadron leader, Lieutenant Asaeda, killed himself in the attack on Biak Island. Oh! Poor Division Leader Asaeda and Sergeant Sugano—I am quite overwhelmed![26]

I wonder how Ashidachihara and Togashi fared?

October 5, 1944, cloudy

My quarters here are really splendid.

The town of Ambonia seems to be some distance away. This time, it turns out that I'll go by "large boat" to Macassar on the eighth.[27]

It appears this unit will be dissolved, and I have no idea what will happen next. I'll go first to the Twenty-third Naval Air Flotilla Headquarters on Kendari.[28] Traveling solo is lonely, but it can't be helped.

October 14, 1944, cloudy

The "large boat" arrived.[29] It's scheduled to go to Macassar tomorrow.

The seaplane will search for the enemy. It has a three-man crew, and I'll go along.

October 15, 1944, clear

We left Ambonia at 5:00 a.m. and arrived at Macassar at 9:00 a.m. as four big ships were moving south.

We went out in the afternoon, and amusing ourselves in a city was unusual for

---

26. See Itabashi's 2/11/44 entry for his memories of Sergeant Sugano.

27. Macassar (now Ujung Pandang) is on the southwest side of the island of Sulawesi (formerly Celebes).

28. Kendari is on the southeast side of Sulawesi.

29. The "large boat" was a Kawanishi Type 97 flying boat.

us, a really rare thing. There was one daytime bombing raid, and eight planes took off in pairs. We are steadily making military gains.

October 31, 1944, clear

Last night there was another bombing raid: B-24s and B-17s.[30] They dropped incendiaries, which were more terrifying than before, and the fires were not put out for two days. Here, Rairai Island, is completely neutral.

November 4, 1944, clear

The pilots who went to "Manila" returned with stories to tell, all of which were unusual.

The recent achievements of the kamikaze special-attack units have been striking.[31]

There are reports of self-destruction units made up of Comets and Vals. I bow my head low to them.

November 8, 1944, clear

In the afternoon I had a phone call from Commander Masuda, the vice-commander of the North of Australia Group, and met him at the Navy Club. He told me all sorts of stories.

There are few pilots left. The division leaders flew off to Kokubu Air Base.[32] I went to the First Air Fleet Headquarters in Manila, and my fate has been decided.[33]

November 15, 1944, clear

I learned I'm in the same divine wind special-attack squadron as Second Lieutenant Kunihara and Sergeant Asao Hiroshi, which surprised me.

The 503rd Air Group has been decimated. There are just a handful of survivors. Like the others, I'll go off on a special attack. Everyone wants to join his friends. I'm just amazed by the strange tricks fate plays on us.

---

30. Itabashi identifies the bombers as *consori* and *boingu*. The former refers to the Consolidated B-24, and the latter probably refers to the Boeing B-17.

31. The navy first used what it called "special attack" (J. *tokkō*) tactics in late October 1944 in the Philippines, and the first successful sortie, led by Lieutenant Seki Yukio, took place on October 25, 1944.

32. Kokubu was the site of a naval air base on Kyushu, the southernmost of the main Japanese islands.

33. Vice Admiral Ōnishi Takijirō, who oversaw the creation of the first navy special-attack units, commanded the First Air Fleet at this time.

November 22, 1944, clear then cloudy

There was a P-38 bombing attack. Four planes were shot down, and a pilot was captured at Rairai Island. He was hit with two powerful uppercuts and then handed over to the Special Defense Forces.

November 25, 1944, clear

I was coming down with a cold, so I took it easy.

The military situation on Leyte has improved.[34]

There was a report that seventy B-29s bombed the imperial capital, and I was furious over the ineffectiveness of the home guard fighters.[35] What is three downed planes?

November 28, 1944, clear

We've made some military gains. Kamikaze units attacked and sank an aircraft carrier and a cruiser. I heard from Superior Flight Petty Officer Nishide, just back from Manila, that my older brother Origasa died recently in an attack on an aircraft carrier. I was quite overcome with emotion and couldn't speak.

January 3, 1945, cloudy then clear, rain in the evening

We've had stews for the past three days. Today's was the most delicious, perhaps because it was made with a miso broth. I couldn't stomach the strange smell of the herring roe, though.[36] The roe would have been fine if it had been soaked in water for two or three days. Serving things that even the Payroll Department couldn't eat was just for show and was irresponsible.

Take-yan read my fortune with cards.[37] According to what he said — in the tone of a real diviner — I would be poor and struggle, and my social standing and advancement were uncertain. My future was exceedingly uninteresting. Will Dad die before me and Mom live on? Even if I had a romantic relationship, he told me, I'd be completely rejected and defeated. He says that I absolutely will not be bound to anyone and that a man I would approve of will appear, steal her heart, and steadily captivate her. And apparently I will die young. Well, that

---

34. American forces invaded Leyte in late October 1944.

35. On November 24, 111 B-29s attacked Tokyo.

36. What Itabashi describes as a "stew," or *zatsuni* in Japanese, was probably made by simmering the herring roe in a mixture of miso, fish stock, sugar, and soy sauce. The roe (J. *kazunoko*) usually is salted or dried and must be soaked in water for several days before it can be eaten.

37. Itabashi uses the suffix *yan*, common in the Kansai dialect, instead of *san*.

can't be helped, and besides that's my basic wish. What's strange is that she's going to die young, too.

If he's this sort of diviner, he doesn't need to borrow any cards. When I laughed and said, "If you offer fortunes like this, your business will fail," he said, "Because I do it only when asked, I don't give discounts or do it for free." He nonchalantly and noisily began to eat a pomelo. He gazed longingly at a second pomelo that was big and looked like a head, and he finished that off, too.

I remember that it was two years ago today that I got a thirty-six-hour pass and went home, together with a student pilot at Yatabe, my chest festooned with seven medals. A send-off party was held, and lots of saké was poured. My older brother Kitarō made a speech. I recall that he pointed out that it was the anniversary of the fall of Manila.

I'd like to reflect on that. It's been a full three years since the fall of Manila. Hasn't Manila been transformed into the site of frontline fighting? In that time there was the change of course at Guadalcanal. There was the *gyokusai* at Attu Island. The *gyokusai* at Kwajalein and Rota. The many infuriating results continue: the *gyokusai* at Tarawa and Makin and more recently the *gyokusai* at Saipan and Tinian at this time last summer. But we are not defeated. We're winning. We are definitely winning this war. While everywhere we rout two or three times as many enemy and achieve splendid victories, resistance is hard, quantitatively, and we go off to commit *gyokusai*, pledging resolutely to save the country for seven lifetimes. Decisive battles are now taking place in the Philippines. At the moment, Japan will make a comeback with this last stand, break the enemy's nose, and push with irresistible force, push to the end.

Both the army and the navy have formed special-attack units and are continuing the intense and endless battles. I believe that 1945 is the autumn of emergencies when the Yamato race, one million strong, will choose death and make a last stand. I am overcome with emotion as I remember my send-off two years ago.

January 4, 1945, cloudy

In the morning a seaplane returned from Ambonia, and the two men—Nishiwaki and Fuku—who attacked the enemy airport at Futagojima and Maru were aboard.

Last year I entrusted to Nishiwaki the personal belongings (cough drops, letters, and magazines) I wanted sent to Manokwari, but because there were no special flights there, he gave the cough drops to soldiers on Anbonia and personnel at the Bobane base. And although it couldn't be helped, that bugger burned my cache of letters. I was furious. Having once been a poor correspondent, I now was writing letters that were five or six pages long and displaying a rare patience. I couldn't bear the thought of my letters being torched and no longer wanted to write any more. I had intended to comfort the soldiers on Manokwari but gave up on that idea.

In any event, Nishiwaki is a jerk who enjoys burning other people's letters without their permission.

At 8:30 I hitched a ride on the same seaplane and left nostalgic Macassar.

We flew straight to Surabaya, arriving there at 2:30, and I reported for duty at East Indies Airport.[38] I went straight to the air staff officer at the Second Southern Expeditionary Fleet headquarters, and although I was counting on him for a letter, the word was that I had to apply to the air transportation clerk at the Twenty-first Special Base Force Headquarters. I was disappointed and returned to my quarters.

January 14, 1945, cloudy

I read a newspaper. In the three-day period from the seventh through the eighth and ninth of this month, the enemy started to come ashore at Lingayen Bay on Luzon Island, with 350 transport ships and warships protecting them.[39] Enemy military forces were said to be four or five divisions strong.

In response, army and navy special-attack units, surface vessel special-attack units, and army units have been in a certain death mode for several days and have been transforming themselves into virtual fireballs and mounting frenzied attacks.

The headline read "Reckless Advances Are Our Plan," but it wasn't the time to say such facile and soothing things.

Isn't it time for us all to join special-attack units and crash our planes into the enemy? Have I forgotten my pledge to so many of my war buddies? I really have to think about this.

At the moment, I am full of the spirit that will make it easy for me to become a member of a human bomb special-attack unit. Mine is not empty energy.

We cannot not win. To help us prevail, I'd happily see my little five-foot body smashed to pieces.

In last August's issue of *Bungei shunjū*, Ishikawa Tatsuzō wrote an article en-

---

38. Surabaya is on the northeast side of Java, which the Japanese still held.

39. American troops actually began to come ashore on January 9 and proceeded to take Manila as Japanese forces retreated to the mountains in northern Luzon.

titled "The Way of Fluid Speech," in which he wrote, "Prime Minister Koiso speaks of Yamato united. Without believing in the people, what is Yamato?" I'm in a war zone and know absolutely nothing about the Koiso cabinet and the policies that Prime Minister Koiso is carrying out. But reading this article made me feel strangely uneasy. That is, for someone who is just a writer to dash off this sort of thing, it must contain some truth.

There was a time in the past when political parties and politics were quite the thing, but now we're provisionally under a regime positioned for decisive battles. We must fight resolutely with our prime minister at the center! In any case, I don't know whether Prime Minister Koiso's reputation among the people of our country is good or bad, but I believe that ex-Prime Minister Tōjō had much more political skill. Having said that, none of this really matters for those of us fighting for the Great Righteousness.

February 11, 1945, clear

Today was the anniversary of Emperor Jinmu's ascension.[40] I was reminded of times past. It was the same day last year when I was training at Kisarazu. Everyone said something or other and then went outside. A few people in my unit stayed behind, and that group made a test flight. We worked ourselves into a funk and drank as though our lives depended on it and got roaring drunk. We went to the command center, put on our flight uniforms, and merrily danced around. There seemed to be a lot of us — Sergeant Yoshimatsu, Kumatani, Sergeant Sugano, and others. Morimura was there, too. He's a cute guy. We made our test flights, reeling from side to side, and then suddenly descended on Kisarazu Town and played around at superlow altitudes. All the people who flew test flights that night are no longer in this world. All have brilliantly scattered.[41] Oh! If only I had done the right thing and asked for Sergeant Sugano's address. Sergeant Takagi sacrificed himself at Saipan, and I wonder what he felt when the enemy came ashore. They probably fought brilliantly to the death. And let's join them and then we can talk about old times. I can almost hear Sergeant Sugano singing his specialty, "My Beloved Steed."[42]

---

40. Emperor Jinmu was a legendary figure reputed to be Japan's first emperor and is said to have ascended the throne in 660 BCE.

41. Itabashi uses "scatter" (J. *chiru*), as in the scattering of a flower's petals, a standard wartime epithet for dying.

42. "The March of My Beloved Steed" (Aiba kōshin) was included in collections of war songs distributed by the War Ministry.

February 20, 1945, clear then rain in the afternoon

There was a report that we caught the enemy task force that bombed the home islands in southwest Kanto, attacked viciously, and sank twenty-three ships before breaking off.

Is this a lie? Is it true?

The seaplane *Clear Skies*, bound for the home islands, was carrying a lot of air transport guys, and I couldn't get on.

February 22, 1945, cloudy, light rain

A day of memories. It was on this day last year that forty Comets from the 503rd Air Group grandly departed Kisarazu and flew to the front. The gloriousness of that day is as clear in my memory as if it were happening right before my eyes: the weather that day was exceptionally fine at Kisarazu, and we took off with great dignity, with hundreds, thousands, of well-wishers waving their caps as we gunned our engines so they made that distinctive roar.

As the lead plane in the No. 2 Division of the Second Squadron, I had the five planes on my left and right firmly under control, and we flew straight to the decisive battlefields to destroy the enemy.

I resolved not to survive and never to set foot on the soil of the homeland again.

A light rain covered the mountains of the Bōsō peninsula, and dimly visible above the mist was Mount Fuji. I controlled my emotions and flew southward over the vast Pacific, arriving at Nakama Air Base on Iwo Jima at 1:00 p.m.

It's been exactly one year, a long year, since I left Japan, but then it also feels like a very short year, during which the war situation has changed dramatically.

Now the enemy has come ashore at Iwo Jima, and a great and intense battle is raging.[43] Why? What is this?

Not one of my wingmen is left, and not a single war buddy has survived.

It's like a dream. Isn't this all a dream? No, no, it would be fine if it were a dream, but . . .

None of us should feel that our unfavorable military situation is because we failed to work hard enough. . . . It has been, to be sure, a painful war, and an unreasonable war.

It would have been good if I had been able to die. I'll be satisfied if I'm able to destroy myself. It's probably survivor's guilt. But then again, I'm still alive and must fight.

---

43. Allied forces went ashore on Iwo Jima on February 19, 1945, and secured the island by March 26.

The day when I offer up my small five-foot frame is approaching. When I catch up with my war buddies, I won't be late. I'll just exhaust my death power and advance to annihilate the enemy. A sea eagle wrote the following verse:

> Though I don't regret my body's scattering,
> My thoughts are on the future toward which the country moves.

The poem has a logic. I find it congenial. Yet what sort of state will exist without victory? Will the Yamato people still exist if we're completely defeated? We'll give up our lives for the sake of victory. Happy and laughing, we go off to crash — one plane, one ship — and there is nothing quite as powerful as the decision to die. What are physical objects? One absolutely doesn't expect that things fashioned by human hands can't be destroyed by human hands. When all is said and done, victory resides in the self. This is simply a story of my giving up my life to lead the way to victory.

February 23, 1945, clear then rainy

I was summoned to the Twenty-eighth Naval Air Flotilla Headquarters and had an interview with the maintenance staff. Judging from the way they were talking, returning to the home islands is out of the question, and it looks as though I was to be transferred here officially. Apparently the Comets will arrive by carrier shortly, which is what I had hoped would happen. I was just thinking that I want to board an aircraft as quickly as possible and fight. This for sure!

All of this means I'll soon join my war buddies.

If it were in a special-attack unit, that'd be even better.

I want to climb into my beloved Comet right away.

In the evening, they showed films behind the headquarters building — *Umontorimonchō and the Curse of a Hundred Thousand Ryō* and *A Prayer for a Winged Victory*.[44]

Both were good. I thought about the evanescence of human life. The moment of scattering is important, especially for warriors.

February 24, 1945, clear then cloudy

We had an enormous air raid from about 9:40 a.m. with about 120 or 130 B-29s

---

44. *Umontorimonchō and the Curse of a Hundred Thousand Ryō* was released by Nikkatsu in 1939, and *A Prayer for a Winged Victory* was released by Tōhō in 1942.

attacking.[45] The naval port was the target, but today only Shōnan City was badly bombed.[46] Huge fires broke out, and their smoke turned the sky black.

At the urging of my mischievous colleagues, I painted undiluted creosote on my ringworm, but it made it swell up, and all I could say was, "No, no, it hurts but it doesn't hurt," and hop around.

They didn't think it would affect me this way and suggested the creosote partly as a joke. It'll probably take about a week to heal. It's a real annoyance.

March 4, 1945, clear

We left Saigon at 10:00 p.m. on the third. In a long night flight we went directly to Tansui on the northern edge of Taiwan. We arrived there at 8:00 a.m. on the fourth, but the situation was bad, so we flew back to Tōkō on southern end of the island. We arrived there at 9:30 a.m. and spent the night at the navy hostel, which cost fifteen yen. As far as going out was concerned, the electric lines had been blown up and the streetlights were out and it was pitch black. The air units based at Tōkō had taken a vicious beating.[47]

March 5, 1945

We left Tōkō at 4:00 p.m. Before we left, Kōyū was bombed, and it was still burning when we took off and smoke was visible in the distance.[48] We arrived at Kagoshima at 10:00 p.m., and I planted my feet on the home islands at 10:10 p.m.

It was cold. The white plums were blooming. It was the homeland I had missed.

We stayed at the Taien Inn.

As scheduled, I went to the air base at Kokubu and met my former division leader, Lieutenant Commander Takeda, but he told me that I wouldn't be able to transfer. I was disappointed, but on my way back I met folks from the Kō Thirteenth Flying School class and ate lunch at the cafeteria, which I had forgotten about. As a service, they gave us twenty bottles of beer. I thought to myself, Japan is truly the best place!

---

45. On February 24, 105 B-29s attacked the Empire Dock area of Singapore, destroying 40 percent of the warehousing in the vicinity. See Carter and Mueller, *Combat Chronology*, 581.

46. When the Japanese occupied cities, they renamed them, and Singapore became Shōnan, which means "Illuminated South."

47. Tansui and Tōkō are Japanese readings of the Chinese names of the cities of Tanshui and Tungkang.

48. Kōyū is Kaohsiung.

We were scheduled to leave around noon the next day, but unfortunately it started raining in the evening. It would be great if tomorrow were clear.

March 6, 1945

We went to the airport at 9:00 a.m. but the weather was poor, so we turned around. Our departure was postponed for a day.

I exchanged military scrip—a total of 770 yen—at a Bank of Japan branch. After I had lunch in my quarters, I went into Kagoshima and did some sightseeing.[49]

I found small bolts of pure silk with a beautiful design at Yamagataya Department Store. When I got irritated because they said they didn't have many more, they gave me two and said, "How about getting the others from the other young salesperson?" There was a female salesperson, who, when I asked for more silk, quickly produced thirteen bolts. Shopping in my flight cap and flight boots seemed to help. A single generous person gave me six bolts of silk.

Kagoshima is a fine place, and I was touched by the warmth of the people there.

March 7, 1945, cloudy

We left for Yokohama at 10:00 a.m. and arrived there at 2:00 p.m.

People seem to be having quite a hard time.

We went right away to Yokosuka and entered a marine unit for the time being. It was 6:00 p.m.

March 8, 1945, clear

In the morning I went to the Naval District Personnel Office, told them my situation, and asked them to decide on my next assignment.

I telephoned the personnel office at the Naval Aviation Department and requested a special-attack unit.

March 9, 1945, cloudy

In the morning I received an order to transfer to the No. 1 Air Attack Squadron of the 601st Air Group at Katori Air Base.[50] After lunch I finally left my group.

---

49. Kagoshima is about thirty miles from the air base at Kokubu.
50. Katori Air Base was located in Chiba Prefecture in eastern Japan.

I visited Toshiko at the Technical Aviation Research Center in Oihama and was surprised.[51]

I went to Kisarazu and was supposed to stay for the night but changed my mind on the way and stayed over in Narutō. There was a bombing raid in the middle of the night, and incendiary bombs were dropped on the neighboring village. It was horrible! The Tokyo area appears to have been hit really hard.[52]

March 17, 1945, clear, snow in the evening

It's been ten days since I've been back to the home islands. Having gone here and there, it has seemed like a really long ten days.

Today I drilled with Sergeants Yamanouchi and Minami who arrived from the skies over Usa — we sat three abreast.

It was my first special flight in some time, and it felt wonderful. All things considered, I really do like the sky best of all.

In the afternoon, five aircraft returned from an air transport mission. After dinner, I had a phone call from my older brother who's in the Takeyama Marine Detachment — I hadn't heard his voice for well over a year and some months.[53]

March 18, 1945, cloudy

An enemy task force made up of three different groups has appeared in the vicinity of Tosa Bay, and the Fifth Air Fleet has been attacking it.[54] The outcome of this battle should be clear by evening. Six carriers and one cruiser have been attacked and sunk. And there were more.

We were scheduled to evacuate to Matsushima Air Base in the morning, but it was decided that we should stay on alert.

I had the chills in the afternoon and rested. It turned out to be a full-blown case of malaria. I've had the chills really bad on alternate days — the fourteenth,

---

51. Toshiko is Itabashi's sister, and it appears that she had been mobilized for war work. He doesn't tell us why he was "surprised." The Technical Aviation Research Center was a navy facility devoted to research on aircraft materials, engines, optics, weapons, and the like.

52. On March 9, 1945, 279 B-29s based on Guam, Saipan, and Tinian in the Marianna Islands attacked Tokyo, for the first time dropping incendiary bombs from a relatively low altitude — 4,900 to 9,200 feet. This had an utterly devastating and deadly effect, killing around 83,000 people and destroying 267,000 buildings. See Carter and Mueller, *Combat Chronology*, 594.

53. This might be the brother identified as "N" in Itabashi's August 20, 1944, entry.

54. Tosa Bay is on the south side of the island of Shikoku, one of the four main Japanese islands.

sixteenth, and then today — and my fever rose from thirty-nine to forty degrees centigrade.

Tomorrow five aircraft are scheduled to attack in the Kyushu area. Might it be because the aircraft there are all gone? It's a sad story.

March 20, 1945, clear

The recent attacks on the enemy task force do not appear to have produced very dramatic results. Apparently the report that six carriers were sunk the day before yesterday was false.

There were extensive air raids in the morning, and everyone was evacuated, but air operations resumed midday. On the first go-around, we did pilot training in the new Model 33, no. 10, Comet.[55] When I climbed out of the aircraft, I suddenly had the chills and a malarial fever. I was examined and told to stay indoors.

This was the end of that unusual pleasure called a holiday. I accepted my fate. Although I say I accepted my fate, it wasn't because I wanted to return to the home islands. After all, I had assumed I wouldn't go home any time before my death. I've had a lot of battlefield requests for letters, and I'll spend tomorrow writing them.

Today the Comet squadrons began night flights.

March 21, 1945, clear

Today is the spring equinox, which means it has to warm up. This morning my fever dropped, and I felt decent. I wrote letters to send here and there. Nishiwaki asked me to write some, as did Eguchi — I have a bunch to do. By evening I will have written ten of them.

I recently had a phone call from Makoto, [one of] my older brothers, who said that when things were back to normal I should write a letter to Mitsu-chan.[56] Today I gave some thought to this and calmly wrote to her.

After I appealed to my unfailing emotions, I expressed my thoughts. I said even if ours was a one-sided romance, I was still satisfied. My feelings had changed a lot from what they were a year and some months ago, before I left for the front.

---

55. The Model 33 Comet had a new, air-cooled, fourteen-cylinder engine — the 1,560-horsepower Mitsubishi MK8P Kinsei 62 — and a flexible, thirteen-millimeter, Type 2 machine gun.

56. Itabashi's relationship with Mitsu, who is a woman, is unclear, although this diary entry suggests that his affection for her was not returned.

War at the front has made me wild, and I think it's because I was always thinking about Mitsu-chan's feelings. Having only people who were not blood relatives comforting me, I realized, was something I should be grateful for and not resent. When I think about it, though, it's strange. Even now the person I know as Mitsu-chan has the same figure as the person I knew six or seven years ago and the same heart. One might say it was my bad luck not to see her grow up, but it actually may have been good luck. There's no greater happiness than going off to die brilliantly with that pure white lily image engraved on my chest.

When I reflect on this, I'm sure of the happy principle of unrequited love.

March 22, 1945, cloudy, strong winds

It was finally announced that all the members of the Iwo Jima garrison committed *gyokusai*. This had been predicted, but my blood still boiled.

I will avenge them. I definitely will avenge them.

The cost for the enemy was 33,000 deaths. We must not let the brave warriors who committed *gyokusai* die a dog's death. Whether right or wrong, Japan must win!

March 23, 1945, cloudy, strong winds

The noncommissioned officers I roomed with asked me to tell them the story of my forced landing.

So I described how the brave warriors of Biari Island had three *kanpan* a day as their main food and a rice allotment of one rice ball for dinner. When I talked about accepting that one rice ball, filling our canteens with the water that dripped into our bunker, and men going off on raids every night, the brave warriors, all of them combat veterans, sniffed and blinked through tears.

Those who hear my story cry. I once told this story on a train to Kokubu, and everyone sobbed. The Yamato people are brothers and sisters. Japanese citizens are united and facing their national crisis together. Japan absolutely cannot be defeated. If the basis for my life is the eternal peace of the Yamato people and progress, how can this little body have any regrets?

March 24, 1945, clear

A blood test confirmed that my recent illness was "three-day tropical malaria."

Perhaps because I've just gotten here, I feel lonely. My inability to make friends may be the biggest reason for my loneliness. I'm the most senior pilot and thus am responsible for bringing along the younger group and instilling in them the will to win battles. I assemble them every night and give them advice and make them listen to my stories. I go to some pains when I do this so others can't say of me, "That fellow Itabashi may be advanced in rank, but he still is young and probably not able to train most of them." I doubt, however, that my men are as serious and attentive as I think they are. Because they are Japanese as well as navy fliers with a tradition and because they ache for a real battle and long to perform brilliantly in combat, I may not need to say very much to them. And don't I have to train myself so my performance doesn't fall below theirs?

Whenever I feel lonely, I can't help but long for my former war buddies in the 107th Squadron of the 503rd Air Group.

I had a pure air base unit education. Most of the First Air-Attack Squadron pilots, in contrast, had a carrier-based education, and it's hardly surprising that they're not used to air base life and flying.[57]

After getting into bed at night, I think quietly about my long stay in the South Seas, my traveling alone and my extended sojourn in a corner of New Guinea. I feel as though I learned something from that experience, but that's just my gut feeling. I doubt that this experience really has become a part of me or my consciousness. Even when I think about it now, it seems that nothing related to these experiences is mentioned in my diary. I'm a little calmer, but this doesn't mean I've developed any courage. I can say that I don't have a single pleasure, and to this, I can add my loneliness.

March 25, 1945, clear

Today a letter and a package arrived from mother. It contained rice cakes, dried persimmons, shirts, and the first volume of *The Light of the House*. Right away, four or five of us roasted the rice cakes and ate them—they were delicious! Although my mother is this way all the time, I still bow my head in gratitude for her worrying about me.

I packed up a bunch of things that for some time I've been thinking about sending home—suitcases, shoes, white shirts, etc. They came to two packages.

To Mitsu-chan, I'll send the things I got in Kagoshima—the beautiful obi material with the pure white rose pattern.

I wrote:

> Embracing the perfume of the pure wild rose
> the decks of enemy ships
> I will smear with my blood.

Tonight I intend to ask for an inspection. It seems that air units will be attacking in the Kyushu or Shikoku areas. I may have to go.

---

57. Itabashi is referring to his new unit, the First Flight Echelon of the 601st Air Attack Group. See his 3/9/45 entry.

Having come so close to home, I'd like to stay here a bit longer, but personal feelings are not permitted.

March 29, 1945, cloudy, strong winds

On a clear day when the 601st Air Group's fighter-bomber squadrons and attack units were scheduled to sortie, young Nemoto mistakenly opened fire from a turret gun, killing fifteen or sixteen people, wounding thirty around his aircraft, and causing a huge ruckus.[58]

Young Nemoto is still a pure-hearted, red-faced boy.

When I think of him, I can't help shedding a few tears. He felt responsible for what happened and was the first person to grab a fire extinguisher and to try to put out the fire raging in his beloved plane. It already was too late, and the flames got worse and worse, fanned by the strong winds blowing at that moment, and quickly spread to the airfield grass. It became a blazing inferno! A 500-kilogram bomb just being loaded caught fire, and there was a huge boom and explosion. It was the very picture of hell!

Young Nemoto survived but never showed his face in our presence again.

His classmate, Superior Flight Petty Officer Ushio, transferred from the Kure Naval Corps. There was a report that he saw service in the South Pacific as a radioman on the command aircraft of the Third Air Fighter Group. Some of his classmates came to see him, which was reassuring to him.

March 30, 1945, clear

Yesterday the remaining flight echelons advanced to Meiji Air Base. I finally became a senior noncommissioned officer with thirty crewmen under my command.

Some of my subordinates say they've never been in a Type 99 Carrier Bomber, and others specialized in carrier fighters.[59]

They've been spirited students, and in another month, they'll become crewmen who can make war. I have a really big responsibility. I'll do the best I can.

March 31, 1945, clear

I boarded a plane for the first time in ten days. It was a test flight for no. 16. I had Ushio get into the rear seat, and after mercilessly swinging from side to side, I flew to Tsuchiura, teasing the student pilot the whole way.[60] It was fun.

---

58. It was probably a turret gun on a Mitsubishi G4M attack bomber (Betty), the sturdy medium-range bomber used through the war.

59. The Type 99 Carrier Bomber also was known as the Aichi D3A (Val).

60. Tsuchiura is in Ibaraki Prefecture and was the site of Kasumigaura Naval Air Base.

In the afternoon we were told we'd have to pick up aircraft at Kaminoike Air Base, and I went with Lieutenants Takabatake and Yanagihara and Sergeant Funakoshi. We landed at Sahara at 10:00 p.m. and stayed for the night. Thanks to beer and wine, we got to feeling pretty jolly and traded war stories. Although our hosts spoke of doing daring things, what do student officers with 100 or 150 hours of flying time really know? Just living it up.

April 1, 1945, clear

This afternoon we returned with two Type 99 Carrier Bombers and two Comets. Lieutenant Takabatake and I flew the Comets. After all, our base is the best. Ushio and I get along famously. Wherever we go, we're together.

April 2, 1945, clear

Today we had bombing practice. For the first time I flew in the back seat behind the pilots from the carrier-bomber attack squadrons, and we dropped bombs, but I was alternately surprised and angry at their ignorance of the thing called bombing. We landed right away, and this time I piloted the plane and made them get into the back seat. I was so appalled I was speechless. When I put them into the back seat, they couldn't read the altimeter when I went into a nose dive. If they don't do better, it'll be bad news! What a surprise!

April 3, 1945, clear

I rode in the rear seat of the Type 99 Bomber and gave instructions to the group that had never flown Comets before. Among those I was training, some didn't complete their training runs, and some did the unthinkable—they descended and landed.

Next, I flew the no. 1 plane in the formation, and we did the no. 25 test flight in the afternoon. I put young Iimura in the back seat and did special flights for as long as I wanted. Today, I spent the whole day in an aircraft. Because I was pretty worked up, I didn't get that tired.

April 6, 1945, clear

We've had insane drills for several days and nights. With the attack close at hand, engines roar in the sky over the base all day long. This, in fact, will be the decisive battle.

The military situation is increasingly grave, and Japan is now encircled by the enemy. Superior Flight Petty Officer Ushio recently has been freaking out a little, and I believe I'm the one who understands his feelings best.

Having served as a radio operator on three-man aircraft for two years in the

South Seas, he has skills that he and others recognize, but his having to be a first-year student learning to be the scout on a carrier bomber is nuts. If we could move him to a three-man aircraft, we could use him right away. He says it would be best if he could show all his stuff and then go off and die. That is the truth!

April 7, 1945, clear

At long last, we received the order we've been waiting, and hoping, for. We'll go to Kokubu. The appointed day is the day after tomorrow.

Banzai! I'll do it!

This will be to avenge my several hundred war buddies from the 503rd. I'll do it. I'll be decisive!

April 8, 1945, clear

In the morning we practiced dropping thousand-kilogram practice bombs. One bomb was twenty meters off the target, and a second misfired.

The engines of our planes were in great shape, and we were in good spirits.

Preparations for the attack.

This time—I'm definitely not expecting to return alive.

No, it's not that I don't expect to return alive. I simply intend to body-crash, and thus my dying can't be avoided, can it?

I'll get myself ready, write my last letters, and make arrangements for the things I'll leave behind.

In the end, my life will have been twenty-two years long.

I'll smear the decks of enemy warships with this teenager's blood. It'll be wonderful!

Last letter

Parents,

Yasuo is happy and will go off to die laughing.

All I can do is aim my aircraft, and it may not be something I can laugh about, but I expect to be laughing at the moment I crash. In any case, please try to imagine this.

I wasn't able to do anything filial and apologize for this.

Next, about my financial affairs, please use all my money to pay the cost of constructing a plane.

Thank you for all the things you did for me.

I'll seem a complete stranger if I say this, but from the bottom of my heart, thank you for your many kindnesses.

Japan definitely will win!

I will happily go off dreaming of the day of victory.
Please put up a good fight until the day of the final victory.
Finally, I pray for my honorable parents' good health.

Good-bye.

Attached to the No. 1 Attack Air Group.
Superior Flight Petty Officer Itabashi Yasuo
Older Brother Kitarō and Everyone Else

The long-hoped-for day has come at last.

I have the feeling I'll be the happiest of my siblings.

What? You say, "It's not that big a deal," but no, it's true. Because I'm saying it, there's no mistake.

Kitarō and Older Sister . . .

Please do what you can for the family. No, no, as for the family, or aside from that, please do what you can for the country. Toshiko, Masako, Kenji, Noriko, and Shigehiko—study hard and become people who can fight for the country as soon as possible.

If you look at what is not said, you'll never become a superb student.

That's not acceptable!

Well then, everyone, please be well. I've decided to stop writing.

Good-bye.[61]

---

61. At 2:15 p.m. on the afternoon of August 9, 1945, Itabashi took off on his "special attack" from the naval air base at Kokubu on the southern island of Kyushu as a member of the No. 4 Great Shield Corps.

Bittersweet | The Wartime and Postwar
Diary of an Ordinary Kyoto Person

Tamura Tsunejirō was born in 1870 in Hamabun subvillage in Kawakami Village in Shiga Prefecture, the second son of Sugihara Ihei, who was in the dry goods business and also worked at the local post office. Tamura attended the Tōka School in Fukashimizu, graduating in 1882. While in his teens, he was adopted by his aunt's family and worked at their dry goods store until he decided one day to run off with some of the proceeds. He then had a series of jobs: he worked as a peddler for a time, a house boy, and a policeman; and he even painted designs on lacquerware and ceramics.

In 1895, he married Tamura Ei and was adopted by her family, which owned a seafood-import business. They had nine children — three sons and six girls — but lost three daughters in the early 1900s. When the seafood-import business went bankrupt in 1914, Tamura moved his family to Jōzenji in northern Kyoto, where he started a konbu-import business and opened a billiards parlor. In the 1910s and 1920s, billiards was very popular, and by the 1930s, Tamura owned four parlors.

In 1936, however, he closed two of them. Then when Japan invaded China in 1937, the authorities cracked down on youth-oriented amusements like billiards, and this, together with the wartime blackouts, rationing, and financial hardships caused by the war, forced him to close a third parlor, leaving only Iroha in Kyoto. At the time, Tamura's family consisted of his wife Ei, two sons (Shinkichi and Fujihira), and four daughters (Tsuru, Mie, Toshie, and Haruko), and a granddaughter (Sumiko), all of whom appear in his diary.

Although Tamura kept a diary from the 1910s until June 29, 1950, there are substantial gaps. For example, there are no entries from May 16, 1945, to April 9, 1946, and none for 1947 and 1949. After Tamura died in 1951, his family sold his diary to a wastepaper dealer, who in turn sold it to a used-book dealer. Oka Mitsuo, an economic historian who taught at Dōshisha University in Kyoto, bought the diary at a used-book sale. In 1979 Oka published a month's entries from the wartime section of the diary as *Senjika Kyōto no shimin seikatsu (The Wartime Life of a Citizen of Kyoto)*, and a year later he published the entries from July 9, 1944, to June 29, 1950, as *Shinsan: Senchū-sengo Kyō no ichishōmin no nikki (Bittersweet: The Wartime and Postwar Diary of an Ordinary Kyoto Person)*. The portion of his diary translated here is from the latter publication, from July 9, 1944, to May 15, 1945.

July 12, 1944, Wednesday
Tormented by Heat and Mosquitoes

The rainy season is over, and it's suddenly gotten hot. The mosquitoes' nightly attacks are worse than those of the enemy planes. With no incense or mosquito net, I spent a sleepless night waiting for dawn.

July 15, 1944, Saturday
With No Rain I Think of the Farmers' Plight

It is hot, hot, irritatingly hot, and the sun is blazing. When did the rainy season end?

In the old days people used to say the rainy season was over when you heard huge claps of thunder, but today it's completely different. No one utters these old sayings.

The farmers struggle to produce more food. But they have lots of rice paddies that are parched [because of the heat and the drought], and they have not been able to do their planting. I hear they are making a big to-do about rainmaking rituals in the countryside. The farmers probably want rain and cool weather. Increasing production is the first concern, and the sun is so hot that clear skies are hateful.

It's quite nice this afternoon. Toshie must be getting off from work, and I thought I'd better overlook my hunger and rush home.[1] At the moment I'm in Takatsukibe.

I believe the endurance by a million citizens of the hardships caused by the wartime food situation will mean victory, and I myself practice simple economies, filling up only 70 percent of my stomach's capacity, putting in a [full] day's

---

1. Toshie was Tamura's sixth daughter and one of four surviving daughters. She was born in 1918 and graduated from Ōtsu Prefectural Girls High School. During the war she lived with her parents and worked at Iwata Enterprises in Osaka.

Tamura Tsunejirō, date unknown.
Courtesy of Tamura family.

work, and returning home pooped. There was nothing to eat to comfort myself and, of course, nothing sweet.

My only pleasures and comforts are roasting soybean residue and adding *bancha* and listening to the lively conversation of Osaka businessmen.

At 9:00 a.m. I went to browse in the open-air stalls on Shakadō, but there wasn't a single thing I needed to buy. I took an old chestnut-wood tray to sell and was offered twenty-five yen. Because of my old-fashioned way of thinking, I couldn't decide whether to sell it. Is this just gibberish? Has the heat driven me mad? If I said it was an expensive tray, would they think it's good and buy it? If I said it was cheap, would they see it as poor quality and not take it? Surprised, I returned home at 10:00 a.m.

July 16, 1944, Sunday
Recent Prices

With the drought continuing day after day, the water was shut off. They'll probably urge us to conserve electricity. At the Senrotō bathhouse, there's no hot water in the tubs after two or three minutes, and customers leave quickly. I think this is rather sad for business. Now you might want to take a bath at home, but there's no fuel to heat up the water.

Today's food prices have a front and a back. There are the "public" prices of the black market. As they do with rice, the food supply corporations handle potatoes, which are regarded as a food substitute, and the distribution price is eighty-five sen for one *kan* of potatoes, and two to three days worth is deducted from a person's rice allotment. The black market price is forty yen in gold for ten *kan*, and one *kan* is being bought and sold for four yen.

July 1944
Prices

Commodity	Public Prices	Official Black Market Prices	Black Market Prices
Rationed rice, 2 qts.	4 sen	12 sen	15 sen
Third-grade saké, 2 qts.	3 yen, 5 sen	15 yen	40 yen
Sugar, 1.6 oz.	45 sen	13 yen	17 yen
Adzuki beans, 2 qts.	45 sen	6 yen	NA
Chicken, 13.2 oz.	2 yen	6 yen	NA
Beef, 13.2 oz.	1.8 yen	7 yen	NA
Clothing ticket	NA	35 yen	NA
Charcoal, 33.2 lbs.	3 yen	18 yen	NA
Potatoes, 8.3 lbs.	85 sen	4 yen	35 yen
Paulownia-wood clogs	NA	30 yen	NA

July 17, Monday
Cancellation of the Gion Festival

The farmers are planting quite late. The rice paddies are parched, and they can do nothing but wait for rain. Even when they pray to the gods for rain, none falls. I can imagine they're worried about the future.

An order was issued calling off the Gion Festival because of the war.[2]

Even though each day's meals are expensive, there's nothing. There's no rice, no fish, no miso, no soy sauce, no oil, no sugar, no matches, no clothes, and no soap. It's not that these things don't exist but, rather, that there's no point in buying them on the black market.

The rich can do anything with the money they have, and they buy up the

2. The Gion Festival, Kyoto's most famous festival, honors the deity Gozu Tennō and is held every year on July 17.

lower classes' goods and food and circulate them back to the black market. This is why there's no festive mood this year.

July 18, 1944, Tuesday
Predicting the Defeat from Food Shortages

There has been no distribution of fish for some time, and you can't get a single herring or snag a sardine tail. Because my body is not getting enough nutrients, I tire easily. Most of my countrymen are going through the same thing. Perhaps because the American and British enemy know we're suffering from food shortages and starving to death, they've devised a strategy for not rushing the war. In this situation, Japan will probably be defeated, won't it?

July 19, 1944, Wednesday
Sadness about the Decline of Morality on
the Occasion of the *Gyokusai* on Saipan

The American enemy has occupied Saipan, and I hear that Japanese civilians on the island, together with the military, committed *gyokusai*.[3] Facing south I prayed for the souls of the dead.

In the midst of a great war, you don't expect the lives of your countrymen to be as they are normally. Because you can't make money selling at official prices, production has ceased, and people must hunt for scarce commodities. Merchants have surpluses and are trying to make a killing. The honest ones who respect the laws and regulations are disappearing, and the dishonest ones who break the laws and regulations are making money. Morality has declined. I don't think the black market can be abolished.

No matter what one says, isn't this the moment when the state will survive or disappear? Complaints and unhappiness are forbidden, so one has to be discreet. With apologies to the government, I'll simply follow the doctrine of three evils.

July 21, 1944, Friday
Impressions of the Collapse of the Tōjō Government

The world is in desperate straits! How will things turn out? We'll probably die.

We depended on Mr. Tōjō to the end, but I hear he just up and resigned.[4] What a shame!

---

3. Saipan, one of the Mariana Islands, had large Japanese military and civilian populations. Allied forces landed there on June 15 and took the island on July 9.

4. General Tōjō Hideki was war minister from July 22, 1940, through October 16, 1941, and then prime minister from October 18, 1941, to July 18, 1944.

I'm sorry, but as far as the emperor is concerned, there's no reason for Tōjō's resignation, and how should I comfort his Absolute Eminence? The world has become too repulsive. Enemy aircraft, come quickly and attack! Please end this awful situation.

July 23, 1944, Sunday
Burying the Tōjō cabinet

Because Prime Minister Tōjō is an army general, he wears a military sword at his waist, but with his whole cabinet resigning, he has acted like a coward and betrayed our hopes.

We believed in him but were misled. With small fry like him, there won't be military victories or a resolution. Quickly bury what should be left behind. The sound of a bell clanging.

We've all been betrayed: Agricultural Minister Uchida Nobunari, my father who knew hardship, and I myself. Our stomachs are getting emptier and emptier! I don't think we can survive on six-tenths pint.[5] A bell clanging. This poverty may bury Agricultural Minister Uchida! Good-bye small-fry cabinet Buddhist priest! *Namu amida butsu, namu amida butsu!*

A bell clanging.

July 24, 1944, Monday
Getting Angry at Greengrocers' Black Market Sales

The greengrocer's allotment was just one Kamo eggplant and one Japanese radish. The good things are saved and will be distributed to Yoshida, Kataoka, and the banks in our ward.[6] For us poor people, the eggplant and radish cost eighteen sen. They say this should be enough for side dishes for five people. With a surplus of produce, the greengrocers are making a killing and pretending not to notice. They make people with children on their backs buy just a little bit and scold them. In this situation, can one speak of the equality of our one million countrymen?

July 25, 1944, Tuesday
The Loneliness of the Kitano Tenjin Street Stalls

My first pleasure today was to visit the Kitano Tenjin Shrine, and I allowed myself one yen to spend on bargains as I browsed among the stalls there. This is my one

---

5. Tamura is complaining about the rationing system.
6. Tamura does not identify Yoshida, but he and Kataoka, the head of the local community council, appear in other entries.

pleasure every month. But the stalls are controlled, and I stopped after visiting a third of them. The prices are illegally high, too high for me. Nor were there any food stalls, and I left for home at 10:30 a.m.

July 26, 1944, Wednesday
Eating a Meal with Salt as a Side Dish

Daily side dishes. I used to think the ancient saying "The secret of thriftiness is living by licking salt" was a myth, but I don't today. Every day our five-person household is short on side dishes, and each person licks a little salt. As the war situation gets worse, salt licking is for the dogs. The only other thing you can do is to tie a rope around your neck and die. To save rice, let's resolve to repay the debt that we owe the country. We have experienced the happiness of the world.

Grandma happily went off to buy what was being distributed today, this day of many happinesses.[7] "I got four ounces of potatoes—it was a fine distribution," she beamed. "Thanks to you, we're saved." I'll never forget the wonderful taste of those potatoes. Fish flooded the black market, but we don't eat it anymore.

Grandma is old and eats a little too much *okara* and *mamemeshi*. She goes back and forth to the toilet and runs to the Itō Nōeru Pharmacy on Senbon Avenue. She has to do this to control her aged stomach.

Then Toshiie had diarrhea. Grandma carefully inspects the food, but the person in charge had the runs because it was not a good idea to add sugar to the *okara*. Two eggplants for one yen on the black market.

Two eggplants for one yen is no laughing matter. I wondered whether this was a way for farmers to prevent hoarding, but Otsuru said, "No, no, two eggplants for one yen. I'll happily go and buy some."[8] Grandma was surprised. Today's entrée was a single eggplant for each of us, and it was even roasted. The cost of today's side dishes was two yen, fifty sen. In this situation we'll be eating only salt. I'm not ashamed to say we use sesame salt, which costs forty sen a bottle, for ten days' worth of side dishes. Divided up among five people, it'll disappear (the following appears next in my July 28 entry: "I'm revising this because there is a story circulating in Osaka that two eggplants are going for one yen.")

---

7. "Grandma" is Tamura Ei, his wife of forty-nine years.
8. Otsuru is Tamura's oldest child and one of four surviving daughters. She was born in 1896 and lived with her parents after her husband was killed in Manchuria. She stayed with them for the duration of the war.

July 27, 1944, Thursday
Asking the Welfare Minister to Pass Out Six-Foot Loincloths

I have something to ask of Hirose Hisada, the welfare minister in the new cabinet.[9] There's a saying "Tight loincloths are best," but recently no one wears six-foot loincloths. Stringed loincloths and drawers are more typical. When we say "Yes!" and plant our feet firmly and exert ourselves, I think it's most important that we not give up. When our countrymen are giving their all on the battlefield and fighting resolutely, I think it's appropriate to distribute six-foot loincloths to the people. The true Japanese male requires a six-foot loin cloth. I, therefore, humbly ask Hirose Hisada, recipient of the Second Order of Merit and minister of welfare in the new cabinet, to distribute six-foot loincloths.

Although I'm ashamed to admit this, hunger comes first. This aging body's sole pleasure is eating. Both Grandma and I could be buck naked, but we'd still exchange an eighty-point clothing chit for ten quarts of white rice. It's now the height of summer and fine to do this, but when it gets freezing cold, we may regret it. We don't know what our fate will be tomorrow, but chowing down comes first. We'll exchange the clothing chit and put something into our empty stomachs.

July 30, 1944, Sunday
Penetrating the Contradictions of the Control of Fish

It came to us as a gift from Osaka. On the Day of the Bull in the Doyō season, we received a broiled eel.[10] It made for a wonderful feast, and I couldn't help but feel it was undeserved good fortune for us poor folk. In addition, Mr. Tamura Shirō of Takakeya Ward sent us a crate of onions weighing about twelve pounds. We also received lots of tomatoes.

There hasn't been a distribution of fish for two months, so we haven't had even one. Buying on the black market is pointless. One sea bream is forty yen. They say fishermen are both flooding the local market and selling on the black market so they don't have to pay for boxes and straw mats and for sending the fish to Kyoto. If one portion rots, they just throw it away and still make a profit. Why doesn't the Kyoto Fish Industry Corporation know about this? They'd do well to raise the public price, buy high, and then distribute the fish. Isn't that a bit of a problem?

---

9. Hirose Hisada (1889–1974) had a long career in the Home Ministry and served in two cabinets before he joined the Koiso cabinet.

10. The Tamuras probably received an *unagi* that had been basted with a sweet sauce and grilled.

The air defense emergency meeting began at 8:30 a.m. Kataoka, the head of the community council, talked about the various functions of young, middle-aged, and elderly people, and it was that rare thing: a packed house. The evacuation sites are, first, the post office in front of the Karaku School in Imadegawa; the second is the forest on the Kitano Shrine precincts; and the third is the forest at Jūjiin. The meeting ended at 10:00 a.m.

August 1, 1944, Tuesday
Getting Angry at Prime Minister Koiso

I browsed in the morning market at Shakadō, but there was nothing I wanted. The street stall operators brought nothing they could sell, and I wasn't tempted to buy anything.

They tried to mollify us with moving war stories. So it's come to this. At this rate our country will be destroyed.

Prime Minister Koiso told a newspaper journalist there would be no victory without divine intervention. This is evidence of a demoralized cabinet. We're dying. We don't eat the food we have, and it's just a matter of time before we'll dive into attacking enemy planes and commit suicide.

Tōjō Hideki, the prime minister in the last cabinet, army general, holder of the Senior Third Rank, Second Order of Merit, and Order of the Golden Kite, First Rank, called up the first reserves. What a spineless general! I hear that he'll go to the Ise Shrine today, and no doubt he'll shed tears and express his gratitude for being allowed to resign safely. Small-fry generals have rusting swords that probably can't be drawn.

A circular came today. The Wartime Health and Physical Education Sports Meet will take place on August 20. This is thought to be necessary for the morale of everyone in Jōzenji-machi, and the whole family is asked to participate.[11] From our household, Toshie probably will participate.

August 2, 1944, Wednesday
Feeling Sympathy for the Departing Student Soldiers

The departure of the brave young conscripts was glorious: they were sent off with enthusiastic shouts of banzai, and they offered a rousing greeting as a veritable human wave and then left for the front. With the recent *gyokusai* on Saipan, theirs is not an enviable position. Yesterday I saw a soldier in his forties leaving with no one to send him off. He was saying good-bye to his parents, wife, and

---

11. Jōzenji-machi is in Kita Ward in northern Kyoto.

children, who watched forlornly as the train disappeared in the east. In the past it was said that a human life lasted for fifty years, but the lives of today's student conscripts and young people last barely twenty-five. Words like these are prohibited as "dangerous thoughts," but they're a sign of exasperation.

You brave old warrior, I pray, from the bottom of my heart, for your success in war. Oh, you young ones! I feel pity for you, born in a difficult time.

October 7, 1944, Saturday
Wanting to Eat Fish until My Stomach Is Full

The tiny wife of our neighborhood association leader, Mr. Ono, called out in a booming voice, "Fish distribution!" A bowl fell from the shelf and shattered. "Salmon! Salmon!"

Sumiko was all smiles.[12] When there's talk of "distributions," Otsuru and even Sumiko instinctively get excited as though we were getting something for free. This is maddening! At such shockingly high prices, it's maddening to hear talk of a "distribution," which sounds as though things were being given away for free. Let's think about, and be wary of, people [aged] around fifty.

Although what I say is reasonable, a stomach of greens every day does little to help me regain my strength. Good god! Do I want to eat fish! I want to be treated to a whole salted *sanma*. Whether it's expensive or cheap is of no concern. I want to eat until my throat gets dry.

With my head lowered and my hands folded [as though I were praying] to Buddha, I bartered for sweet potatoes from Yodo to Terada. Saying it was a secret, they gave me one *kan* of sweet potatoes for thirteen yen. If I give them sugar, I get the sweet potatoes for eight yen. Seven to eight Terada potatoes make a *kan*. Don't be shocked! It comes to one yen a potato. I took the day off, paid my train fare, escaped the notice of the police, and bought them on the black market. If I weren't interested in eating potatoes, we wouldn't be getting things to eat. The income of farm households has reached levels unheard of in earlier times.

October 8, 1944, Sunday
Visiting Imamiya Shrine

On the morning of the scheduled visit to Imamiya Shrine, Community Council Captain Kataoka came to urge us to participate. We had a responsibility to do this. We had to pray for the success of Inao, who enlisted and was being sent to

---

12. Sumiko is Otsuru's daughter. She was born in 1928 and lived at the Tamura residence with her grandparents and mother.

the front.[13] We couldn't say we can't go because it's raining . . . and luckily we got Toshie to go off at 7:30 a.m. and stand in for us and march to the Imamiya Shrine with the people from the community council.

October 11, 1944, Wednesday
I Ate the Sweet-Saké *Manjū* in Front of Daitoku Temple and Wanted to Die

When the chrysanthemums are in full bloom, my aged body's only pleasure is food. My interest in sex has disappeared. It's a wartime period that isn't conducive to searching for food. Every year the Respect-the-Aged Association at the Karaku School has a celebration at which you're treated to good food, but ours is a city at war.[14] We're prohibited from eating more than three-fifths pint per person, and both our minds and stomachs are controlled. Being blessed with things from one's children is wonderful and exceeds one's expectations. While I know this is bad for my stomach and bowels, like a child, I can't disregard my hunger. Because this delinquent oldster is a burden on the country and being beaten to death for the sake of the rice-rationing campaign, I'll probably be made a Buddha. But please wait. Tamura Tsunejirō has regrets about the present world. I won't leave this world until I've had my fill of the sweet-saké *manjū* at Daitoku Temple.[15]

October 14, 1944, Saturday
A Rice Ball from My Son

A clear Japanese autumn day! Fujihira dropped by.[16] He was on his way home from Nisshin Electric — he had worked all night — and although he must've been hungry and sleepy, he came at 7:30 a.m. As always, the company used hunger as a lure for all-night operations. They gave him a loaf of bread, two rice balls (four ounces each), and two kilograms of Tanba chestnuts. Instead of eating these himself, and wanting to please us, he came seven or eight blocks out of his way to give one rice ball to Grandma and one to me. Because of his kindness, I thought I shouldn't just gobble it up, so I poured a cup of *bancha* and ate half my rice ball. While I ate it, I told him the latest war news, and we enjoyed ourselves.

---

13. Inao is Tamura's grandson; see the 4/14/45 entry. His unit was sent to New Guinea, where he was killed in December 1944, although the family was not informed of his death until October 1946.

14. Tamura graduated from Karaku School in 1882.

15. The Daitoku Temple *manjū* is a special delicacy.

16. Fujihira is Tamura's second son. He was born in 1903 and worked briefly at one of his father's billiards parlors before he started at Nisshin Electric during the war.

October 15, 1944, Sunday
Matsutake Mushrooms

How are they? No doubt the splendid *matsutake* mushrooms with no "insect hair" are delicious.

It appears that thirteen-ounce mushrooms do exist. A thirteen-ounce mushroom without bargaining is six yen cheaper. At one point the first *matsutake* were eight yen, fifty sen. Now that upper-class people have had their fill, *matsutake* will come to us in dribs and drabs, but we can't afford them at six yen, fifty sen. We can't even collect two gallons of chestnuts, and although there was a bumper crop of *matsutake*, sadly we can't go hunting for them in wartime, and thus a bountiful year is the same as a poor year.

October 16, 1944, Monday
The Barber's Admonition

"Mr. Tamura, I haven't seen you for some time, and you've changed, haven't you? Is anything wrong?" asked Yagi, the barber. "No . . . nothing's wrong." "You've changed; you've lost weight. It's because you're not getting much nourishment. It's like cats. When they don't eat fish, the color of their fur gets bad, and they waste away." "I see. That makes sense." I'm probably right to think Yagi said what he did because he thought I was about to collapse.

October 17, 1944, Tuesday
Running Out of Matches

Not having any matches is more painful than running out of cigarettes. There's been no distribution this month, and I think everyone is inconvenienced.

Grandma went over to the Isokawa residence to borrow matches, which was more painful than being cut off, but we can't do without matches for even a day and let the fires go out. She borrowed five or six matches for each of us, which will hold us for about three days.

Yesterday, Yoshida mooched off me, and I made tea for him with my own stock. Today I had a customer I wasn't close to, and although I wanted to give him a cup of tea, I didn't have any matches, and so I asked, "If you happen to have any matches, could you spare one or two?" "That's too bad," he answered. "We're all in a bind, but luckily, because I'm a seaman I have some I got in Manila, and I'll give you half a box." His generosity will be hard to forget. I eagerly accepted the half box—a Buddha in hell. I quickly made some *bancha*, and he talked about Manila and then left.

When you trace the lineage of Hamabun, Kawakami Village, Takashima County, Shiga Prefecture, you discover that several famous people were born there. It's known as the birthplace of Ishida Mitsunari, a spearman at Shizu-gatake.[17] Currently, Hamabun is called "Ishida Village" and consists of only thirteen households. Hamabun residents Ishida Koyuemon and Ishida Yozaemon have surnames that make one pine for the good ol' days.

Half their livelihood comes from farming and half from fishing. They fish for Ishida River sweetfish once a year, from October to November. When it gets cold, the small fish swim upstream. When the sweetfish swim upstream from the lake into the Ishida River's pure waters, the fishermen go off with square nets draped over their arms. When they drop their nets into the river, more than a gallon of silver scales dance in the small hand nets, and the fishermen skillfully scoop up the fish. Then they simply drop their nets into the water again and scoop them up without waiting—it's that easy. There are so many sweetfish, you can't see the rocks and gravel on the river bottom.

If, for the heck of it, you threw a rock into the water, it would kill five or six fish.

They say the river is half river, half sweetfish. When one goes upstream, it's incredible: the fish are jumping in puddles.

Candy merchants from Otsu and Kyoto quickly set up eight-gallon cauldrons, and they roll candy and make candied sweetfish with long bamboo chopsticks. They send their candied fish to the silk market and the Osaka area. Candied sweetfish, a Gōshū specialty, is a year-round business.

When the sweetfish swim upstream from the lake to lay their eggs, they eat gravel and stones and thus are not edible. The part of the Ishida River that can be fished is about the length of a block. So if you go two or three blocks upstream, you will beat out others in the hunt for fish and don't have to worry about whose territory you were fishing in.

As soon as I got home from the Tōka School, my best friend Yamaguchi Ka-metarō and I would run to the upper reaches of the Ishida River, baskets hanging from our belts and scoop nets in hand. Although we were just kids, we usually came home with eight or ten quarts of fish. We sun-dried the sweetfish that had eaten gravel and used them as fertilizer for mulberry trees and things planted in the fields. We skewered on bamboo sticks the ones that had not eaten gravel, three at a time, roasted them, and kept them in straw bags until the winter, when they were used to flavor radish dishes and various kinds of soups.

Our small catch was the work of children at play, and I carried the big basket

17. Ishida Mitsunari (1560–1600) was the retainer of Toyotomi Hideyoshi who, after his lord's death, led a coalition of western lords into battle with Tokugawa Ieyasu at Sekigahara on September 17, 1600, and lost.

on a pole together with my older brother Yasusaburō, and Dad gave me a Bunkyū tsūho coin.

At one *rin*, five *mō*, per skewer of fish, our catch came to about twelve and a half pounds, which was half a string of coins. When I went to the Ishida River fish market, they'd say he's the son of Mr. Sugihara Ihei from Katsura Village and generously fill my basket. Dad would pour a little saké on the sweetfish and roast them, so their bellies split open and yellow eggs popped out. They were memorably good. They were so good I was sorry I had gotten full on rice. For three or four days I ate only sweetfish and didn't eat a single grain of rice. Mom and Dad worried that because I was eating only sweetfish and no rice, my complexion would get bad, and I now appreciate their concern.

October 18, 1944, Wednesday
Discovering Life in the Music of Autumn Insects

The autumn insects seemed to have forgotten yesterday's heavy rains and cheerfully cried out in their thin voices,

> "*Jijō, jijō*, silly old man die, die
> save rice, save rice."

The autumn insects don't know they'll die before this silly old man. Your lives are as ephemeral as the dew! Yours is a tragic life that won't know spring, winter, or summer.

"Oh, oh, despite that, the *hōbori* is born in the morning and dies in the evening."[18]

They made their case.

With all the heavy rains we've had recently, the proprietors and growers of the famous Terada potatoes, fearing they will rot, want to sell them and are searching for buyers.

Because one *kan* is going for three to four yen, they should be able to find buyers, and I hear that Osaka people are coming to buy them for thirteen yen. This story doesn't mean I actually went to Osaka. I heard it from someone.

October 19, 1944, Thursday
Hankering for *Matsutake*

There was a bumper crop of *matsutake* mushrooms this year, and no matter how poor you are, you want to have at least one. I still haven't been able to eat

---

18. I haven't been able to identify this insect.

any because the rich people are paying eight yen for a hundred *monme*. My complaints about not getting any chestnuts or *matsutake* in this bumper crop year are understandable.

October 20, 1944, Friday
Distribution of Carp into Reservoirs

In this morning's newspaper, I read that carp released in a water supply reservoir have grown to weigh one to three pounds. Prompted by their paternalistic feelings that these carp should find their way on to the tables of ordinary citizens, the authorities lowered the sluice gates early this morning, and carp swam into the Kamo River, where people trapped them. I'm licking my lips.

Although people may scold the authorities for doing this, having carp is a real luxury for those who can't eat even one *matsutake* mushroom. Life can't go on without the nourishment of carp in miso soup.

At the lake at Takashima in Gōshū, Minamoto Gorō pickled carp and ate well, didn't he? Because they say there'll be a citywide distribution today, regardless of whether or not we get any, I understand the mayor's intentions and am pleased.

October 21, 1944, Saturday
Mocking Agricultural Minister Shimada

It's been two months since Agricultural Minister Shimada assumed his post, and this old Seiyūkai Party power broker, famous for his passion and grit, asked, "Doesn't it take talent to make existing foods and goods seem not to exist and to make nonexistent foodstuffs seem to exist?[19] Even if the people empty their stomachs, as is happening now, [they] can't do a thing. Even if we steadily eat up the stored foods before they rot, when they're eaten and gone, what will we do?" This is an agricultural minister's stock argument.

Yes, Mr. Shimada is a worldly man, and the food situation has greatly improved since his appointment. In addition to rationed rice, three days' worth of wheat

---

19. The Rikken seiyūkai (Friends of the Constitutional Government Party), one of the major political parties of the day, was founded in September 1900 by the great Meiji statesman Itō Hirobumi. The Seiyūkai was progovernment, and most of its supporters were well-to-do landowners. It was dissolved in July 1940, and its members formed the government-sponsored Imperial Rule Assistance Association. Shimada Toshio (1877–1947) was elected nine times to the House of Representatives, the lower house of the Diet (parliament), and became a stalwart in the Seiyūkai. He served as the agricultural minister in the Hirota and Yonai cabinets before assuming the same position in the Koiso cabinet on July 22, 1944.

flour is a common special-distribution item, as are canned goods. But canned goods this delicious are things we can't eat. Next, I want to eat a can of something or other, but because there is an air raid, I'll eat it again. This corresponds to the meaning of welcoming the enemy.

This is an exaggeration. My mouth will be the source of my undoing, and I'd like to erase what I just said as a slip of the tongue.

October 22, 1944, Sunday
In Chaotic Ages the Ecology of Birds Changes

In a small, not very good, picture, the bird is called the *misosuri*, its city name, but in my home village it's called the *sanzai*.[20] It's smaller than a warbler and moves so quickly you can't see it. Its call is *chun, chun*. When the snow piles up, this little bird comes searching for insects and then flies off for long periods to look for quick-moving insects. It's a loner and a cute bird that always comes every morning seeking the shade of the same tree. Today it went off searching for food near the *yamasasa* at the imperial tomb. When the world's at war, the birds change their habits: the *sanzai* now comes before we see snow, and haven't we forgotten that the cuckoo sings before the camellia blooms?

No matter how bad things are, if I don't read the newspaper for a day, I don't feel whole. The war situation and the economics of daily life produce misperceptions that can't be easily corrected. Although they're not reliable, the articles on the incomparably loyal and brave imperial army and the world of constant changes are splendid, living texts that I can't do without, not even for a day. When I finish reading the newspaper, it's discarded as wastepaper, and I've thought about clipping articles and using them for reference, but there's no paste, and it would be a shame to toss out the things I took the trouble to clip.

October 24, 1944, Tuesday
An Increase in Public-Bath Prices

Notice of Public-Bath Increases

From October 25:

Adults	10 sen
Children	6 sen

From November 1:

Adults	12 sen
Children	7 sen

These price increases follow union rules.

---

20. Tamura is referring to the *misosazai*.

Kyoto City Public-Bath Union
Gentlemen:

The public bath entrance fee is eight sen, but it will rise incrementally: after the twenty-fifth it will be ten sen for a five-day period and then twelve sen from November 1. Quite a dramatic rise in prices.

October 25, 1944, Wednesday
Receiving Sweet Potatoes from the Prince

It was the day of the Kitano Shrine.[21]

Shinkichi came over with two big sweet potatoes, the likes of which I'd never seen. He's proud of the Terada Honjo potato. Apparently he didn't say a word. Just plopped them down and left. The two potatoes weighed around six pounds. Grandma quickly cut one in half and added it to the rice porridge she was making for dinner, and it became a meal for a five-person family. It had a wonderful flavor, and we smacked our lips as we ate it.

Having put half a sweet potato into the dinner porridge for the five of us — me, Grandma, Otsuru, Toshie, and Sumiko — Grandma will boil the other half for breakfast tomorrow, and it'll be plenty as a side dish. It's big, isn't it? We'll probably do the same with the remaining one.

In Osaka, eighteen yen will buy a *kan* of sweet potatoes, but the "official" black market price in Kyoto is thirteen yen. Because it's a rice substitute, the police watch things very closely, and when you arrive at Terada Station, you're immediately put into the clink and the goods are confiscated. Even Otsuru was thwarted, and all she'll say is, "It was terrifying! Terrifying!"

So even if one wanted to eat a sweet potato, it was impossible. Luckily Shinkichi gave us these Terada potatoes, and they were a great treat. The distributions mean profit and loss, involve money and authority, and lead to confiscations and thievery, and poor folks like us don't get good things. Because there's discrimination even in our imperial country, I think speaking of the equality of the country's ten million people is pure semantics.

My Son Suffered from the Preparation of Industry

Shinkichi is troubled. He has six children waiting with open mouths. All he worries about from morning to dusk is that day's livelihood. At one point, he bought paddy and dry land in Mizuguchi Ward and had eight or nine hired women rolling kombu for a large market. He even had dealings quite far away — in Korea and Kyushu.

---

21. The Kitano Shrine was built in 947 to placate the spirit of Sugawara Michizane (845–903).

He finally had come into his own. During the war, he had to sell the Mizu-guchi Ward land for what the authorities called "industrial preparation," but he never asked his parents for help, or for anything at all. I can imagine that Shinkichi probably will be bitter about all this. If the prosperity had continued for two more years, he would have become his own man. With a wife crying over illness and two sick daughters, the life of this family of eight was a sight to behold.

October 28, 1944, Saturday
The Distribution of Sardines the Size of Minnows

There was a distribution of sardines this morning, and, I thought, I'll finally eat with gusto. Yet it was all in vain. Three sardines the size of minnows were on Otsuru's tray. They made fools of us.

Toshie complained a lot but said, "I'm off," and went to work in Osaka.

Grandma had not been feeling well for two or three days and is sleeping. With twice as many empty stomachs, unbearable discomfort and complaints, and our treatment as hanger-oners, I have begun to have vengeful thoughts, but they don't come to anything.

The sweet potato distribution offered about twenty-one pounds for eighty-nine sen.

November 2, 1944, Thursday
The Pleasure of Receiving *Matsutake* Mushrooms

It took some doing to get the *matsutake* mushrooms I ordered, and they called Iwata Enterprises to say I should come get them. Toshie went to the Ōnishi residence in Ōmiyaji at 6:30 a.m. They were a little expensive but . . .

The top grade of mushrooms, those with a lot of perfume, were selling at a *kan* for fifty-five yen. Shigesaburō remarked, "Isn't that cheap? On the Osaka black market, you'd pay eight yen (for a hundred *monme*)."[22] The mushrooms were distributed to ten employees of Iwata Enterprises, but unfortunately when we drew lots, I was third, and two exceedingly fine specimens, which weighed sixty-eight *monme*, were sold for three yen, seventy-eight sen. I wasn't disappointed.

Kyoto is the home of *matsutake* mushrooms, but they're shipped to distant Osaka and then come back to their source. "No matter what one says, the world is governed by money, and when a *matsutake* is selling at one *kan* for ten yen, that's fine."

---

22. Tamura Shigesaburō is obviously a relative who lives in Osaka.

This is connoisseurs' talk — it's the way Tamura Shigesaburō and the Osaka gluttons talk — and this is impossible in stingy Kyoto. This *matsutake* mushroom was the first of the year for me and probably will be my last. Now I'm looking forward to savoring *matsutake* rice for the last time.

November 4, 1944, Saturday
Cigarettes Will Be Rationed

Now cigarettes will be rationed. In Kyoto, after November 1, cigarettes will be rationed: men who smoke will get six per day. Today, in Jōzenji Ward, neighborhood association captain Iobara told us that we'll get one Asahi, one Hikari, and a total of thirty cigarettes for a five-day period. Any more than that is prohibited. Grandma, Otsuru, and Toshie have been living in a smoker's paradise, but no more.

We should have expected this. If wives were allowed to smoke, then the authorities would have to recognize black market transactions, and the monopoly office would have to make up for the shortage of raw materials and workers.

The peacetime price of a pack of cigarettes was seventeen sen. The wartime tax alone is fifty-three sen. If it were peacetime, it would be just seventeen sen, but because of the war, it's seventy sen. One Asahi is three sen, five rin, and until today I put up with waiting in long lines. Because I put out an empty box and spend two to three hours to buy one cigarette, it's still a plus. I wondered whether these had been distributed a little early.

Seventy sen for a box of Asahis is not expensive! Up to now, when I had time, I made a show of collecting my salary and then lining up three or four times to buy one-yen cigarettes, and making a profit, in my spare time. Those who deal in cigarettes will have to switch to other businesses. I think I discovered another good idea.

Pharmacy Telephone Center Number 4219, "Going to Die"

For two or three days I've been coming down with a cold, and my head has been hurting. Last night I coughed continuously and was up all night. It's painful, and blood is about to come out of my throat. This Sunday morning is beautiful, and Toshie said that my condition was good, and I asked the Itō Nōeru Pharmacy for some medicine. "When I am able to get up, I don't cough much, but when I sleep, I start coughing."

The ironist Itō said, "Isn't the venerable Tamura seventy-five? My store's phone number is 4219, going to die.'"[23] This is why the aged are lonely.

---

23. Tamura's pharmacist is making a macabre pun: the number 4219 is pronounced *shi-ni-i-ku* in Japanese, which also can mean "going to die."

Kataoka, the head of the Jōzenji community council, and others gave us a bottle of Yōmei saké and five yen in sympathy money for Grandma, who is bedridden. We really appreciated this gesture. Since Grandma is recovering and now doing needlework and cleaning, Otsuru wondered what we should do with the sympathy money. We can't very well return what was brought, so we decided to keep it.

November 5, 1944, Sunday
Granddaughter Drafted for Volunteers Corps

An order came drafting Sumiko for service in the Kamigyō Girls Volunteer Corps. For five years, from the time she was thirteen up to now, I have scolded her a lot about how she did things, and although I think she wanted to become more refined, inborn habits die hard. She helped the family business a lot, and although we're losing her, we'll muddle through. We'll truly miss her, but in wartime you have to work for the state, if even just a little, and because complaints are undemocratic and forbidden, I'll send her off with strict orders to work hard.

. . . For only one day, the eighth, you'll go alone to Kyōgoku: I release a caged bird, and I warn her not to impose on her close friends and want to give her a little spending money.

Wherever the operations are, when she's not around, things will be gloomy and it won't be surprising if they go out and it's pitch black. Besides being ready to work, this seventy-five-year-old will start working, and my unromantic body will probably be comical. Sumiko, good-bye, good-bye.

At 11:00 a.m. an air-raid warning was issued. It was lifted at 12:20 p.m. First of all, everything was fine.

I delivered the entertainment tax of twenty-five yen, sixty sen, to the office on Ichijō and paid one yen, five sen, for one package of *sencha*; one yen, fifty-six sen, for a ration of split firewood; sixty sen for cough medicine; and one yen, fifty sen, for supplementary food.

November 11, 1944, Saturday
The Aged Have Neither Gods nor Buddhas

We've had glorious weather, but it's been cold, very cold.

With no firewood, no split wood, and only a little charcoal — it's a life-or-death situation. Two bundles of charcoal are left. There's no end to our feelings of hopelessness.

Without the distribution of even one fish, I've forgotten what a fish is. We've consumed our three-month ration of soy sauce and miso, and this means we have to ask repeatedly and beg for pity. At this rapid rate of consumption, do we say our situation is grave? In the rapid rush — there is no reason, no complaint, or no making a case. In this autumn of emergencies, when the life or death of the state is at issue, the weak have become food for the strong, and even the tobacconist is closed, and people are upset. The problem is how to survive in this bleak society. Standing on top of the rock of desperation, those of us who are old pray to Buddha and the gods, saying, "If I have life, . . ." but at the moment our strength is exhausted, and joining our hands in prayer is the height of idiocy.

November 18, 1944, Saturday
Black Market Cigarettes

I never imagined, not even in my wildest dreams, that the tobacconist would deal on the black market. Official black market prices for cigarettes are one box of Hikari (ten cigarettes) is three yen, fifty sen, in Osaka and three yen in Kyoto; and one box of Kinshi (ten cigarettes) is three yen in Osaka and two yen, fifty sen, in Kyoto. There are various black market prices for other commodities, and the tobacconist is asking for quite a lot. I never knew black market dealing would generate such huge profits. There are no distinctions in the black market's "public" controls. The prohibition on women's smoking, which is based on the rationing system, is just a hollow law.

November 19, 1944, Sunday
A Friend Who Spent Twenty-five Years in Shanghai

I met Mikami Takejirō again.

He and his wife unexpectedly showed up after twenty-five years. It appears they succeeded in Shanghai, and they're nostalgic about their birthplace. It's been twenty-five years, and he's now fifty-four. He lives in Higashi Funaoka in Murasakino in Kamigyō Ward and has been living there for some time, so we said by all means come over, and he did, with Okuni.

Mikami was a customer at our billiards parlors and less a fan of the game than a devotee of the polite arts, and an old pal of mine. His wife, Okuni, a samisen artist from Rokken-chō in Imadegawa, is from a family that made a living as performers of traditional song. Even though Mikami has aged, his sexual perfume lingers, and he's still charming and just as he was in the past. Mikami was a handsome man, and he and Okuni were lovers who caused many scandals. Hearing how they went hand in hand to Shanghai twenty-five years ago made us nostalgic. They said they'd call on us again, and left.

November 20, 1944, Monday
Skyrocketing Prices and Prospects for Death

Two quarts of supplementary rice is now twenty-five yen. A two-gallon bag of rice is worth a thousand yen. Seventeen pounds of sugar is forty yen, and an old bathrobe that's falling apart is eighty yen. The lives of us lower-class folk is oppressive. We simply are waiting to starve to death.

Neither the diarrhea nor the coughing will stop. Suffering from these maladies, I can only plan on a time to hang myself. I'll end my morning and evening salutations with this and impolitely put down my brush for a time.

November 24, 1944, Friday
The Attacks by the American Aircraft Have Begun

At noon an unromantic bell began to toll: *pu-pu-pu-*. What? Have they come again? It was a type of American aircraft whose name I didn't know—get it quickly before it escapes!

Suddenly at 12:10 p.m. an air-raid warning was issued. The warning broadcast on the radio made us nervous. The Central District Army announcement: an enemy observation plane was sighted on the twenty-first. Because today's raid had bombing as its ultimate aim, completion of the air-defense system is desirable. As we were calmly preparing, the Central District Army announced that ten enemy aircraft had attacked the Ise Bay coastline.

Then, one after another, the planes in the attacking squadron passed over the lighthouse at Shionosaki and required the appropriate vigilance. At 1:30 p.m. they turned east of Ise Bay, then north. At 1:50 p.m. the warning was called off. What a relief![24]

November 30, 1944, Thursday
Rumors of Sweet Potatoes in Kameyamamachi

It's raining hard. There was a distribution of rice: it was four yen, fifty-six sen. Toshie left for work in Osaka at seven this morning, and Otsuru went out in the rain to buy vegetables.

If one goes to Kameyamamachi, which is a short distance from Nagoya and famous for its sweet potatoes, great stores of steamed potatoes are piled up everywhere.[25] There's no need to pack a box lunch, and it's unlimited buying: a *kan* of potatoes for two yen. Every day a herd of foragers arrive from Kyoto, and

---

24. On November 24, 111 B-29s attacked Tokyo. See Carter and Mueller, *Combat Chronology*, 505.

25. Kameyama is about thirty-six miles from Kyoto.

each person takes home five to six *kan*. With a round-trip train fare of six yen, the buyers are ecstatic. They have you eat steamed potatoes until you're stuffed, and Otsuru told us stories of quick profit. This is why she doesn't ask anyone to go with her and why I can't go.

The three women talk only about eating and don't care a whit about how the business is doing or why there's no profit. The women are irresponsible.

December 1, 1944, Friday
The Deeds of the Special-Attack Units

Wartime December 1 has arrived. There were pictures in the *Asahi* newspaper of the Wild Eagles Squadron, who were either students or teenagers who had just turned twenty and who once had a future, and pictures of the brave warriors of the Yasukuni Squadron being toasted by their unit leader. Seeing these pictures made me realize that it's impossible for us to express our complaints and unhappiness about food anywhere.

Yet the stomachs of the elderly weaken, and their diarrhea won't stop. Without the distribution of even a single fish, their diarrhea doesn't stop, and the elderly are regarded as very accommodating.

December 3, 1944, Sunday
Trouble over the Forced Delivery of Cotton

The beautiful weather was glorious, but it suddenly turned cold and nothing could be done without a fire to warm ourselves. We've used up most of the charcoal, and the fuel situation is pathetic. Three days earlier, Iobara, the captain of our neighborhood association, ordered us to make a forced contribution of four hundred *monme* of cotton. Grandma gave up 390 *monme* of cotton futon, and I remember her saying she'd do something to find another hundred *monme*.[26]

Yesterday Iobara came and said because our house had not been able to deliver more than half its cotton allotment, we'd have to come up with the remaining five hundred *monme* by this morning. Although we produced 390 *monme* [sic] of the allotted four hundred *monme*, were they going to overlook what Iobara called "half"? Where was the 190 *monme*? Although she felt only half-well, Grandma's sense of uprightness emerged. When the 190 *monme* was accounted for, she'd gladly produce more than five hundred *monme* — what is half?

My colleague Moriguchi Hanako from Daikyō came over and reported that detectives burst in three or four times in one day, rebuking her for having customers. As a result, the customers stopped coming. Later the tax office came to

---

26. Tamura is referring to *shikibuton*, the futon laid directly on the floor and slept on.

do a survey, and they levied a tax of three yen per table, and because there were three tables, it was nine yen. They hypothesized that we had made profits, and we were closely investigated. I found the thought of continuing my business beyond this point rather unappealing. Not long afterward, my boss got a job in Fukui City working with expropriated cars, and I considered moving as well.

Because he was a young person with a future, he recognized his situation and cut his ties, encouraging me to do the same. "Why don't you move to a more meaningful occupation?"

Going to the Formal Introduction of the Company at the Minamiza

On a very cold and clear day, I took advantage of Toshie's day off and asked to be allowed, as an old person's solitary pleasure, to see the formal introduction of this year's kabuki company at the Minamiza on Shijō.[27] I went off after lunch at 12:30.

As I looked at Shijō from the trolley, I was surprised to find that everything from Horikawa Ward on had been transformed into inelegant rental units. The conductor shouted hoarsely "thirty sen change" but didn't give any change. Even making change seemed to be a bother, and the two things surprised me.

I wonder whether the current inflation policy and the overissuing of 150 million yen in paper currency is slowing the movement of goods and services within society and causing us to see money as wastepaper. I don't eat what there is to eat, and as an old-fashioned type I retain mistaken ways of thinking. But seeing the now exceedingly inelegant Shijō Avenue, I realized I must change the direction of my thinking from now on, even if just a little. The Minamiza's response to the war was a fighting drama with Ichimura Uzaemon and Nakamura Baigyoku.[28] They even abolished the old conventions and performed with a smaller troupe. First-class tickets were exceptionally cheap: two yen, five sen. But because the wartime tax was 100 percent, the entrance fee was five yen for a first-class ticket.

The curtain was raised at two o'clock. The first piece featured Sawamura Tosshi and . . . Ichikawa . . . as Genroku martyrs who performed the Isogai Jurozaemon suicide. This was a lineup of the young actors. Sawamura Tosshi and

---

27. The Minamiza is the big kabuki theater in Kyoto and is located at the corner of Shijō and Kitayama Avenues.

28. Ichimura Uzaemon XV (1874–1945) was a popular actor who specialized in romantic roles and was famous for his role as Togashi in the play *Kanjinchō*. Nakamura Baigyoku (1875–1948) was a leading *onnagata*—performer of women's roles—in the Kansai area.

Totoki Denyuemon performed a one-act play whose noble scenes were a little disappointing.[29]

December 8, 1944, Friday
Cutting Firewood and Air Raids

I cut down one of the pepper trees left in Mr. Isogawa's care.[30] Cutting it down took a lot of effort, and considering my age, it is something I am proud of. Because I couldn't expect to find anyone to cut a tree for less than seven or eight yen, I made one cut every morning, and after I had done this for five days, I brought it down.

Central Headquarters suddenly issued an air-raid warning at 11:35 a.m. There was the unsettling *bu-, bu-*. At 11:40 a.m. it was reported that enemy aircraft were coming to attack the Harima Shallows area and we were to be on our guard.[31] What? When? It was like being tricked by foxes and badgers. What a relief! It was like water thrown in a drunk's face or relieving oneself.

I didn't expect any customers, and I still had to find something good about the suspension of our business. Today I had to live with no income.

December 9, 1944, Saturday
Shortages of Goods and the Bombing of Tokyo

It's clear and cold, very cold, but there's no charcoal. With no fuel to burn, nothing's quite as hard on old bodies as the cold. Although New Year's is coming, we haven't had a single rice cake. If we eat three pounds of rice cakes, it's deducted from our rice ration. So we can't have any. This year, too, will be a New Year's without a distribution of rice cakes, and I think it can't be helped. Even if we ate rice cakes, it wouldn't be a typical New Year's when you're being attacked by the enemy.

It was Tokyo's fourth attack, and now there are completely burned-out areas in that city.[32] The fires continued from noon until 5:30 p.m. They say six thousand people died and their bodies filled the underground passages of Mitsukoshi Department Store, but they still couldn't handle them all. It occurred to me

---

29. Sawamura Tosshi was an established actor. Tamura gives only the surname and not the given name of an actor named Ichikawa. I have not been able to identify Totoki Denyūemon.

30. The *sanshō* (*Zanthoxylum piperitum*) is a Japanese pepper tree.

31. There is no record of B-29s attacking the Japanese home islands on this day.

32. Nearly seventy B-29s attacked Tokyo on December 3. See Carter and Mueller, *Combat Chronology*, 513.

that we haven't known anything this tragic. The New Year's ceremonies have become funeral ceremonies. It appears that Akita Kiyoshi, Nagai Ryūtarō, and Inoue Tetsujirō were killed in the bombing.[33] The reverberations make the hair on your body stand on end, and even New Year's is trembling and the Tōkaidō Line is not running.

Customers don't come during a blackout, and it always happens that the collectors show up when there's been no income. Oh, how I'd like to forget the world! Mine is the utter humiliation of having bees attack even a tearful face. I'm just unlucky! Enemy planes, come! Kill me! Then I'd forget the world! *Namu amida butsu, namu amida butsu*!

December 15, 1944, Friday
Making Rice Cakes is an Ancient Dream.
Now We Just Fall on Our Duffs

If this were a peaceful age like those in the past, we'd be starting to prepare for New Year's. First, we'd make rice cakes. In normal years we'd hire rice pounders, three or four husky men with red headbands inscribed with the "in and out" stone emblem, calling out "*Hoi! Hoi!*" and "*He-*, this year too will be bountiful!" We received two quarts of glutinous rice from farmers as payment for our night soil. I washed the rice three or four days earlier, and as I did, I heard the propitious sound of rice cake pounding next door. I gave the neighbors on both sides of our house my pride and joy: a rice cake filled with bits of azuki bean, a rice cake experiment, and I did this as a gesture of my appreciation. My intention was to share generously the brilliant lifestyle of the mundane, and my repaying my neighbors' generosity with experimental rice cakes became a greeting. That sort of easygoing age was miles away from what was left of my dream.

I no longer can hear rice pounding next door. The New Year's glutinous rice allotment is an act of love—just over a quart per person. When you've eaten up this quart of rice cakes, you can only cry, holding a stomach one quart less full, because the New Year's rice will be subtracted from the rice allotment on the tenth. We weren't eating the ceremonial rice cakes: we were eating the cry-

---

33. Akita Kiyoshi (1881–1944) served in several prewar cabinets and was an adviser to the Imperial Rule Assistance Association; Nagai Ryūtarō (1881–1944) was a well-known politician, journalist, and educator who served in several prewar cabinets; and Inoue Tetsujirō (1855–1944) was a philosophy professor at Tokyo Imperial University who is best known for introducing German Idealist philosophy to the Japanese academic community.

ing rice cakes. Celebrating the New Year with the potatoes Otsuru bought at Kameyama is probably more in keeping with the war spirit.

Yesterday Nagoya was hit by air raids, and half of Ginza Avenue in Tokyo was destroyed.[34] The Tōkaidō Line is not running. Today enemy aircraft came to reconnoiter Osaka and Kobe. All of a sudden someone in back of us just started making rice cakes, and his making rice cakes sitting down is probably because of the war.[35]

December 21, Thursday
Carrying Night Soil to an Empty House

I got up at 6:50 a.m. They haven't come to collect our night soil. I was desperate because I was unable to bear the stench and the filth, so I came up with a solution. I carried our four buckets to the toilet at the empty old "Krober" house.[36] While Mr. Isogawa was asleep and after holding out for three or four months, I made a profit of three or four yen, a smelly, smelly profit.

December 26, Tuesday
The Electrical Light Company That Illuminates
Us Is Dealing on the Black Market

At the end of the year, we found out that the electric light company has been operating on the black market. Our house paid thirty-seven yen, sixty-five sen, for October as well as a fine for exceeding our quota, which was extremely painful. We were prohibited from using more than six lightbulbs.

In November, electrical workers came and took off the sticker that had been pasted on the house, releasing us from the six-bulb limitation, and I welcomed the long-awaited lifting of the restriction. They said, "From now on you're released from the limitation, so go ahead and use electricity as you please," and then left. I inquired about this strange affair, and I heard it came together with the end-of-the-year bonus and was a special marketing strategy. I learned for the first time that this sort of shady black market dealing is rampant in the well-lit electric light companies of our time. Even though wartime provisions and so forth are hard to come by, the black market cannot be wiped out completely.

---

34. More than seventy B-29s attacked Nagoya early on the morning of December 14. See Carter and Mueller, *Combat Chronology*, 520.

35. Instead of standing to pound the cooked glutinous rice, which is how it usually is done.

36. I have not been able to identify "Krober."

December 28, 1944, Thursday
Exchanging Saké for Firewood

As a kindness at New Year's, we received daily distributions of various goods, including coupons for two quarts of third-grade saké. Even if I do receive two quarts of saké, I can't drink the sweet stuff. Matsushita Makoto had three bundles of firewood, and because one bundle was worth three yen, fifty sen, three bundles were ten yen, fifty sen. I suggested an exchange and handed over the saké coupons. I decided to do this on the condition that he give me three-fifths of every two quarts of saké that he gets.

December 31, 1944, Sunday
End-of-the-Year Thoughts

At long last, today is the last day of 1944, and when the new day dawns, we'll greet 1945, the Year of the Rooster. The enemy attacks are a daily affair, and there's no New Year's spirit. I got up at eight, but there were no sounds of tatami being beaten.[37]

The crowing of the neighborhood roosters is pathetic, as though their lives were being sucked to the bone.

Toshie and Haruko put on their clogs and cleaned the planks laid out over the mud.[38] Up until two years ago, as a morning exercise, they polished the area between the Iroha signs with oil until it was smooth, but in no time, this area, which guests were once reluctant to walk on in their shoes, had become muddied and dirty.[39] It was New Year's Eve, and not a single cent was owed me, no loans had to be repaid, no end-of-the-year gift to be given, and nothing coming in. When I thought about this strange, unprecedented sort of New Year's Eve, I simply accepted the fact that it felt good, and that was enough.

New Year's Day
Impressions of a Sweet Potato New Year

Wartime conditions have come to prevail with extraordinary speed, and the weak have become food for the strong. How will we survive in this harried world? The new year promises to be one filled with problems.

It was unusual, but even the enemy planes seemed to have some humanity. On New Year's Day alone, we're not worrying about air raids over our heads. First

---

37. At New Year's, tatami mats are taken outside and beaten as part of a general, once-a-year housecleaning.
38. Haruko is the youngest of Tamura's daughters. She was born in 1932.
39. Tamura's billiards parlor is named Iroha.

of all, although it was a small matter, there was *mazetakīmi* rice, some bamboo shoots, and saké. I'm seventy-six, and although I'm of no value for the honorable country, today I realized my humanity, and it felt like an old-style New Year's.

It was a sweet potato New Year's. Otsuru must not be surprised. She went to a place about a mile east of Shimokameyama in Mie Prefecture to buy fifteen or sixteen loads of sweet potatoes. What made this possible was the fact that the potatoes were black market goods. We've developed good relations with the farm families, and we came to buy sweet potatoes at one *kan* for three yen; even with the train fare included, one *kan* cost only three yen, eighty sen.

When we eat glutinous rice, we have to sacrifice one month's worth of rice, and as a rice substitute, the honorable sweet potato is full of nourishment.[40] Under the circumstances, while both Toshie and I are in the house, it's strange for us, rather than Otsuru, to be searching for, and eating, food.

January 4, 1945, Thursday
I Want to Know the Truth about the War

We've gotten accustomed to the frequent air raids occurring day after day and are no longer surprised. Since Japan is taking the offensive, I think there's a chance we'll win. I now realize that the government's not revealing the truth about the war could be a way to win the support of the general population.

Some people are patriotic and discuss the war in the most optimistic terms, while others are very pessimistic. All of this because the truth can't be made public.

January 7, 1945, Sunday
A Kite for the Return of Peace

The Wild Eagles of the imperial forces are in a decisive battle against the American aircraft attacking Nagoya, Shizuoka, and Tokyo, body-crashing from ten thousand meters, day after day and night after night.[41] Fighting for the life or death of the imperial country is not like flying kites in peacetime. I flew mine at a mere two hundred feet, and because it didn't reach the fighting, I could only stand on one leg, wind up my string, and wait for the return of peace.

Thinking about the ferocity of the fighting in the Philippines, it seems that

40. Sweet potatoes are rich in vitamins C and E.
41. "Body-crashing" (J. *tai-atari*) refers to the suicidal tactics used by pilots in the special-attack squadrons known in the West as the kamikaze; see Tamura's 12/1/44 entry. Fifty-seven B-29s attacked Nagoya on January 3; see Carter and Mueller, *Combat Chronology*, 538.

those who die have a step ahead on becoming the Amida Buddha and those left behind will fight as hard as they can.

January 8, 1945, Monday
My Daughter's Sweet Potato

With the train to Kameyama in Mie Prefecture not running, Otsuru went to Tokyo, but even the unlimited selling, which took place at a famous site of sweet potato production after the official distribution, there was a backside to the noisiness. In November and December this year and last, one could buy sixteen loads of sweet potatoes, and at three *kanme* per load, one could buy forty-eight *kanme*.[42]

This price was popular with Kyoto and Osaka people, and they came by electric and steam trains to buy sweet potatoes. The result was that the price kept going up, and today one *kanme* was selling for two yen, fifty sen. I went to buy some on the third day they were available. I bought forty-eight *kanme* for forty-eight yen. Apparently the round-trip fare for the electric and steam trains was only five yen, and so I used only eighty yen. The total was 128 yen.[43]

These potatoes have become a food substitute and snack, and although by the end of the year, the entire family had wasted away and suffered, Toshie and I, around October when we bought the potatoes, actually gained weight. Our regaining our health is, of course, the blessing of the gods, but Otsuru's labors were truly exceptional.

In the morning we had sweet potatoes in our rice porridge, and Toshie put one *kanme* of potatoes in our box lunches, and I, too, had a *kanme* of Otsuru's potatoes. Except for Otsuru, who worked in Osaka and was hungry from being sent on business to other areas, our sweet potato box lunches had more than enough supplements and were just fine.

Haruko cannot be expected to be full from the seven spoonfuls of food provided at school. When she gets home from school, I roast one sweet potato in the ashes and fill her up. In the evening, I close the business at ten and when anyone feels hungry, I fry sweet potatoes in a saucepan or boil them. Toshie likes *kin kin ni* and sweet potato appetizers: the two most delicious dishes. Since we are given vegetables for side dishes, in addition to the rice ration, Otsuru alternately buys Japanese radishes and carrots. We finally are managing to eke out an existence. This is the story of an old person's sweet potato New Year's.

---

42. Three *kanme* are about twenty-five pounds, and forty-eight *kanme* are four hundred pounds.

43. It appears that Tamura had help.

Of course, as a substitute food, sweet potatoes are rich in nutrients, and we had to buy Otsuru's hard work. Sweet potato New Year's, coming as it did as the war intensifies in 1945, is also a gaseous New Year's.

We thanked Otsuru again for her hard labor and then farted away 128 yen.

The details of that story are in my precious diary entry:

> There is embarrassment within the
> darkness/black market
> A front and a back to things.

We get a scant five or six stalks of green onions and one Japanese radish from the greengrocers as the side dishes for five people — anyone hearing about this would have a good laugh.

Otsuru went off to buy in the Toriba area and did this with incredible secrecy. The arrogance of the farmers this year: turnips — don't be shocked — are eighty-five sen. Even Japanese radishes and green onions, firewood, and soy sauce for five people costs about two yen.

January 15, 1945, Monday
A Child's New Year

Recently, enemy planes have been attacking a lot, and I reminisced about the New Year's celebrations in the old days, when I was sixty-four years younger. January 15 was "Little New Year": rice cakes were added to azuki bean porridge as part of the morning's festivities, and we ate until our stomachs were full.[44] Then we got up on Japanese stilts and went over to the neighboring village, playing along the way in the four to five inches of snow that had accumulated.

It was a festive day at the household of Sugiwara Ihei in Katsura Township, Kawakami Village, Takashima County, Shiga Prefecture. Persimmons hung under the eaves on the south side of the house — red, sweet, and perfect. Getting back up on our stilts, we picked about twenty persimmons that were too high on the tree for anyone to reach and made short work of them, licking our lips in appreciation.

Mom made sweet saké from malted rice — she liked sweet saké — and she drank four or five bowls of it every day, drawing it from a narrow and deep tub.[45]

---

44. "Little New Year" (J. koshōgatsu) is celebrated in the countryside on the first day of the lunar calendar.

45. Amazake, translated here as "sweet saké," is made by mixing the mold used to make saké into a pot of cooked rice and simmering it from twelve to twenty-four hours. Sugar and ginger are added before it is served.

There is an old saying that it isn't pleasant to drink sweet saké because it makes your stomach swell.

We assembled at the shrine for a "Little New Year's" ceremony in which we first wrote *tenmangaki* (the first writing of the year) and then burned them. Matsumoto-sensei treated us to a feast of unrefined saké, but I didn't drink any of it. I dreamed about "Little New Year's" in the countryside.

Unforgettable Humiliations in My Life

I was up all night depressed. There wasn't a single customer. It was an unusually cold night, and I turned on the light in the hall so I could see my feet during a fire prevention drill. Unfortunately, unbeknownst to me, the Karaku civilian air-raid warden was making his rounds. It was dark and I was grubby, but I thought he was a customer. "Please come in," I said, which was the wrong thing to say. At that instant I felt sharp pains in my chest, and before too long someone shouted, "Hey! Who's in charge? Don't you know about the Civilian Air-Raid Patrol? What's this fire? This is not allowed today! Come to the station! Now!"

"I'm sorry. Now if you'll let me, I'll put out that light right away!"

"No! That's not permitted. Come to the station!"

"Don't you think the Matsubara bomb damage was a terrible shame?"

"You idiot! Don't you know that it's because of one house that many are inconvenienced?

An overbearing guy with a drooping moustache came in from the street and shouted.

"This old guy is still not the age when he'd be senile. Isn't there a young person here?"

Were these the words of a fellow human being? Because I recognized that I was in the wrong, I fell to my knees and lowered my head, but he insisted, "This old guy's not senile." Seeing Toshie with her hood and *monpe* on, he said, "Hey! You've got rouge on your cheeks and are dressed in these clothes—why?" When human beings become this coarse, right or wrong, they're beyond judgment. Since I didn't turn on the light purposely but just forgot, I expected him to be a bit warmer.

In my seventy-five years, I've never been called a "senile old guy" or humiliated to this extent.

Toshie looked pathetic, and since there was no way to respond to that barrage of words, she said nothing; and the two of us, crying and fuming, put up the blackout curtain.

I couldn't sleep a wink the whole night. They'll come from the station to summon me; they're sure to come. All I can do is apologize.

January 16, 1945, Tuesday
Bombing and Social Conditions

Enemy American aircraft have been bombing day and night, dozens of times —
Tokyo, Nagoya, Shizuoka, and especially the munitions factories outside Nagoya,
which produce more than 60 percent of our munitions and are number 1 in our
imperial country.[46] The bombings have cut Japan's productive capacity, and the
indiscriminate bombing is intolerable.[47]

The furniture and household objects being moved to the Tokyo suburbs got
more and more expensive at one point, but after two or three months, high-class
items like paulownia-wood chests, once 1,200 to 1,300 yen, were selling for just
fifty yen. They say the market for household items, no matter what, has no bottom. At present, just to survive, people are moving foods from black market to
black market. It's the age of the strong eating the weak.

Those who die precede the rest of us to Amida's Pure Land, and there's no
telling whether the survivors can bear the home-front misery and the pain and
suffering of battlefield carnage. I hear that indiscriminate bombing from far
above the heads of a million city folk caused a lot of damage to the Higashiyama
Line to Matsubara.

January 18, 1945, Thursday
Bomb Damage at Matsubara, Kyoto

At 3:00 p.m. Haruko returned from the Demizu School.

What the teacher in charge told the students in writing was that a lone enemy
plane came today, and because issuing an air-raid warning would have slowed
munitions production, no warning was given. The Matsubara bomb killed or
injured 270. The students also were told that those with futon over their heads
were not injured.

January 19, 1945, Friday
Bowing and Falling over with Vegetables in Hand

As the fires of war get worse, you eat to survive, but everyone knows that you can't
live on greengrocers' distributions alone. My daughter dashes off to the southeast
for carrots, turnips, and radishes. This one turnip, which she begged for, was

---

46. Fifty-seven B-29s attacked Nagoya on January 4; seventy-two attacked Tokyo on
January 10; and forty attacked Nagoya on January 15. See Carter and Mueller, *Combat
Chronology*, 538, 543, 546.

47. The attacks on January 3 and 9 targeted urban areas.

eighty sen. This radish was fifty sen. From now on, I won't deal with anyone who doesn't bring saké.

Needless to say, our daily earnings and expenditures don't stay in balance. Our income has gone further and further south, together with enemy planes. First, the warnings will be called off.

January 21, 1945, Sunday
Giving up Sightseeing at the Higashidera Market

Browsing at the Kōbō Daishi Market is one of my monthly pleasures and a hobby.

But starting this month, conductors won't let you on the train if you're not in uniform, even if you've waited in line. If you get on, they'll push you off. For this billiards player to be pushed off—this rejection is not a problem. Although I was sorry about this, I had no choice but to give up my monthly pleasure.

January 23, 1945, Tuesday
Bombing of the Shimabara Gas Company

A bomb fell on the Shimabara Gas Company with a huge boom![48] First, there was an explosion and then a violent ripping sound, followed by a horrible shock wave. When people dashed into the street or looked out their windows, it was the Shimabara Gas Company burning bright red at one in the afternoon. The full extent of the damage is a secret and can't be released, however. Incendiary bombs also fell on the Ryōanji and Renkadō, but the fires were put out quickly.[49]

The teachers in charge of the Demizu School reported to the students that 270 to 280 were killed or wounded on the night of the fourteenth at Matsubara on the Higashiyama Line. This seemed about right. Today's bomb was the second one dropped on Kyoto. It was a shame that lots of people were killed or wounded. I clasp my hands and chant *namu amida buddha, namu amida buddha.*

January 24, 1945, Wednesday
Granddaughter's Homecoming and Life in the Senshin Corps

It was a servant's holiday for Sumiko, now a member of the Senshin Corps, and she came home from Banda City. As gifts she brought cute clogs for Toshie and Haruko and lots of sweet potatoes and dried cuttlefish for the rest of us.

Her work is secret, and although she didn't say a word about what she's doing,

---

48. There is no record of an attack on Kyoto, although sixty-three B-29s did attack Nagoya and other targets on January 23. See Carter and Mueller, *Combat Chronology*, 554.

49. The Ryōanji, a Zen temple famous for its rock garden, is located in western Kyoto.

not even to her parents, it's thought to be munitions. She gets up at 5:05 a.m. and bathes at 8:30 p.m., and after that it's lights out and to bed. Her monthly salary is just twenty yen, which doesn't allow her to buy any rationed goods. Her board is ten sen for breakfast and fifteen sen for lunch and dinner, and her meals consist of vegetables and potatoes, and fish every fourth or fifth day. Even with food substitutes, she couldn't hope to have enough to be full. Every day, enemy aircraft attack and she's buffeted by explosions, and she says you don't feel as though you're alive. Next month she'll be evacuated to Tomiyama, and for two years it'll be very hard for her to come home.[50] She'll return to the Banda arsenal on the twenty-sixth at 6:30. Otsuru will see her to Kyoto Station. In this cold season the old man is well — Sumiko, good-bye.

January 25, 1945, Thursday
Air-Raid Life

I've been holed up in my house and haven't gone out for some time.

With the cold and the frequent attacks of enemy aircraft, I haven't bathed or washed my face. I sleep in my clothes and eat quickly in bed. A truly human existence has been impossible for some time, because I have only one bowl of rice and a watery miso soup with greens floating in it and live like a pig. I've gotten quite thin and lack the energy to go out.

January 31, 1945, Wednesday
New Year's Next Year

In this wartime New Year's, it'll be February in one day. Every night makes me realize that if my daughters die, at least we'll be together: these are a parent's feelings.

I took down the sacred straw ropes that were put up at New Year's.[51] The demons may laugh, but next year I'd like to have a peaceful New Year's to please the children.

Pray to the gods, present arms.

February 2, 1945, Friday
Living on Beans Is a Forward-Looking Thing to Do

It's the equinox. Last year we celebrated with soybeans distributed by the city, the one-pint allotment that each household got for the year-crossing celebration, beans filled with parental affection. This year there're no loud celebrations. A

---

50. Tomiyama is in Chiba Prefecture.

51. Tamura is referring to *shime nawa*, the woven straw ropes that are used in Shinto ceremonies and hung at New Year's.

life lived under the bombs that enemy aircraft drop every day is not even what is described as "happiness within and the devil without."[52] Of course, one doesn't expect a distribution of soybeans from the city, nor will there be the commotion of celebrations. Living on beans, one doesn't look ahead very far.

February 5, 1945, Monday
Forgiving the Bathhouse Black Market

The bathhouses, too, tend to run out of fuel and close often, so when one happens to open for business, it's packed. In the long lines of people waiting for the bathhouse to open at four o'clock, all you hear from three o'clock on is "Don't push, don't push." I came up with a shrewd plan. Bathhouses would secretly let in customers from a back street starting about two o'clock.

It would be a black market business! Without the police or unions knowing, bathhouses would do an overflow business that could charge fifty sen per adult. In the illicit one-yen-per-adult bathhouses, everyone is hostile in what is a dog-eat-dog situation. I thought it'd be wonderful to pay fifty sen and spend a leisurely hour warming up, secretly entering from the back and going into the bath.

Then the union changed things: beginning today, one day will be set aside for male bathing, and the next for female bathing. Because the bathtub was used by both sexes up to now, a hundred people would come in at one time, and now they've divided the days that one can take a bath. Also, dividing up the schedule for the bathhouses was a good method.

In order to compensate for the fuel shortage, they'll close from four to five o'clock and from six to nine, and the bath fee will continue to be the twelve sen it's been up to now, and this to control the black market. Black market bathing soon will be forgotten.

Because up to now the bathhouse black market had transformed backwashing into a business and made the owners a lot of money, those who did an illicit business will do business within the law for some time. No matter what one says, because it's a business that washes things away, from now on the bathhouses probably will do a one-handed business.

February 16, 1945, Tuesday [sic]
The Black Market Price of Yodo Turnips

Because we were running out of the makings for side dishes, Otsuru said she was going to the Yodo area to search for vegetables.[53] A farm family she knew said

---

52. "Happiness within, the devil without" is a Japanese proverb.
53. Yodo is several miles south of Kyoto.

they would not sell vegetables for money any more. They said bring something, anything, even clothes. We have thirteen turnips, and if you're willing to pay a lump sum of thirty yen for those that are edible, we'll sell them to you. That meant each one would cost two yen, fifty-sixty sen, and Otsuru, afraid that father would scold her, gave up. A housewife who was a regular happily bought them for thirty yen and said, "If only you had some goods, I'd be happy . . . ," before she snatched away the turnips. Disappointed, Otsuru returned home.

One mackerel is twenty-five yen and has reached the "public" black market price in Osaka. There's no value in our eating a twenty-five-yen mackerel. Like the whole mackerel, everything was selling for twenty-five yen. We'll be self-sufficient starting around April, and the extravagant Osaka consumers realize that we'll lick salt to survive.

February 18, 1945, Sunday
About the Black Market Price of Green Onions, Chicken, and Eggs

The greengrocer's distribution was two stalks of green onions for ten sen. Facing three days with no distributions, we could hardly expect to feed a family of five with two stalks of green onions.

So this morning, Otsuru turned to a good friend in Yodo, and when she really begged for green onions, she got one *kanme* for five yen, fifty sen. At that price, it was like a gift, and she returned home with the onions, very pleased. She and Grandma counted the number of onions, and there were sixty-five, which meant that one green onion, with train fare included, cost fifty sen.

A hundred yen for a chicken wing. At that price, it was fine, and the roots of the wings could grow and fly away. As for eggs, even university and municipal hospitals charge ten yen for three. I produce paper currency, and they leave, as always, three eggs — what a terrifying world this has become.

February 19, 1945, Monday
The Life of a Night Soil Collector

Grandma finally found a night-soil collector.[54] The fee for one load is one yen, fifty sen. At that price he took away four loads, and it was six yen. Even though he didn't take more than three loads, he called it four, and the buckets weren't even half full, and he made what was light seem heavy. He's probably a . . . person.[55]

"Old man, doing this job that doesn't pay, I work from five in the morning to four in the afternoon, and I make twelve to thirteen yen, but one can't live on

---

54. See Tamura's 12/12/44 entry.
55. Either Tamura or the editor of his diary left out or deleted part of this sentence.

one pint of rice. If one eats black market rice, it's twenty-five yen for two quarts. If one eats a pint and a half, then just over half a pint of supplementary rice is three yen.

"About a drink in the evening: saké offers comfort for the day's work: I drink only a pint. Isn't a pint of saké, even low-grade stuff, about ten yen?

"I have a wife and three kids, and I'm ashamed because I can't feed them. I thought of doing something else, but I don't have the things I'd need for a trade, or the capital. I've spent my whole life in sewage. Indeed, when I hear 'Check your weights,' hey, it's less than one sen."

February 20, 1945, Tuesday
Exploring the Military's Responsibility for the Fall of Iwo Jima

Amid the mountain of corpses, the rivers of blood, and the tragic and hard-fought four advances and four retreats, the enemy has begun to invade Iwo Jima.[56] We're silenced by the phrase "Leave the war to the soldiers." Our attacking squads, our attacking squads that go off like cattle — what are they doing? "Body-crashing," "body-crashing" — what's that? What responsibility does army headquarters bear? We can no longer take the safety of our country for granted.

February 25, 1945, Sunday
Bombing on a Snowy Day

It was the day of the god of the Kitano Shrine.[57] The falling snow was more than four inches deep, and the wintry scene of snow falling on the tomb was exquisite. It was this year's first snow, which was unusual.

Many formations of enemy aircraft were moving north at about 3:00 p.m. in the sky over the Dōjōji.[58] The enemy aircraft bombed indiscriminately.[59] Although the Yamashiro area was on alert, when the planes suddenly appeared overhead with their telltale drone, it made people feel exceedingly anxious. When they headed east, we thought, whew! A close call!

At 4:00 p.m. we fled south, and then the alert was called off. A sticky snow

---

56. Iwo Jima, the largest of the three Volcano Islands, has an area of about eight square miles and is located 660 nautical miles from Tokyo. American forces landed on Iwo Jima on February 19, 1945, and, after very hard fighting, secured the island on March 26.

57. Sugawara Michizane (845–903) was a noted Heian-period official and scholar who was exiled to Kyushu by his political opponents, the Fujiwara family.

58. The Dōjōji is a Buddhist temple located in Wakayama Prefecture. See Tamura's 3/10/45 entry.

59. More than two hundred B-29s attacked, with 172 bombing Tokyo and the thirty others bombing other targets. See Carter and Mueller, *Combat Chronology*, 582.

clattered as it fell. Everything above ground was a silvery world, and the silver of five inches of snow was unexpected in the capital.

February 26, 1945, Monday
Regulating the Sweet Potatoes of Kameyama, Mie Prefecture

Otsuru agonizes over every day's side dishes, and I doubt that there's anyone as lonely as a cook in a kitchen whose daily expenses outstrip revenue. Even for an unusual meal, Yaokō's distribution for bodies on vacation was two stalks of green onions at eleven sen on every third day.[60] As a result, we lack protein and our feces are the color of green vegetables. One speaks casually of life on the home front, but it's unbearable.

As is usual when we go to Kameyama, we started out at 3:30 a.m., walked to Kyoto Station and went to the end of a long ticket line, and luckily were able to get tickets. We got off the train at Kameyama and asked an old man we know from Kasado Village to help us feed our old father and mother, but darn it, a policeman was monitoring Kyoto's purchase of potatoes.

"Hey! Are you aware of today's battles in the Philippines and Iwo Jima? You unpatriotic young woman, you come to buy potatoes and are destroying the equal distribution system for a million citizens. Go home! If I find you here again, I'll throw you into the clink and have you punished!"

With this scolding voice . . . yes, yes.

They say a Chinese meal for eight people in Osaka costs a thousand yen, which is absurd! When I asked Takayama about this, he said one could have a Chinese meal for ten in Kyoto from a thousand yen.[61] So this means the extravagant ones are not just in Osaka, and there's Chinese food in Kyoto for a hundred yen a person. Like me, he's a frog in a well and knows nothing about other places. This means that the "unpatriotic" ones are among the privileged and elite upper class, and the result is the loss of the Philippines and Iwo Jima.

February 28, 1945, Wednesday
The Lives of the Black Market Nouveaux Riches

At this time when the enemy American devils have invaded Iwo Jima and the imperial country is in crisis, those who step out on the town, determined to satisfy their hunger and need for arrogance, are the ones ruining the country. They're most numerous in Osaka, and they're pathetic. Old me, I polish off two quarts of grade 1 saké every day: grade 1 saké is two hundred yen.

---

60. Yaokō appears to be the local greengrocer.
61. Tamura does not identify Takayama.

The distributed rice is horrible, and I can't eat it. The pure white rice I get from Hiroshima Prefecture, which resembles crystal rice, is fine. Two gallons is three hundred yen. Because I have to have two quarts of rice, the daily rice bill is thirty yen.

For hors d'oeuvre I eat only meat — it's the most nutritious food and increases one's energy. If I polish off nearly a pound of meat, it's twenty-five yen. On occasion I have pork, and when I don't have a yellowtail dish, a wind blows up from my navel and the chill depresses me.

As far as my stomach goes, if I don't spend about three hundred yen a day, I don't feel alive.

Our world is interesting. Shall I go to the licensed quarters in Shinmachi and rest my head on a geisha's knee and recite Chinese poems out loud?[62]

March 5, 1945, Monday
Shortages and Preparing to Starve to Death

It has warmed up. With this year's charcoal shortages I thought people would freeze to death, but the gods are generous when one is desperate. It'll probably depend on my navel's capacity for restraint. Mysteriously, two straw bags of hard, resistant-grade charcoal were mixed in with our charcoal allotment, which was still warm when it was delivered. If we tough it out, we'll survive through March with three straw bags of charcoal, and I think if I stretch my neck, there might be a rejuvenation.

The rice ration is three-quarters of a pint for people over sixty, but I'm a big guy and that's not enough. I can't bear to have an empty stomach day after day, and it's only because of others' thoughtfulness — my children, for example, kindly make concessions — that I escape starvation. Hearing today's bad news about the military situation, starvation finally is right before us! We hear the government will distribute salt starting in April, but the prices of side dishes have soared, and we no longer have the strength to buy on the black market. With a single radish now selling for one yen, will we be able to survive by licking salt? I think surviving on moderation will be hard — as was the case with charcoal.

March 8, 1945, Thursday
A Second Draft Notice for the Beloved Tama Family

A second draft notice came to Matsumoto Masao, Nishijin billiards champion of the beloved Tama family. It's just a husband and wife without parents or

---

62. Shinmachi was the licensed quarter in Osaka and one of a hundred that had emerged in Japan by 1697.

children. They're very well off and have suffered few privations. He's going off in high spirits, and I'm not prohibited from secretly feeling sympathy for him. You should fight hard for the state! Good-bye, Matsumoto. He leaves in the morning at 6:20 a.m.

When Toshie passed the Sennichi business district while running an errand for Iwata Enterprises, she noticed a suspicious-looking man standing in front of a temple, cradling a nest of boxes as though they contained something important.[63] Smiling sinisterly, he called, "Hey you! They're delicious! Won't you have any? Three fingers are three yen. Do you understand?" He halved a sweet potato, and a student held out a ten-yen bill. "I'll take two." Osaka's culinary hedonism was offering half a potato for three yen, and people were going off, eating and muttering, "Delicious! Delicious!"

In no time he'd sold five boxes, and sticking out his tongue he returned to Kyoto.

Wow! Talking about wheeling and dealing. He fooled the police. What a frightening, horrible world!

March 10, 1945, Saturday
The Battle of the Elephant and the Rat

I thought the enemy aircraft that appeared over the southern part of the Kumano coast and passed over the Dōjōji in Kawachi were coming to Osaka, but they turned toward Nara Prefecture, raced in the direction of Miyazu, then turned from Fukui Prefecture to Shiga Prefecture, and then came back to Kyoto. They turned right above Senbon at low altitude, making a horrible rumbling sound — this is no joke! Hey! Don't take the Anglo-Saxons for fools.

I didn't know this, but 103 B-29s burned out Tokyo: Kanda, Fukagawa, and Honjo were bombed from a thousand meters high and completely leveled.[64]

Although I thought I was ready for this, I was shocked when I heard that the dead and wounded numbered several thousands [the death toll was 100,000].

My first thought was to joke about this, and I'm embarrassed for myself. Corpses, arms, and legs were hanging from the electric wires; household goods were strewn on railroad tracks; the interiors of houses were burned out; and only their unburnable foundation stones remained — there's just emptiness. For a

---

63. Sennichi is in downtown Osaka.

64. On March 9, 1945, 279 B-29s carried out a devastating bombing raid on Tokyo, dropping more than 31,000 tons of incendiary bombs and killing 83,793 people and injuring 40,918. Twenty B-29s bombed other targets. Tamura misquotes the official account, which described the March 9 attack as the work of 130 aircraft. See Carter and Mueller, *Combat Chronology*, 594.

day and a night the survivors were surrounded by madly raging fires, fires that couldn't be put out, and there was no helping them. Children cried out for their parents; parents searched for their children; and the height of the tragedy was that it was a living hell. How could there be a living heart in all this?

There is great resentment of the brutal American enemy and lots of grumbling.

It's a struggle between a rat and the elephant he's jumped on, and I assume this was obvious from the start. The enemy won't accept the idea that their bombing is a brutal and violent violation of the treaty. I don't think we have any choice but to fight by repaying violence with violence.

Although we protest that the American enemies are ignoring the treaty, they say it's a peacetime treaty and not relevant during a war.[65] I'll just grab my gold and jewels and move about as I please. The military's incompetence in the south is the butt of jokes, and now, after a respite, it's sure to start up again.

March 11, 1945, Sunday
Resenting Those Who Wage War

This world of ours has become hateful. Every day the poor cry because of their hunger, and the powerful in the government make war, resign, and feign ignorance. I hate it! I hate it! The black market prospers, morality has declined, and demons feast on the flesh of the poor. Living this tragic short life we've been given is hateful. Who started this? I resent what they have done. The politicians with their bravado give us nothing to eat.

Today there were no customers and thus zero income. That's natural and to be expected. When I think about the damage caused by the enemy attacks, the burned-out areas of Tokyo and the several tens of thousands who have died, it's not the time for an educated Japanese male to be playing pool. I'm embarrassed that I'm even open for business.

March 12, 1945, Monday
Central Military District Command Announcement

A warning and alert were suddenly issued at 8:50 in the morning.
Enemy aircraft no. 2 will soon arrive in Settsu and Naniwa.
Enemy aircraft no. 2 has entered Japanese airspace.
We don't recognize aircraft no. 3.

---

65. It is not clear what "treaty" Tamura is referring to. Earlier in the war, American and German leaders had exchanged notes on what constituted suitable targets for aerial bombing, but there was no international treaty governing this issue.

The warning and alert were canceled in Tokushima Prefecture.

At 9:04 a.m., enemy aircraft no. 3 is heading toward northern Itami.

It's now 9:04 a.m.

9:08 a.m. — enemy aircraft no. 2 is flying over the Shinoyama area.

It is now 9:14 a.m.

9:15 a.m. — aircraft no. 2 is moving toward the Tajima area and is now in the central district.

9:20 a.m. — aircraft no. 2 has changed direction and begun to head from Fukuchiyama toward Fukui.

9:23 a.m. — aircraft no. 2 is flying north to the skies above Amanohashidate and will require an alert in Fukui Prefecture.

It's now 9:24:5 a.m.

9:27 a.m. — aircraft no. 2 is proceeding in a southeasterly direction, passing over Hirayama in Ōmi.

9:30 a.m. — aircraft no. 2 is going over northern Ōtsu in an easterly direction.

It's now 9:33 a.m.

9:35 a.m. — aircraft no. 2 has advanced from the center of Ōmi to the Inland Sea area.

The warning and alert were called off in the Kinki area.

The enemy aircraft has entered the Inland Sea area. It's now 9:43 a.m.[66]

The House of a Rich, Absent Soldier

Yesterday Toshie was invited to dinner by Kimura Yoshiko, a former classmate from Shiga Prefectural Girls High School and the daughter of the family that owns the Tanaka Dry Goods Store in Hishiya Ward in Ōtsu.[67] She had dinner there and got home at 8:30. The absent husband of this rich friend is an army lieutenant who went off to war and is serving in the southern islands. She's had no letters from him. His monthly salary from Mitsui Heavy Industries in Osaka is 160 yen, and his military pay is more than 120 yen, and twice a year Yoshiko receives his three hundred–yen bonus. In addition, she's living in a house owned by her father and thus is not paying any rent. She's a friend whose carefree life is everyone's envy. She said, "Tamura-san, no matter how expensive things are on the black market, it's OK, so I shop around and buy goods and foods. If there's a distribution at Iwata Enterprises, I'll leave it up to you, so please buy [whatever]."

---

66. There is no record of an attack on the morning of March 12. The aircraft may have been reconnoitering targets.

67. Ōtsu, the capital of Shiga Prefecture, is located on the southwestern edge of Lake Biwa and is about five miles from Kyoto.

She entrusted Toshie with a hundred yen. Toshie then returned home. Even though they were classmates, there was such a dramatic difference in lifestyles. We were envious.

March 13, 1945, Tuesday
The Tragedy of the Osaka Air Raid

The city of Osaka was almost completely wiped out by a nighttime air raid.[68]

The wreckage of an enemy aircraft and the corpses of four American airmen that lay on the road where they had fallen lined the road to Toyonaka, and charred bodies of men whose uniforms had burned off, and the stench penetrated our nostrils. Horrible-to-look-at corpses with their penises exposed were piled here and there. The living look for relatives and they do so without having had a grain of rice or a drop of water, searching with bloodshot eyes. It was a scene of incredible carnage and was overwhelming.

The area from Sennichimae to Dōtonbori was reduced to ashes in one night, and Kabuza, Nakaza, Naniwaza, and the various entertainment districts were razed and were little more than burned-out fields. I understand that at the time of the Great Kanto Earthquake, you could see the area from the burned-out parts of Shitaya Ward and Okachi-machi to Kyōbashi and Nihonbashi, but at that time building materials were plentiful, and the reconstruction was quick.[69] Today Japan lacks both building materials and food, and reconstruction will be hard.

March 14, 1945, Wednesday
Issuing an Air-Raid Notice

At 11:15 p.m. several formations of enemy aircraft attacked Osaka, dropping a rain of bombs and incendiaries, and then flew over Kyoto.[70] At that instant, an air-raid alert was issued.

The signal at the Karaku School shelter blared noisily.

Toshie's clothes had been laid out, and since she had to spring into action before anyone else, she went straight to the air-raid tunnel and was out of breath. Was she acting out a comedy of gestures?

Haruko found it hard to leave the leg warmer, and even when scolded, she

---

68. In the early morning hours of March 14, 1945, 274 B-29s dropped incendiary bombs on central Osaka. See Carter and Mueller, *Combat Chronology*, 597.

69. A 7.8 magnitude earthquake hit the Kanto area at 11:58 a.m. on September 1, 1923, killing more than 100,000 people and injuring more than 50,000.

70. Tamura appears to be writing about the March 13–14 air raid.

stayed put, saying that the shelter was cold and that she had decided to tough it out. Grandma loudly announced that she was hungry, so we fed her, and when we did, she seemed hungrier than people usually are during air raids. She said, "I can't evacuate if you don't feed me."

I myself thought it'd be better to be killed instantly in one's own haunts, so I didn't move.

Because Otsuru was hungry, too, she asked whether we could make some rice.

"What? Isn't it 11:20 at night?" Glutton! The fact is that although I scolded her, saying, "We absolutely cannot light a fire," I was hungry too.

The skies to the south were bright, and radio broadcasters kept asking, "Have you prepared your air-defense water? First of all, incendiary bombs are water." It's 1:50 a.m., and the dogfights involving friendly aircraft have begun in the skies above Osaka. One plane fell to earth, another was forced down, and still another, spewing fire and smoke, climbed into the sky. The incredibly bright, lightning-like flashes of the battle reddened the smoke in the southern skies as far as the eye could see.

The enemy aircraft, in several formations, were as numerous as the stars, and I didn't know how many there were. But I didn't get excited. I asked only that the fire and air-defense crews be careful. We shouted ourselves hoarse, and the radio broadcasts urged caution.

Besides the darkness, there was rain leaking from above our heads in the shelter and our *zabuton* got damp.[71]

The attack lasted until 3:30 a.m., and we got virtually no sleep. We passed the night listening to the warnings broadcast over the radio. There must have been evacuations in Tokyo and then Nagoya, too. For the first time, we understood the drills that demonstrated the inadequacy of our preparations.

First, bank and postal account passbooks, the *inkan* bag, the whistle for calling to others, ointment, paper bags, matches, several candles, an iron bar, pliers, cash, bonds, a sword and dagger, and as for food: there was a little rice but not enough to be of much help. Next, we had to take some care in stuffing the valuables into socks.

The air-raid alert was called off at 3:30 a.m.

Well! We got a taste of an air raid, and somehow or other our endangered lives were saved.

---

71. During the war Japanese often covered their head with a *zabuton* during air raids.

At 4:27 a.m. Otsuru cooked rice, but it didn't fill her empty stomach, although her having some rice was no joke — it disappeared into her stomach.

At 7:27 a.m. Toshie went off to work at Iwata Enterprises in Osaka as usual.

At 8:00 a.m. Haruko left for Demizu School in the middle of a downpour.

Matsumuro and Yoshida came over.[72] By 9:30 a.m. Osaka had been burned up by the enemy attack that rained bombs on that city, and it was a burned-out field. It was a repeat performance of what happened in Tokyo and Nagoya.[73] I half believed and half doubted.

Matsumuro and Yoshida, it's now 5:30 p.m. We'll know more when it's 6:20 p.m., because Toshie will return from Osaka. For some time and until we hear the facts, it's hard to predict what will happen next, but I believe Kobe or Kyoto will be next.

Somebody made a joke, and we parted.

March 16, 1945, Friday
Evacuating Kyoto

I went to Shichiku to look at a rental house.

When I looked it over, I found the kitchen was absolutely first class, so I decided to rent it. The rent was twenty-eight yen a month, and I paid three months' rent as a deposit, interest free. The landlord was a serious man (Funagoshi Makitarō of Shibano, Nishi Kita-machi 7-1) who resisted the urge to build a splendid house, and I was surprised by his wife's devotion: she had no maids and did all the cooking herself. When I asked, I was told that a renter had made various renovations at the landlord's request.

Those evacuating continue to do so, and there are lines of eighteen- and nineteen-year-old women pulling long-handled carts loaded with dressers and chests. Where are they going? Those who value life? When I looked out from the second floor of the evacuation site that Aeba and I rented at Jōmon-machi, 21-ban, in Shichiku, there was a murderous look on the faces of those leaving homes that had been in harm's way since the Osaka air raid and evacuating to the north, south, and east.[74]

Tokyo has become a burned-out field; Nagoya is weeping over a similar fate; and corpses are piled up in the burned-out fields that is now Osaka — Kobe is probably next. No, no — Kyoto will be first. A gentleman moving his household goods was dripping with perspiration in the cold — it looked like a bad painting.

---

72. Tamura does not identify Matsumoro.
73. Tokyo had been bombed eleven times, and Nagoya seven times.
74. Aeba Seyoshi was married to Mie, Tamura's daughter.

It's because life is dear, and our household belongings and money, too, that my Kyoto has been thrown into an upheaval!

March 18, 1945, Sunday
A Distribution of Vegetables Fit for a Sparrow

Yaokō's distribution was the opposite of a bad picture: a radish for a small house-wife, and only the bottom half at that. I went to the Municipal Office to pick it up and was breathing hard through my nose when I was told, "Tamura-san, yours is a five-person family, and because the allotment is seven rin per person, you get a fifty-seven sen, five rin, allotment. Thus, weighing this, it's four sen for delivery, and today's a day off." We don't have any sparrows. Half a radish divided up among five people for two days. The human stomach can't survive on so little.

March 20, 1945, Tuesday
With the Evacuation, No One's Here

The evacuees' luggage was moving south, north, east, and west. All the people in the east, west, south, and north had to evacuate, and no one was in Kyoto. Everyone had evacuated. It's a fad! First, enemy aircraft throw expensive bombs at us, and the matchboxes simply burn. Second, I think I can cheerfully take a bath. [On this day, the entire family left him and evacuated to Shichiku.]

April 1, 1945, Sunday
Had a Boil on My Arm Operated On

A boil appeared on my old arm. The superb nursing care of Toshie and Otsuru had no effect, and the boil got steadily worse and stank so much I couldn't ignore it any longer.

I . . . the research of a general practitioner of good reputation, a Dr. Nakani-shi Teijirō of Ōmiya-dōri, 5-tsuji, 2-chō agaru, Nishigawa.[75] According to the old doctor, "This is a serious problem! If you'd just left it alone, we'd have to amputate the whole arm. It wouldn't seem so bad on the outside, but it would start to affect your internal organs. If that had happened, you'd be the worst of today's patients."

"Let's cut it open," and there I was, lying in a strange bedroom, the old doctor cutting away with his scalpel, audibly, and then finishing by sharpening it — the sound of a knife being sharpened was hard for my ten organs to hear. With no

---

75. The verb is missing in this sentence.

anesthetic I gnashed my teeth, crying "Ouch! Ouch!" He completed the operation while scolding me — "Because it's gotten to this stage, it would've been OK with me if you hadn't come." Otsuru paid seven yen, and we returned home. What was that? It was like being a carp on a cutting board.

April 14, 1945, Saturday
A Draft Notice for My Son

A draft notice came for Fujihira, saying he was to enter the Thirty-seventh Fujinomori Unit.

We're optimistic, since the Thirty-seventh is a cavalry unit, and the cavalry has no function at this point in the war. That our son, an old soldier of forty-three, would leave behind a wife and children for the sake of the honorable country and eagerly serve was truly a happy occasion.[76]

Before this, the Tamura house was represented by my grandson Inao, who was a member of a unit sent to the southern islands. Sending off Fujihira was a real honor for the house and a source of infinite pleasure.

May 3, 1945, Thursday
A Hundred-Yen Tip

When I went to Shichiku for breakfast, Aeba and Mie were beaming and looking like the god Ebisu. Aeba said, "Father, I've been in the moving business for four years, and today for the first time I got a hundred-yen tip." The fee for transporting seven bags from Kyoto Station to the Miyako Hotel on Sanjō is twenty-five yen, and a hundred-yen tip was added to that fee.[77] "I thought the bill I was given was a little big for a ten-yen bill, and it turned out to be a hundred-yen bill! The young people at the Miyako Hotel don't wrap their wad of bills in paper, but pull them out one bill at a time." The extravagance of genteel upper-class society surprised me. When the ministers from each country gathered for a meeting in Tokyo, I wondered whether the sort of extravagance we just witnessed would allow Japan to win the war against the American and British enemy and whether it was appropriate for upper-class leaders to do this sort of thing.

May 8, 1945, Tuesday
As One Ages, There is No Greater Pleasure Than Eating

At 5:30 a.m. my aging body, which has no other pleasures besides eating, walked along most of Senbon Avenue to the east of Kuramaguchi and then to Shichiku.

---

76. Fujihira was stationed in Korea and survived the war.
77. The Miyako Hotel, located on Sanjō Avenue, was the grand old hotel of prewar Kyoto.

Panting and gasping as I walked up the hills, I breathed in fresh air and helped bring on the dawn.

This is my greatest happiness every day. "Father's come, hurry! Come quickly!" I'm sorry, once again, that mine is a body with no parental obligations.

Otsuru and ever filial Mie and Toshie wash my face. I shall never forget Mie's kindness.

This one bamboo shoot was, lo and behold, an unusually big one! It weighed about one *kanme* and cost one yen, eighty-five sen. We cooked one as a breakfast side dish, and nothing was left for dinner.

Otsuru — even though the earnings and expenses will not continue for long — eat lots! This year there was a bumper crop of bamboo shoots, and we'll have them for twenty days, both morning and night, and bamboo will seem to sprout from our mouths.

If Grandma gets up, she'll have no tolerance for this sort of crude rumor mongering. She's like the deaf. No matter what those around her say, she doesn't hear them. When it comes to eating, however, she says only, "It's delicious," and gobbles up her portion.

May 15, 1945, Tuesday
The Black Market Prices of Various Goods

It's the Imamiya Festival, and 120,000 men have landed at Okinawa — What are we going to do with the American and British troops?[78] Even in our wartime lives and in our depopulated household:

One mackerel is twenty yen.
One sardine is two yen, fifty sen.
Two quarts of sushi rice are fifty yen.
Two quarts of first-second-grade saké are a hundred yen.
and a piece of chicken is two yen.

If this is the case, then it's time to jump off the terrace at the Kiyomizu Temple.[79] If one doesn't go to great lengths to buy these things on the black market, they won't find their way into our mouths.

---

78. Tamura's estimate is low. The invasion force consisted of 290,000 men.
79. The Kiyomizu Temple is nestled in the side of the hills that form the eastern edge of Kyoto, and the main hall is surrounded on three sides by a platform that is two hundred feet above the ground.

The Diary of a Defeated Japanese Soldier

Nomura Seiki was born in Kōchi City on the island of Shikoku in March 1922. He graduated from higher elementary school in the 1930s and then attended a government-sponsored youth academy that provided both vocational training and what he later described as "military education." As a youth, his real passion was kendo (Japanese fencing), and much of his time was spent at a local fencing academy. He worked briefly for a prefectural cooperative before he was drafted into the Imperial Japanese Army. He saw action in China and then was transferred to Okinawa in August 1944 as a member of the Twenty-sixth Shipping Engineering Regiment. He was assigned to a communications unit and helped maintain the telephone lines that connected the Japanese bunkers. He miraculously survived the Allied invasion of Okinawa but was wounded in July 1945, and hid out until September 14, 1945, when he and his fellow stragglers were persuaded to surrender. Nomura began his diary on March 23, 1945, just as the Allied invasion force was gathering off Okinawa, and wrote until September 13, the day before he surrendered. He later added a long and detailed description of his surrender.

After the war, Nomura worked briefly at a shipbuilding company and was the head of a labor union youth group. In January 1947 he resigned from the company and gave up his position with the union and started working as a guard at Kōchi Prison, which led to a career in law enforcement administration. He got married in December 1949 and had two children.

Nomura's diary was published as *Okinawasen haihei nikki: Gyokusaisen ittōhei no shuki (The Diary of a Defeated Japanese Soldier from the Battle of Okinawa: The Notes of a Private First Class in the Fight-to-the-Death War)* by Taihei shuppansha in 1974. The part of his diary translated here runs from August 1 to November 10, 1945.

August 1, 1945 (Wed.), clear

Just before dawn, one group returned from Tametomoiwa.[1] The yield was approximately thirty-five kilograms of rice, four kilograms of red beans, three kilograms of sugar, two bags of powdered soy sauce, seventy-five boxes of Golden Kite cigarettes, and ten cartons of small matchboxes.

According to what everyone says, it seems that the number of friendly troops in the Tametomoiwa area is increasing.

Evening. I went to visit Lance Corporal Shinohara in the square of the village ruins, but he wasn't there. I then thought I might have Spectacles treat me, but Jihei fiercely opposed this, and since I was uneasy about doing this, I didn't do it.

August 2, 1945 (Thurs.), partly cloudy and hot

Morning. It was something that happened long after we had crossed the southern pass. With a definitely unpleasant look on his face, Jihei had asked, "Won't you have someone look at your wound?" According to what he had heard at dawn, Lance Corporal Shinohara was living with locals in a cave at the western pass.

I can't imagine why Jihei is encouraging me to have my wound treated, perhaps because I wonder whether he really is concerned about me. I wished he hadn't started to treat me as though I were a burden.

I left Jihei without saying a word and started out for the cave where Shinohara was, and when I found the opening of what looked like the cave in a stand of trees, I slid downhill and landed with a thud.

Luckily, he was there, and I had my wound treated. Since it would be unpleasant to return to Jihei, I stayed put and spent the night with the lance corporal and the locals.

August 3, 1945 (Fri.), clear

Since Lance Corporal Shinohara appeared at Aragaki, my relationship with Spectacles has cooled. Remembering that there were protocols for asking someone for treatment and that such requests were regarded as selfish acts, I felt guilty. But Lance Corporal Shinohara's seasoned techniques and his character — he never asked to be compensated — attracted me to him.

This was fine psychologically because I rarely had face-to-face contact with Spectacles, who, as before, never emerged from the ruins of the houses in the west.

---

1. Tametomoiwa is located on the site of old Urasoe Castle in Urasoe City, which is about three miles northeast of Naha and Shuri.

*Nomura Seiki, sometime
between 1937 and 1945.
Courtesy of Nomura Seiki.*

August 4, 1945 (Sat.), partly cloudy

The numbers of those coming north has gradually increased. They know the American line of defense is at Kishaba, and they are coming toward the Aragaki Hills.

During the day, you can see people trying to hide in the trees and shrubbery at the base of the cliffs. They're doing this because all the good places have been taken by those of us who were here first. As a result, the village ruins become pretty lively at night.

This is most unfortunate. To those in hiding, the growing numbers of people in the area increase our chances of being discovered.

August 5, 1945 (Sun.), partly cloudy

If, by some chance, friendly troops are assembling in the direction of the Kunigami Mountains . . . this can't be! This thought, together with my anxiety about being left behind, are overwhelming.

Moreover, the anticipated breakthrough at Kishaba seems absolutely impossible for this body of mine. There's no point in getting anxious about this! All we can do is wait. I decided that more than anything else, healing my wounds was my priority.

August 6, 1945 (Mon.), clear

There are those who complain that "Japan started a reckless war!" Although we heard this occasionally in the midst of intense fighting, even more radical thoughts occur to a straggler.

On the other side is the view that Japan probably had no other choice but to do what it did: Japan's enemies supplied weapons to China; these Allies schemed to dissipate the power of Japan, Germany, and Italy; they set up an economic blockade to bring about our country's self-destruction, etc. American and British pressure on Japan right up to the outbreak of hostilities was maddening and unacceptable.

August 7, 1945 (Tues.), clear then cloudy, rain at one point, hot and humid

Several days ago, an old captain appeared on the hill. He was accomplished in the martial arts and knew things like osteopathy, acupressure, faith healing, and exorcism. His own wounds had healed, and apparently many have received his acupressure treatment.

When it gets dark, the captain practices with his sword in a meadow near the village ruins. Some call what he does the "arts of masters," but having once dabbled in the martial arts, I disagree somewhat.

Our country's martial arts are really the techniques of barbarians. Seeing the captain making a display of his prowess, I recalled battles in which hands and legs were lost, and it made me sad.

August 8, 1945 (Wed.), clear then cloudy, rain at one point

Jihei gradually seems to be distancing himself from me, and it can't be helped. In the evening, I went down to the village ruins, but the whole time I was there, he treated me as though I were polluted. He's quite solicitous toward others but thoroughly unpleasant to me. This morning he approached the base of the cliffs. Last night Lance Corporal Shinohara was gone, and I couldn't get any treatment, which made Jihei get angry at me. He told me to find Shinohara, but Shinohara's whereabouts are unclear because he often sleeps in different places in response to the requests of the wounded. When I seemed puzzled, he blurted out, "If you wait, no one will look at you. You've become a complete mess." His words pricked my chest like needles. I was furious and turned away.

I knew that Spectacles was somewhere above the cave occupied by Sergeant Itokazu and others. It was hard to have to depend on Spectacles, but I had no choice. Spectacles was with the usual group of soldiers in a small rock cave off to the side of the little road that hugged the mountain. When I begged him to treat me, he did, and as always, I remembered to roll tobacco leaves for him.

Afterward, I slept in a thicket above the rock cave where I found Spectacles.

After lunch, it clouded up and then rained hard. It was the first rain since the *gyokusai*.[2] I took refuge in Spectacle's cave and stayed there until the rain let up later that evening.

August 9, 1945 (Thurs.), light rain then clear

Last night, a group of soldiers arrived, accompanied by women. I don't know where they came from, but bewitching colors and smells wafted into the Aragaki Hills.

Perhaps the women were like the "Fervent Nurses" (military nurses drawn from the Okinawan female population). Even in fierce battles, I had seen large numbers of them holding hands and falling back together from the front lines. . . . Somehow, even as thoughts of envy wafted over me, I also felt contempt for them.[3]

August 10, 1945 (Fri.), rain then clear and windy

I heard stories about officers and men who shouted, "Long live the emperor!" and then went off to their deaths, and I felt even more than before how futile this was. . . . This I could never do.

If people say that we as citizens of Japan never cease benefiting from the emperor's generosity, had the emperor's power and virtue really been that sort of thing up to that point? I wasn't persuaded. . . . The emperor was too distant, a presence that had nothing to do with me. Somehow I just couldn't get used to the idea of shouting "banzai!" and dying for him. I have fought not for the emperor but for the homeland where [my] more familiar parents and siblings, relatives, and friends live and for the ancestral country. Even now, my thoughts about the emperor haven't changed.

Nor was this view mine alone. Except for the officers and men who shout "Long live the emperor!" — isn't this how most officers and men think?[4]

---

2. When Nomura uses the word *gyokusai*, he is referring to the Japanese attempt to break through Allied lines in late June 1945.

3. The women may have been the so-called comfort women (J. *ianfu*).

4. Nomura was right. Most Japanese felt as he did, according to Home Ministry surveys conducted during and after the war. See John Dower, *Embracing Defeat: Japan in the Wake of World War II* (New York: Norton, 1999), 302–303.

August 11, 1945 (Sat.), light rain then clear

My right hand has started to get better, and this morning I undid the sling holding my elbow. I was able to eat with [my hand] and no longer stumbled. If it's
this good, I thought, it'll be normal soon.

After dinner, Lance Corporal Shinohara treated my wound in the square in
the village ruins, and afterward I visited the red-roofed mansion just to the south
and had a nice chat with the locals.

August 12, 1945 (Sun.), light rain then clear

As the number of people in the area increases, there is an outpouring of opinions
about the war. Of course, there's no way for us to know the current military situation, but based on what has happened militarily in the past and on our experiences on this island, few speak of Japan's superiority or its sure victory.

Yet no one speaks of Japan's defeat. That's because we've lost all hope of surviving. It's a distant hope, but everyone hopes for the day when under the bright
white sun, the imperial army's fortunes will be reversed. Most revealing of our
true feelings is the fact that everyone prays for an end to the hostilities. This is
natural. Aren't humans basically peace loving?

August 13, 1945 (Mon.), rain then clear, a little cool

In the evening, those of us who went down to the ruins we always visit discovered
that the food we had hidden in a thicket in back had disappeared and been carried off. We made a great fuss about this. With the growing numbers of people
in the area, thefts are unending. Knowing this, it was stupid to leave the food
there.

Sergeant Itokazu immediately had the locals at the red-roofed mansion di-
vide up their rice, and this filled everyone's stomachs. Then with five people,
not including me, he left to procure food at the friendly troops' bunker near
Tametomoiwa.

August 14, 1945 (Tues.), light rain then clear

Before dawn, Sergeant Major Itokazu and the five men returned from Tametomoiwa carrying food on their backs. The fruits of the battle were approximately
forty kilograms of rice, seven kilograms of red beans, five kilograms of sugar,
two bags of powdered soy sauce, five hundred grams of *bancha*, 102 Golden Kite
cigarettes, twenty small boxes of matches, three packages of U.S. Army biscuits,
six boxes of tobacco (Suricassuru), and three small books of matches. The U.S.
Army biscuits, Suricassuru, and matches were booty taken from a jeep that had
had an accident and was abandoned on the road to the Tametomoiwa area.

According to everyone's stories, enemy soldiers came every day to the Tameto-moiwa area and lobbed white phosphorus grenades and attacked with gasoline.[5] The unease is gradually finding its way to Aragaki.

August 15, 1945 (Wed.), light rain then clear, hot and humid

For several days, it's rained lightly in the morning and then let up in the afternoon. It rained lightly today, too.

At dusk, we gathered in the garden of one of the ruins and watched with some pleasure as our first mountain sheep in some time simmered in a cauldron. All of a sudden, there was a huge explosion that made the earth shake. Tracers streaked across the sky in all directions, and the inhabitants of our hill got quite upset. The attackers were using weapons we hadn't seen up to that point.

Someone said it was probably a big attack of special-attack aircraft;[6] others said it seemed like the dropping of airborne troops. Thrust as we were into the jaws of death and yet wanting to live, we pinned our hopes on everything that happened, and it was easy to hope for unexpected good fortune.[7]

August 17, 1945 (Fri.), cloudy

Recently it appears that Yonabaru in the south, which had been the battle line for U.S. forces, is undermanned, and the number of those coming north increases daily.[8]

With growing numbers of people arriving in the area, new reports and false rumors are coming to us. We learned that our commander, Lieutenant General Ushijima Mitsuru, together with his chief of staff, Lieutenant General Chō Isamu, committed suicide with daggers at the army headquarters cave at Mabuni just before dawn on June 23.[9]

Transmitted as well was the news that the American commander, Lieutenant General Simon Buckner, was killed by friendly fire on June 18 on a hill above Maezato Village.[10]

---

5. "Attack with gasoline" may refer to the Americans' use of flame throwers.

6. The "special-attack planes" flew one-way missions which ended with their crashing into enemy ships. They are known in the West as the *kamikaze*, "divine wind."

7. At noon on August 15 the emperor announced that Japan had surrendered to the Allied forces, but Nomura and his fellow stragglers are unaware of this.

8. Japanese forces had made their last stand near Mezato, Komesu, and Mabuni at the very southern tip of Okinawa but were routed in late June.

9. The information about the deaths of the Japanese commanders is accurate.

10. Lieutenant General Simon Buckner was killed by friendly fire on June 18, nine days before the Allied campaign on Okinawa officially ended.

We also learned most of the island's civilian population had come under the control of American forces.

Among these reports was one about a lot of Japanese becoming prisoners of war, and this was unexpected. As someone who'd chosen the path of death for a time, I definitely did not want to become a prisoner.

I didn't know how many Japanese troops had survived, but I heard the incredible story that after the *gyokusai* of our comrades, there were, as before, soldiers hiding out in the mountains and bunkers in the southern part of the island, including several named units.

August 18, 1945 (Sat.), cloudy

Lately I've been thinking about my rank, and it's depressing. Ever since the breakout from Yonabaru, I had forgotten about rank, but if I go to Kunigami, I will be, after all, a soldier, and it makes me sick to think about having to do the bidding of commissioned and noncommissioned officers.

No matter how low your rank, you're a member of the imperial army. When all is said and done, I have to go to Kunigami. I don't want to be called a coward.

August 19, 1945 (Sun.), cloudy

Recently I have felt that Aragaki has become a den of defeated soldiers. We now number more than eighty.

As our numbers increase, the situation gradually changes, and some commit shamelessly selfish acts. They visit others' hiding places in broad daylight, and worse yet, they boldly climb to the top of hills to survey the enemy's situation. At night, groups gather in the village ruins and sing and carry on, and the carousing often lasts until dawn.

Don't they understand the basic principle that as our numbers increase, we become more conspicuous, and there is greater danger? It seems our growing numbers give them a false sense of security. I alone am angry, and I can't do a damned thing about it.

This is dangerous! The American troops will be sure to attack in force. Even though I realize this, I don't have enough resolve to leave Aragaki. Our lives, no matter where we go, are in jeopardy.

Even after the honorable death of our comrades, special-attack aircraft flew over us from time to time, but they no longer appear. I wonder how things are back on the mainland.[11]

---

11. Nomura obviously has not heard that Japan surrendered on August 15, 1945.

August 20, 1945 (Mon.), partly cloudy

In the evening, I was terrified and listened for any telltale sounds. Jihei concentrated on one spot and listened intently. . . . Gunfire reverberated in the area. It kept up for a time, stopped, and then continued for quite a while. It came from the village ruins.

When it got dark, two people went down into the village ruins. Sergeant Major Itokazu said the two officers that Jihei and I met when we first came to Aragaki had gone off toward Tametomoiwa to get provisions and were just approaching the road below the hill to the east when they ran into American troops. They fled into the hills and were pursued.

We were furious about the two officers' stupidity, but the damage had been done. Since American army attacks were sure to come tomorrow, several groups left the mountain to go somewhere else, where they didn't know. And for us, our new address was, suddenly, uncertain.

August 21, 1945 (Tues.), rain then cloudy

In the cave that evening, Jihei quietly made the following announcement: "This morning on the way back, I talked to Sergeant Major Itokazu and Sergeant Nishi, and this evening, Yanagimoto and I will go off to Tametomoiwa. We'll get provisions and survey the situation. Depending on how things go, we probably won't be back for two to three days."

Jihei and I hadn't talked much until very recently. With the growing pressure in Aragaki, I kept thinking that Jihei seemed to be abandoning me, and as he talked I simply nodded. Some time later, Jihei and I went down into the village. The sergeant majors uttered the usual hackneyed "Well, be careful, and off you go" to Jihei and Yanagimoto, and their disinterest suggested they didn't approve of the pair's rash actions. Unconcerned about these reactions, Jihei and Yanagimoto left Aragaki.

August 22, 1945 (Wed.), light rain then clear

Even after it got light, Jihei and Yanagimoto still hadn't returned. A light rain began to fall, and I hurriedly crossed the western peaks with Sergeant Major Itokazu and others, then broke away from the group to return to my cave.

During the day, gunfire close by disturbed my dreams. I could hear the voices of American soldiers, and I tried to locate them and then realized they were at the cave of Sergeant Major Itokazu and his group.

When the gunfire stopped, hand grenades exploded continuously. The American attacks were persistent.

When things quieted down, I had strange, foreboding thoughts. Rain was falling silently.

In the evening, the rain stopped. When I made my way to Sergeant Major Itokazu's cave, a lot of people already had gathered. Everyone, from the sergeant major on down, was safe.

According to Itokazu's story, several American soldiers emerged without warning from the shadows of the trees in front of the cave. They moved toward the mouth of the cave firing their automatic weapons and throwing hand grenades into the cave. The sergeant major and Sergeant Nishi, who had been napping, responded immediately with hand grenades and beat back the Americans. But Lance Corporal Shinohara, who also was in the cave, sensed danger and dashed out through a rear entrance and into a ravine. Just before the American soldiers pulled back, a hand grenade exploded in the ravine, and we wondered whether he had been wounded and committed suicide. When we went to take a look, it was as we thought: he was lying facedown and stretched out in a field of ferns at the bottom of the ravine. His face and hands had been blown off, and everything from his chest down to his thighs had been hollowed out. Without thinking, I looked away.

Mournfully, we went down into the village ruins. While it was still dark, many people left in search of safe places.

August 23, 1945 (Thurs.), clear

We passed the night in an uneasy state, and still no sign of Jihei and Yanagimoto. Sergeant Major Itokazu, Sergeant Nishi, Ishikawa, Fujiwara, and I avoided walking directly on the ground and instead trod on grass so we wouldn't leave footprints on the freshly rained-on mountain road and made it back to the caves undetected.

The Aragaki Hills were gloomily quiet again. Those who had hidden in the grove below the cliff until yesterday had gone off somewhere else, and I could hear neither whispers nor footsteps.

In the midst of the silence, my heart was darkened by the strange and ominous thought, more an expectation, that the American troops probably would come today . . . today!

Then suddenly, Fujiwara and Ishikawa clambered up the cliff. Had the sergeant major's cave become unsafe? They smiled wistfully as they entered the cave to the east of mine.

I did as I always did: I took off all my clothes and stared at the forests and the sea spread out below the entrance to the cave, and as I did this I had the wildest fantasies about an impending attack. I spread my uniform on the rocky floor and threw myself on it.

It was something that happened several hours later. Suddenly, something made the cave shudder, and gunfire reverberated nearby.

Surprised and wide awake, I jumped up, and although I was stark naked except for my loincloth, I got quite excited.

Mixed in with the gunfire, I could hear the shouts of American soldiers directly overhead at the top of the precipitous rock face.

Without warning, two Japanese soldiers appeared at the mouth of my cave and scampered toward the west, with the nimbleness and speed of monkeys, along the face of the cliff. Then an old soldier with a finely trimmed moustache and a gun appeared at the mouth of my cave. Then he turned his back to the front of the cave and stopped. He seemed unaware of the American soldiers up above. He recklessly exposed his head and was in a state of complete agitation. Right at that moment, gunfire from above exploded in my ears. Simultaneously, he pirouetted a half turn, uttered an anguished "Ow!" and then fell backward down the face of the cliff.

Japanese soldiers were running into the grove beneath my cave, and American soldiers were firing and throwing grenades at them from above.

Running out into the open at this moment would hasten my death. I had no choice but to leave my fate in heaven's hands. Thinking the end was near, I resolved to die as well as I could. I nimbly put on my uniform, carefully inspected everything down to my thigh buttons, and then studied my situation . . . the sounds of gunfire and exploding grenades echoed throughout the hills, and American planes circled overhead.

When I looked at the cave to my east, Fujiwara, Ishikawa, and an old soldier I didn't recognize were standing and then crouching. They were terribly upset and carrying on. The old soldier suddenly brought his hands together and began to pray, shouting at the top of his lungs "Namu myōhō rengekyō. Namu myōhō rengekyō. Namu myōhō rengekyō."

This was a bad idea, I thought, but I couldn't stop him. I prayed that his voice wouldn't reach the ears of the American soldiers at the top of the cliff. The old soldier continued to chant sutras for some time, unconcerned about those around him.

I then thought about my own situation. I assumed that I wasn't visible to the Americans up above and that there was no way for them to come down to my cave. Even if they threw hand grenades at me, they'd fall all the way to the bottom of the cliffs.

But if the American soldiers started out from the forest below the cave and came to the base of the cliffs, then it was all over. I looked, for a second time, at the cave to the east. This time three people were wildly lobbing grenades at the American soldiers up above on the cliffs.

Their resistance from inside the cave was about as stupid as trying to throw stones onto the roof of a house from inside the house.

In a rocky corner deep in the cave, I hitched up one corner of my portable tent and let the rest hang down. On the other side of the tent, I left a space big enough for one person.

I crunched up and entered that space, and then kneeled. I made tiny holes in the canvas right at eye level. Then I took out of their bag three grenades that had been intended for the grenade launcher and set them down right at my knees. I concealed myself in this way so an American soldier coming into my cave would think the tent had been left by someone who had once lived here.

I sat quietly watching the movement of the shadows made by the light entering the cave. . . . When I had the urge to urinate, I took care of that with my canteen. In the afternoon, the attack let up, but from time to time I could hear the voices of American soldiers up on the peak.

What had happened to the three people in the east cave? There wasn't a single sound.

I thought I'd be safe when it got dark, but it was still a long, long time until dusk. Under the bright sun, the trees and ocean were deathly still.

At some point, I don't know when exactly, an American soldier's cigarette butt tumbled down from above and landed on a fern frond just to my right, and blue smoke danced silently from side to side. There was a burned odor and a faint perfume in the air.

As the sun finally began to go down and dark shadows crept stealthily into the spaces between the trees at the bottom of the cliffs, the American soldiers called out and answered one another, their voices echoing throughout the hills.

After a while, I no longer heard any voices, and then I heard the roar of several trucks at the base of the hill. When they had left, the hill returned to its original silence. The American troops appeared to have left.

Ever cautious, I clung to the inside of my tent, and didn't move. As the twilight gradually darkened, I ventured out for the first time to visit the eastern cave.

The three of them were sitting in the deepest part of the cave, just sitting there and holding their knees, and they seemed to have recovered from the shock of the attack. When they saw me, they crawled out without saying a word.

Together we quietly made our way down to the village ruins. Near the road we could make out in the shadows of rocks the bodies of soldiers, some lying flat, others squatting.

August 24, 1945 (Fri.), clear, humid, and hot

Last night most of those from Aragaki who survived the attack had gone elsewhere. Unsure about whether we should move, we spent the night in the village ruins.

Before dawn, Sergeant Major Itokazu and Sergeant Nishi came back to the Aragaki Hills. Together with Fujiwara and Ishikawa, I moved to the hill on the north side of the road that ran below the village ruins and hid in a thicket in front of the hill.

After sundown, the three of us went back to the village ruins at Aragaki. We talked things over with Sergeant Major Itokazu and Sergeant Nishi and decided to move south toward Shuri.

Itokazu and Nishi concocted this plan this morning after hearing from a soldier who had come to Aragaki that both Jihei and Yanagimoto had made it to Shuri. We decided to put off the impossible breakthrough to Kishaba until the typhoon season began.[12] Our reasoning was that moving south to Shuri was a smart thing to do, since we'd be going against the suddenly increasing flow of Japanese soldiers coming north and through a blind spot in the American line.

We left Aragaki, fourteen of us, including the sergeant major and nine local youths.[13] This group was well accustomed to foraging for food and pushed southward along a moonlit road with little concern about the enemy.

In the distance a lone American plane, with its signal lights on, flew across the sky in the same direction that we were moving in. We could hear distant explosions that the darkness seemed to muffle, and slowly falling shooting stars scratched lines across the night sky.

A little later we passed a group of ten or more Japanese soldiers moving north on the road that skirted the side of the mountain, and among them was Private First Class Suzuki, one of the Youth Corps soldiers from the Dawn Unit. Since we were moving quickly in different directions, we could only call out to, and then pass, one another, disappointed at the shortness of our meeting.

We kept meeting Japanese troops coming one after another from the opposite direction, and it became clear that for several days, American troops had been carrying out a massive mopping-up operation.

---

12. The typhoon season starts in late summer and ends in the fall.
13. The "local youths" were Okinawan boys.

August 25, 1945 (Sat.), clear

Just before dawn, we reached a plateau overlooking the lights of Yonabaru, and while we were searching for a hiding place, we saw what looked like Japanese soldiers at the foot of a small hill.

We approached them using the password "mountain river," and they turned out to be men from an engineering unit (Sixty-second Division) of the Ishi Unit (Divisional Engineering Unit). It was a sergeant, three of his subordinates, and a marine, and they lived in the field artillery unit bunker right behind where we happened to be standing. We decided to try to get them to let us stay with them.

In the course of swapping various bits of information, we learned that Jihei had stopped here several days earlier and said, "If a person named Nomura from the Dawn Unit comes from Aragaki, please help him out." He then returned to the Genya military storage bunker in Shuri. I was able to say that we both were being pursued, and although I harbored quite a lot of resentment about his leaving Aragaki, hearing this report made me grateful, as always, for his friendship.

We then entered the field artillery unit bunker. After we crawled through a small opening blasted out of the rock, the engineering unit sergeant stayed behind to wipe out the footprints we left near the entrance. He followed us in, moving a big rock to block the entrance. The interior was shaped like an "H," and the corpses of Japanese soldiers were scattered about the central meeting area.

The engineering unit sergeant explained that these were the bodies of those who were seriously wounded when horse-riding American troops attacked but who managed to escape during the intense fighting.

Mysteriously, the corpses had not decomposed but instead had hardened into a mummylike state, and each body showed signs of an agonizing death.

After the sun had gone down, the engineering unit sergeant and others started cooking rice on the path leading up to the entrance to the bunker. The rest of us emerged from the bunker and savored the delicious, fresh air. Looking up at the stars in the night sky, we reveled in our feelings of liberation.

After dinner, the whole group went out into the meadow in front of the bunker and chatted. Small hills undulated like waves in the area, and blackened mountain ranges pressed up against the night sky.

There was a road about thirty meters in front of the bunker, and off in the distance at the foot of the mountains were the lights of Yonabaru. And from time to time, the ocean breezes even carried music blaring from radios up to where we were.

August 26, 1945 (Sun.), clear

During the day, I woke up to a faint shusssssing sound in the silent darkness of the bunker.

I wondered whether the enemy was pumping in poison gas. I listened intently and breathed through my nose, sniffing for telltale odors.

Right at that instant, there was a commotion in the bunker, and a light went on, revealing everyone's strangely tensed faces. Then suddenly, "It's this! It's this!" "I'm sorry," said the sergeant from the engineering unit who dangled a rubber pillow from one hand and scratched his head with the other. The pillow had been losing air.

The light went out, and the bunker returned to darkness and silence. Watching for the enemy all day put us on edge, and it was a comedy none of us could laugh at.

August 28, 1945 (Tues.), partly cloudy, windy

Since coming to the heavy field artillery unit, my wounds, which had been healing, began to fester. It was probably because with the large number of people in the bunker, it was stuffy, humid, and hot.

As a way of getting some fresh air, I decided, beginning tonight, to line up wooden boxes at the bend in the passageway near the bunker entrance and to sleep on top of them.

August 29, 1945 (Wed.), clear

After the sun went down, everyone wolfed down his dinner and went off to forage for food. I was left behind with Private First Class Matsumoto Hajime (a native of Fukuoka Prefecture) from the Iwao Unit who had been bitten on the knee by a *habu* and thus could only limp about. We sat down together in the meadow in front of the bunker.

As we sat there, two Japanese soldiers approached from the right on the road that ran in front of the bunker. One of them left the road and approached us.

It was Jihei. I remained silent. Seeing me, he shouted "Nomura!" and rushed over. He sat down in front of me, grabbed both of my shoulders, and could say only, "How wonderful!" as if he were suppressing his real feelings. He peered into my face.

Jihei explained that he didn't come back to Aragaki because the road back from Tametomoiwa had been cut off by American soldiers, and he simply couldn't get back. He talked quickly and didn't sound like the old Jihei.

But I couldn't accept his words at face value. Was it my suspicions after being wounded? Jihei, who had distanced himself, was now in front of me, but I was cool toward him. Despite the situation on the day of the mopping-up operation when he was visiting Aragaki, I couldn't say anything about my survival that wasn't sarcastic.

After a bit, Jihei got up and said, "Give my best to everyone. I'm now on my way to the Tametomoiwa area and will come back to see you in the near future." He then went off with his companion, who was waiting at the side of the road.

I could no longer believe his words about coming back to see me. A certain distance between us had emerged, and our earlier intimacy was gone. Yet I couldn't really hate him. Each of us was living a life of uncertainty. Even as I prayed for his good fortune, I said good-bye to my memory of him.

August 30, 1945 (Thurs.), partly cloudy

It was past noon. I was sleeping at the bend in the passageway near the bunker entrance when I was awakened by the sound of falling earth. Without thinking, I got up. The passageway just opposite the entrance was illuminated, and what looked like the beam of a flashlight shone on the wall of the bunker. I could faintly hear the sound of footsteps.

It was the enemy! In an instant, I felt as though I had been doused with cold water. I realized that if I didn't wake everyone sleeping in the central rest area or do something, we'd all be killed, and I hurriedly tiptoed through the dark passageway.

I reached the rest area and shook and awakened the person nearest me, whispering, "Hey! The enemy has come! Wake up everyone!" and he called out excitedly, "Hey! The enemy!" It was the voice of one of the country boys. "What?" "The enemy!" "The enemy has come!" In an instant the boys were up and agitated. "Be quiet!" When they heard the commands of Sergeant Nishi, the engineering unit sergeant, and me, they beat down the closest door, kicked over empty cans, and competed with one another to run to the back of the bunker.

It happened just as all this was taking place. ". . ." ". . ." There was a strange cry near the bunker entrance, the sound of a lot of feet moving helter-skelter, and then it all stopped. It seemed that the commotion inside the bunker surprised the American soldiers, and they bolted.

Had the Americans entered the bunker without knowing we were there? In any case, now they knew we were here, so an attack was sure to come. Ours was a bunker with no escape. I just sat there, staring at my navel, lost in the thought that the situation was beyond repair.

Yet in the wake of this uproar, I wasn't sorry about being with the local boys we had brought along. When I thought about it, it was clear that even if they hadn't made such a ruckus, the result would have been the same.

I lit a candle. Predictably, Sergeant Major Itokazu, the engineering unit sergeant and his three men, Sergeant Nishi, Ishikawa, and Fujiwara, all were sitting at their own places, their ears alerted to any sound, and unusually tense.

In the meantime, the country boys who had rushed to the back of the bunker returned to the central area, and we talked about how we might respond to the enemy . . . but we couldn't agree. Would we be burned to death by gasoline? If we're attacked with phosphorous grenades, it'll be the end. Escaping from the bunker during the day was impossible. Exhausted by this debate, we agreed if the enemy came, we'd retreat to the back of the bunker, and although it would be no match, we'd fight back with hand grenades. Having reached this conclusion, we put out the light and readied ourselves for whatever happened.

Once again, I withdrew to my place near the entrance. Several hours passed, but the American soldiers didn't appear. Finally, it began to get dark in the passageway in the front of the bunker, and I was just thinking that sundown was at hand.

Suddenly, ZUZUNN! The earth reverberated with a terrifying sound, and amid all the confusion and shouting, I could make out human groans. When I turned on the light in the central part of the bunker and ran over, dirt and sand were scattered about, covering everyone. Fujiwara was at our feet, looking upward and toward us. He struggled to get free, and Ishikawa let him grab hold of his wrists and pulled him out of the rubble. The cave-in had crushed Fujiwara's left and right thighs, and Ishikawa's left wrist was broken. I lamented that ours was the ironic fate of the pursued.

After the sun went down, we debated whether we should leave the bunker but, in the end, agreed with the engineering unit sergeant and his men, who said, "No matter where we go, it's the same!"

. . . After dinner, Sergeant Major Itokazu suddenly assembled the country boys and announced, "We're going to Tametomoiwa to get provisions," and then left the bunker.

At the same time, Sergeant Nishi announced, "I'm going to the field warehouse bunker in Shuri where Jihei is," and left.

Their going off and leaving those of us who were wounded—Fujiwara, Ishikawa, and me—was a little strange, or so I thought. I realized I had no choice but to accept my fate. Suppressing the loneliness and resentment I felt at being abandoned, I saw them off.

August 31, 1945 (Fri.), clear and a bit cool

Last night, I spent the whole night talking with the engineering unit sergeant who had said, "No matter where we go, it's the same. Let's do as well as we can in this bunker!" . . . As expected, Sergeant Major Itokazu and the others didn't return.

. . . All day long we lived in terror of the impending American attack, but mysteriously they didn't show up today. All we could do was to wait for Fujiwara and Ishikawa to recover and for Jihei's help.

September 1, 1945 (Sat.), clear

American soldiers didn't appear today either.

Both Ishikawa and Fujiwara were in good spirits, and we had dinner together. After dinner, I left them in the bunker and went out with the engineering unit sergeant and his three men.

There was a gorgeous moon in the middle of the night sky, and the lights of Yonabaru were visible in the distance. It was a typically quiet evening. We plopped ourselves down in the meadow where we always gathered after dinner and passed the time talking about this and that.

I looked forward to Jihei's visit, but at midnight he still hadn't come.

September 2, 1945 (Sun.), clear

Today came and went without incident.

Both Ishikawa and Fujiwara were in pretty good spirits. Still no sign of Jihei. Four nights have passed since I last saw him. Since Sergeant Nishi had reached Shuri by now, Jihei was likely to pop in suddenly. . . . Or had he also forsaken those of us who were wounded?

September 3, 1945 (Mon.), partly cloudy

Jihei didn't appear tonight either.

Not wanting to become an unwelcome guest and to presume forever on the hospitality of the people in the bunker and encouraged by the recovery of Fujiwara and Ishikawa, I asked the engineering unit sergeant for directions, and the three of us decided to go off tomorrow night to visit Jihei in the former military field warehouse bunker in Shuri.

September 4, 1945 (Tues.), clear

After dinner, the three of us bid farewell to the people in the heavy field artillery bunker and left.

We had walked only four kilometers by the light of the moon when we found ourselves in a ravine about a hundred meters below the ruins of Shuri Castle, a ravine that the engineering unit sergeant had mentioned, and as luck would have it, there, sitting on the side of an artillery shell crater filled with water, was Jihei.

He ran over and said, "I was just thinking I should welcome you." Ishikawa and Fujiwara were ecstatic and talked a mile a minute, relating how Itokazu and the others had abandoned them. With no chance to speak, I just stood silently at their side.

When Jihei finished hearing their story, he guided us to the military field warehouse bunker at the foot of Mount Tokuzan.

We entered through a small entrance blasted out of the rock, and the interior of the bunker was surprisingly spacious, with passageways running in all directions and good ventilation, all of which surprised us.

At the end of one passageway, we used a four-meter-long hemp rope to climb up into a hiding place. There was a door made of wood planks painted with earth which closed from above like a cover, and even if you looked up at the door from below, you'd have trouble distinguishing it from the bunker wall.

Then Sergeant Nishi and Yanagimoto appeared. Yanagimoto talked about why they couldn't return to Aragaki, and Nishi, why they hadn't come back to the heavy field artillery bunker. None of this mattered to us anymore.

All we could think of was that we finally had a safe place. They had a lively conversation with Ishikawa and Fujiwara, the first since their parting, but I couldn't talk to Jihei and felt vaguely uncomfortable.

As the night wore on, a soldier named Uchimura (a fictitious name) from the Ishi Unit (Sixty-second Division) came over to where we were. He was the oldest occupant of the bunker and a childhood friend of Jihei's. Gesticulating as he talked, he told us how, about a month earlier, civilians, together with American soldiers, had approached on the road below the bunker and urged them to surrender. . . . This bunker was certainly not safe.

Although I could accept this for what it was, when I thought about civilians calling out to the men in the bunker, I felt an inexpressible loneliness and rage. That Japanese civilians had become puppets of the enemy and came to call us out—had all the civilians deserted us?

September 5, 1945 (Wed.), clear

When dark shadows stole into the southern observation post, the lights were switched on, and Uchimura began to play his harmonica.

Our free evening had arrived. Uchimura played his harmonica as if he were singing the evening's praises, and he did a medley of popular songs, movie scores, and *naniwa bushi* with obvious enthusiasm and confidence; and for his finale, he even imitated American soldiers, singing in falsetto.[14] Each unit had at least one or two talented fellows like Uchimura who were not shy about performing.

After his solos were over, three of us, together with Uchimura and others, went out to the kitchen area on the south road that ran right up to the bunker's lower entrance.

Uchimura and others carried buckets of water relay-style from the craters in front of the bunker up to the kitchen area. And then, for dinner, we made *gomoku* rice and *zenzai* soup. After eating, we all went outside. In front of the bunker entrance identical mounds of earth left by explosive charges revealed doors to storage bunkers, and although the view was not as good as it was in front of the heavy field artillery bunker, we still had a good time gazing at the stars in the night sky, breathing the fresh evening air, and simply enjoying our liberation.

September 7, 1945 (Fri.), clear

Food and clothing had been left behind in the field warehouse bunker, and there wasn't a single thing we lacked. Even my rather serious wound, which had worsened while we were in the heavy field artillery bunker, had begun to heal more quickly since I arrived here, thanks to the good ventilation.

Not all was well, however. My relationship with Jihei was lousy. It may have been my own prejudices, but I felt he was overly formal in his dealings with me. Moreover, although Uchimura hasn't openly revealed this in his attitude toward us, I must not imagine that he's beginning to treat the three of us — Ishikawa, Fujiwara, and me — as though we were problems.

My complaints about my current situation probably should be regarded as a form of self-indulgence.

September 10, 1945 (Mon.), clear, windy, with fast-moving clouds

In the evening, I went out with all the others, but unfortunately it was raining. After being holed up in the bunker for the whole day, we looked forward to the pleasure of being outside at night, but if we left any footprints near the bunker entrance, we'd give away our whereabouts to the enemy. Therefore, everyone ate his dinner quickly and returned without complaint to his seat in the bunker.

---

14. *Naniwa bushi* were narrative ballads about historic events that were sung to the accompaniment of a samisen. Although the genre developed in the early modern period, it became popular again in the late 1930s, thanks to modern recording and the radio.

It was something that happened sometime after midnight. I was away from my seat and having Fujiwara treat my wound. Others were asleep in their respective places, turning and shifting. Uchimura had gone to the kitchen but hadn't come back yet.

At that moment, Uchimura shouted from the bottom of the passageway we used to go up and down from the top level of the bunker to the lower one. "Hey! A crowd has come to the front of the bunker and is demanding rice."

Everyone jumped up at once and dashed toward the entrance to the passageway. With my companions shouting, "What . . . how many?" "More than ten!" "Damn! Drive them away!" we excitedly went down the passageway.

I slowly followed Fujiwara, who stopped the treatment and hurried out. The rain had let up at some point, and moonlight shone in through cracks in the bunker entrance. Everyone gathered at the entrance.

As I approached the group, Sergeant Nishi said, "They've left," and turned around to look back at me. I stepped out in front of everyone else and stared at the entrance.

In the vicinity of what I thought was the forward storage bunker, I could make out the shadows of people milling about. Now that the rain had let up, the moon was a pale white.

When I thought about how carefully we had suppressed our own wants, how fastidious we had been, how this was being ignored and how footprints were being made right before my eyes, I began to feel an anger that I usually reserved for the enemy.

After a time the human shapes became a column and marched off right before our eyes.

All of us vented our indignation and then made our way back to our seats. Dawn was approaching, so we turned off the lights and lay down.

It was right at that moment. Suddenly, there was a tremendous explosion! It seemed to move from one place to another, shaking the very bowels of the earth and reverberating throughout the bunker. Everyone knew the explosions were occurring in the storage bunkers in front of ours, and we were upset.

Without question, what had happened was that the gasoline and gunpowder stored in the bunkers had exploded. The group that came for rice must have left a candle in the area where the gasoline cans were stored, igniting them.

The American troops will blame the storage bunker explosion on Japanese soldiers hiding in this area, and they'll be sure to come on a mopping-up raid to our bunker. We had to think about what to do at daybreak.

None of us could sleep a wink until the sun went down, and we just whiled away the time. But strangely, the American soldiers didn't do what we thought they would.

Everyone was relieved, and we went about our usual evening's work. Someone suggested that we move to another hiding place in the morning, but since we'd find ourselves in the same situation no matter where we went, a plan for doing this never materialized. In the end, we decided to stay in the military field warehouse bunker.

September 11, 1945 (Tues.), partly cloudy and windy

Today passed without incident. Unlike my experience in the heavy field artillery bunker, we seemed not to agonize over the enemy. This being the case, I thought the military field warehouse bunker was fine for the time being.

Although our uneasiness about the enemy on the outside diminished, unpleasant things happened inside the bunker. Uchimura's inclination to treat the three of us who were wounded as though we were a burden became more and more obvious. I kept my feelings to myself, but Uchimura's attitude really got to Ishikawa and Fujiwara, who were civilian employees in the army.

Today Uchimura complained that Ishikawa and Fujiwara, who were asleep some distance away from him, were snoring and threw rocks at them. I found myself clenching my fists in response to Uchimura's pettiness, but given my status in the bunker, I could only grit my teeth and put up with it.

September 12, 1945 (Wed.), partly cloudy and windy

After sundown, Jihei, who was on cooking duty and had gone outside, came rushing back into the bunker.

He was holding three boxes of U.S. Army field rations and a piece of paper. "This was left at the entrance," he reported as he held out the paper to Sergeant Nishi.

Everyone moved forward all at once and surrounded the sergeant. Without thinking, I too got up from my seat and stood behind Sergeant Nishi and strained to get a look at the piece of paper in his hand.

The following had been written with a pen in a fine hand:

> I have heard from a group leader who was in the former heavy field artillery bunker in Yonabaru. I will visit tonight, so I beg you not to attack me. (The password is "mountain and river.") 9/12/1945
> From a former war buddy
> To everyone in the military field storage bunker

My immediate thought was that the next thing American forces would do is to recommend that we surrender.

Was everyone else suspicious, too? Instantaneously, a feeling of unease filled the bunker. This was not a time for us to relax. Our American counterparts were probably already approaching the entrance to the bunker.

Although I was at odds with Uchimura and Jihei and didn't speak to them, I couldn't just sit by quietly and watch. Both Ishikawa and Fujiwara came over to where I was. The message on that piece of paper elicited various responses: if they come, should we kill them? Could we escape somewhere before they arrived? Or should we hear what they had to say and then take action? It wouldn't be too late. We reached a conclusion: we'll attack them and blow them up.

It was at around nine in the evening. Jihei and Uchimura, who had been waiting outside, guided two middle-aged men into the bunker. Both were wearing American uniforms. One looked like a nisei, and the other was a bespectacled intellectual.[15] As they said hello and smiled, they distributed cigarettes and caramels to each person in the bunker.

Then the bespectacled one slowly started to speak, choosing his words carefully. He began by saying,

> I am someone who, like all of you, fought American troops here on Okinawa. But now, wanting to help even one of my many brothers, I became a member of an American forces pacification team and have been doing this work.

He then explained that Japan had surrendered unconditionally to the Allies on August 15 and that because our obligations as military men were over, we had to return to reconstruct our ancestral land — each of us — and the sooner, the better. Military units from the continent and points south were already returning, one after another, to the homeland. And he explained our position and the action we should take.

"Japan's unconditional surrender!!" I was shocked by these words I never expected to hear. Although I'd known the war situation was not favorable, I had hoped against hope for a cease-fire. "Unconditional surrender" were words I couldn't believe.

Their answers to our questions were clear, and there was no room for even a shred of doubt. In response to our questions about the situation of our buddies who had already surrendered and, of course, questions about the war, their state-

---

15. A nisei is a second-generation Japanese American. Typically, nisei have immigrant parents but were themselves born on U.S. soil. Several thousand nisei served in both the U.S. and Japanese military during World War II and saw combat in both the European and Pacific theaters. Many served as combat interpreters in the Pacific, as was the nisei who came to the bunker.

ments were reasoned and coherent. . . . But we still weren't inclined to believe everything they said.

This was the first we'd heard about Japan's surrender, and we couldn't respond quickly. We asked to be allowed to think about this until tomorrow evening, and everyone asked the pair to be sure to tell American troops in the area not to attack, just for tomorrow. They said, "This is eminently reasonable. Tomorrow night we'll bring proof so that we can convince you, so please think carefully about all this. And we'll be sure to communicate with American troops in the area," and then left the bunker. Although overwhelmed by feelings of desperation, we saw them off. "Japan's unconditional surrender." If this were true, then our interpretations of the actions that American troops were taking against us were dead wrong. We thought about how they hadn't sent any communications to the soldiers of the surrendering country and how they'd renewed their attacks — this could not be allowed. When we thought carefully about all this, the detailed knowledge of Japan's surrender made it difficult not to interpret our actions as resistance to American troops carrying out mopping-up operations in the area.

September 13, 1945 (Thurs.), clear and windy

We talked all day, half-believing and half-doubting what the pacification team members told us last night. I lay down alone and dozed. No matter how much we talked about it, without seeing the evidence the pacification team said they'd bring, conversation was pointless. I didn't like talking.

It was around eight in the evening. The same two members of the pacification team who had come last night arrived with conclusive evidence of imperial Japan's surrender.

First, letters from our war buddies in units that had been attacked and surrendered were distributed to each of us. The letters explained Japan's unconditional surrender and urged us to surrender right away. Then they showed us copies of the "Potsdam Declaration," which Japan had accepted;[16] the emperor's "Surrender Rescript"; and the "Surrender Instrument" from the deck of the USS *Missouri*.[17] There also were orders from Douglas MacArthur, Supreme Commander of the Allied Forces, the top official overseeing the occupation of our country, and issues of the *Asahi*, *Mainichi*, and *Yomiuri* newspapers that had pictures and articles

---

16. The Potsdam Declaration contained the Allies' terms of surrender and was sent to Japanese leaders on July 26, 1945. Japan formally accepted these terms on August 14.

17. General Douglas MacArthur accepted the Japanese surrender on the USS *Missouri*, which was anchored in Tokyo Bay, on September 2, 1945. Foreign Minister Mamoru Shigemitsu led the Japanese delegation.

about the August 9 "Soviet Invasion of Manchuria," the "Damage from the Atomic Bombs" dropped on Hiroshima and Nagasaki, and the "Failed Suicide Attempt of Prime Minister Tōjō.[18]

The seven of us stared silently at the evidence — its meaning was all too clear. I felt as though my whole body had suddenly collapsed and I were being attacked by a dark loneliness.

Then after recovering from this feeling of loneliness, I was assailed by an inexpressible anger. Who or what in the world was the object of my anger? I couldn't say.

I stamped my feet on the floor like a child and screamed words of anger. I felt the urge to run like a cannonball right into the center of the American camp.

In the end, even as I was being attacked by these violent feelings, I agreed with everyone else that we should surrender.

Frankly, even if I acted alone and raced out of the bunker, the surrender of Japan as an actuality wouldn't change, and the mop-up operation the American troops would launch in the wake of such an action would be directed continuously at all the Japanese soldiers in the vicinity of the military field warehouse bunker.

Rather than rant and rage, I kept my thoughts to myself, left the group, and slowly walked to the back of the bunker.

September 14, 1945 (Fri.), clear [19]

Just before daybreak, seven of us, with Uchimura in the lead (he volunteered to be our leader), climbed the small hill in front of the bunker to wait for the American troops coming to meet us. Uchimura had on a white headband and wore a uniform with a warrant officer's insignia on the collar.

When we got to the top of the hill, the five men who had been hiding in the field artillery bunker joined us.

The twelve of us went out, all together, to the edge of the hill and sat down in the grass . . . the sky gradually began to brighten.

To someone accustomed to living in a bunker, the bleak landscape seemed unreal. Off to the right, at the foot of a hill in the distance, a lone farmer wearing *kuba* grass on his head was using a horse to plow a field.

This world existed just one step outside the dark bunker where we lived face-

---

18. The *Asahi, Mainichi,* and *Yomiuri* were the leading Japanese newspapers, comparable to the *New York Times,* the *Washington Post,* and the *Los Angeles Times* in the United States.

19. Nomura's September 14, 1945, entry was added after he was taken into custody by the Americans and is interesting as a postsurrender text.

to-face with the threat of death. We stared at the peaceful farmer as though he were a real oddity.

At that moment I heard the faint sound of an engine behind me, and when I turned around, a large olive green truck was bouncing across a grass field and rushing toward us.

Everyone now saw it, and a feeling of unease immediately swept through the group. It was an American army truck.

They really were coming! I felt as though I were being attacked by a loneliness I can't begin to describe. As the truck drew closer, those feelings intensified and overwhelmed me. I could only think of the phrase "Do not give up under any circumstances" in the *Field Service Code*.[20]

I was now facing a humiliating fate I never could have imagined, not even in my wildest dreams, and blankly stared at the truck. I could see that the pacification team members from last night and two American soldiers were on the truck. As it approached, Uchimura and Jihei got up, and I did the same, though not very enthusiastically. The truck stopped at the bottom of the small hill. The two pacification team members and four American soldiers with automatic weapons slung over their shoulders waved to us and jumped off the truck.

We went down the hill in single file with Uchimura in the lead and Fujiwara, Ishikawa, and me lagging behind.

We lined up in front of the four American soldiers, forming a single line with Uchimura at the far left, then Sergeant Nishi, the engineering unit sergeant, Jihei, and myself in that order. We were a pitiful sight, and an icy wind blew through the grass as if it were mocking us.

The American soldiers read us instructions, which the pacification team members translated into Japanese.

The soldiers then tossed all our weapons into a large artillery shell crater filled with water, and we got on the truck. The pacification team members told us our destination was Ishikawa.

We were astonished by what we saw! The original village was now a scorched field; the surrounding hills had been removed, and there was absolutely no trace of them; nearby mountains had been cut into; wide roads ran in all directions; and cars streamed by.

Once again I was amazed at the American army's massive mechanical power. The pitiful sight of a vanquished soldier like me, now exposed on the road in

---

20. The *Field Service Code* (*Senjikun*) was adopted by the Ministry of War on January 8, 1941, and was distributed to all Japanese servicemen.

broad daylight, was unbearably embarrassing, and I couldn't bear to show my face. It may have been my imagination, but everyone else seemed to be looking down at their feet, too.

American aircraft flew overhead from time to time.

As we drove along, we passed truckloads of young island boys and girls probably going to work on American military projects, and when they saw us, the girls cried out in shrill voices and waved.

Truly indescribable feelings ran down my spine. Not one of us responded to the waving girls. We turned on to a road at the foot of the hills and could see the ocean on our right. The traffic finally seemed to end, perhaps because we had come to the eastern shoreline. American aircraft flew in formation in the sky. Then we could see a line of American military barracks shaped like *kamaboko* at the foot of the hills to our left. When we got to a small road that led off from the main road and ran like a branch toward the barracks, the truck stopped. Uchimura said, "I'll go with the pacification team," and got off the truck with the two pacification team members.

His actions seemed strange. Everyone looked at him suspiciously, and even after the truck started up again, he seemed not to notice and just followed the pacification team men down the small road to the barracks.

The truck kept going for some time on a road that skirted the seashore.

When we got to an area next to a broad field, there were American army tents in the valleys on the left and the right. Then the truck stopped again, and Ishikawa, Fujiwara, and Yanagimoto got off the truck with an American soldier. There seemed to be a military internment camp across the way.

At about 9:00 a.m., the truck, with the remaining eight of us aboard, arrived at an open space in front of the Ishikawa Prisoner Internment Camp.

The camp had been built in a broad sandy area at the foot of the hills and was surrounded by two barbed-wire fences with towering sentry boxes placed at intervals. American soldiers with rifles in their hands kept watch.

An American soldier stood guard in a sentry box in front of the barbed-wire gate. Beyond the gate was a passageway about eight meters wide running straight ahead for such a distance that it disappeared in a haze. In the fenced-in areas on both sides of the passageway, we could see people who were probably Japanese army prisoners, most of them wearing olive green American army fatigues, and lines of tents in an open area behind them.

After a short wait, two American soldiers emerged from the wooden barracks next to the truck and had us get off the truck. We were made to walk in single file toward the gate of the internment camp.

As we approached the gate, Japanese army POWs in fatigues immediately gathered on both sides of the passageway and called out, "Where are you from?" and "What was your unit?"

Still overwhelmed by a sense of shame, I couldn't raise my head. Nor did anyone else.

The seven of us were then ordered to disrobe, right there on the passageway, in full view of the throng of POWs. Once we were naked, we were dusted from head to foot with a fine white disinfecting powder. Then all our personal belongings were confiscated, and we were given American army clothing. When we put on the fatigues, we looked like all the other POWs. Then, for the first time, I realized that "POW" was stamped in black ink on the back of my shirt and on the inner pocket of my pants. The mark of a prisoner.

An American soldier who seemed to be a nisei approached us from behind. He asked detailed questions about our original rank, name, unit, where we had been up to now, and whether we had any wounds. Then leaving behind Matsumoto and me, who had wounds, the others were led away by the two American soldiers who had been with us from the outset. Jihei turned and said, "Take care of yourself!" "Yeah, you too," I answered. It was the first time my words to Jihei were sincere. These words undid the knot of emotions that had existed until that moment, and the two of us smiled wistfully at each other and parted.

Guided by the American soldier who looked like a nisei, Matsumoto and I walked down the passageway toward the interior.

One by one, Japanese army POWs appeared on both sides of the passageway and called out to the two of us, but we hid our faces and just walked on.

Finally, following the American soldier, the two of us entered the fenced-in entrance of a tent filled with sick and wounded patients. It was located on the right side of the center part of the camp. Inside, five or six former Japanese soldiers wearing armbands were working at a line of desks, and the American soldier called one over and told him to take charge of us and then left. The POW then guided us to one of the many tents lined up inside the fence. Fifteen to sixteen former Japanese soldiers lived together in the tent, and they were sitting on blankets spread over wooden boxes of canned goods and chattering when we entered. When our guide said he had brought two new people, everyone gathered around us, and all at once they began to ask about our original unit and what we had done.

I felt unbearably shy and couldn't say much. While I recognized that they were Japanese soldiers who had become prisoners before I had, I still couldn't look them in the eye when I spoke. What I most feared was that someone I knew would make me talk.

I felt a certain self-reproach about my surviving and becoming a prisoner, and an unbearable guilt.

That evening, I wasn't able to get to sleep and went outside. The surrounding tents were bathed in moonlight, and this, together with the deathly silence, made it seem like the bottom of the sea.

Directly in front of me and beyond the fence that was white in the floodlights, I also noticed two fires in the hills that looked like bonfires. The fire on the right was higher up, the one on the left was lower. Their red glow looked like the flowers of the Chinese lantern plant.

Instinctively, I strained to get a better look. . . . The next day my tentmates said, "From time to time, we can see stragglers' cooking fires in the hills over there." Without a doubt, these were the cooking fires of Japanese soldiers.

Seeing those red fires, I felt an impulse to start running. There was freedom in the hills. And everything that had happened to me up to now came back. . . .

But these memories of life in the hills were suddenly obliterated by the roar of an American aircraft in the sky behind me.

The plane had its lights on and seemed to be drifting toward the hills in front of me.

The nostalgic lights in the hills suddenly seemed lonely and ephemeral.

I assumed that those who lit those fires were Japanese soldiers who would be killed — when, I didn't know — by American soldiers. When I thought about how they, like us, had no idea that the ancestral country had surrendered and were doing their best to persevere, I felt an utterly indescribable emptiness.

November 10, 1945

Today, with the help of American soldiers, I visited the field storage bunker at Shuri and was able to recover the diary I left in the back of the bunker the night before I surrendered on September 14. This was a wonderful find. I have followed and recorded my memories of the day that brought things to an end for me as a Japanese soldier, and this is the end of this diary.

From the Start of the War

Takahashi Aiko was born in Tokyo in 1894. She attended schools in the Tokyo area and graduated from Utsunomiya Girls High School. Her family immigrated to the United States in 1916 or 1917, and Takahashi spent her twenties and early thirties here. While living in California, she met Takahashi Shōta, a physician practicing medicine in Little Tokyo in Los Angeles, and married him in 1922. They had two children, a son, Nobukazu, and a daughter, Emii. In the fall of 1932 they returned as a family to Japan, and Takahashi's husband opened a medical practice in Tokyo. During the war they lived in Hiroo, a fashionable area in central Tokyo not far from Sacred Heart Girls High School, where their daughter was a student. Takahashi and her husband may have chosen Sacred Heart because they were Christians, and we learn from her diary that she also had a younger sister living nearby.

Takahashi began her diary on February 18, 1942, and continued it through 1955. Apparently, she started keeping it so her children would know what the family went through during the war. The wartime portion of her diary is included in Agawa Hiroyuki et al., eds., *Shōwa sensō bungaku zenshū* (Tokyo: Shūeisha, 1972), vol. 14, *Shimin no nikki*, 322–357.

February 18, 1942, Wednesday

Because Singapore fell, a Great East Asia celebration was staged on a huge scale.[1]

Prime Minister Tōjō sat on the throne of the various countries of East Asia and looked splendid. The entire Japanese people gained self-confidence from their country's newfound power, and they were deliriously happy. But why couldn't I share these feelings? The fall of Singapore and the brilliant victories achieved since the start of the war mean that we are protected, but I don't know just how grateful I should be. While I feel gratitude and joy, the things that have affected me most directly lead me to ask about the state of my own daily life, and this is something I can't ignore. Having said this, I can't simply feel comfortable when I think about the shortages caused by the war—that we don't have enough to eat, that we don't have anything to wear, and that we're not able to go sightseeing or mountain climbing. Without these sorts of things, the meaning of my own life is found in my wanting things to be like so or my feeling that they must be like so, in other words, its meaning is in those very needs. Regarding my basic ideals as a human being, because there's a war going on, things are all different, too different, and I feel dissatisfied and sad about the oppressive atmosphere of daily life. Although I enjoy the same position as those pleased with our military victories and am neither a foreigner nor a person of a different race, I feel different and experience the loneliness of someone with no one to talk to about the sadness of living each day so unhappily. Even if a person like me, who has no redeeming qualities and is like a weed, should die by the roadside, my death would not have the slightest impact on anyone, an unbearable thought to a human being. I really feel I could find comfort if I were able to express these feelings to someone. Every day I wonder who, among my friends, would respond kindly to my agony, but I also want the person who will give me answers to be someone who is, in present-day Japanese society, famous in some sense, or put differently, someone important. Among those I know, I can't decide who would be good and whom to pick. I am tired of thinking that some would see this as an imposition and that others would not see my discontent as a problem at all. With no one to talk to, I didn't even consider that it might be an imposition and picked Mr. Arishima Ikuma.[2] Today's Greater East Asia War celebration aside, I

1. The government declared February 18 to be "Victory Celebration Day," and 100,000 people gathered in Hibiya Park in Tokyo to express their gratitude to the officers and enlisted men who took Singapore. See Kōdansha, comp., *Shōwa: Niman nichi no zenkiroku* (Tokyo: Kōdansha, 1989), vol. 6, 130.
2. Arishima Ikuma (1882–1974) was a painter and writer who spent many years in Europe and returned to Japan in 1910.

spent all morning writing a long letter to Mr. Arishima and then sent it to him. I feel sure he will rebuke me for my poor manners, and I think he will find my writing to him an imposition.

February 21, 1942, Saturday

Although I wondered whether I would hear from him, I had a response from Mr. Arishima this morning: an oil-painted postcard. His postcard read, "I sympathize with your agonies about the current state of affairs. Rather than say this or that, I have sent a translation of something I wrote. Please read it."

Today I went again to Shinjuku to search for food. In one corner in a department store basement, someone was making tempura. I didn't know what kind of fish was being fried, but she was dipping it in batter and throwing it into bubbling oil. I happened to go by at a good time and was so happy my heart danced. Lately when I have gone out to search for food, if I find anything that seems palatable, I feel so triumphant. When was the last time we made tempura at home? It seems like a long time ago, and I honestly can't remember when it was. Thinking that I would buy some tempura and please everyone with something they hadn't had in ages, I went to the end of the long line. Finally my turn came, and I bought some and carried it home, feeling quite proud of myself. I set it out on the dinner table. But when I tried a piece, whew! It had the horrible smell of something that had begun to go bad and was inedible. The pleasure I had been denied for some time and so looked forward to proved to be an illusion. I was surprised they were selling something bad.

March 13, 1942, Friday

As a result of the noisy debate about the writing of Japanese characters — one of the issues I raised in my recent letter to Mr. Arishima — Yokoyama Taikan and others overcame the opposition of the Imperial Palace, and the problem that went unresolved during the Meiji, Taishō, and Shōwa periods finally has been resolved.[3] It has been decided that Japanese will be written horizontally and from left to right. This was broadcast on the radio in the evening. I was so happy! Although I speak of happiness, I wasn't gloating just because those I agreed with prevailed. It was the pleasure of seeing a theory realized and the correctness of realizing that theory. Proceeding from the simple and easy to understand, the theory that one plus two is three, the fact that an easily solvable problem has remained unsolved for three eras — Meiji, Taishō, and Shōwa — confirms that

---

3. Yokoyama Taikan (1868–1958) was a contemporary artist who painted in traditional Japanese styles.

the country is inclined to ignore theory and that oppressive forces exist among the upper classes.

April 18, 1942, Saturday

It was Saturday, and so at noon I was waiting for the children to return from school and was busy in the clinic. Lunch was late, and it was about one-thirty, when the servants finally were having their lunch. All of a sudden, I heard the terrifying sound of explosions—boom! boom!—and what I thought were windows shattering. Everyone stood up and looked about in confusion. "What was that?" "What happened?" We ran to the front of the house and then to the back to find out what it was. I wanted to know where my husband was, and I went to the clinic and then dashed up to the second floor, but he wasn't there. I became even more anxious and upset and rushed to the inner garden, but he wasn't there, either. Then when I went around to the front garden, he was standing under the stone gate of the inner entryway. When the explosions occurred, he was just looking toward the Mizuno house, and when he looked up at the sky, there were telling black smoke puffs two or three feet across, which he was studying. "Oh, you were here?" I asked, staring at him. There was nothing to say except "What was that?" "What might that have been?" The people at the factory next door stopped their machines, and all of them ran outside and climbed up to the clothes-drying platform on the roof and were just standing there. "It's an antiaircraft gun!" they shouted shrilly. At that moment we realized that the puffs of smoke in the sky were exploding antiaircraft shells. If that was so, then we knew that there must have been an enemy bombing raid, and our fear intensified. To be targeted from the sky without warning, no matter where you were—didn't that mean that those on the ground had nowhere to flee or hide? Some time after the antiaircraft guns opened up, Japanese aircraft appeared, flying in three-plane formations.[4]

At around that moment, an air-raid alert sounded—for the first time.[5]

The weather has been bad for the last five or six days—it has rained and been windy—but this morning was exceptionally clear. Because it was really beauti-

---

4. Takahashi is describing what it was like to be on the ground during the Doolittle raid on Tokyo. Lieutenant Colonel James Doolittle led sixteen B-25 bombers that had been transported to within five hundred miles of Japan on the carrier USS *Hornet*. Twelve aircraft bombed Tokyo, killing fifty people. Three others attacked Yokohama, Yokosuka, Nagoya, and Kobe. Fifteen of the bombers then crash-landed in China, and the sixteenth flew on to Vladivostock in the Soviet Union. See Carter and Mueller, *Combat Chronology*, 13.

5. Air-raid alerts were called "yellow alerts," and air-raid warnings were "red alerts."

ful, the children talked incessantly about how they wanted to go out to play. How could we imagine that the first air raid would occur on such a beautiful day? After lunch, Nobukazu said he had to go off to buy the carpenter's tools he needed for school but also to enjoy the good weather, and he went off on his bicycle, and I was frantic with worry about him.[6] But he came back quickly, and I breathed a sigh of relief. Then he went out through the gate with his puttees on and his telescope slung over his shoulder.

The air-raid warning sounded sometime after the bombs were dropped and with no prior alert. In the wake of the battle, Japanese aircraft flew about in the sky that the enemy aircraft had just left, and at three thirty in the afternoon a siren sounded, signaling the lifting of the air-raid warning.

When the warning was lifted, the first person to show up at the clinic was the man who came two or three times a year to sell slippers. Apparently when he came to our neighborhood, he found himself in the middle of the ruckus and evacuated until the all-clear sounded. "Is it true, Doctor? Is it, Doctor?" he asked excitedly. "You know, Doctor, can you believe that American planes would come on a gorgeous day and in broad daylight? Can you believe that? If this is really true, you know, and if our brave warriors who attacked Pearl Harbor are military gods, then what should we call these brave American warriors? Perhaps we should call them the gods of the military gods?" His face exuded a confidence that said that today's incident was not an American attack, and he laughed it off. I had the feeling that these sorts of people who know only their own personal views and get worked up are like the characters in popular Japanese stories and storytellers' tales, characters who exhibit the faults of Japanese. This is what his words brought to mind. While we practiced with great drama what to do in a preliminary alert, after the air-raid warning sounded, and when these warnings were lifted, I wondered what in the world the meaning of today's incident was. I wanted to know the truth.

June 8, 1942, Monday

Because the battlefront is spreading daily and expanding to various islands in the south, we opened our maps once again and looked at island groups and place-names. What in the world are we doing extending the battle zones to such distant places? Are there enough supplies of critical material to wage war effectively? We were studying our maps with a distinct unease when it was reported that our troops had landed in the completely opposite direction—on

6. Nobukazu is Takahashi's son.

Attu in the Aleutian Island chain — and we were surprised.[7] Our daily lives are subject to shortages, but when it comes to the military's extending the battle line to the south and the north, it is because they have made adequate calculations and have realistic expectations and prospects for victory that they were able to make the breakthroughs they did. There are stockpiles in the military that we don't know about, but we're still surprised at the military's enormous power. We couldn't help but think about the soldiers who landed on Attu and how they were probably suffering in the severe cold, and we prayed for them.

Attu Island aside, here in Tokyo we are enjoying the season that gives us the first glimpses of summer. It is the best time for the roses blooming on the fence here at home, and they are really beautiful. Yet every year I am utterly amazed at the flower thieves that my roses attract. Some even bring their own shears. I am troubled by Japanese who don't see stealing others' roses as bad. Although I condemn those who take the flowers we are so devoted to, it is true that they are called "flower thieves" and that from ancient times flower stealing has been seen in our country as an elegant and tasteful thing to do, not a crime. If we complain, we are criticized for lacking elegance. To me, this is a truly bizarre elegance. One cannot garden in Japan in the way that one does in the West: one can't plant flowers along the side of the road to enhance the beauty of one's house and to share that beauty with passersby.[8] It seems if one has money, one has no choice but to surround one's property with a sturdy wall that no one can peer over.

June 27, 1942, Saturday

The rain that had been falling for four or five days straight finally stopped, and the morning sun shone beautifully. Because officials were coming to inspect our air-defense equipment, a neighborhood association circular instructed each of us to compose a detailed list of what we had and to post it where it could be seen easily. In response I made a list that read:

> 2 fire hoses
> 2 steel helmets
> 4 fire dampers
> 1 ladder

---

7. Admiral Yamamoto Isoroku designed a plan to create a forward defense line running from Port Moresby in Australia, through the Solomon, Gilbert, and Marshall Islands; Wake; Midway; and the Aleutian Islands. In accordance with that plan, 1,200 Japanese troops went ashore on Attu in the Aleutians, and 350, on Kiska on June 6 and 7, 1942.

8. Takahashi spent her teens and twenties in California.

3 fire extinguishers
2 boxes of sand
1 hose
3 metal buckets
2 shovels

and posted it on the back door. In the afternoon, two officials with stern faces conducted the inspection. I really don't like the attitude of these sorts of people and their way of speaking. In the evening the physicians' neighborhood association was meeting at Dr. Kōno's house, and my husband went to the gathering and returned at eleven.

July 23, 1942, Thursday

Beginning today and continuing for three days, the neighborhood association will have air-defense drills. As always, the air-defense squad leader lined up the *monpe*-clad women and directed the bucket relay with total seriousness.

September 16, 1942, Tuesday

Today, I worried when Emii didn't come [right] home from school. In time she did return, but she looked very upset.[9] Surprised, I asked, "What's the matter? Were things that bad?" but she didn't answer and slunk down the hall and threw herself on the couch in the living room, and sobbed. The story I heard in dribs and drabs through her tears was that the sisters of the Abbey of the Sacred Heart were taken from their classrooms today and made to board trucks and go off with Japanese officials. I wondered how seeing this might have wounded these girls' pure hearts. Emii went up to the second floor and throwing herself down in front of the altar in her room, she seemed to pray for some time.

September 30, 1942, Wednesday

Today was the day of Emii's graduation. It also was Nobukazu's day to go to camp at Narashino. The graduation ceremony was to take place at ten, so my husband and I left together for Sacred Heart Girls School. If this had been a typical year, we would have seen the sisters with their radiant faces, beaming and moving about — a scene one sees only at this school — but sadly this was not the case this year. The sisters had been interned just two weeks earlier. Why didn't the government consider interning the sisters after the graduation ceremony?

---

9. Emii is Takahashi's daughter and a student at Sacred Hearts Girls School in Tokyo.

What was the rush? I couldn't understand this government measure. Interning the sisters of the convent: I acknowledge that this would be possible in a foreign country, too.[10]

March 27, 1943, Saturday

Today, we had an air-defense drill again. The community council big shots put on their pompous clothes and their pompous faces and strutted about with a pompous number of people. Each time there is an air-defense drill, we are made to line up in single file, call out our names, and roll is taken, with lots of muttering about which houses are not represented, who was late, and which wife sent her maid in her place. On evenings when there are blackout drills, people are roused from bed and there's a lot of shouting: "the glow from your cigarettes is visible," "light is leaking out through knotholes," "moonlight is reflected off glass planes and showing," and "have you turned out the lights?" There always is quite a commotion. One night there was an air-raid drill while it was raining. Voices were raised on the street right in front of our house, and there was a real ruckus, so I looked out. A member of the civilian defense corps was holding a six-foot pole across his chest and blocking the way of a car that had come up the hill. He was ordering the car to stop. While he was arguing with the people in the car, the all-clear sounded, and suddenly three or four cars began to move uphill. When they found their way blocked too, the drivers got out of their cars. A fight broke out, and people scuffled with one another. I didn't understand why they were fighting, and my husband went out to have a look. When he returned, he said, "He's a worthless jerk! The civilian defense corps guy is drunk and absolutely insufferable!"

We couldn't tell whether the intentions of the group directing us were sincere or true. They just struck us as overly dramatic. And so rather than feeling that we really had to carry out these sorts of practices and drills, we simply felt displeasure or pain at being bossed and pushed around and being made to do this and that. With less physical strength because of the food shortages and with a shortage of help in every house, we wonder how much of our time and energy will be wasted as the neighborhood association orders us to do this and that. The things they ask of us are really a burden.

April 21, 1943, Wednesday

When we read the morning newspaper, we learned the cabinet ministers are suddenly being reshuffled. The prime minister, of course, will continue, but the

---

10. Takahashi may be thinking of the U.S. government's internment of Japanese Americans, which took place earlier that year.

home minister, foreign minister, education minister, and agricultural minister have been reshuffled, and Prime Minister Tōjō will serve also as education minister. Perhaps there were differences of opinion within the government. What exactly is happening? It's like picking colors in the dark, and for better or worse, there is no criticizing the government. It simply makes us uneasy.

That evening Kazuide-chan brought over some thread.[11] This was a great help. Recently, whenever you wash newly made clothes, they have to be mended or patched before being worn again. We need thread for garments that are falling apart, but we're really in a fix because none is available. I just used red thread on a black background and stitched some white material with black thread, but since everybody is having to do this, this is perfectly OK.

When it was evening, Rei-chan came to pick up the rice-hulling stick.[12] Somebody thought of a way to hull the brown rice distributed to us: you put the rice into a beer bottle, filling it up halfway, and then beat it with a stick until it turns white. Most households do this—at night or when someone has a moment. The newspapers tell us ad nauseam that brown rice is good for the body, and although it is indelicate to say this, if one looks at one's excrement after eating brown rice, the brown rice is still there. With food and such in short supply and with less protein, this seems like such a waste, and it's a pity we can't laugh about this. We hull rice using the beer bottle method until blisters begin to form on our hands, our sleeves start to tear, and we get tired. We use the fine powder that the hulls leave in the bottle to make flour and then steamed bread, which everyone eats. When humans reach this point, perfectionists are seen as a peacetime luxury.

April 29, 1943, Thursday

Today is the emperor's birthday. The Japanese people are offering up their bodies to this deified emperor. As part of the emperor's birthday celebration, Nobukazu was ordered to march to demonstrate the formidable power of Japanese youth, and he was gone all afternoon.

June 10, 1943, Thursday

Today again, a procession of soldiers being sent off to war came up the hill in front of our house heading toward the train station. At the start of the war, these processions were accompanied by a band and waves of fluttering flags, and continued for one or two blocks. But now as the war intensifies day by day, our daily lives are more and more straitened, and we have fewer hands. In the processions that pass now, there still are people holding the well-used flags but also some

---

11. Takahashi does not identify Kazuide-chan. She must be a neighbor.
12. Rei-chan also must be a neighbor.

not holding flags; the war songs lack power; and those seeing off the troops are relatives and neighborhood association folks who are required to show up. The processions have become rather pathetic affairs. The processions pass often because our house is close to the station. As I look at them, I have the wrenching thought that today once again, a funeral of living people is passing and youngsters with their sleeves rolled up are being sent off to die.

June 22, 1943, Tuesday

Our clothes are in tatters, and it's almost as though we've been defeated in battle, with our swords bent and our arrows spent. Our pots also are falling apart, and we can't find substitutes. Today the bottom of the pan I use to wash dishes dropped out, so I couldn't use it any more. Thinking I would find a replacement, I went shopping but couldn't find one. What I did find was a strange thing called a wooden bucket, and I returned home pleased with my discovery. When I tried using it, however, the water just ran through it.

Socks get holes in them the first time they're worn; clothes fall apart after being worn two or three times; and things break when you use them — recently everything has been artificial, and I'm furious. Even things that don't work require raw materials, human labor, and time, and yet they're still unusable and useless — what is going on? It is an unimaginable psychological situation for Japanese to be in.

September 2, 1943, Thursday

Our household is on neighborhood duty for the month, and this is causing us a lot of anxiety. The reports that enemy planes will be coming increase daily, and if this should happen, we will have full responsibility for the neighborhood association. For those who are not very good at leading people, the thought of having to do this is depressing. Although it must seem quite irresponsible to have these thoughts, we are terrified and pray that nothing will happen during our month of duty. When a commodity has to be distributed, the person on duty, representing the neighborhood, picks it up and divides it up among the various households based on the number of people in each family. Is there a circular to be sent around? Do we have to have someone run around the neighborhood? I have everyone come to get the various commodities but am at a complete loss as to the vegetables distributed by the greengrocer. When dividing things up based on the number of people in a household, I find that if I don't include the bundled straw sheaths and the completely yellowed leaves, the distributions don't work out by weight. But if I do include the straw and the dried leaves, I have the feeling I'll hear the criticism "she's probably taking the good ones for herself."

This is irritating to everyone, and it's really unbearable and difficult for us. When you're on monthly duty, you can do what everyone else has done, but you can't do anything about people who think about things only from the perspective of the present. You can't become a god who thinks of everything, nor can you do something for the sad people and show compassion. In distributing things in this way, you waste a lot of time and have hurt feelings, and you go to pick up things at the distribution center and have to work hard.

When a notice arrives saying there are goods to be distributed, you have to go immediately, leaving rice cooking on the stove and hot water for laundry boiling, even though fuel is scarce. When you get to the distribution center, you have to stand in a long line, bite your tongue over the way the distribution center personnel puff away on their cigarettes while staring at you, and then just wait. If you ask the distribution center people what's going on, they just say they're waiting for everyone to get there. Whether it's rice, miso, soy sauce, fish, or meat, the distribution center people bow deeply and say unnecessarily flattering things to you. So what about that? Although we talk about "distributed goods," they certainly are not free. We pay money and buy these goods, but exchanges are not possible, and the distribution center personnel act as though they're doing this as charity, and as a result conversations with them are most unpleasant.

When Japanese are haughty, it's because others have been haughty to them, and they seem not to understand the relationship between the pleasure they derive from being haughty to others and their own displeasure at others' haughtiness.

In this morning's newspaper, there was a report about enemy aircraft bombing the southern islands before dawn yesterday.

September 9, 1943, Thursday

On September 4, there was a news report that England has landed troops in Italy, and today, in the afternoon, there was a radio broadcast that Italy had surrendered unconditionally. Some people blanched when they heard this report and were surprised, and yet when the Mussolini government was overthrown a month and a half earlier and the Badoglio government was established, the surrender was just a matter of time.[13] Is there really any need to be surprised just because we hear that Italy has surrendered? Nonetheless, the newspapers report that although Italy has surrendered, Mussolini is holed up in the north and has proclaimed the establishment of "North Italy." Thus nothing has changed in the

---

13. Marshal Pietro Badoglio (1871–1956) was a career military man who succeeded Benito Mussolini in July 1943 and negotiated an armistice with the Allies on September 29, 1943.

secure three-country [Axis] alliance.[14] Recently, all newspaper reports have been written in this style, and thus we have to use intuition and much more when reading the papers. If we don't work at discovering the truth, we may see all this as incredible mistakes, but I feel that nothing is more dangerous than this.

Even so, though, the collapse of one of the countries in the three-country alliance of Japan, Germany, and Italy makes us feel more and more uneasy.

Even if the collapse of one corner of a castle causes us to question the prospects for recovery and to contemplate defeat, and if we surrender quickly or if the castle defenders fight to the death, won't the leaders who will be held accountable feel that the people, no matter what they think, must be pushed to the very end? I think this is a terrifying thought.

October 21, 1943, Thursday

There was a minuscule two- to three-line article in the newspaper about Prime Minister Tōjō's visit to the Imperial Palace on September 7. Ever hypersensitive about everything we read, we wondered whether a change was about to occur, and then Italy surrendered on September 9.[15] Next we noticed that the number of those going to the front seems to be dramatically increasing. All able-bodied males between the ages of eighteen and forty-five are being drafted, and it seems that the Japanese home islands are being emptied.

Today, a send-off party was held at Meiji gaien for those who are already draft age and those whose graduation was speeded up—they all are being sent to the front as student draftees. Unpropitiously, a light rain has been falling since morning, and several thousand, or several tens of thousands, of students wearing their school uniforms and with rifles on their shoulders assembled for the send-off.[16] Nobukazu was one of those seeing off the draftees, and he went to Gaien. He was seeing them off but not being sent off himself because of a slight difference in age. I got choked up as I thought about what the students and their relatives and friends were feeling. Rain fell steadily on the meeting ground as though even heaven was moved by the spectacle.

We had a letter from Yanagii, who normally sends us *matsutake* mushrooms in the fall. He wrote that he was just going to send us some mushrooms, but the post office turned him away and told him they no longer handled such small

---

14. Japan signed the Tripartite Pact with Germany and Italy on September 27, 1940.

15. Italy surrendered on September 29, not September 9.

16. The government kept secret the number of student draftees sent off that day, but 65,000 people—relatives, fellow students, and friends—were on hand to see them off on a cold and rainy fall day. See Kōdansha, comp., *Shōwa*, vol. 6, 264.

packages. Even though *matsutake* mushrooms could not be sent because of the war, we were glad to know he was safe.

November 11, 1943, Friday

Nobukazu heard that someone was selling sugarcane near Ebisu Station and was told you could make sugar from it, so he bought some. Looking at the cane, it was exactly like corn in thickness and shape. When we licked the cut end of the stem, sure enough it was sweet. Nobukazu bought ten pieces, each about a foot long, and we cut each into one-inch pieces, but because the stem was hard and difficult to cut into pieces smaller than thirds, our palms got bright red and blisters formed where we held the handle of the knife. Determined to make sugar, we endured the pain and succeeded in cutting each length of cane into small pieces, which we then prepared to boil. Using our precious firewood, we boiled the pieces, and the hot water turned brown. Because it looked exactly like water in which brown sugar has been dissolved, we talked about how much sugar would be produced and were very pleased with ourselves. Nobukazu had been told he should add lye to the brew at this stage and boil it some more. Because we didn't have medicinal lye and thinking that ash was okay, we added ash. When we did that, the liquid suddenly turned clear. Nobukazu had been instructed to keep boiling this clear liquid, and although it took a lot of time and firewood, we did this. But no matter how much we boiled it, the liquid did not become sugar. When we tasted it, it was strangely sweet but smelled like ash, and it was like tasting a poisonous soup. Where did our enthusiasm for making sugar go? Staring at our swollen palms, we felt utterly defeated. In the end we had no choice but to toss out the soup that made us want to throw up.

January 4, 1944, Tuesday

We had an unusual visitor from the countryside. This person came to Tokyo for medical treatment, and we learned a lot about the prosperity of the countryside.

In the past the daily lives of farmers were not blessed in any sense, but now they suddenly hold the key to our lives — food — and sit in the kingly position of lords of production. By selling on the black market, they are enjoying extraordinary prosperity. To survive, city dwellers take this and that to the countryside. Establishing relationships with country folk — by taking a bride or groom from the country — is seen as a necessary means of survival. Day by day the contents of city dwellers' dressers are finding their way into country folk's dressers. And city people have found new ways to flatter country folk. As to how people feel about this reversal of position, it's hard to say who is right and who is wrong. When you realize that it also may be payback, despising each other is really sad.

February 22, 1944, Tuesday

This morning when we opened the newspaper, there was an article reporting that Prime Minister Tōjō also would serve as the chief of the general staff. Is there something going on again? Perhaps something big is about to happen. Even a short, two- or three-line article like this puts us on edge.

March 10, 1944, Friday

The cold is turning the rain into snow. Recently there haven't been any newspaper articles about the war in the South Pacific. What in the world is happening? Enemy planes seem to be coming more and more on reconnaissance flights, and this is really creepy.

March 22, 1944, Wednesday

An experimental drug for blood typing arrived, and we determined the blood types of people in the neighborhood association, acquaintances in the neighborhood, and everyone in the family. We did this because it was required, but when I thought about how the moment when this might be needed had arrived, I felt an unspeakable loneliness.

July 18, 1944, Tuesday

Last night the heat was oppressive, and it was a sleepless night. Yesterday a change of navy ministers was announced, and it made us wonder whether something terrible was about to happen.[17] Just as we were thinking that, we heard the sad report that our troops on Saipan had committed *gyokusai* and were annihilated. Apparently for six or seven days after the decisive battle, the survivors hid in trenches before deciding on the sixteenth to commit *gyokusai*. As the stepping-stones leading to Japan are occupied one by one and the hand-to-hand fighting comes closer, our unease is unbearable. Although this is what we feel, the reports in newspapers and magazines boast that giving up these islands is a tactic for drawing in the enemy and that the enemy is doing what we want.

No matter how favorably you look at the war situation, after the fall of Singapore, it's been impossible to imagine that Japan enjoys the advantage. Hearing about our troops' *gyokusai* on Saipan makes us angry. We should have the courage, come hell or high water, to give up the fight.

---

17. Prime Minister Tōjō Hideki and his entire cabinet resigned on July 18.

August 29, 1944, Tuesday

The second son of Dr. Umehara from the neighborhood association physicians' group has received his notice to be shipped out. Oldest sons already were inducted last October, and since they were sent off on January 9, reports and communication have recently tapered off. We were just noticing that if you count the days, it seems to have been from around the time of the Saipan debacle that the second sons were sent off. There is no question how Umehara's boy felt, but when we imagined how his parents felt, our words of consolation seemed hollow, and there really was nothing to say. All his father could say was, "If it is for the country . . ." The government has cut the number of years for graduation from college and no longer waits for college students to graduate. They are rushed to the battlefield. Young students say, "A normal life span is fifty years, but isn't ours only twenty-five?"

September 13, 1944, Wednesday

It was one of those invigorating, clear fall mornings that come right after a rain. My younger sister's husband, Mr. Iwase, came over to visit. He announced glumly that "now that we are threatened by air raids, we may die, and if we should be unlucky enough to die, then what? I have written a will in which I ask you to look after my family. . . ." He came over just to make this request. For all us parents who have children, this is the saddest thing to contemplate and what we think about most carefully. "If this should happen," we say to one another, "I'm counting on you."

September 30, 1944, Saturday

We learned from an announcement made at five this afternoon that all our troops on Tinian committed *gyokusai*.[18]

October 6, 1944, Friday

Mr. Tōyama Mitsuru had been bedridden, and today it was announced that he died.[19] Mr. Tōyama was a "black curtain" person, and it is said that although Prime Minister Tōjō holds sovereign power and that a certain general is the leader

---

18. American troops landed on Tinian on July 24 and secured the island by August 2.

19. Tōyama Mitsuru (1855–1944) was a pioneering Japanese ultranationalist who consistently espoused Japanese expansion on the Asian mainland beginning in the 1880s, when he founded the Gen'yōsha, up to his death in 1944.

of Japan at the moment, Mr. Tōyama was, in fact, the most powerful person in Japan today, not a politician or a military man.[20] Everyone depended on, and was manipulated by, him. Rumor has it that only Mr. Tōyama could appear before the divine emperor and act as he pleased, or even ignore the emperor. One of the things he said still rings in my ears. It was something he said after the war started, when no one said much about America as the enemy: it was his words "I have fought the enemy America all my life." I don't know what was behind this statement, but apparently Mr. Tōyama believed that America was his enemy from the time he was sentient and lived with this as his credo. I can't help but think that if the actions of Mr. Tōyama, who went off in one direction and lacked intellectual discernment, caused Japan to be ravaged in the way it has been, rather than ask about his responsibility for this, we must not blame the Japanese for their stupidity. I also was truly sorry that Mr. Tōyama died. [Now that] the specter of Japan's imminent defeat has appeared before our eyes, I am sorry that Mr. Tōyama will not have to face his country's ultimate sadness and that he alone was able to say and do what he pleased. His dying comfortably in a hospital bed was too easy. In pictures he is always wearing Japanese clothes, and some Japanese worshiped him like a god. At ninety he died today, without taking responsibility.

October 19, 1944, Thursday

When I turned on the radio tonight, the announcers were making a big deal about an evening of victory celebrations on Taiwan, but Taiwan had actually been attacked, and there was no celebration. I couldn't help but feel contempt for the authorities who treat us as though we were stupid.

February 25, 1945, Sunday

As had been predicted, the enemy attacked the imperial capital early this morning, with six hundred carrier-based aircraft and 130 B-29s.[21] It was just as the Mass my husband and Emii were attending ended, and they were on their way home. I also worried about Nobukazu, who had gone off to work at a factory, and when he returned safely just after five, I breathed a sigh of relief. My biggest fear is that the family will be separated during an air raid. During today's air raid, my nephew Toshimitsu had to evacuate. Because it was broad daylight,

---

20. "Black curtain" (J. *kuromaku*) refers to those who control the situation from behind the scenes.

21. Early that morning, 172 B-29s bombed Tokyo. See Carter and Mueller, *Combat Chronology*, 582.

we couldn't see the flames reflected in the sky, but apparently the *shitamachi* area got hit pretty hard.[22] After the all-clear sounded, the radio reported that the palace had been damaged but announced over and over that both the emperor and the empress were safe. It is both amazing and frightening to a Japanese to imagine bombs falling on the palace. How much of what we're getting in the public reports in the newspapers and on the radio directed at the general population is true? We wondered about this because sometimes we couldn't believe the reports, and it just made us more uneasy.

March 8, 1945, Thursday

Yesterday I had an unexpected phone call from Mr. Masamune's wife.[23] She's come down from Karuizawa and will be returning right away, but she asked if I have time, could I come over to see her? So at about seven thirty this morning, I went to her house in Ōokayama.[24] It was the first time we had met since she evacuated to Karuizawa.[25] Neither one of us knows what tomorrow will bring. Perhaps because of our feelings at being able to meet again, safely, in a world like ours — we were so happy at the instant we met that our eyes teared up. With nearly everything shipped to the evacuation site, the inside of her house felt like a vacant house and was lonely. As always, we sat in the sun room and were having one of those conversations that never ends when, rather inconveniently, an air-raid siren sounded. I decided to say good-bye and start for home. As I rushed home, I prayed for our houses and my own safety. When I got there, my husband was typing out the pledge for his Catholic baptism on the coming eleventh.

March 10, 1945, Saturday

It was the morning of a long-awaited dawn.[26] After twelve last night we were wakened by air-raid warning sirens, and when we looked in the direction they were coming from, the sky over Mr. Kume's mountain — on the north side of our house —

---

22. *Shitamachi* refers to the area in central Tokyo located within the Yamanote Railway Line. The lower-middle-class and working-class people living there have a distinctive language and cultural style. As in other cities in early modern Japan, *shitamachi* was where warriors forced artisans and merchants to live and work, away from where the warriors lived.

23. The wife of Masamune Hakuchō (1879–1962), a renowned naturalist writer.

24. Ōokayama is in Meguro Ward.

25. Karuizawa is a resort town in the Japan Alps where before the war, well-born and rich Japanese spent the summer.

26. Early on the morning of March 10, 279 B-29s attacked Tokyo, dropping nearly 20,000 tons of incendiary bombs on a twelve-square-mile area of central Tokyo, killing 83,793 people and injuring 40,918. See Carter and Mueller, *Combat Chronology*, 594.

was red. Everyone was standing at their windows looking out. I was shocked by the size of this air raid, which covered a broader area than the earlier ones had. I was speechless and could only watch as the fires died down. From time to time, flames appeared in the stand of pines in Mr. Kume's garden. In the last air raid, one part of Mr. Kume's mountain had burned, but this time nearly one whole side of the mountain appeared to be painted bright red. It was probably just past three o'clock. After the enemy planes left, the color of the flames reflected in the sky got paler, and I took off my air-defense gear and was about to go to bed when someone knocked furiously at the front entryway. I hurriedly opened the door, and two Sacred Heart Girls High School students stumbled in. "Both the Sacred Heart Girls High School and the convent have been hit. Please let us stay here!" "What? You say Sacred Heart has been hit?" Both my husband and I were in shock. It had been that close. Because the fires had come so close, I thought it was really odd that no one was aware of them. Apparently the splendid Sacred Heart buildings stood out among the surrounding buildings and did not burn down until the end. I took the two girls up to the Japanese room on the second floor, made a bed for them, and had them get some rest. Then I had my husband bike right away to Sacred Heart. All the trains running to Sacred Heart had stopped, and the two girls were lucky to get to our house. As they were escaping to areas where there were no fires, they remembered Dr. Takahashi's house and ran as if in a dream. The other people living in Sacred Heart dormitories, all of them, fled in every possible direction, and the girls said they didn't know who was where. Because they were separated, physically, from their parents and living in dormitories, feelings of pity welled up in my chest, and I felt so sorry for these two girls that I wanted to hug them. With just the clothes they were wearing and with no time to bring anything else, they shook, crying. Just when it began to feel like dawn, my husband returned. "When I got there," he reported, "Sacred Heart was already a sea of fire, and I couldn't get very close. It seems that the chapel was saved. All the sisters living in the convent were safely evacuated to the nearby houses of parishioners, and I was glad to hear no one was hurt. And I also gave them the names of the two students who sought refuge at our house." Just three or four hours before Sacred Heart burned down, my husband had gone there to chat with Father Rogan about arrangements for his baptism on the eleventh.

When dawn came, I hurriedly made breakfast, and my husband and I went to visit the homes where the people from the convent had been evacuated. We took anything and everything, worn-out and old things — black stockings, black cotton, and gauze, bandages, and absorbent cotton from the clinic. Perhaps be-

The convent before it burned down on March 9–10, 1945. Courtesy of Sacred Heart Girls School.

cause they are servants of God, everyone looked cheerful and seemed energetic, which made us happy.

My sense is that this air raid hit more than half of Tokyo, and for the first time, I began to be afraid.

March 11, 1945, Sunday

The chapel at Sacred Heart, thanks to the sisters' heroic efforts, miraculously escaped being destroyed, although parts of the hallway had caught fire. After hearing how the sisters had fought the flames in that sea of fire and protected the chapel, our respect for them deepened.

The chapel was saved and the hallway was kept from burning down, but they were now full of people, and my husband's baptism was impossible. So it took place at Saint Miki in Azabu. Since there was no public transportation, the rest of the family could not go, and my husband went alone on his bicycle to be baptized.

April 10, 1945, Tuesday

It is finally cherry blossom–viewing time, but there aren't many blossoms this year, and it's rather sad. Yet the fact that there are any cherry blossoms at all for us to see this year is rather unexpected. It occurred to me that for the several tens of thousands of people who died in the bombing raids because they were in the home islands and not in the battle zones, last year's cherry blossoms were their last. As I did last year, I looked at our cherry tree from the Japanese room on the second floor. I never get tired of looking at it, and I wondered wistfully whether I'll see these blossoms in next year's flower-viewing season. I looked at them for some time, lost in my thoughts. Just when you think the cherry trees have begun to bloom, the petals begin to scatter, one by one, even when no wind is blowing. For no reason at all, I began to cry.

April 15, 1945, Sunday

It seems that even in Christian countries, there is no Sunday during a war. An air-raid warning was issued at about 9:30 in the evening; air-raid sirens went off at about ten; and there was a report that two hundred enemy planes were attacking the imperial capital.[27] Following the military's orders, we painted white buildings black, were careful about burning grass, and observed complete blackouts. Despite this, the enemy comes repeatedly to reduce the city to ashes, one ward after another. Up to now, the areas of destruction have been mostly where there are big factories or the densely populated *shitamachi* district, and although terrifying, I simply watched from a distance. The other day, however, the convent at Sacred Heart was hit, and tonight as I look down the hill in front of our house and beyond it to a valleylike depression and what looks like a hill, one part of the area is in flames, which makes the burning hill float up in the night sky. I finally feel the danger threatening us. I thought about when the next squadron of attackers comes how it'll be our turn to be hit, and we'll have to sit quietly in underground rooms, not our own rooms, and if we venture out, we'll get hit. We have absolutely nowhere to go.

The mountain in the Kume garden, right across from us, could be climbed from the street, and when one climbed it, the top was level, and so, as though by prior arrangement, people were evacuating there in a steady stream. Feeling that the Kume mountain was the safest place, we decided to vacate the house and go there as well.

At the foot of this mountain, a tunnel had been dug, which served as an air-raid shelter. I had long intended to take a look at it, and when I did go over at one point, it was really awful. There was human excrement everywhere near the entrance to the tunnel and soiled papers were scattered about, and I doubted that anyone would be able to get even one foot in. I accepted the Japanese people's lack of public virtue but was speechless.

It was lucky I had gone to take a look at the tunnel. It would have been terrible

---

27. That evening 109 B-29s bombed industrial targets in Tokyo, and 194 B-29s bombed similar targets in nearby Kawasaki. See Carter and Mueller, *Combat Chronology*, 629.

if I stepped into the shelter in the middle of the darkness not knowing what I now know. So although there was a tunnel just down the hill from our house, we didn't go in. With our bodies exposed, if even only one fragment fell, it would be a direct hit, and this made us uneasy and frightened us.

It appeared that the area being bombed was growing. The sky was enveloped in black smoke, and the fires on the ground were reflected in the sky, painting it black and red, an indescribable color. Although we couldn't see the enemy planes, we could hear them, and their tremendous roar intensified our fear. Was it safer to go right or to dodge to the left? We couldn't decide even that. I slid down into a hollow clutching Emii, and we made ourselves as small as possible and prayed to God. Where had all the people come from? The top of Kume's mountain was crowded with people fleeing the fires. The red and black burning night sky pushed people on the ground into the dawn brightness, and among the evacuees milling about in fear was a solitary housewife who was about fifty. She was well dressed and held a long sword in her left hand and a small crepe bundle in her right. She stood apart from the crowd of people with knapsacks and beggar bags slung over their shoulders. As I looked at her, I noticed a youth with a beautiful face at her side. Were they parent and child? I didn't know, but they stood out. When I asked about them, it seemed they were of noble birth.

We weren't able to hear anything over the thunderous roar resonating around us, and because we couldn't hear a radio broadcast, we simply waited for the all-clear siren to sound. We got irritated when it didn't sound, but then someone said, "It sounded! It sounded!" and everyone let down their guard and began to go down the mountain.

We breathed a big sigh of relief, celebrated our surviving unscathed, and went back into our house. People who seemed to be victims stopped on the road in front of our house and stared at the sky over the hill across the way where the flames were still raging. I heard a male voice just below the window of our study saying, "Look, those eggs, I should have made you eat them last night. . . ." Without thinking, I craned my neck to look out, and it appeared to be a father with two children, aged five or six, in tow. Seeing this made my chest hurt.

April 25, 1945, Wednesday

It appears that the Soviet army marched into Berlin two or three days ago.[28] While both American and English forces continue to occupy the important

---

28. Takahashi's information is incorrect. After several failed attempts, Soviet forces succeeded in reaching Berlin's outer defenses on April 21 and surrounded the city on April 25. Lieutenant General Karl Weildling surrendered on May 2.

points, they also have gone north to Berlin, and thus if the fate of Germany has been decided this early, I can't think it is good.

May 15, 1945, Tuesday

Nearly all primary school children and almost all the elderly have been evacuated from Tokyo; the young people have been drafted; and various specialists and scholars have been pressed into service and sent to the front.[29] Those like our children who just graduated from middle school — one is a girl and the other is a boy who is too young to be drafted — have been directed to work sites and put to work as part of the state's mobilization program. When Emii returned from school today, she said she would have to accompany evacuated children as a student monitor.

May 24, 1945, Thursday

I thought for sure that our house would be hit during the next air raid, but I was surprised by the one that took place from midnight until dawn this morning.[30] The other day, looking west from my house, the hill across the way was just a line, and the sky was burning red. In the air raid this morning, the fires consumed the hill, came down this side of it, and destroyed the valley below. Our house is midway down the slope of the opposing hill, not far from the top, and the Meguro River is at the bottom of our hill. Somehow the river seemed to stop the spreading fires, and the basin separating us from the river was a sea of fire. Those fleeing the fire came up our hill in a steady stream passing right in front of our house.

I heard a *za, za, za, za* that I believed was the sound of falling incendiary bombs, and all at once fires broke out over a wide area. What shall I call this scene — heartbreaking? Tragic? I was witnessing the conflict of people against people in the human world, and it should not have been happening. I felt a fear tinged with bitterness. We had no time to sleep a wink before it was dawn. After carrying water and lugging our things around, there was no time to clean up, and the house was a mess when Nobukazu, who had been at a work site, suddenly showed up. He came home because his departure wasn't until tomorrow. The direction of the fires made him think that our house had been hit.

When he got to Meguro Station, he thought that if things were as they always

---

29. By April 1945, the last of the children were evacuated from Japanese cities.
30. On that day, 520 B-29s attacked Tokyo, dropping incendiary bombs on both industrial and residential areas south of the imperial palace. See Carter and Mueller, *Combat Chronology*, 654.

were, he would go downhill and after half a block, where the road angled left, he would see our house. But today our red-roofed house was not visible through the dense smoke. Convinced that our house had been hit, he descended the hill in a daze, and as he did, it appeared before his eyes, still standing, and he was ecstatic. Both my younger sister's house in Ōokayama and the empty Masamune house were hit in the air raid, as we learned from a phone call from my younger brother's family in Ōmori.[31]

May 26, 1945, Saturday

The enemy is persistent. The air raid at dawn quickly moved across the Meguro River, and the Hinode Girls High School, which was located in a basin just half a block away, burned down. The fires were so intense that if you poured water over yourself, your clothes would dry out in no time. My husband shouted in a shrill voice while carrying buckets of water, "It's all over. Everyone, keep your eye on this house." The neighborhood association's emergency bell was clanging madly. Good God! The house of a neighborhood association member caught fire, and we passed buckets from hand to hand, but this turned out to be a mistake by the person on duty. Relieved, we returned home.

That today's air raid spared our house was like a dream. A lot of incendiary bombs fell on the five or six houses in front of ours, and we fought the fires that broke out and worked to put them out, narrowly escaping danger ourselves. After the all-clear sounded, we walked around the neighborhood and discovered that a one-block area that formed a circle around our house had survived. It looked as though we had been encircled by fire. The strangeness of our being spared made me feel a deep reverence.

From the time the all-clear sounded, the injured were carried one after another to the relief station. At the time of the air raid on the twenty-fourth, the relief center headquarters could not handle all the injured, so three patients were brought to our house. This morning, too, the injured were brought to us. I heard the injured were being lined up in the hallways at the relief center headquarters. At our house, which had been made an auxiliary relief center, there was no rest, even after the all-clear sounded. I was exhausted both mentally and physically, and it was already past seven in the morning when I crawled into bed on the verge of collapse. When I was finally able to lie down, physical pain and nervous fatigue mingled, and I had just entered a kind of fog when I heard my younger

31. Takahashi's younger brother, Nobuo, lived in Ōmori, which is on the southern edge of Tokyo. See her 8/10/45 entry.

sister's voice. "Older sister, you were lucky, weren't you?" She had come to see how we had fared. Her house is in the basin on the other side of the Meguro River, and she thought for sure we had been hit and, in fact, had come to offer her sympathy. Sparks were still raining down from both sides of the road, and it was really hot, making the road impassable, and she thought she might not make it. I was surprised she had come.

Even our neighbor's house had caught fire, and it appears we had fought off the fires and saved it. From my younger sister's house, it looked as though everything on our hill had burned down, and she was sure we had been hit. We rejoiced over both of us surviving the air raid unharmed.

Our house is on high ground, and because of all the fires, water stopped coming out of the tap. My younger sister's house is on low ground and still had water, and so although it was some distance away, we went over to get water. Some neighborhood association houses had wells, but since everyone was drawing from them, the water in the wells had no chance to accumulate, and there was a real hubbub as everyone had to get water from others. My husband calculated that the wells would not be used in the evening, and he loaded buckets on the red wagon he had bought for Nobukazu when we were in America, crossed the Meguro River, and went over to Meguro Primary School. He scooped up water running out of the water pumps in the burned-out areas, and made several trips to fill our bathtub. In the evening, the electricity went out completely, and we lit candles and passed the time thinking forlorn thoughts.

May 27, 1945, Sunday

A truck from the city came to pick up the patients at our clinic. As I watched the crummy old truck from the second-floor window, it was hard for me to see the patients, lined up like cordwood in the bed of the truck, as living beings. I had never seen such pathetic figures, not even in medieval hell screens. Humans had done this to other humans.

Mr. Masamune suddenly appeared with a companion in our darkened entryway, where the electricity didn't go on.[32] Apparently he came down from Karuizawa today to see the burned-out remains of the Ōokayama house. We had a simple dinner in the candle-lit dining room for Mr. Masamune and his companion, a Mr. Horiki. Because Mr. Horiki's house had not burned down, only Mr. Masamune stayed over.

Life in a city with no gas, electricity, or water is sad. From the point of view of the victims, however, we were kings, and our situation was enviable.

---

32. See Takahashi's 3/8/45 entry.

June 17, 1945, Sunday

The plan was for Emii and the students going with her to Okaya to assemble at Sacred Heart at seven this morning, so she and her father attended Mass.[33] Since we decided she would go on to school after communion, without coming home, I made her a breakfast. But when my husband got back, he said Emii's departure time had changed and now would be in the evening. So Emii came home, and because our house was close to the station, the students were going to meet here. I was happy to have this unexpected time with her, although it was only a few short hours. Around the time we finished dinner, the students, accompanied by their mothers, who seemed to be feeling the same parental affection as we did, began to gather in front of our house. It was an evening graced with a bright moon. Emii stepped out through the inner entryway, stood in the road, and said, "Everyone, please line up here." Hearing that voice, I thought "Dear me!" and was quite moved. In an instant Emii had become an adult. Be strong! Be strong! Like the honorable heart of God. . . . I turned away from the moon and quickly wiped away tears. We decided to have Nobukazu stay with Emii and see her as far as Shinjuku. He got home just before midnight. And I prayed for her safe arrival at Okaya.

July 11, 1945, Wednesday

In this hell of unremitting anxiety and sadness that threatens us day after day, something completely unconnected with the war brought us pleasure and made us smile. We discovered that swallows had built a nest on the light fixture in the middle of the inner entryway and were raising cute babies.[34] Two or three days ago they all left the nest and flew away, and yesterday I wondered whether we would see them again. Just as I was thinking that, I discovered the yellow-beaked babies in the cherry tree in our yard.

When the parent birds brought food, the baby birds flapped their little wings, opened their yellow mouths wide, and gobbled it up. I didn't know whether other people's swallows were burned up in this human conflict, but the swallows who nested under our eaves were really lucky. I hear it's auspicious to have nesting swallows, and even though they dirtied the entryway, they were cute and made us smile.

---

33. There is an Okaya in both Gumma and Nagano prefectures, and it is not clear which was Emii's evacuation site.

34. Because the barn swallow habitually returns to the same nest year after year, it is thought to bring good fortune. In the Tokyo area, it appears in late March and leaves in the fall.

July 25, 1945, Wednesday

Just as I was thinking that only one enemy plane came today, half a large metal canister fell from the sky into the lot behind us, burying its nose in the dirt and scattering propaganda leaflets all over our neighbor's yard. Our neighborhood association went into a frenzy. The leaflet was an *ukiyo-e*-style picture of a woman with a cat or some tigerlike animal at her throat, and it had a caption that read "Deceived by military authorities."

There was a great commotion because we had been told that whenever something dropped out of the sky, no matter what, it should be taken to the police and not shown to anyone. There was a real ruckus.

I went to the *shitamachi* area for the first time in quite a while and surveyed the damage. Tokyo has changed completely. Fires usually leave charred wood strewn about, but the air raids left completely burned-out remains that were gray with a faint red hue.

Looking out over the gray plain, only concrete buildings survived, but they were hollowed out and rather pathetic structures. In the distance, fleecy white clouds floated in a cobalt blue sky above a distant forest. The devastation was so bad that I wondered whether I was really in the center of Tokyo. Since the city was, with the exception of a few government ministries, mostly wooden structures, it had been completely leveled. Many hundreds of years ago this area probably was an uninhabited plain like this, but what I saw seemed fantastic and like a dream.

Apparently the enemy came today to bomb the Osaka area.[35]

August 9, 1945, Thursday

This morning Nobukazu went off to Gōra and returned in the evening.[36] When he finished dinner, he had to leave again—this time to board a nine o'clock train to Karuizawa, his school's evacuation site. And so after he finished dinner, he left the house. It was about seven.

The same sort of strange bomb that was dropped on Hiroshima three days ago was dropped on Nagasaki today, and it was wiped out. This bomb possesses extraordinary power. Photographs showed that Chinese ideographs written in black on signs at train stations had burned, and it was explained that white things wouldn't burn. Up to now, we've been ordered not to wear white garments, not even when it was hot, because they were easy for enemy planes to see. Now we're warned not to wear black garments because they burn easily.

---

35. On July 24, 570 B-29s bombed several cities, including Osaka. See Carter and Mueller, *Combat Chronology*, 679.

36. Gōra is located in Kanagawa Prefecture.

So what in the world is safe for us to wear? We don't know anymore. The thought of a single aircraft destroying a large city in an instant is driving us to nervous breakdowns, and I feel as though we have no choice but to die or go crazy. I can't help but hate those responsible for placing human beings in this situation and continuing the war. At this point, continuing the war will save neither us nor our country. When one comes to this point and when those responsible realize that they have no escape and contemplate the punishments they will surely receive, I believe they will continue the war because they simply don't know whether or not fighting until the last Japanese falls is a good idea. In this country, where human morality is based on the relationship between masters and followers, we submit to our leaders' will and simply do as we are told. Because ours is a country in which each person lacks any kind of individuality and because our citizenry doesn't realize that they themselves have the power to revere their own individuality, we have fought this unprofitable war right up to the present, muttering all the while, "We will win, we will win." At the very start of the war, Japanese declared in unison, "Today we take pride in our good fortune to be born a Japanese." I myself could only lament "my misfortune at being born a Japanese today."

If Japanese had not been cursed by this sort of feudalistic thinking, I believe we could have expected our country to have ended the war sooner than Germany or Italy did. At the beginning of the war, I predicted that we would lose in the way that we have and worried about it. My arguing that we should have stopped the war at Singapore was an earnest and heartfelt plea. Those of us who thought this way were called traitors; our beliefs were regarded as unthinkable; and we were seen as potential spies. I blamed this on the ignorance fostered by feudalistic thinking. No matter what, I can't accept the fact that my own life has been taken from me for the sake of the lawless promoters of this feudalistic way of thinking, and I am not happy about it.

August 10, 1945, Friday

In the afternoon, Nobuo came over from Ōmori, and as soon as he sat down in the living room, he said, "There's 'big news,' but it's absolutely a secret.[37] We've been saved." "What?" we asked, moving closer to him. Lowering his voice, Nobuo explained, "Apparently Japan will surrender sometime around the fifteenth." "What? Is this really true?" Having been stretched to the limit psychologically and having known only disappointment, my sudden sense of relief did not allow me to believe what I was hearing. If this were true, what kind of happiness might

---

37. See Takahashi's 5/24/45 entry.

this be? I thought I must share the news with Emii and Nobukazu right away, but I certainly couldn't do this in writing. Nor could I tell them something that was hearsay. Today Nobuo delivered the message of a gracious God. With our long, long suffering, I had begun to lose the strength to endure and feared that my life was being threatened by my passivity. As I looked ahead, despair was all I could see. And now, despite all this, it seems we will be rescued.

The people around me know nothing about the surrender, and their faces are as they were yesterday, severe and pitiful. I feel so rejuvenated by my happiness that I worry that although I'm doing my best to conceal my secret thoughts, I may unwittingly relax the expression on my face.

August 14, 1945, Tuesday

A radio broadcast informed us that there would be an important announcement at noon tomorrow which we should listen to. Finally, the long-awaited day has come. When we heard this, we breathed a deep sigh of relief.

We went to bed in a relaxed mood for the first time in a long while and attended to the lives we had regained and fell asleep. But in the middle of the night the sound of sirens shattered our dreams. When we put our ears to the radio, we learned that 250 enemy aircraft were attacking Japan.[38] It was as senseless as having a pistol thrust into one's body. What was this? I had no idea what was going on, and the all-clear siren sounded at 2:57 a.m. There was no damage anywhere. We relaxed and agreed that the enemy's coming when we were quietly asleep was probably "the grand finale of the parade."

August 15, 1945, Wednesday

Many people believe the rumor that the emperor's important broadcast at noon probably will be to encourage the general population because the war has intensified and an enemy invasion is imminent. Having prepared themselves for the moment when the enemy invaded and practiced attacking with bamboo spears and overturning tanks, the people said the long-awaited moment has come and assumed fighting poses. As for starting the war—I couldn't help but pity the people of this country: before they knew what was happening, they were led into the war, and even now the war was about to be ended without their knowing it.

This morning the usual broadcast of last night's fires was not heard, and I wondered why not. It was reported that 250 carrier-based aircraft attacked and

---

38. More than seven hundred B-29s bombed assorted targets in Japan, and thirty-nine more mined the harbors at Hamada, Miyazu, and Nanao, as well as the Shimonoseki Strait. See Carter and Mueller, *Combat Chronology*, 688.

that there were hostilities until a little before midnight. Would there really be a broadcast ending the war? I began to have my doubts. In order to hear the broadcast at noon, we had our lunch early. When everyone gathered in the living room, Mr. Iwase, who worked at the neighborhood bank, came over during his lunch break because he wanted to hear the broadcast on our radio.[39] Hearing the emperor's voice, a rarity in earlier ages, was an awe-inspiring event for a Japanese.

Noon arrived. I don't remember who got up first, but everyone rose to their feet in front of the radio. The emperor read the surrender proclamation without feeling, gravely and in a trembling voice. As each word and phrase was etched on my heart, my eyes got quite warm and tears welled up, and I had to wipe them with a handkerchief.

Sadness and happiness. Happiness and sadness. I wondered how I should separate these mixed emotions and then how to rejoin them. Today, now that the end has come, you'd think we'd have a lot to say to one another, but I was not in the mood to say much to anyone.

39. Iwase is married to Takahashi's younger sister. See her 9/13/44 entry.

Until the War Ended

Yoshizawa Hisako was born in the Fukagawa district in Tokyo on January 21, 1918. We have little information about her childhood and education but know that she graduated from Bunka gakuin (Culture Academy) with a degree in the liberal arts. In 1941 she began working as a stenographer and lived in Asagaya, just west of Shinjuku in central Tokyo. At some point during the war she became the personal secretary of Furuya Tsunetake (1908–1984), a man with literary interests. When Furuya was drafted in November 1944, he asked Yoshizawa to keep a daily record during his absence, which she did. Her last entry was dated August 21, 1945, six days after the emperor's surrender announcement.

In 1946, Yoshizawa married Furuya and had a very successful career as a feature writer, specializing in women's issues, domestic life, and the home. She has written fifty-four books to date, including *Utsukushii kurashi o anata ni* (*For a Beautiful Life*), *Kaji o tanoshimu watakushi no hōhō* (*My Methods for Enjoying Household Chores*), and *Toshi o toru tanoshimi* (*The Pleasures of Growing Old*).

Yoshizawa's diary was first published in January 1947 under her husband's name. Exactly why it was published under his name is unclear, and it may have had to do with the censorship policies of the Occupation authorities or perhaps his reputation in the publishing world. Her diary is included in Agawa Hiroyuki et al., eds., *Shōwa sensō bungaku zenshū* (Tokyo: Shūeisha, 1972), vol. 14, *Shimin no nikki*, 322–357.

November 30, 1944

It started raining in the morning and didn't let up all day.

I felt uneasy when I left the house. The people boarding the train from Shinjuku Station and beyond looked like victims.[1] I couldn't bear to look at them. It was painful to see children with bare feet exposed to the winter rains.

Bombs have fallen on Kanda, Kōtō, and Shiba.[2] Apparently incendiary bombs fell just thirty houses away from O's house.[3] They say the bombs looked like falling wind chimes.[4] The explosions shattered the windows at Kanda Station. The destruction was considerable in Mitoshirochō, Nishikimachi, Kandabashi, the Kamakura shoreline, Tamachi, and Tsukasachō. For no particular reason I pitied those searching for random things in the burned-out ruins. Their harsh voices were offensive, and there were many sightseers. My head started to ache.

I was much relieved that the railway lines were not damaged.

It made me think about "happiness." Perhaps because I live in the midst of this uncertainty that persists day after day, my own life has been greatly simplified. When I examine my own life, I find that the household goods I'm using now are those of a peaceful age. When I think of the clothes boxes and wicker trunks of warrior times, it's clear that things like present-day dressers were invented to arrange and separate one's belongings in a peaceful age not riven by conflict. I *think it's wonderful* that we've been given a chance to reflect on the complexity of these lives in which we've grown accustomed to using these sorts of goods.[5] November is already over.

December 3, 1944

On Sunday, we had clear skies for the first time in a while. I spent the morning tidying up my dresser. I packed kimonos and other things into trunks and made emergency moving boxes and emergency food packets.

Just before two o'clock, an air-raid warning sounded, and a bombing raid followed. The sky was beautiful today, and I could see the American planes clearly. They were at too high an altitude for me to hear their engines and flew

---

1. Yoshizawa is referring to stations on the Chūō Line between Shinjuku and Tokyo Station.

2. Twenty-four B-29 bombers bombed industrial areas and docks in Tokyo on November 29–30, 1945. See Carter and Mueller, *Combat Chronology*, 509.

3. Yoshizawa does not identify O, but she mentions him often in her diary.

4. Yoshizawa is referring to the long, thin M-60 incendiary bomb, which was first used against targets in Tokyo on November 29, 1944.

5. Passages in italics are emphasized in the original.

along at a leisurely pace in single- or multiple-plane formations.[6] For nearly two hours they came, more and more of them. I pulled out something that needed mending, and since there was no take-cover signal, I just kept sewing. Bombs appeared to be falling nearby because fire trucks sped by. Glass was breaking. I could hear the sound of things falling—just like in the newsreels. The American planes were directly overhead, but nothing fell. I was entranced by their glittering, white, and beautiful bodies. All we could do was to look at the advancing American planes, which seemed to be pulling the moving patterns of flying clouds. I wasn't troubled at all. I just thought this was war. The radio said that five planes were shot down and two airmen bailed out. It seemed strange to me that the enemy, flying over the skies of the main island, would entrust their lives to parachutes. Was this national character? Or was it differences in the instilled ways of thinking about life and the nation? At this time I reflected on the fact that my attitude toward life and death had become frivolous.

Around the time the sun began to set, the air-raid alert was called off, and the setting sun shone on the areas that had burned so furiously, as though nothing at all had happened. When I think of how the sun will continue to shine for several thousand, or several tens of thousands, of years, I can't help feeling that humans are rather pathetic creatures. No doubt the sun is unimpressed by all the great things achieved in Tokyo. After all, the people in the planes were trying to exterminate those of us on the ground as we entered and exited air-raid shelters. And the sun probably will continue to shine in this way without changing.

December 14, 1944

Recently, I have been anticipating nighttime air raids and have been going to sleep earlier than usual.[7] It's a shame that I'm spending the long winter nights unproductively, but it can't be helped.

There was a report that at about three o'clock this morning, a few American planes circled Edogawa Ward, dropping incendiary bombs.[8]

Recently we have been making preparations based on the direction of the American planes' attack. If there is an air raid, I'm terrified, and I can't help complaining.

---

6. Nearly seventy B-29s attacked Nakajima factories in Ōta and Musashino on December 3, and Yoshizawa does not hear their engines because they were flying at more than 20,000 feet. See Carter and Mueller, *Combat Chronology*, 513.

7. B-29s bombed industrial targets and dockyards in Tokyo on November 24, 27, and 29 and December 3. See Carter and Mueller, *Combat Chronology*, 505, 508, 509, 513.

8. There is no record of an Allied attack on targets in Tokyo on this date.

It can't be helped, can it, that I always think first about my own well-being. Nor can it be helped that I get angry at those who maintain their own daily lives and complain only about the reality in front of them.

December 19, 1944

Was it because the cold suddenly appeared? This morning we had a heavy frost, which made the leaves on all the trees in the garden droop. Because their blooming seasons are close at hand, the camellias and daphne have red, swelling buds.

It made me acutely aware of how naturally perfect the vitality of living things is. Yet when I compare the vitality of the grasses and trees, which never forget the seasons, with the vicissitudes of human life, the grasses and trees seem more reliable than humans, which makes me realize that I may not be feeling what I should be. We had air raids again today, and I was quite moved by the thought that the newly formed buds might drop and just stared at them.[9]

January 6, 1945

Things have taken a turn for the worse at Leyte, and Luzon will become the next decisive battlefield, which makes me wonder what will happen militarily after that. I haven't been very pessimistic, but after reading the newspapers every day, my views have gradually changed bit by bit. There now are full-scale attacks on Taiwan and Kyushu, and some say the day is approaching when both places will become battlefields. This is definitely no longer just idle speculation.

Although we're now told at work to give everything we have, I worry every day about whether this will be enough. The factories don't have enough raw materials. Factory owners have to use the workers sent to them as mobilized labor, but poor management has caused problems—all this is very depressing.

The fatigue brought on by the sleep deprivation caused by the air raids is leading to a brittle sort of self-interest that makes boarding and getting off trains frightening. Try as I might to remain calm, my nerves are on edge.

Today, a friend who recently joined my company reported that her aunt doesn't clean house much because she said, "If [the house] catches fire during an air raid, it won't matter." Recently, life in the capital has been "day-to-day," as they say, which sums up what we city folks are feeling.

---

9. There is no record of an Allied attack on targets in Tokyo on this date. But seventy-three B-29s attacked aircraft factories in Nagoya, which may have triggered the air-raid alerts in Tokyo. See Carter and Mueller, *Combat Chronology*, 524.

January 12, 1945

Last night again, we had three nighttime air raids.[10]

Recently, we've been getting up so many times during the night that our bodies are showing signs of abnormality. Recently I've gotten used to sleeping with my *monpe* and everything else on so I'm able to sleep soundly. At two o'clock and then at four, my eyes suddenly opened, and I waited for an air-raid signal.

How will the war turn out?

Most people no longer believe in victory. My only thought is that it will be pathetic if we're defeated. Even rural folk believe that if we're as deadlocked as this and still fall short of our goals, there's no reason to think we can win. Listening to the conversations of people at the company, I gather that we Japanese have obediently done what the army and the government have instructed us to do. So if we're defeated, the authorities will not say that it's because the Japanese were bad. When things go well, they say, "Leave the war to the soldiers." When things don't go well, it's an all-out war for every Japanese. People say this just won't do.

What should we do about the ambivalence that people have about the war? Of course, our rulers are depressed, but they have done nothing to clarify the progress of the war. Is this because of conflict at the top of our government?

Recently, I haven't been able to stop being irritated not just at stupid people but also at those who just don't get it. When I become a little more important, I'll resolve this, but . . . my lack of sleep and the fatigue resulting from having to go out and deal with people have all come together and are getting to me. *Recently what has been most perplexing is my being criticized for complaining about [what is happening] to the country and for my words of concern about the present; I am criticized for making judgments based on my own limited knowledge. My critics ask whether I am really Japanese. I feel that things are out of control. I think it's a shame and realize that it can't be helped.*

January 14, 1945

T visited.[11] I asked how everyone viewed the war. She said no one will talk about it. *They seem only to talk about it.* Apparently everyone thinks this way, and some say that when we acknowledge that Japan will be defeated, we will deal on the black market.

S's wife came over at about ten o'clock to return charcoal she had borrowed.[12]

---

10. There is no record of Allied attacks on Tokyo or nearby areas.
11. Yoshizawa does not identify T.
12. Yoshizawa does not identify S, who appears to be a neighbor.

She said she was going off to stand in line for *udon* scraps. With a ten-person household to support, she stands in line to buy *udon* scraps to supplement their rations. When I calculated the time and energy she expends doing this, I thought I must do something. It bothered me that I felt powerless, and I was troubled by this.

January 18, 1945

I recently made an interesting discovery.

When there's an air-raid warning, I feel like singing a song. I thought it was just me, but when I inquired at the company and elsewhere, it seems everyone has these feelings. Is it because we're excited? Or is this to distract ourselves?

January 22, 1945

Today I heard that the radish we grate for one meal now will be our vegetable allotment for three days. I've been thinking a lot lately about food. Doesn't having a lot of just one thing reduce our dissatisfaction? With staples, for example, there are no complaints when we have something or other instead of rice and when there is enough salt as a soy sauce substitute. No matter what the commodity, if it's available, all is well. But at present, with the fish we get every eighth day and the vegetables every fourth day in short supply, what are we to do?

For those of us who must work to defend the cities, self-sufficiency is impossible, and besides, there's no land. The control laws keep down the salaries of those of us who have to stay in the cities to work, and there are taxes to pay as well. There are distributions of bonds, but when taxes are raised even on the goods available, we have absolutely no way to buy things on the black market, although it looks as if the black market is prospering. Articles about the eighty-sixth session of the Diet will appear in the newspaper beginning today. Things are bad. I have the feeling there's nothing Japan can do at the moment. These days, everywhere I look, young, rosy-cheeked youths are being appointed executives of companies. It would be fine if Japanese politics, too, were entrusted to young, dangerously young, people.

January 28, 1945

Apparently there was quite a lot of damage from yesterday's air raid.[13] Today is really windy, and I worry about would happen if there were an air raid.

---

13. Seventy-six B-29s attacked Tokyo. See Carter and Mueller, *Combat Chronology,* 557.

An air-raid warning sounded. It appears to be one plane. It's probably surveying the damage from yesterday's air raid.

From ten in the evening until dawn there were three air raids, and five from noon. I'm gradually getting depressed. The words "I don't have any idea what my life will be like tomorrow" are hitting home. I have no desire for money or material things.

It's strange to think that I am more troubled by things caused by my fellow humans. I have no problems with the effects of what I do myself, and when I think about dying, humans seem pathetic. Aren't these the creatures who are the lords of the earth and the most advanced animals? Some other animals may be willing to die for their offspring. I regard with sadness this thing called war. If this much energy were expended for humanity and human culture, think of the wonderful things that would be possible. Sad thoughts filled my heart.

January 30, 1945

Although people may feel they don't need money or clothes, don't they still hate to lose what they do have?

Doesn't saying that all this is due to the war make people more and more dissatisfied? I find the current sort of exhaustion unbearable.

Today was a day of peace. I feel lucky to have survived for another day, *but I have absolutely no hope.*

February 20, 1945

It was clear. An air-raid siren wailed as I awoke at about seven o'clock.[14] I wondered whether these were carrier-based planes again and tensed up. Then there was a report that the warning was issued because vigilance was required in the south, and I breathed a sigh of relief and left the house.[15] The alert was called off. Today was mercifully quiet, which was fine.

Teacher Y's wife asked, "In the current situation, is it best to marshal what extra strength we have left and do something, or should we simply persevere with what spiritual reserves we have?"[16] Teacher Y replied, "Each option has merits and demerits, and our persevering reveals the exceptional spiritual power of the

---

14. Early that morning, 150 B-29s attacked Tokyo. See Carter and Mueller, *Combat Chronology*, 576.

15. "South" may refer to the dockyards and factories in southern Tokyo that were targeted in the bombing raid.

16. Since the 1930s, the government had disseminated the notion that the spiritual power or spirituality of the Japanese made them superior to all other peoples, and it was now arguing that this would enable the country to prevail over its enemies.

Japanese. The complete exhaustion of the nation's strength is extraordinary. Although it's exceedingly rational to do something, it's not a good idea in terms of spiritual power."[17] My concern is that having completely expended our physical strength, shouldn't we, for the time being, treasure our spiritual reserves? I am a Japanese, and I hope my country will flourish forever. After exhausting all our strength and throwing ourselves completely into the conflict, if we can't prevail, we must not think we've lost the strength to rise again.

Looking at the newspapers recently, the words "the way of the emperor exists within me" and "a way of humans exists within humans" *recur, but one must not regard these as words directed at an opponent who can't be opposed.* These sorts of conceptions are familiar to my fellow Japanese, but against an enemy who doesn't see things in this way, shouldn't Japanese hold views like those of our enemy? In Japan, there are Japanese reasons, and war is something one does with strength, and more strength. Although we might appeal to spirituality, it's already too late.

During air raids, I always think about the destruction of what humans believed would enhance their own lives and took many tens or hundreds of years to create. Why do humans exist? Creatures of the same species kill one another, and we lose our lives because of the machines that our fellow humans have made. I no longer understand why human beings and living things have been born.

However, when I think of the entire cosmos, human existence is an earthly achievement of the smallest magnitude.

I can no longer understand this.

February 22, 1945

This year snow has fallen heavily all over the country. The snow continued to fall all day, and when the wind picked up in the afternoon, it began to form drifts. It made me think of the February 26 incident and what happened on that day.[18] In the evening, a power outage stopped service on the outer track of the Yamanote Line and the Chūō Line, and after considering the situation and realizing that service was not likely to be resumed, I decided to take the city trolley home.[19] I

17. Yoshizawa does not identify Teacher Y.

18. On February 26, 1936, 1,400 men of the First Division of the Imperial Japanese Army attempted a coup d'état: they attacked several cabinet ministers, including the prime minister and imperial officials, and demanded the formation of a new cabinet, one that would implement their proposed reforms. The emperor refused to condone their actions and instead ordered that the coup be put down. The conspirators were tried, and seven were executed.

19. The Chūō and Yamanote lines are the two major commuter rail lines in Tokyo.

left Sudamachi at 5:00 p.m. and arrived at Shinjuku at 7:40 p.m.[20] The national railways were said to be running, so I went up to the platform. The train was late, and the crush of people was terrible. I couldn't get on until 9:30 p.m., and when I did and breathed a sigh of relief, we were let off at the next station, Okubo. It took until 10:00 p.m. to get to Higashi-Nakano, and then we stopped in front of Nakano Station and waited for some time but the train didn't leave. A few people jumped out through the windows, and when the doors finally opened, we jumped down too. I worried that there might be an air-raid warning and was very happy when there wasn't one. By this time, it was 11:00 p.m. The trains were not reliable, and I had no choice but to go to M's aunt's place.[21] Because M's aunt was in charge of the house during M's absence, I felt that it was not up to me to open it, and it bothered me, but I had no choice. Her aunt had been asleep but got up and was gracious. I was grateful and slept for a bit.

Here are my impressions of the day. On the platform at Shinjuku Station, when the trains were late and couldn't be boarded, the female station attendant announced in a slightly hysterical and high-pitched voice, "Because of an accident, the trains are running a little late, and the next train has left Yotsuya. If you are not able to get on this one, please wait for the next one." People were not the least bit convinced, and they looked more and more irritated. After some time, perhaps because the female attendant had been replaced, a male voice announced, "The trains will be coming very quickly, so please step back and wait." Once again, no one believed this, and everyone burst out laughing. The situation called for some humor.

I heard a rumor that our gas would be turned off tomorrow, and I had a premonition that something, an incident of some kind, would occur in the not so distant future.

February 26, 1945

It was clear. I was deeply moved as I looked at the expanse of burned-out buildings.[22] It was an area that bore the imprint of the many years that countless numbers of people had spent there. I was sad, too, because the coffee shop we used to go to burned down. Living each day amid this destruction has become unbearable. Is this natural selection?

---

20. It appears that Yoshizawa worked in Sudamachi and took the Chūō Line to and from work.

21. Yoshizawa does not identify M.

22. Two days earlier, on February 24, 172 B-29s attacked Tokyo, dropping incendiary bombs and causing extensive damage. See Carter and Mueller, *Combat Chronology*, 582.

Seeing figures trudging along in *tabi* on snow-covered roads and piling burned futon on carts, noticing people's blackened faces and hands, and witnessing the movement of troops, *somehow I can't feel that our country is winning the war. After all is said and done, I may not be able to bear the war any longer. I can't live a life without hope. While waging war with the very fate of the country at stake, not to have any chance of success is to have no hope.* I thought of Miyazawa Kenji's words, "Individual happiness is unattainable until the whole world has achieved happiness."

February 28, 1945

At the company today I heard the following rumors: the first one went like this. When someone mentioned that no one in the neighborhood association had eaten tofu for some time, the wife of a lieutenant who had just joined the group heard this and asked, "Hasn't anyone had any tofu? In my house we eat it every day. Shall I order some?" She made a call and a truck full of tofu arrived. Everyone in the neighborhood was furious. The second rumor went like this. Someone mentioned to a soldier that he was having trouble getting heating oil. The soldier made one phone call, and a military truck drove up, piled high with wood that could be used for firewood. The whole lot cost only five yen.

These rumors reveal the weakening of people's trust in the military. Most of the rumors I've heard recently are like these two, and soldiers appear in many of them.

March 6, 1945

Rain. My shoes got soaked, and I had no choice but to go to work in my *monpe* and trusty old clogs.

They made me very aware of how unstable but beautiful and flimsy Japanese clogs and umbrellas are. When I wear clothes like these, I feel as though everyone is looking at me. They weren't gorgeous clothes. Over my *monpe*, I wore a *meisen* silk jacket and a black *meisen* coat, but perhaps because nowadays few people appear in public wearing pleated garments, people naturally stared. I had the feeling that it's not just because they're busy but because people have abandoned any thought of dressing beautifully or making themselves attractive.

War has changed people's thinking in this way. I expected Japanese to find beauty in every object and to show the quality of their taste.

March 10, 1945

The wind was strong. In the morning the Ministry of Transportation broadcast an emergency statement that the national railroads were not running in two places.[23] They said the Tōkaidō Line was running from Ōfuna and the Jōban Line from Matsudo. I left for work with a certain resolve: I took the city trolley to Shinjuku. Then, because the trolley ran only as far as Yotsuya-mitsuke, I went to the national railway station there, but it was closed. Soldiers were standing guard there, and only people with passes were allowed to enter.

I waited and waited and finally took the national railway to Iidabashi, and between Ichigaya and Iidabashi I glimpsed the remnants of last night's fire. Kudan was still burning, and the Kokugikan was slowly being shrouded in smoke. Yaesu Avenue was burning from Nihonbashi toward Kyōbashi, and they were still hosing down the fires in Ōtemachi. Shirokiya had burned down.[24] One of the waitresses at the company was unaccounted for. They say the dead in Honjo and Ryōgoku are piled up in the streets.

I wondered how many dead and wounded there were. How extensive was the damage? I can't bear to think about it any more. You use your wits to protect yourself as well as you can, and it can't be helped if you burn to death. My feeling now is that neither life nor death is an issue. When the whole country is reduced to ashes, I believe an unimaginable strength will emerge. When I lose everything, I'll probably have a new strength.

We're already way beyond not believing in our rulers or being dissatisfied with them. Now that these feelings are widely held by my countrymen, I *must be ready for the next thing and I must survive.*

March 11, 1945

Sunday morning there was a notice from the community council saying that we should assemble quickly at the captain's house. At nine o'clock we gathered at the local auditorium. Suginami Ward had a quota for 60,000 victims, but it's become 30,000. Our community council has a quota of 540 people, and each group is to handle ten to fifteen. The special assembly started, and it was decided that each family's allotment would be one person. The plan was to have the visitors arrive at the sericultural experimental station until about noon and then to greet and guide them to the local auditorium.

Then they said to take futon and china to Tenri Church, and at some point the 540 people became a tenth of that: fifty-four people. We heard that things

---

23. Early on the morning of March 10, 279 B-29s attacked Tokyo, dropping 1,700 tons of incendiary bombs. The Japanese authorities later reported that sixteen square miles of central Tokyo were razed and 83,793 people were killed and 40,918 injured. See Carter and Mueller, *Combat Chronology*, 594.

24. The Shirokiya Department Store is located in Nihonbashi.

would be collected at one place, but it was clear by evening that no one would be coming today. We cooked and prepared meals together, and one group fired up the bath, but the coordination was not very good. I got angry at what the officials did, but everything was fine in the end. When I visited each family, everything—from the bathroom and the bath—seemed to require special effort. If it wasn't that, then "it was because we haven't finished providing for our children"; "what with two generations living together . . . ," or "it was because of the confusion over preparing for evacuation." They had lots of personal matters to attend to and that alone would have been fine, but I felt that all our preparation was ignored.

Today, too, an air-raid warning sounded. Perhaps because of our skittishness, clouds were mistaken for aircraft, and a warning sounded.

March 14, 1945

The apartment of a friend who had gone to work for a newspaper company had become dangerous to live in, and so he moved, together with an associate from the company, also a victim, to his older brother's empty house.

Today I had a day off from work, and the three of us packed things into knapsacks and carried them out.

I saw what remained of my friend's neighborhood after the bombing. The faces of the people moving out of the houses that had been destroyed revealed no certainty about victory. All the talk in the streets was about the air raid. The sight of bombing victims overflowing into the narrow streets and people carrying stoves and cobbler's benches was really depressing.

Today there were no air-raid warnings, and I went to bed at ten.

March 22, 1945

I heard that a wife, together with an infant and another child, were evacuated to her husband's family home in the countryside, but she and her relatives didn't get along, and so she returned to Tokyo.[25]

I thought "what completely, outrageously irresponsible people" and couldn't help getting upset. People are mostly unconcerned about the rationing system, and when they talk about the rice shortages, all they say is, "It's horrible, isn't it?" The fact that even money won't help means there is nothing to look forward to.

---

25. Beginning in October 1943, the wartime government had encouraged the evacuation of those in the cities who were not involved in war work—chiefly women and the elderly—but it could not make such a move compulsory. In contrast, children were forced to evacuate, with the first wave of evacuations occurring in August 1944 and the second in March 1945.

As to how things will be if martial law is imposed, I worry only about how it will affect my own life and am completely indifferent to what might happen to the country.

I am furious with myself! Why can't I see the big picture?

In the final analysis, it's because we Japanese have had no training in losing battles. I know only about winning and don't understand losing, or being a good loser. Even if one is defeated in battle, there still are mountains and rivers. And the Japanese people will continue to exist. I think that we'll need extra strength to recover.

March 26, 1945

It was clear and windy. Compulsory evacuations were under way along Asagaya Avenue, and the atmosphere was electric. Since furniture couldn't be taken, people who didn't know what else to do simply put their furniture out in front of their houses and tried to sell it. Hibachis were lined up in front of a bookstore, and bamboo baskets and empty cans were arranged in front of a Western goods store. It was a veritable secondhand market. They were selling *mizuhiki* at the candy store. Ceramics and beautiful deep blue pots were lined up in front of the store that sold tropical fish, and although I wanted some of the pots, I thought that even if I bought something, I didn't know what would happen [to it].

As I gazed at a city that had become a war zone, I was moved by what I saw, and it occurred to me that we Japanese had never practiced losing battles even once. This is why we were such a happy people. I thought, too, about how we always had had peace and *about the small things I had been proud of, but now all this seemed a thing of the past.*

Facing this harsh reality, *those of us whose minds and bodies have been steeled for battle must create the next age, a truly stable age.* Let's forgo all our demands and just live and realize the day.

March 27, 1945

It was clear and windy. Lately I've wondered whether there would be air raids if it was windy. I hear there are massive attacks twice a day in Kyushu — at dawn and at night — and there are reports that American troops have landed on islands near Okinawa.[26]

Earlier I also tried to imagine what daily life would be like if there were air raids every day. Initially I wasn't the least bit confident about how I'd handle

---

26. On March 26, American troops went ashore on Kerama Atoll, which is twenty miles south of Okinawa, and on March 27 and 28, more than 150 B-29s bombed targets in Kyushu. See Carter and Mueller, *Combat Chronology*, p. 610.

204 YOSHIZAWA HISAKO | UNTIL THE WAR ENDED

this. Yet even with air raids every day, I've been calm and able to work. Was this the mystery of the human heart? As the days and months passed, I've been able to make the necessary mental adjustments.

Recently I've even thought that I could live my own life with a certain serenity. To do my very best and to live the life I was given as beautifully as I can — if that and that alone constitutes my life, that's fine.

March 29, 1945

It was clear and windy with strong southerly winds. It wasn't cold, but something made my heart feel cold. Recently whenever I go to the company, everyone — and I mean everyone — looks so glum. I find it hard to maintain my composure. As for myself, my family, and our household goods — we'll just have to make do. We can't do a thing, so I wonder constantly about what I should do, but actually there's nothing I can do.

Some think only about their own self-preservation and do so secretly. Others openly admit their preoccupation with their own self-preservation. There are, in fact, all sorts of people.

Lately I've felt that it's now OK to express all sorts of raw feelings. How is it that one simply criticizes others' faults? The unhappiness of "a life of many complaints" saddens me.

March 30, 1945

Today we had our regular company meeting. There were warnings about both commuting time and work schedules, and this was a very difficult matter. I thought about how one needed real political skill to manage both a company and a family.

At this moment, the invasion of Okinawa wasn't much of a concern.[27] I think I'll always decide on my own course of action together with that of the country. When one speaks of the importance of "scattering purely," it becomes a criticism of those intent on surviving at all costs.[28] Everyone tends to criticize others, but what we need is for all people to be considerate and to reflect on themselves.

However, it seems I've come to learn and feel a variety of things. If this sort of existence continues, I'll probably become quite a wonderful person.

March 31, 1945

It was clear, and the end of another month.

---

27. American troops landed on Okinawa on April 1.
28. Yoshizawa uses the wartime term "scattering purely" (J. *kiyoku chiru*), which means to die willingly for the emperor and the state.

I'm frightened by how hardened I've become. I don't care about anything and believe that anything is fine and can't be helped—this is bad. Those who busily strive to protect themselves and their things might regard me as someone who enjoyed a solitary purity, but as I reflect on myself, I wonder whether this isn't a way of purification inspired by precisely the sort of hard-heartedness that frightens me.

Everyone was warned about leaving the company. I'm probably not the only one who is impressed with the beauty of correct regulations, but I still dislike being controlled by regulations. And yet when I hear people say, "If things are expressed so harshly, then rather than not doing something, it's simply that this can't be helped," their thoughtlessness is obvious, and I immediately feel a certain repulsion.

I'm too exhausted to do anything and go to bed right after dinner. Not being able to complete things at the end of the month is bothering me.

Tomorrow is April, and it'll be spring.

April 8, 1945

Cloudy. I went to the regular community council meeting. It was held to introduce the newly appointed officers, but we discussed one or two other matters as well.

If the evacuations increase, it appears that the community council's revenue will shrink, and the authorities are now saying we have to prepay the community council's expenses for a half or a whole year. Opposing opinions were expressed, and a lot of time was wasted. While I was getting irritated at the stupidity of those bickering over details, the doctor who heads F clinic and who also was a new group head, said he couldn't bear to discuss old issues. He asked whether these sorts of issues couldn't be left to the community council, and as he said this, there was applause, and I knew what everyone was feeling. When you think about that response, *you understand how our countrymen feel about the government and their dissatisfaction with useless debate and temporizing.* I keep wishing for someone who has the power to carry us along. I want someone who will do this without empty rhetoric. I've been reading about Komura Jūtarō and Miyazaki Tōten, who gave everything—heart and body—to the nation, suppressed their own feelings, and did their jobs.[29] Their power made me work. There is the feeling that politicians just want people.

---

29. Yoshizawa's invocation of Komura Jūtarō (1855–1911) and Miyazaki Tōten (1871–1922) is revealing. Both men actively promoted Japanese involvement on the Asian mainland. Komura did this in his capacity as a diplomat serving in Beijing, Manchuria, Korea, and the United States and during two terms as foreign minister. Miyazaki first was sent by the Foreign Ministry to gather information on anti-Manchu activity in China and later actively supported Sun Yat-sen.

M's aunt came to ask me for advice about the two evacuation sites — Isawa and Kunitachi.[30] The word is that a month's rent will be ten yen per tatami mat. In addition, you have to provide your own firewood, and neither site interested me. Even if it were OK for a year or two, the absence of any plan for the future made me uneasy, but it couldn't be helped. It seems that the current cabinet regards the Koiso cabinet's rushing evacuation as too hasty and shameful.[31] Where would it be good for our countrymen to go? Even admitting that the problem of victims' livelihood is a serious one, the government's irresponsibility has given us much to be angry about.

April 14, 1945

It was clear. The national railways were not running, and the city trolley was so full I couldn't get on. To get to work I went to Eifuku-chō and took the Teito trolley to Shibuya, then the subway to Kanda.

Yesterday I was able to go west and north with the Teito trolley — I use the words "able to go" because recently Sensei's younger brother, who is house-sitting with me, and his friends use it a lot. Fires broke out at the Imperial Palace, the Ōmiya Palace, and the Meiji Shrine, and there were reports that both the shrines and the inner sanctuaries burned down.

Unlike the March 9 evening air raid, the streets were not overflowing with victims.[32] I hear that 160,000 houses burned down. My sense was that it was different from the time when Honjo and Fukagawa burned down, even for the victims. Perhaps because these areas are so different. This time everything between Kōenji and Asagaya, Ōkubo and Shinjuku, and Shinjuku and Yotsuya burned down, and the areas from Ōji, through Itabashi and Arakawa, burned as well.

This time, people not on important business could not buy train tickets.

April 25, 1945

It was clear. Although it was the end of April, the cold was penetrating.

There was just one air raid during the day, and one aircraft.

---

30. Both sites are well out of Tokyo: Isawa is in Yamanashi Prefecture, and Kunitachi is on the eastern outskirts of Tachikawa City.

31. General Koiso Kuniaki succeeded another army man, General Tōjō Hideki, on July 22, 1944. The Koiso cabinet was dissolved on April 5, and a new one was formed by Admiral Suzuki Kantarō. Suzuki was a graduate of the naval academy and the Navy War College, saw action in the Sino-Japanese and Russo-Japanese wars, and became chief of the Navy General Staff in 1923. He was the last wartime prime minister.

32. Yoshizawa's observation is correct: although 330 B-29s bombed Tokyo on April 13–14, dropping incendiary bombs, their targets were not residential, as they were on March 9–10. See Carter and Mueller, *Combat Chronology*, 627.

Today I went to the company carrying flowers from my garden—Indian red-wood and azalea blossoms. As I walked in town carrying my flowers, everyone looked at me. There isn't much color on the streets these days.

I got my hands on some powdered green tea, which I hadn't had for some time, and relished the thought of making some.

April 30, 1945

It was clear. This year the flowers were late, and by now all their blossoms have scattered and the azaleas sit proudly in the greenery. Even the *akagirenge*, the earliest of the azaleas to bloom in spring, has only a few withered blossoms. The hydrangea leaves have gotten big, and the young leaves of the Indian redwood are just emerging. The azaleas are at their peak. And the oleaster is decorated with balls that look like buds.

Today, at lunchtime, I saw the god of fire at Meguro for the first time.[33] I was visiting M's home, which was near by.

It was reported that two hundred planes in a military bombing formation attacked this morning, and all of them went to Tachikawa and Hamamatsu.[34] I returned with some parsley roots. Nowadays, after a big air raid, air-raid warnings prompted by a single airplane are greeted with emotionless and completely expressionless faces. This year, too, I've lived through another April.

Lately, I've had strange feelings about my day-to-day existence.

No matter what happens, I'll try to live a life that has not lost any of its optimism. I'm ready to die tomorrow but will try to live today full of hope. I'll do this to ensure the brightness of my surroundings.

May 1, 1945

Cloudy and windy.

I walked around in the burned-out areas around Shiba. The wind made the dust and ash spiral upward in little twisters, and pieces of tin roofing sailed through the air.

In the midst of all this, a man who seemed to be deranged furiously dug holes in the ground. He inserted pieces of wood in the holes, and it looked as though he intended to live there. Will hole dwellings become a part of city life? This is what I've been feeling about Tokyo recently.

Lately when I've seen people in the process of moving, they're doing it all

---

33. The god of fire (Fudōmyōō) statue is at the Rōsenji Temple in Meguro in central Tokyo.

34. More than 126 B-29s attacked aircraft plants in Tachikawa City and numerous other targets. See Carter and Mueller, *Combat Chronology*, 642–643.

The god of fire is housed in this gate at the Rōsenji Temple in Meguro. Author's collection.

themselves. They remind me of insects building a nest, and it just seemed odd that they were moving themselves and strange to see people carrying things over their heads, the way ants do.

It rained in the evening.

May 10, 1945

It was clear.

Now with the end of the war in Europe, what might Japanese be forced to consider?[35] Won't the yearning for peace intensify? My outlook brightened. It was my sense that our ties with Germany had been resolved beautifully and Japan now could take a freer course of action. Mentally, we Japanese have the narrowness of an island people and so although we're honest, our thinking is too limited. I sincerely hoped our diplomats would be broad-minded. No, more than that, it made me sad that there were no politicians willing to take real risks.

---

35. Germany surrendered unconditionally to the Allied powers on May 7, 1945.

May 23, 1945

It was clear, then cloudy. With all the rain we've had recently, the garden was an intense green, which was comforting.

At midnight I went to bed. At 1:00 a.m. a preliminary alert sounded, and then an air-raid warning.

There were fires in the southeast. It was mostly an incendiary attack.[36] The closest fire was in the Mabashi area (later when I asked — the entire Suginami Garage area), where a B-29 was shot down, and there were fires and the black smoke from burning gasoline.

When the planes passed overhead, I worried that one might fall and start fires.

An American plane that took a direct hit flew on for some time trying various maneuvers, but I thought it was done for. Then at full throttle it turned toward the central part of the city that was ablaze and went down. While it was just an enemy plane, it was like the sky clearing. This sort of fighting spirit exists in all people, and the patriotic spirit that demands that the fight must be fought surely must exist in Americans, too. Haven't we gone too far in disliking and resenting Americans? That feeling intensifies when one thinks about postwar management.

The air-raid warning still hadn't been canceled when it began to get light, and I heated water on an electric heater, made some tea, and drank it.

I stayed in bed during the air raid.

The sun was shining brightly, and nature favored us with another day, as it always does, and those of us who survived the air raid began our day as we always do. Unavoidably sad thoughts filled my heart, however. It'll be heart wrenching tonight when I think of the people who have lost their homes and belongings. Is it OK for us to remain silent and do our jobs in the face of war's harsh realities?

For the first time this year, we had a morning that really seemed like spring.

June 1, 1945

It was clear. If this were a typical year, the rays of the sun would be strong, shining and brimming with hope, but there still are cold spells. The fields of ripening wheat where people worry over every inch of land is an autumnal color and the heads of grain hang down, broken. It is a deeply felt sadness.

---

36. On May 23, 528 B-29s attacked Tokyo and dropped incendiary bombs on industrial and residential areas. See Carter and Mueller, *Combat Chronology*, 654.

Our house probably will burn down and even if it doesn't, the day when we have to move out may not be far off.

No matter what happens, I'll continue to exist with the same state of mind and the same face I have today. I've been thinking a lot lately about how I don't really want to live an extravagant life, just a quiet one. It's probably my total exhaustion that leads to these feelings.

June 4, 1945

Yesterday, K came over, and I thoroughly enjoyed the visit.[37] The reason is that no matter what your daily life is like, joy is joy, and there must be joy in your life. My younger brother and his friends had the day off, so we played records on our phonograph and had a concert. We all seemed to enjoy ourselves.

We've all been pretty exhausted lately, and everyone turned in early tonight. I did a little sewing and then went to bed. Thinking that I'd go to sleep, I turned off the light and after I did that, the strangest thoughts ran through my head.

Astrologers and all sorts of other people have been telling me, "You'll find happiness in your later years." Seeing all the people living in air-raid shelters, I now think pleasure is spreading out two futon, wearing a nightgown that won't get soiled, and getting a sound sleep.

How long can this life continue?

I suddenly thought about how all of us had no means of transportation and remembered the people I saw walking in small groups along the Tōkaidō and Tōhoku highways, going somewhere. If you're already separated from your family, now that these separations seem to be final, human life is unspeakably wretched.

My younger brother and his friends were talking in the bedroom next door, and although I wasn't really listening, I could hear what they were saying. "Don't you think about calling your wife and children back from wherever they were evacuated and having a family again? It would be nice to tease the children while drinking saké, wouldn't it?" said O. My younger brother responded, "Yeah, I was about to say something about my wife and kids and was thinking about how I wanted to drink saké with them."

I listened sympathetically. When you let down your guard, it's hardly a surprise that the world is so horrible.

June 29, 1945

Clear, hot.

There was a letter from Sensei from his unit in Kōchi and it included a poem:[38]

---

37. Yoshizawa does not identify K.
38. I believe "Sensei" is Yoshizawa's mentor, Furuya Tsunetake.

The southern mountains are brilliant in the sun.
The loquats ripen red in my eyes.
Faintly black the soil, the Dutchman's-pipes
White flowers bloom the color of earth.[39]

Nothing extraordinary happens in the mornings and evenings in a barracks full of men waiting for American troops to land: everyone makes minute observations about this and that and calmly takes everything in. Looking at my own daily life, there is so much to reflect on.

This got me thinking. Recently I've felt a lot of confidence about my own life.

As a Japanese who never experienced defeat up to now and who lived through the China incident, which was a complete victory, my feelings about the current war seemed to have matured.

The letdown after Guadalcanal continued, and I was depressed at the time of the fighting on Luzon.[40] Victory and defeat in war are pursued when opportunities suddenly appear, and I heard that the vanquished are those who can't stand in the end, and this is what I thought. Looking at the example of Germany in the last great war and the current one, what is described as being carried along by the forces of the times might, to a surprising degree, be unconnected to decisive power. Especially when it comes to power, different situations make this sort of thing conceivable. The feeling that I had to do something now makes me impatient, and yet I find it sad that I can't do anything. The war situation gets worse by the day: most cities have been completely destroyed, starting with the imperial cities and extending to the middle-size and small ones, and before too long American troops will come ashore, landing in a Japan that has not been attacked by a foreign enemy in three thousand years.[41] Yet when I think about this, why am I so calm? It was a strange calmness.

Living in Tokyo as it is now, I'm full of hope. In last night's air raid, there were no accidents on the line that burned all the way to Makuragi, and the trains were still running. In the smoldering ruins, people built semi-subterranean huts with tin roofing to protect themselves against the elements. The next day, netting was stretched across frames, and laundry flapped in the wind. Immediately after some areas were razed, bright green garden plots appeared and extended as far as the eye could see. Children who had slept until yesterday on tatami were now sleeping on a single straw mat. They were not the least bit unhappy

---

39. Dutchman's-pipes are flowering plants known as *uma no suzukusa* in Japanese.

40. American troops landed on Guadalcanal in the Solomon Islands on August 7, 1942, and, despite stiff Japanese resistance, secured the island by February 1943.

41. Yoshizawa forgets that an army consisting of Mongol and Korean troops had invaded Japan twice, in 1274 and 1281.

and made their own toys and played contentedly. Trains had fewer cars, and you waited longer. I saw three girls who looked like underclassmen sitting on the train platform and playing to kill time, and I admired them. While the waiting irritated me, the children were having a lot of fun. The truth is, I thought, I'm unimaginative and small-minded.

No matter what happened to me, I was confident that my fellow Japanese would be able to get up the next day and carry on. I wouldn't be so sure of this if I hadn't seen what I had seen with my own eyes.

It made me think of how the intellectual class has been criticized since the war started. Of course, I'm not denying that some think it's terrible for anyone to have these thoughts, but I can't be stupidly patriotic and insist that simply believing in Japan's victory is good. The intellectual class has gone through a lot, and when they begin to think confidently about the country, I believe that Japan's victory truly will come.

Although we've worked our way up to the point in this war where we can say we have not been completely defeated, everyone now realizes there will be no "victory." I realize that nothing can be done about this, but I do believe that all Japanese will do what is asked of them. Then I can work with all my body and soul. I am completely convinced that *more than the confidence and joy of a so-called victory, my fellow Japanese will grasp something at that moment that is more valuable and more stable.*

June 30, 1945

Rain. It has rained hard since midnight—the first big rainstorm in some time. Since my rain boots and umbrella burned up when I evacuated, I've really come to hate rainy days.

When I got to Asagaya, a warning and alert had sounded, and although I didn't know what had been reported, I went ahead and boarded a train. It appears to have been a B-24.

I spent the morning writing a total of six replies for Sensei. I cleaned the office toilets, and after I had been at it for a while, one of the office boys came to help.

In the evening I did my household accounts. This month's expenditures came to 832 yen, 88 sen. I'll be in the red.

I remembered what S-sensei, then recently returned from Beijing, had said.[42] "The female teachers invited to Beijing were told to live within the recom-

---

42. Yoshizawa does not identify S-sensei.

mended daily budget, which none of them found very realistic," and it's now become impossible to live within a budget.

The value of the paper currency probably will fall further, but isn't it nice to return with a trunk filled with one's salary? In any case, I have to be grateful for being able to live quietly this past month.

July 1, 1945

Rainy-season cloud cover, Sunday. Since I intended to join the evacuation, I packed manuscripts and handwritten notes: thirty boxes' worth.

Ten B-29s and B-24s attacked from different directions, apparently dropping mines.[43]

Today, a friend of my younger brother's asked me to send a telegram for him, so I went off to Nakano Station to do this, but they wouldn't take cash, and nobody nearby sold the stamps I needed. Another woman had come to send a telegram, and she too was perplexed, so the two of us had no choice but to take a train to the main post office in Suginami Ward. She said she simply wanted to inform relatives of her grandmother's death and was overwhelmed by all the rigid rules.

She said that when someone dies now, their relatives have a terrible time getting a coffin. She told me how a relative's father died recently, and because there were no coffins, they had to do something — after all, it was Father, they said — and so for the wake they put him into the best wicker basket they could find. Then there was an air raid, and thinking that it would be too bad if they burned up together with their father, they loaded the basket onto a cart and started out. But in the confusion of the moment, someone stole the cart. The family reported the theft to the police but the cart still hasn't been found. What a horrifying story! I tried to imagine the look on the face of the thief who stole the cart when he opened the basket, and this put me in a strange mood.

July 7, 1945

Clear. Last night Aunt M stayed over, and this morning we left the house together. Recently, general passenger tickets are not sold during rush hour, and since I had a pass but Aunt didn't, we parted ways at the station. This morning I joined in our company's clearing of areas for war gardens. When you dig in the burned-out areas, you find all sorts of things. I found a bottle opener, a curling

---

43. On July 1, twenty-four B-29s dropped mines in Shimonoseki Strait and the waters off Nanao and Fushiki on the western coast. See Carter and Mueller, *Combat Chronology*, 670.

iron, charcoal, a pair of tongs, a camera, and much else. Everything we dug up showed signs of being used, and I wondered about the owners of these objects. They've scattered here and there. Where were they living now?

Yet when you consider what blossoms even in the burned-out areas, you come away impressed with the power of nature.

August 4, 1945

Clear.

Lately, because I haven't been sleeping much, I stand while I work. I have virtually no reason to sit on tatami, and so I think of myself as a pole, and once in a while I do get a little strange.

Last night my brother-in-law stayed over. He knows absolutely nothing, and I envy his obliviousness.

He works hard, eats heartily, and sleeps soundly.

Recently we've been working hard, eating little, and not getting enough sleep, and it's really beginning to be a source of concern.

Let's try to put up with whatever happens.

I've gotten used to not thinking about tomorrow, and as a result I haven't been that anxious at all.

August 9, 1945

Clear. Today was a historical day both for us and the country.

I was ready for the Soviet Union's declaration of war, and the long-expected day finally has arrived.[44] I was speechless as I listened to the news.

O returned close to midnight. He reeked of alcohol and blathered, "Wake up every body!"

It turned out to be as I thought. We expect a statement from the imperial government tomorrow. We have two choices — we can accept the Allies' July 26 offer or continue to fight until the country is reduced to ashes — and we have to pick one.[45] Apparently the new bomb used on Hiroshima was an experiment.[46]

If we receive that sort of bombing for several days, they say that little Japan, all of it, will be reduced to ashes, and the *gyokusai* of the people will occur on more than just an emotional level. Will we be able to accept the Allies' whole offer?

---

44. The Soviet Union declared war on Japan on August 8, 1945.

45. On July 26, 1945, the Allied powers sent Japanese leaders the Potsdam Declaration, which contained the terms of surrender.

46. Yoshizawa is referring to the atomic bomb dropped on Hiroshima on August 6, 1945.

I can't even decide what I should be feeling. For the last several years I've had various experiences, but haven't my personal discoveries become completely meaningless? I absolutely refuse to lose the will to work myself to the bone for the recovery, but I'm uneasy about how much I actually can do.

I must prepare myself physically and mentally.

I can't wait for tomorrow's announcement.

August 11, 1945

Clear.

The word was that today was the day of an important cabinet meeting on the American side and that they'll respond to the Japanese offer.

The newspapers were already telling the nation what should happen soon.

We will stake our lives, and the work to be done will begin. As far as the birth of the new Japan is concerned, I believe our duty will be to bear the pain of this delivery.

August 13, 1945

Clear. An air-raid warning sounded early in the morning, at a little past 5:00 a.m. As I was putting up supports for the pumpkin squash and checking the controls on the stove, there was a report that carrier-based aircraft were approaching.

The air raid got everyone up early, and we had *dojo* and string beans simmered in saké and soy sauce for lunch. Our sense that we were living for the moment got stronger.

After some time, at about 10:00 a.m., the all-clear sounded, and I set out for work, but the trains weren't running, so I gave up and came home. I went back to putting up supports for the ripening pumpkin squash and did other odd jobs in the garden. For dinner, I added unfiltered soy sauce to some peeled cucumber and mixed it with boiled fiddlehead ferns. Everyone said it was delicious, very delicious, and ate heartily.

At about nine that night, O returned from the newspaper company. The report was that the Allies had accepted the Japanese offer. Apparently the emperor graciously and without hesitation announced that this course of action would save the people. Because the military did not accept this, it was reported that the cabinet had been meeting since 4:00 p.m. this afternoon, and it's gotten late.

No matter what happens to Japan, if these are the emperor's words, we will follow them. From the military's point of view, however, if there still are reserves, they probably will want to fight on for some time.

I myself have nothing to say except that on the question of how to proceed in building the next age, we will have to work as hard as we can.

For some time, food may be our biggest problem. We'll have to create more gardens for the coming days.

One can expect that all sorts of things will happen: there will be outbreaks of horrible illnesses, and the immoralities that arise out of decadence will become popular.

How am I to work and exist in the midst of all this? But I believe that my health will survive all this and I'll handle everything that comes my way.

No matter what happens, I'll always have my life.

I'd like to live as someone who never overlooks the beautiful things in life.

August 14, 1945

It was clear. I went to work as usual.

Early this morning, I thought carrier-based planes were attacking, but the report was that it was a single B-29. Although it's not clear, the rumor was that the B-29 was dropping leaflets that read "The emperor is hoping for peace."[47]

I was already calm, however. I thought we'll work for the day when Japan recovers.

At long last there were reports of a final announcement tomorrow.

The long-awaited-for day has come, I thought to myself, and I must be brave.

Mrs. H heard the nine o'clock news, and we wondered together what tomorrow's important broadcast would be like.[48] We agreed that if the newspaper companies knew what was coming, we wanted them to tell us. We talked for some time, and then she went home.

There was an air-raid warning again.

August 15, 1945

Clear. At 5:20 a.m. there was an air-raid warning announcing the attack of carrier-based planes.

At 7:21 a.m. we were told that the emperor would make a special broadcast at noon. At long last His Majesty himself will offer, in his own words, a solution for the current situation. I thought of what he must be feeling and teared up.

As I walked down the street, I could hear whispered conversations, every one of them about what would happen if the war ended. I remembered a conversation I overheard this morning: the grandmother next door announced to her

---

47. Takahashi Aiko reported that leaflets fell on her neighborhood on July 25. See Takahashi Aiko nikki, 7/25/45.
48. Mrs. H appears to be a neighbor.

grandchildren, "If the war ends, I'll make you bean-covered rice cakes with real, sweet sugar."

In the morning, various rumors circulated in the neighborhood. People were saying that the banks probably would stop giving out money.

At fifteen minutes before noon I went outside to listen to the broadcast on the neighborhood public address system. I went out because I wanted to hear the emperor's broadcast in the streets. Half the crowd seemed to understand what was about to happen, [and] half had puzzled looks on their faces, looks that said they expected the worst.

Five minutes before the broadcast, then four, and as the noon hour approached, people gathered. They paid their respects to the emperor, removed their hats, and said "Please let us hear. . . ."

A siren went off, and we heard the emperor's voice. People silently bowed their heads, and in an instant the streets were dead quiet, and various thoughts ran through my head.

Word by word, the emperor's voice reached us, and tears ran down our cheeks. My only thought was that from now on we would have to work as hard as we could so our fellow Japanese would not fight among themselves. Let's get to work.

The streets were quiet.

People's faces had no particular expression. Perhaps they were exhausted. As to how they felt about the war ending, an unmistakable brightness in their faces told the story. Wasn't this what I was feeling? It wasn't that I didn't trust my own eyes.

I had a slight headache in the afternoon.

Because of the change in the military situation, there was a meeting at my company at around 3:00 p.m. We were a company that didn't need to burn and destroy documents, so we didn't know what to do next. The emperor's announcement meant that the military units would be disbanded and that we, too, would be discharged. We burned all incriminating materials.[49]

I couldn't imagine the coming hardships, but I thought I would survive on my good health and willpower.

August 16, 1945

The expressions on people's faces haven't changed much at all. When one meets

---

49. They were probably doing this to obscure the names of those in positions of responsibility.

people, instead of uttering the usual greetings, they blurt out, "What's happened is terrible."

This morning there was an air-raid warning and alert.

At the company, we were told that female employees would be on vacation until there was a better sense of what would happen next. Whether I'm in the mountains or wherever, I just want to stay in touch. Apparently, government offices will tell us what procedures to follow. What in the world are they thinking of doing? I expect there is a mountain of serious problems, but what are the officials managing the country getting so excited about?

Haven't they lost their power and been defeated?

The military is calling for complete resistance and appealing to all citizens. This is a very difficult problem. The true nature of a people is apparent when they lose a war, rather than when they win, and the day has arrived when we should reveal Japan's greatness.

Now that we've been defeated in war, *I'm eager that our national identity as a people not be completely ruined.*

August 17, 1945

Clear. Beginning today and for some time, it was OK to stay home from the company, but because I was the only one who knew how to handle mail transfers, I went to work. There were reports that the young military men haven't accepted the peace and were still active, and wild rumors circulated. We were fearful of what couldn't be foreseen, perhaps because we were hearing that everything was in chaos and that people were uneasy about the evacuation of women and girls and because as a people we had never experienced defeat.[50]

Today leaflets were dropped from friendly aircraft.

At Kanda Station I saw a flier plastered on a wall that read, "Both the army and navy are fine and believe that the people will endure," and people had signed their names. As far as the feelings of military people were concerned, I thought this was not unexpected, but we already had had a statement from the emperor. If we are to build the future, don't we have to begin clearing a path today? Dying is cheap. In the long history of the state, this defeat probably will not amount to very much, whereas the reconstruction that was about to begin could end up as a great achievement.

What was there to say? We did our best and were defeated. Only those who did not work as hard as they might have would feel any regret.

---

50. There were rumors that Allied troops would rape Japanese women and girls.

Take C, for example. While he was in the city, he was angry about everything and said he wanted to go off, even to the mountains, and I was surprised by the narrowness of his perspective.[51] That may be a purist position to take vis-à-vis the country, but it was only his own personal philosophy, one that was too beautiful, and it really hadn't taken root or spread. C's philosophy made me feel the need to broaden my vision.

August 18, 1945

Clear. There was a distribution of *kanpan*. Mrs. A and I went to get some.[52]

August 21, 1945

Clear. A letter arrived from Sensei, who is in Kōchi. This probably will be the last I'll receive from the military. Sensei's worried about my going off to work and providing for the two men while the house was empty, and he wondered whether I was taking care of myself. His letter made me realize that recently I've had virtually no chance just to sit on tatami for a whole day. As a result, when I crawl into my futon at night, my feet are hot, and I feel that it can't be helped and probably is just exhaustion. But if I were to get sick, it would be terrible, and I simply haven't given this much thought. The time for me to help Sensei and to work hard had arrived, and thus, I had to take care not to catch cold.

G visited and was completely pessimistic about postwar life, especially the food situation.[53] Hearing this, I thought I would do my best to make a garden for the family, even if only a small one.

O's return was late because of an announcement from imperial headquarters.

At long last, on the twenty-sixth, Allied advance units will be airlifted in, and naval units will enter Japanese ports the day after that. The word is that the army will be airlifted in, coming first, they say, to Atsugi.

According to the story of someone who went to accept the conditions of surrender, the American side was actually gentlemanly. When our side explained the Japanese situation and said that what the Americans were asking was impossible, they immediately made changes. The Japanese side's excuses were pretty lame.

American newspapers described the meeting as follows: "Thick steaks were prepared, and they waited for the seven or eight people they expected. Because seventeen came, they quickly killed some turkeys and showered the delegates

---

51. Yoshizawa does not identify C.
52. Mrs. A appears to be a neighbor.
53. Yoshizawa does not identify G.

with real hospitality before sending them home." When I heard this, my thought was that the Japanese way of doing things was pompous and inefficient. They say the American way of doing things at the time of the interviews was to express misgivings about the issue at hand for thirty seconds and then to move on quickly and deal with that issue. They say that the U.S. attitude toward Japan will be exceedingly generous as long as the Japanese don't oppose them, and if they do, the Americans will strictly prohibit any deviation.

As for the Japanese administration, it's nothing more than an administration of chairs and chops. For example, if an office wants to have an outside group do a particular task, it needs twenty or thirty stamps, and because of this, even though we should regret this situation and fight it, old habits die hard, and in the end it makes no sense not to avoid responsibility.

To be sure, the harsh reality of "defeat" is not an easy thing to stomach, but the day probably will come when we see that because what we thought to be true spread among the people, the results were not completely bad.

The Diary of a Labor Service Corps Girl

Maeda Shōko was born on September 15, 1929, and grew up in Chiran, an up-land town in southern Kyushu that was the site of an army air base. She graduated from Chiran Higher Elementary School in 1943 and was a student at Chiran Girls High School when she was mobilized for war work. Her first year of labor service was spent clearing land for planting flax and cultivating potatoes. The following year she was put to work making sweets for the military and digging and provisioning supply bunkers for the battles that were expected when the Allied forces invaded the Japanese home islands.

On March 27, 1945, Maeda and several of her classmates were led to the nearby air base, normally off-limits to civilians. They were assigned to the quarters of special-attack pilots and told to look after them, which meant cleaning their quarters, doing their laundry, and mending their clothes. Maeda's diary reveals that she and her classmates spent a lot of time with the pilots, talking, singing war songs, and listening to their discussions of abstruse philosophical subjects. When the day of the pilots' final missions arrived, the girls gave them flowers or gifts, accompanied them to the airfield, and saw them off.

After the war, Maeda graduated from Chiran Girls High School in 1948 and worked briefly for the Chiran Agricultural Cooperative. In 1951 she started working as an assistant librarian at the Chiran City Library and completed the course in library science at the Kagoshima University Library in 1954. She stopped working when she got married in 1956.

Maeda's diary covers the period from March 27 to April 18, 1945. It was first published in Muranaga Kaoru, ed., *Chiran tokubetsu kōgekitai* (Kagoshima: Japuran, 1989), 76–89, and was reprinted in Chiran kōjo nadeshikokai, ed., *Chiran tokkō kichi* (Tokyo: Waryoku sōgō kenkyūjo, 1979), 167–181.

March 27, 1945

I got ready for work and then went to school.[1] We heard from Sensei that we'll be going right away to serve the special-attack unit and were surprised.[2] We changed into our uniforms and walked over to their barracks. This was my first visit to the triangular barracks, and everything seemed different.[3] We spent the day learning about the building of the special-attack unit pilots' quarters. The thought of pilots living in such cramped quarters made us ashamed of our sleeping on thick futon.[4] We were deeply moved when we thought about our older brothers sleeping on straw-filled futon with a single blanket in cramped quarters to which they wouldn't return and waiting for the day of attack. We got back at 5:30 p.m.

March 28, 1945

Today I was sent to the quarters of the special-attack pilots, but it was my first time, and I was embarrassed and ran away. I was ashamed of my lack of honor. Beginning tomorrow I'll listen to what our special-attack force older brothers say and wash and mend their clothes as well as I can.

March 29, 1945

I did the pilots' laundry in the morning and cleaned their quarters in the afternoon. As I did this, I heard some of their stories. They are members of the Thirtieth Jinbu Squadron, which is commanded by First Lieutenant Ōbitsu, and are young. Although the unit commander is strict, he is very kind to us, and his subordinates are quite attached to him. They enjoy themselves, singing songs out loud, in their pine grove.

---

1. By this time, teenage boys and girls throughout Japan had been mobilized for work in factories, arsenals, and so forth. Initially Maeda cleared land for cultivation, grew potatoes, and made sweets for the army and was building and provisioning supply bunkers that were being prepared for the decisive battle with the enemy when her work assignment was changed.

2. The sensei was Miyawaki Yoshiko, who taught sewing at Maeda's school. Apparently, she generally accompanied the girls when they reported for work at the special-attack pilots' quarters. Satō Sanae, *Tokkō no machi — Chiran: Saizenkichi o irodotta nihonjin no sei to shi* (Tokyo: Kojinsha, 1997), 128.

3. The special-attack pilots at the Chiran Air Base lived in semi-subterranean A-frame structures located in a pine grove.

4. Throughout her diary Maeda uses polite language to describe the pilots, and although this is typical of a girl her age, it also conveys her respect for the pilots.

Maeda Shōko, first row right, and two classmates, spring 1945. Courtesy of Nagasaki Shōko.

March 30, 1945

Today the pilots will leave. In the morning they received cherry blossoms from the local shrine, and we gave them dolls as our farewell presents. They seemed genuinely pleased. We went by truck to where the aircraft were parked and offered the pilots lots of food. They shouted cheerfully to us, "Take care of yourselves and live a long life!" and climbed into their beloved aircraft. The assortment of dolls adorning their planes and flopping and spinning in the wind marked today as the day of an attack. The planes took off but returned because of bad weather. The pilots were very disappointed.

March 31, 1945

We took it easy today and sat on the grass talking with the special-attack pilots. We asked for everyone's addresses. Lance Corporals Sasaki and Ikeda gave as their addresses:

Kusabakure 3-chōme
Santogawa Ward
Hell Prefecture[5]

Then we talked about life at a girls' school and about our elder brothers' lives in the military. Apparently Corporal Fukuie has a younger sister who is our age, and he talked about her.

April 1, 1945

Today, after I did the pilots' laundry and cleaned their quarters, we all talked. Eighteen-year-old Lance Corporal Imai and Corporal Fukuie peeled off some bark from a cryptomeria tree and wrote on it "Corporal Grumman."[6] (Recently the air raids have intensified, and waves of Grumman Hellcats continue to attack.) It seems that "Corporal Grumman" also referred to the fact that both Fukuie and Lance Corporal Imai soon will be promoted to corporal and will wipe out the American aircraft carriers that dispatched these Grummans.[7] I'll tell the story of these two forever and ever. They asked me to write to their younger sisters and to report that their brothers were smiling as they attacked. Using their own blood they wrote, "I will go off together with the dolls . . ." and handed to us strands of their hair and fingernail clippings, and I cried for these older brothers and their younger sisters.[8]

On the same day I went to the battle command center with Iwawaki.[9]

April 2, 1945

Today was the day of the attack. Second Lieutenant Yokota asked that I be the one to fasten the hook on his undershirt, and because this meant my going to

---

5. This is not a real address but a sardonic allusion to the eighteenth-century warrior classic *Hagakure (In the Shade of Spring Leaves)* by Yamamoto Tsunetomo (1659–1719). A staple in the modern, state-sponsored versions of the "way of the warrior" (J. *bushidō*), *Hagakure* opens with the lines "The way of the samurai is found in death." See Yamamoto Tsunetomo, *Hagakure: The Book of the Samurai*, translated by William Scott Wilson (Tokyo: Kodansha International, 1979), 17.

6. "Corporal Grumman" is a reference to the Grumman F6F Hellcat, a carrier-based American fighter that was used in attacks on the Japanese home islands in the closing months of the war. Designed to do battle with the Mitsubishi A6M Zero, the Hellcat appeared in the Pacific theater in October 1942 and was used through the end of the war.

7. The special-attack pilots were promoted posthumously.

8. It was customary for the pilots to send home strands of hair and fingernail clippings so their families had at least a part of their bodies to cremate, as Buddhist funeral practice required.

9. Maeda does not identify Iwawaki, who was probably a classmate.

the barracks alone, I was embarrassed and went with Mori,[10] Saying that the skies were clear and it would be a good day to fly, Second Lieutenant Yokota shaved off his mustache.

The pilots began to take off at 3:30 in the afternoon . . . and we saw them off waving rising-sun flags, but Second Lieutenant Miyazaki's aircraft returned and landed. Then First Lieutenant Ōbitsu's aircraft and others took off one by one. . . . Miyazaki's aircraft went "U-U-U-U," and his engine sounded bad and coughed fire. It was too bad, but if it had been me, I would have taken off in that condition. A member of the ground crew got into the plane, turned it around, and brought it back. Squadron Leader Ōbitsu's plane was shaking violently from side to side; the bomb on Fukuie's plane fell out of its rack; and Gotō's plane broke down and wouldn't move. Today the squadron leader tried to attack twice but failed both times. He sat alone in the barracks gnashing his teeth. Everyone was in the barracks, and we sang ballads with the special-attack pilots. We sang "The Setting Sun Sinks" as well as our school song.[11] Miyazaki told us stories about philosophy, but I couldn't understand what he was saying, and my head began to spin.

We heard a conversation about what to do if the enemy landed. We intend to follow valiantly in the footsteps of our older brothers and not to forget that we are Japanese women and that we are to kill at least one person before we die.[12] Although the pilots themselves will perish together with the enemy ships, they were cheerful as they talked to us, worried about our futures, and warned us not to die in vain. All we could do was to bow our heads in respect.

Lance Corporal Ikeda sang.

Long ago, oh so long ago, Grandpa and Grandma met
And they got off to a good start.
Grandpa went off to cut grass in the mountains, and Grandma headed to
   the river to do the washing
And they got off to a good start.
Donburi gokko, donburi gokko, it flowed toward them
Grandma gathered it up
And they got off to a good start.[13]

---

10. Mori is probably a classmate.

11. I have not been able to identify "The Setting Sun Sinks."

12. Nine-year-old Nakane Mihōko makes the same point about killing the enemy. See her 6/17/45 entry.

13. Ikeda recites the opening lines of a famous Japanese fairy tale, "Peach Boy" (*Momotarō*).

April 3, 1945

Today was the day of the fourth attack — it was four o'clock. Leaving the Chiran airfield for the last time, First Lieutenant Ōbitsu's plane and ten others flew off to the distant, distant south. They left behind one person, a Corporal Kawasaki, who was sick in bed. Before the attack, when Imai took the camouflage netting off his aircraft, he muttered, "It's gotten this dirty!" and showed how dirty his gloves were. It was an unreasonable request, but he insisted that his plane be cleaned off, and it was. Corporal Yokō was extremely pleased about his last flight and said, "I have no regrets. Kawasaki's being left in the sick bay is the only thing weighing on my mind." That's probably so, I thought, because Yokō and Kawasaki were really good friends. I thought Yokō was a truly fine person for thinking about his sick buddy even when his own fate was uncertain. They say he's a squadron leader who will attack with the bones of his subordinates on his back, and they talk about Second Lieutenant Yokota as well, the one with a mustache.[14] They all treated us like younger sisters, or perhaps like children, and I thought we were very lucky. Iwama wrote some calligraphic inscriptions for us, and when I thought of how we hadn't been able to do anything for the pilots and yet received these words of appreciation, my heart was full of gratitude.

We simply pray that the men of the Thirtieth Jinbu Squadron will body-crash without incident into enemy ships and brilliantly fulfill their great assignment.[15]

April 4, 1945

With just the ailing Kawasaki and the ground crew left, the barracks were eerily quiet. All of us left behind in the barracks shared our memories of how until yesterday, it was "like this and like that." I took a break from nursing Kawasaki and went to get a futon at the guard company. I was accosted by newspaper journalists and talked to them about serving the special-attack unit and shared my impressions, emotions, and feelings of resignation. I was surrounded by a horde of journalists, and it was too much.

April 5, 1945

Since there were no more special-attack pilots left, we asked whether we could do the ground crew's laundry. I was sympathetic because it occurred to me that they probably spent the whole day working on the aircraft and were exhausted at day's

---

14. Special-attack pilots often carried on their final missions the ashes of their fellow pilots who had been killed in training.

15. Throughout her diary, Maeda uses "body-crash" (J. *tai-atari*), the official term for the tactic of crashing an aircraft into an enemy target.

end. They were the ones who got the aircraft to fly without a hitch or breakdowns. We felt for them and thought we should wash their clothes every day.

April 6, 1945

Now that the beloved aircraft he had worked on probably had body-crashed, one of the maintenance staff said, "Today is the day of the squadron leader's death — let's all pray." Mori and I each received a cigarette, and after lighting it and smelling its aroma, we prayed. To the distant south . . . when I thought about how people who had been fine just two or three days ago had body-crashed into enemy ships and wouldn't return to this world, I couldn't work and just helped prepare meals.

As I was listening to a member of the ground crew playing a *shakuhachi*, the personnel of the Twentieth Jinbu Squadron asked us to do their laundry. From the outset, I had been in charge of their washing, but I had been away from the quarters of the special-attack pilots. Because the three people left behind when their planes broke down were in the barracks, it was hard to go there. At the same time Second Lieutenant Anazawa asked me to mend three socks. Others cried out, "Mine too," and that afternoon I had my hands full with mending.

April 7, 1945

When I finished preparing breakfast this morning, four or five people I didn't know were puttering around in the kitchen, and when I announced, "The meal is ready," they turned out to be new people. I mistook them for people I knew and embarrassed myself. They all were second lieutenants, and their group leader was a military academy graduate — a fine, quiet, and reliable person. People whispered, "All the people who're coming now are older. Can pilots that old form special-attack units?" All had dark mustaches and seemed older. The barracks once again became merry.

April 8, 1945

Motoshima gave me some camellia and azalea blossoms. Everyone said having azalea blossoms now was unusual, and we made flower arrangements with the azaleas and pine boughs. As we worked on them, we agreed that the flowers would dry up after Motoshima had attacked and body-crashed. Watai gave me a doll that he had gotten from a girls' school in Shizuoka.

Second Lieutenant Anazawa said, "Why have all of you been staying away from our barracks? We have laundry that needs to be done," and went with us to the barracks. When we got there, there was nothing to be done, and we were mystified. We passed the time talking with Second Lieutenants Ōhira and Anazawa.

It was raining, and because we had come to do laundry, we were barefooted and the pilots teased us mercilessly. We ran out of the barracks.

April 9, 1945

Today we did laundry and cleaning and went to the barracks to see what the pilots needed. Recently, even Kawasaki has gotten better and is able to venture outside the barracks. While we were doing the washing, we went over to watch some of the maintenance people fish. Both Koizumi and Kawasaki fell off the dike into the river. Just when I was in danger of getting soaked, Kimoto grabbed me and stopped me from falling in. Apparently one can use electricity to send sparks into the water to catch fish. When we did this, sending sparks flying from the mouth of a pipe, a fish suddenly floated to the surface, its white belly showing. Because the voltage was low, this method didn't work that well, and all the fish swam away. I wrote a letter to Lance Corporal Fukuie's younger sister about his last flight and posted it.

April 10, 1945

I was able to finish my tasks in the morning and in the afternoon went to see the comfort-troop dancers.[16] I went together with Squadron Leader Ikeda, Okayasu, Motoshima, and Watai, and since we were early, we amused ourselves in an elevated vegetable patch. We sang "Sinking from the Sky" at the top of our lungs, and everyone, even the taciturn squadron leader, joined in.[17] The squad leader, fiddling with a head of cabbage, wondered out loud, "Will this *kanran* roll?"[18] Watai added, "I myself say *kyabetsu!*" and Okayasu chimed in, "I say *gyokusai*."[19] The squadron leader smiled wryly. Watai, while complaining always . . . The squadron leader said, "Try as I might, I'm no match for Watai," and turning to him, he asked, "Do you want to become a special attacker?" The boy answered, "No, I don't. I want to live a long life!" When the kind squadron leader brings the food for the air units, he plops down big sweet potatoes that have just been boiled and are piping hot and that always flatten out. Everyone

---

16. It is not clear whether the women in these "comfort units" (J. *imondan*) were "comfort women" (J. *ianfu*). They are mentioned twice more, in Maeda's April 15 and April 17 entries.

17. "Sinking from the Sky" (Sora kara no chinbotsu) was a brand-new Columbia Records song, released in April 1945.

18. A *kanran* is a kind of cabbage.

19. Okayasu is making a pun on *gyokusai*, which can mean "shattered vegetable" or "shattered jewel."

laughs at this. At that moment a car drove up and the squadron leader ran out to it, and because it was filled with a mountain of five-gallon cans, he climbed in, scratching his head. Then a truck drove up. When Motoshima shouted "Stop!" the truck carrying the dancing girls stopped. We got in and went off to see what was going on. But because of the time, we students came right back. Everyone else went out into town.

April 11, 1945

This morning after we finished washing, sewing, sweeping, and cleaning up the breakfast dishes, five special-attack aircraft from the same squadron were scheduled to arrive, so we went out to greet them. While we waited in the control tower with Squadron Leader Ikeda, Motoshima, Okayasu, and Watai, two aircraft landed. The squadron leader was very pleased, as were his two subordinates who flew in. Since I would be indebted to them from now until the day of their attack, I went to greet them.[20]

The squadron commander said, "Tomorrow is the attack. You've come right on time. Will you attack right away?" The newly arrived pilots replied firmly, "We'll attack together."

That night there was a farewell party at the dining hall for the Twentieth, Sixty-ninth, and Thirtieth squadrons. We received special permission to stay until nine o'clock and serve the men. Until now the squadron leader had written down the pilots' addresses for us and asked us to let their families know that they had attacked. This time we asked for their addresses, even though they all were drunk. With breath reeking of saké, they kindly wrote them down.

We all sang "Sinking from the Sky." I intended to join in and sing with everything I had, but for some reason my voice choked up and I began to cry. Mori said, "Let's go outside," and once outside the barracks we cried to our heart's content. Our tears were not at all tears of regret, though. Although tomorrow they would perish together with enemy ships, tonight they were beaming, drunk, and having a great time. When we saw this, we thought, "Ah! Look at this! Japan is strong!" and cried tears of gratitude.

Okayasu, drunk and hanging on to a car, expressed his gratitude to everyone. Amazing! They were such splendid people. Mori and I held each other and bawled.

---

20. Maeda feels a debt of gratitude to those pilots who were willing to sacrifice themselves for the sake of the country.

April 12, 1945

Today will be a clear-weather attack. They loaded us into a car with the divine eagles who will attack and not return, and we drove straight to the waiting aircraft along Guidance Road. On the way we sang "Sinking from the Sky" over and over. Together with our teachers we pulled the camouflage netting off the squadron leader's plane. The revolutions of the propeller on his plane, the one with a bomb on its belly, were fine. Motoshima's plane made a buzzing sound. That was probably the exceedingly kind squadron leader. We climbed onto the starting car (in those days, when aircraft started their engines, their propellers would not always turn automatically, so many had to be started with a starting car) and went to the control tower to send off the pilots. When I turned around, the squadron leader and Motoshima, both wearing pretty Chinese milk vetch necklaces, boarded their aircraft and looked back at us. A plane covered with cherry blossoms taxied by right in front of us. We thought that we, too, should shower the planes with cherry blossoms and ran back to the barracks. On the way we met Kawasaki, who was riding a bicycle.

We picked as many cherry blossoms as we could and ran back as fast as our legs would carry us, but the planes had gone to the starting line and were about to begin taxiing down the runway. They were far away, and we were sorry we couldn't run out to them. Motoshima's plane was late and went to the starting line right in front of us. Then the squadron leader's plane took off. It was followed by planes piloted by Okayasu, Yagyū, and Mochiki. The Type 97 fighters wagged their wings from left to right, and we could see smiling faces in all the planes.[21] The plane piloted by Anazawa from the Twentieth Jinbu Squadron passed in front of us. When we waved branches of cherry blossoms as hard as we could, the smiling Anazawa, his head wrapped in a headband, saluted us several times.

Click! . . . when we turned and looked behind us, it was the cameraman taking our pictures. When every one of the special-attack planes had taken off, we just stood there for a long time, gazing at the southern sky, which seemed to go on forever. Tears welled up in our eyes.

We didn't feel like talking, and when we were about to return together, we discovered Motoshima and Watai. Motoshima was crying unashamedly . . . when I asked, "What's wrong?" he said, "My bomb dropped off, and I couldn't take off. When I ran over to our squadron leader, he said, 'Motoshima, come later. I'll go

---

21. The Nakajima B5N1 Type 97 Carrier Attack Bomber, which the Allies called the "Kate," had been in service on Japanese aircraft carriers since the late 1930s and was obsolete by 1945.

ahead and will be waiting for you in that other world,' I didn't expect this, and I'm so upset! After squadron leader's plane took off, I just sat alone and cried to my heart's content." Teary-eyed Watai added, "It is really a shame! I'm sorry." All at once, the tears we had been stifling welled up, and we all cried together. They said that tonight was a wake for the squadron leader, so saké couldn't be drunk. Horii, who came today, told jokes, and the men listened, but their minds were somewhere else. Since they cried whenever they thought about their squadron leader, who had such deep affection for his subordinates, and about the way he'd say "Motoshima, Motoshima," they asked us not to say anything at all.

It was unfortunate that Motoshima and Watai weren't able to body-crash together with their splendid squadron leader or to participate in the second general attack.[22]

April 13, 1945

We heard the names of the men from the Sixty-ninth Jinbu Squadron who went off yesterday — Second Lieutenants Yamashita (the assistant squadron leader), Watanabe, Horii, and Nakayama. This raised Motoshima's and Watai's spirits. Everyone missed the squadron leader.

April 14, 1945

This morning, after the breakfast cleanup, the pilots wrote their wills and death poems for us. In the car on the way back, we sang "Annihilating the Enemy."[23] Looking up at the last traces of the evening sky, I thought about those who had died. We drove along the runway and saw the maintenance people hard at work on the aircraft, whose engines produced blue green flames when they turned over. Motoshima acknowledged and saluted each member of the maintenance crew. These were a pilot's salutes of gratitude expressing his thanks to the maintenance crews. The maintenance people do their best to prepare the aircraft for the next day's attack and even stay up all night. Seeing all this right before our eyes, we thought that this is why Japanese soldiers are great.

---

22. Motoshima appeared at the Maeda house that evening at dinnertime and gave Maeda Shōko a cash gift for her "school expenses" and a bottle of wine "for her grandfather." He then went to the home of the principal of the local girls' school and donated two hundred yen to the school. See Satō, *Tokkō no machi — Chiran*, 118–119, 127.

23. The song that they were singing may have been "Until the Enemy Raises the White Flag" (*Teki shirahata ageru made*) whose last line is "Close is the day of the annihilation of the enemy!" (*Teki gekimetsu hi wa chikai*). Columbia Records released this song in December 1944.

April 15, 1945

We prepared for tomorrow's attack and were really busy, fussing over the way we wrapped up the pilots' personal effects, tidying up, cleaning, and so forth. We gave Motoshima the two dolls he asked for. He's very happy that tomorrow he'll follow in his squadron leader's footsteps and go off to that other world. Apparently Second Lieutenant Motoshima lost his mother when he was a child, and he was very sympathetic when he learned that I didn't have a mother either. He said, "After you lose your mother, you have to become a good mother substitute and a good older sister." The comfort group will be arriving.

April 16, 1945

Today, at long last, the attack. Mori came to get me at four in the morning. We rode in the car carrying the special-attack pilots to the airfield. The pilots clutched the remains of those who had died performing their duties, and there wasn't a single sad face in the group. They sang "If You're a Man" and "Companion Cherry Blossoms."[24] On this, and only on this, morning, no matter what, the songs could not sound sad. Our older brothers, looking gallant in their white headbands and white scarves, lined up in front of the battle control center. They all wore the same uniforms and were somber, which I didn't understand. As we searched for the pilots we'd looked after, all of a sudden Motoshima called out, "Good Morning!" Then he shouted, "The Sixty-ninth Jinbu Squadron is assembled!" Everyone was there, and for some time we listened intently to what would be the pilots' last speeches. Motoshima wrapped around his head the floating-chrysanthemum headband that the squadron leader had given him, and Watai and Horii prepared themselves for battle.[25] When we offered fallen double-petal cherry blossoms, they seemed very pleased. Of the two dolls, one went into a beloved aircraft and the other was hung from the flight clock. A car then took the pilots to the flight line. Watanabe kept waving a handkerchief until we could no longer see him. Then the aircraft started to taxi, and they took off. The eastern sky was just beginning to brighten. The plane that had "Motoshima" clearly written on it took off in the morning grayness. When I thought, "Hey! It's Motoshima," the "Watai," and "Horii" planes then took off, too. They formed a

---

24. Both "Companion Cherry Blossoms" (Dōki no sakura) and "If You're a Man" (Otoko nara) are well-known military ballads. The former is an army song about two pilots who train and die together in a special attack, and the latter is a navy air corps song whose recurring refrain is "If you're a man, come along."

25. Maeda uses the expression *tasuki o suru*, which refers to the warrior practice of tying up their sleeves before a battle using a cord called a *tasuki*.

three-plane formation and flew off together. The Horii plane flew at a very low altitude, which gave me the chills and made me break out in a cold sweat. We stayed until the very end and then returned to the barracks. I was lost in thought for some time as I prayed for the success of these divine eagles who left their base for the last time to attack, together with the rising sun. As we talked about what we were feeling this morning, Second Lieutenant Yamashita returned. He just said, "I'm sorry" and handed over a scrap of paper. Five names were on the sheet: Watanabe, Horii, Watai, Nakayama, and Yamashita. These five were not able to make it. This meant that those who actually attacked were Motoshima and Kawamura—the two who had said, "No matter what, I'll attack today!" At 9:30 a.m.—the time when Motoshima and Kawamura would be body-crashing if all went well—we faced south and observed a moment of silence. Even now I seemed to hear Motoshima's voice, his strong voice, singing "Sinking from the Sky."

April 17, 1945

There was an enemy air raid, and we evacuated to an air-raid shelter. Hasebe of the Thirty-first Buyō Squadron bolted without touching his food. Everyone called him a coward, and so he dashed out of the shelter and then returned with food in his mouth, crying "Evacuation! Evacuation!" Watai said, "Has the kid come back? Let's take some time and finish our food," and left the shelter. Then when they heard the roar of the enemy planes, they came running back. Finally, on the third try, Hasebe finished his meal. We were amazed. Watanabe—the kind, girlish, and spoiled kid—didn't bother to leave. Because he had once been bombed and narrowly escaped, Horii kept himself out of harm's way until it was clear that he was out of danger, and he did this until his time to attack. He had a good time alone in the shelter, dancing "Flowers Are Islands of Dew . . . ," which the comfort group had danced when they came.[26] He had wonderful hand and body movements, and without thinking we burst out laughing together with our teachers. Akasaki, who had been resting in the Twentieth Jinbu Squadron's barracks, came barreling into the shelter, saying, "They say it's an attack!" Surprised, Watai got up and said, "Dying quickly would be a blessing! Living on while others have died is hard. It's only because we have to go to Fukuoka." Recently Kawasaki, whose color has improved, still had yellow eyes and was listless! When he heard, "Kawasaki is going too," he just said, "Um . . . OK." We were really getting a good look at the trials of a special-attack unit. In the evening we'll go

---

26. I have not been able to identify this song.

to Sensei's house together with Watai, Horii, and others. We'll play cards and have a good time.

April 18, 1945

They were going to take a train to Fukuoka that left Chiran at 7:00 a.m. We went with our teachers to see them off. To buoy their spirits until the train left, we sang "Companion Cherry Blossoms" and "Tomochan and Shinchan."[27] Other special-attack pilots joined in. They'll be coming back in four or five days, and we consoled them, saying, "Come back quickly." We said goodbye to Kawasaki, and by the time we got to Watai and Horii, the train was moving. We waved handkerchiefs until the faces of Watai, Horii, and Kawasaki, who were leaning out of the windows, got smaller and smaller and the train disappeared in the distance.

As he had asked us to, we carried Kawasaki's parachute harness to the barracks. We'll wait for the return of Watanabe and Nakayama, who left for an attack yesterday. The only ones left in the barracks are Second Lieutenants Yamashita and Hasebe and our maintenance crew. Yamashita will go to Fukuoka in the afternoon. Because there won't be special-attack pilots here for some time, we'll have a vacation beginning tomorrow.

---

27. I have not been able to identify "Tomochan and Shinchan."

The Diary of an Evacuated Schoolboy

Manabe Ichirō was born in 1933 and was a student at Keimei Primary School in Nakano Ward in central Tokyo during the war. In the summer of 1944 Manabe lived with his widowed mother and his teenage sister Kazuko. who had been mobilized for war work. Anticipating the Allied bombing raids, the government issued an order on June 30, 1944, instructing third through sixth graders to evacuate to the countryside beginning in August. Already 300,000 children had left the cities, and 700,000 more would leave by war's end. In compliance with the order, Manabe's school chose the village of Yumoto in Fukushima Prefecture as an evacuation site, a village famous for its hot springs. Manabe and his classmates left Tokyo on August 28. After they arrived in Yumoto, they were housed in local inns, whose proprietors did their best to make the children comfortable. On February 25, 1945, Manabe's section of sixth graders returned to Tokyo for their graduation from primary school, and that evening 172 B-29s attacked central Tokyo. It is not clear whether he survived the attack.

Manabe's diary begins on July 14, 1944, and ends on February 25, 1945, the day he returned to Tokyo. Although it covers only seven months, his diary gives us a vivid picture, as seen through the eyes of an eleven-year-old boy, of the daily lives of ordinary people in central Tokyo, with its many hardships and shortages, and also those of the evacuated children.

A photocopy of Manabe's handwritten diary is included in Zenkoku sokai gakudō renraku kyōgikai, comp., *Gakudō sokai no kiroku*, vol. 5, *Shiryō de kataru gakudō sokai* (3) (Tokyo: Ōzorasha, 1994), and the excerpt in this volume appears on pages 276 to 295.

July 14, Friday, clear then showers
Moving Desks and Pool Opening

The no. 1 group of sixth graders gathered at 7:00 a.m. and loaded onto carts the nineteen desks that were going to a school for evacuated children and moved them to Nakano Station.[1] When I got home after pushing and pulling at those desks, my throat was as dry as a bone. Lunch was tofu and *wakame*. There was a lot of *wakame* in the soup but not much tofu. The rice was what we always had. Today the pool was open from 1:00 to 2:30 p.m. Because of what happened last year, the roll call was taken very carefully.[2] We paired off, and we each had to remember who our partner was. If that person disappeared, we were to notify a teacher. When you left the pool, they wouldn't let you leave if you weren't with someone.

July 15, Saturday, clear

Today the no. 2 group of sixth graders carried desks to Nakano Station. We had bread for lunch. While I was eating my half piece of bread, my stomach felt full, but after I finished eating, I got hungry again. There was a science examination in the fifth period. I could answer all the questions, although half of them were a little unclear to me. Later, from 2:30 p.m., the pool was open for student groups. The water gradually ran out, and it disappeared completely in the end, and we cleaned the pool. Today we received a lot of ice from Yamamoto, who gave us red bean rice, too.

July 16, Sunday, beautifully clear but with sudden showers
Visiting Graves

I thought today was Sunday and slept late. It was really hot starting in the morning, and the heat seemed to be changing into steam. The three of us left the house at about 10:30 a.m. and visited Grandpa Yanaka's grave.[3] I prayed that I might become strong in the way that Japan was victorious at Saipan.[4] Then we

---

1. Students in each grade were divided into numbered "groups" (J. *kumi*) and "sections" (J. *bu*).
2. Manabe does not tell us what happened. It appears that a student drowned.
3. Manabe, his sister, and his mother. His 7/25/44 entry indicates that Manabe's father is deceased. When he died and under what circumstances is not clear.
4. Saipan, in the Mariana Islands, was held by the Japanese at that time and served as the headquarters of Admiral Nagumo Chūichi's Central Pacific Air Fleet. It had just been lost to the Americans, but Manabe does not know this. The Americans began their assault on June 11, and although the Japanese put up a stiff resistance, suffering 29,000 casualties and causing 16,500 American casualties, the Americans secured Saipan by July 9.

took another train to Tama Cemetery. When we got off at Kōenji Station so Kazuko could buy tickets, it got really dark, and there was thunder. We waited thirty minutes, and it stopped, and we went on to the cemetery. There was no one besides us. This bothered me, and I pledged to work at getting people to come. When we got on the horse-drawn cart to return to the station, they had raised the fare from forty to fifty sen, and I thought we shouldn't have gotten on again.

July 17, Monday, clear
A Circular from School

I went to school and moved chairs at about 6:30 a.m. There were 150 chairs, and each sixth grader carried one chair. They were hard to hold, and we walked with chairs slung over our shoulders with a rope. It was just to Nakano Station, but we seemed to get more tired than we did when we moved desks. Lunch was rice gruel. The people from the Sunesan Group had already eaten, so there was not enough, and everyone grumbled about this.[5] There was a lot of stuff in the gruel — tofu, wheat gluten, pumpkin squash, and eggplant — and it wasn't very soupy. The soup came around three times from where Noda was sitting. In the evening there was a circular from school about the children who were going to be evacuated, and because it was a very urgent matter, it was passed around quickly. I went into the pool. Still no examination.

July 18, Tuesday, clear
The Brave Warriors on Saipan Died in Action

We had a library examination in first period and a calligraphy quiz in the second (the Chinese characters for "see," "stretch," "boat," "evening," "stand," and "cloud"). For lunch we had the same rice gruel as yesterday. It had *wakame* and one big piece of wheat gluten in it. We had salmon and pickles too. The piece of salmon was quite small, and the pickle was pickled radish. The rice in the gruel was dry and tasteless. The science examination (from the fifteenth) and the Japanese history quiz (from the thirteenth) were returned. I got ninety on the science test and one hundred on the history quiz. There was a Parents Association meeting about the evacuation at 1:00 p.m. I'll be going in the group evacuation. According to the 5:00 p.m. news, all the brave warriors on Saipan died in battle. I think for sure that enemy planes will now bomb Tokyo.

---

5. Manabe does not identify the "Sunesan Group."

July 19, Wednesday, clear with frequent showers
An Air-Raid Drill

There was an air-raid drill at 4:00 a.m. I was sleepy and just couldn't stay awake. Because they said it was a practice air-raid warning and alert, I quickly put on my shirt, wrapped my puttees around my legs, and put on my air-raid hood. Except for those who were sick, even babies participated, and roll was called. We crept into the shelter and covered it with tatami mats and storm doors. The drill ended at around 6:00 a.m. Today was the anniversary of the founding of our school, and so all we had today were ceremonies. There was a distribution of umbrellas, and we did *jankenpo*. I did it with my neighbor Satō and lost the first time. It was bad. Three won—Hayashi Nobu, Yasukawa, and Nakamura Makoto. We were supposed to have bread for lunch, but there wasn't any. The pool was closed. I asked Oka Taiichi for volume 8 of his Japanese-language text, but when I tried to pay him for it, he wouldn't take any money.

July 20, Thursday, clear then rainy
The Closing Ceremony

Today's closing ceremony was supposed to start at 10:20 a.m., and they said people from my group are saying "Come on!" but the no. 1 group had already assembled. Apparently the groups that practiced assembled quickly. The one yen, ten sen, lunch fee was collected today. I wrote "collective evacuation" on the evacuation application and submitted it. My group has thirty-five students, and nine will stay with relatives. Five students will stay behind. We had rice gruel for lunch again. There was no tofu in it, but there were potatoes. These were the ones we harvested at school. We went through with the closing ceremony and received our report cards. Everyone was there. From now on, I'll persevere and not fail.

July 21, Friday, cloudy then rain
A Distribution of Salted Salmon and the Resignation of the Tōjō Cabinet

Starting today we have summer and fall training, not summer vacation. Radio calisthenics began today, but they were canceled because it was drizzling. Salmon was distributed at 9:00 a.m., but by 8:30 a.m., everyone was waiting at the assembly center, so we went to school. Because the line started at the school gate and continued for a long way toward the Okada house, we went to the end of the line. The teacher said the distribution would be in the normal group order, so we were eighteenth from the front. While standing in line in the way we do for a morning assembly and talking, someone said that the Keimei Collective Evacuation Group would be made up of six hundred students and four hundred will live with relatives. When we got our salted salmon, we were given one slice, the head, and two more pieces. Because the salmon was old, it had lots of fins. Today the whole Tōjō cabinet resigned together, saying they had reasons for doing this. I think they are cowards.[6] That evening it began to rain hard, lightning flashed, and there was a lot of thunder.

July 24, Monday, cloudy

Today I stood in line for rice gruel. I was just in front of the bathhouse, but when they returned my ticket, I was at the corner of the bathhouse. They give just one coupon to children. I thought one child could buy only one portion, but apparently one coupon was worth two portions. There were short-necked clams in the soup, and it was delicious. Hasegawa came after lunch, and when I wondered what was going on, he said he was going to Noda Fumi's house, so we left. They let us go into the icebox and gave us tomatoes that had been chilled — two each. Apparently they were grown at Noda's house, and as we were leaving, they gave us taro seedlings. We went to Kikuyo-chan's house to roll roasted soybeans in soybean flour, but it didn't work out.

July 25, Tuesday, clear

Today when I opened my eyes halfway, I heard everyone calling "Manabe, Manabe" and woke up with a start. It was still early, so people were gathering slowly. Kazuko fought with Mother about something, and saying she was going to buy a book for school, she grabbed a hundred-yen bill and left.[7] Mother immediately went to Kikuyo-chan's house and had them make miso soup and a lunch for Kazuko. Then things were as they always are. In the morning I went to the ward office, and they gave me, as the surviving kin of a deceased father, a ten-yen condolence payment.[8] The Yamamotos next door gave us hotcakes, which were not overly sweet, and some fish tsukudani.

July 26, Wednesday, cloudy then rainy

Today I went again to do radio calisthenics, and I have a perfect record for the last five days. At 10:00 a.m. I went with mother to buy vegetables at Saginomiya.[9]

---

6. General Tōjō Hideki, who had been prime minister from October 18, 1941, resigned on July 18, 1944.

7. Kazuko is Manabe's older sister. She appears to be in her teens, and like other young Japanese her age, she had been mobilized for factory work.

8. It appears that since Manabe's father has died, the family is entitled to condolence payments.

9. Although there is a Saginomiya in Nakano Ward, it appears that Manabe and his mother went to the Saginomiya area in Nerima Ward.

We went to a very big house with a tile roof that didn't look like a farmer's house. The farmer was very kind, but he said that everything had been sold. When we continued along the inner road for a long way, we came to a house that sold us things, and we bought about two *kanme* of tomatoes. They absolutely would not give us potatoes. After lunch, when we returned from Masashi-chan's house, a sparrow flew into our house, and everyone shut the doors, and we caught it easily with a long net. We made a bird cage and began to take care of it. In the evening, the rice store people brought rice: we received just over four gallons for a sixteen-day period, which comes to a little less than two pints a day.

July 27, Thursday, rainy then sunny
Mother Visited the Dentist

Today I got up at 5:30 a.m. Because it rained hard just before 5:00 a.m. or so, I thought the radio calisthenics would be called off, but four or five of us went to see if they were being held. Hara-sensei said there would be radio calisthenics, and we gathered at the school gate. They were called off when it suddenly began to rain. At about 10:00 a.m. Mother, whose teeth have been bad for some time, went to see a dentist in Aoyama. Four of her front teeth were pulled out, and she couldn't speak very well. She was pathetic. I thought to myself, I'll take good care of my teeth and make sure mine are good. After lunch I stabbed a vein in my foot with a phonograph needle. Because I pulled the needle out right away, I think everything will be fine. The sparrow died.

July 30, Monday [Sunday], rain
A Circular from School

It's been damp and rainy since morning. The Yamamotos gave me a *senbei* cracker. Kawachi brought a circular. Under the "Good Mother" recruitment program, graduates of girls' schools who are under forty and in good health will get a monthly stipend of fifty-five yen. Kazuko was punished by the gods, and her foot began to hurt, so at about 2:00 p.m. she got a *jinrikisha* and left the factory early. This is probably retribution for the day before yesterday. Her wound was draining pus, and she went with mother to see Doctor Suga.

July 31, Monday, clear

Today I slept really late. I went for rice gruel at about 10:00 a.m. I had Satō pour it for me. He gave me two portions, and although I thought we wouldn't eat all two portions, it was eaten up. Last night I went to roll boiled soybeans in soybean flour. I went with Masa-chan and Shigeo to a barber called Horie.

August 1, Tuesday, crystal clear

The weather this morning was beautiful. It was like the start of summer. The first female pumpkin-squash flower bloomed today. I cross-pollinated it, but I couldn't get the backs of the pistils to touch, so I had Mother piggyback me, but when she did this, we jostled the plant, and the flower fell off the plant. I got pretty upset. We stood in line for rice gruel from about 9:00 a.m. We were eighth from the front and way, way back. I had Mother come later and she left me with two bills, and I bought enough for four people. Sensei came to the house and then went on an errand to Satō Shigeru-sensei's place. Today I bought my July allotment of sweets, fifteen sen worth. I was made to buy ten sen worth of grilled things and five sen worth of biscuits.

August 2, Wednesday, clear

Lately I've been sleeping very well and sleeping late. Today, there was no rice, so I stood in line for rice gruel. I was behind Ishishi and reserved the eighth place from the front and went home. I got back in line with a pot at about 10:30 a.m. and bought two servings. I crossed one male flower with a female one. So maybe I'll get a pumpkin squash. Today I went to buy ice with Masashi-chan. Because all the ice was sold out and none was available, we went to a place in Araichō. It was an extremely big ice shop, and they sold us about two *kanme* of ice which the shop where we usually buy ice calls three *kanme*. This seems like the real three *kanme*. Mother went to buy tomatoes at Saginomiya.

August 3, Thursday, clear
A Circular from School

Today I stood in line for rice gruel. We made two lines, and I was fourth from the front. It was the same arrangement as yesterday.[10] I bought two portions. The gruel had lots of pumpkin squash in it, and it was delicious. After lunch Kawachi brought a circular, and we passed it on. It included an order to report to school on the eighth at 8:30 a.m., a notice about mosquito nets—if you have more than you need, lend them to others—and two other pieces of business.

August 4, Friday, clear
An Air-Raid Warning and Alert

Today I stood in line for rice gruel. I was sixth from the front. I bought two portions. There were potatoes in the gruel, potatoes that still had their skins on.

---

10. Manabe does not tell us what this arrangement was.

Mother went to buy vegetables at Saginomiya at about 10:00 a.m. She bought tomatoes, eggplants, and cucumbers. The eggplants had just been picked and were shiny, fresh, and looked delicious. The farmer was said to be very good. Today there was a distribution of soap. I ordered one batch and went to Funatsuya to get it. I got two bars of Adeka soap and one bar of bath soap. There was suddenly an air-raid warning and alert at about 7:00 p.m. It seems that the enemy planes are finally coming.

August 5, Saturday, clear
The Cancellation of the Air-Raid Warning Alert and a Circular from School

It was Mother's turn this month to distribute nori, and she went off very early in the morning and was busy. The fifth is a holiday and a holiday for rice gruel, too. On the eighth, Nakamichi's uncle is going off to war, and his aunt and others are going to evacuate to the countryside. Masashi-chan was playing when he suddenly burst out crying and began to run around the garden as though he were crazy. I wondered what was going on, and it turned out he had been stung by a huge bee. Kawachi brought a circular today as well. It was decided that our [Keimei] mass evacuation site will be Fukushima Prefecture. I was completely put off by this, and the alert was called off at 2:00 p.m.

August 6, Sunday, clear
A Visit to the Meiji Tōgō Shrine and a Package from Aunt Masuno

At about 8:00 a.m. I went, together with the Yamamotos' uncle, to visit the Tōgō Shrine, which is on the grounds of the Meiji Shrine.[11] At the Meiji Shrine, soldiers, marines, and sailors come to be recognized officially as military units. After visiting the Tōgō Shrine, we went into the Navy Building. After seeing various things there, I was taken to the dining hall and had lunch and coffee together with everyone else. A person who looked like a navy commander said, "Little boy, come here for a second," and gave me a plate filled with barley rice and potatoes. I should have asked his name, but unfortunately I didn't, and I was sorry about this. Today I bought our July and August rations of matches at

---

11. The Tōgō Shrine is dedicated to Tōgō Heihachirō (1848–1934), a warrior from the old Satsuma domain who rose through the ranks of the new Western-style navy created during the Meiji period (1868–1911) and retired as a fleet admiral. He had a fascinating and diverse career: he was at Kagoshima in 1863 when it was bombarded by the British and was sent to England in 1871 to train with the Royal Navy. He commanded the cruiser *Naniwa*, which fired the first shots in the Sino-Japanese War (1894–1895), and distinguished himself as the commander of the battleship *Mikasa* during the Russo-Japanese War (1904–1905). Later he even tutored the Shōwa emperor on naval matters.

Funatsuya. They're called "Celebration Matches," and they don't go out. That evening Aunt Masuno sent fifty or so peaches.

August 7, Monday, rain

Today it's been raining steadily since early in the morning. At about noon, I added egg white to India ink and wrote out name cards for the collective evacuation. After I had done about five thousand cards, the ink got thick and dark. I went for rice gruel just before 11:00 a.m., but I was at the very end of the line. Satō let me cut in up front. I bought two portions of rice gruel, but there was nothing good in it. Today there was a distribution of tofu and *okara*. In the evening, we made bread with the *okara* and *udon* flour and ate this substitute food.

August 8, Tuesday, rainy then cloudy
Nakamichi's Departure for the Front and a Circular from School

Today was the thirty-second observance of the Great Imperial Rescript.[12] Early this morning Mother had a ceremony and went to the Hachiman Shrine. We kids had a ceremony from 8:00 a.m. The principal, together with Saitō Kansensei and Hirano-sensei, were away conducting surveys for the collective evacuation to Fukushima, and since they weren't here, Yajima-sensei read the imperial edict. I stood in line for rice gruel, but there were only eight hundred portions and lots of people, so each person got only one serving, and I was quite sick of all this. Afternoon — there was a going-off-to-war farewell party for Nakamichi at 7:30 p.m. It was pitch black and a little gloomy. Nakamichi said, "I will fight with enthusiasm!" and eighteen people went as a group with him as far as Kōenji Station. This was to the glory of the fifty-three groups.[13] Kawachi brought a circular. Taira City in Fukushima Prefecture has been chosen as the evacuation site.[14] In the evening, they brought rice.

August 9, Wednesday, clear

Beginning at 10:00 a.m. there were typhoid and diphtheria shots at school for those going off on the collective evacuation. The second diphtheria shot will

---

12. During the war, on the eighth day of every month, all Japanese and Japanese subjects, in the home islands and the colonies, read out loud the imperial rescript announcing the declaration of war with the Allies. It had been thirty-two months since the war started.

13. It is not clear what "fifty-three groups" refers to; perhaps they were the groups at Manabe's school.

14. Taira City is about a mile and a half northeast of Yumoto, the eventual evacuation site for Manabe's group.

be on the twelfth, and the second typhoid shot on the sixteenth. It didn't hurt when the needle went into my skin, but it began to hurt later. They did it on my right arm. I stood in line for rice gruel and bought two portions. In the evening there was a distribution of meat starting at 8:00 p.m. Because we were on monthly duty, Mother, Masa-chan, and I went to pick it up. There was a long line, and we waited a long time. The meat dripped a lot and really stank. One to two people got thirty *monme* for forty-eight sen, and three to five people got fifty *monme* for eighty sen. When I weighed the rice delivered yesterday, it came to about one and a half *to* for fifteen days; with soybeans mixed in, it came to one *shō* a day.

August 10, Thursday, clear
A Delivery of Ovens

Today, it's been very humid since morning. Mother went to Saginomiya to buy vegetables at around 10:00 a.m. Apparently, the farmers were very pleased because she took Western clothes to give them, and they gave her one whole chestnut squash free. She also got tomatoes and eggplant. There was also a distribution of soba today, but because Mother had gone off to Saginomiya, the Yamamotos' aunt and I went to get it at Tomoeya, which is in front of the Nogata police station. They gave two generous portions to those who were a part of the monthly rotation system. Each house got two portions, and each portion cost thirteen sen. In the evening, there was a distribution of ovens (steam ovens). Only two families — the Kurusus and us — had them installed.

August 11, Friday, clear

Yesterday Kazuko suffered from anemia while working at the factory and slept until evening. We had her brought home, and she hasn't eaten anything today and is still sleeping. There is no question that this is divine retribution. At noon, the rice gruel people were on vacation, and there was no food at all, so we cooked rice. We started cooking with the steam oven right away. Fuel was scarce, and when the charcoal began to smoke, it was white, and thus we understood right away. It was a good steam oven. Today was fly-catching day, and we caught twenty-six flies with swatters and nets and took them to Aoyama.

August 12, Saturday, clear
Tatami Turning and Diphtheria Shots

Today inoculations were scheduled to begin at 10:00 a.m. We went off to play at about 9:30 a.m. Sensei said it had been decided that the Keimei Group's collective evacuation site would be Yumoto in Fukushima Prefecture.[15] After some time, they said the sixth graders should come to get their shots, and I went to the end of the line. The needle went way in. When I was rubbing the spot where the needle went in, Akiba-sensei rubbed the area far below the injection spot. Mr. Kiguchi from the tatami shop came to turn our tatami mats at about 7:00 p.m. Because we've changed them every sixth year, the tatami are white and made us all feel good. We changed the tatami in the living room, too. The Yamamoto family had theirs changed as well. Mr. Kiguchi did about two houses a day, and we were impressed by how good a job he did.

August 13, Sunday, clear then cloudy
Obata's Visit and a Parents Association Meeting

At around lunchtime, Mr. Obata suddenly appeared. Because he hadn't let us know by postcard that he was coming, there was a great commotion, and we had nothing good to serve him. We gave him a little wheat flour in a bag. Today I had wax taken out of my ears. A large piece was taken out, and I was surprised at how big and thick it was. When I touched it, it seemed damp.

At 1:30 p.m. there was a Parents Association meeting for the parents of those going in the collective evacuation. The no. 1 group of sixth graders, all thirty-four of us, will be at the Shōhakukan in Yumoto, Iwaki County, Fukushima Prefecture.[16] The no. 3 group of fourth graders will be there, too. Yanagisawa-sensei, who is said to be a nice person, will be the teacher in charge. Apparently the Shōhakukan is a very nice inn.

August 14, Monday, clear
Submitting a Change-of-Residence Report and a Circular from School

Today I've felt dizzy since morning and didn't feel like eating. I also had a bad case of the runs. I got my luggage ready for the collective evacuation. Just my books and notebooks alone came to twenty-four volumes, and I worried about whether I'd be able to squeeze in other important things. After lunch I went to submit a "moving report." Beginning today, only two people will be counted for rationing, and Mother and Kazuko will receive a lot less. With charcoal and so forth, there is a big difference between the distributions for two people and those for three, and if the winter is cold, I will feel sorry for them. There was a

---

15. Yumoto is located in the southeastern corner of Fukushima Prefecture in north central Japan and in 1935 had a population of just over 17,000.

16. The Shōhakukan is a *ryokan*, or Japanese inn, and is still operating.

distribution of candles, and this time they were called "thousand-year candles" and were extremely useful. I bought stamps — seven-sen stamps — at the post office and paid money to Ta. . . .[17] It was sixty-two yen, fifty sen. The circular that was passed around had to do with the protective association's member fees.

August 15, Tuesday, clear
Going to the Waseda University Pool and a Circular from School

At about 9:00 a.m. Ii—— and Okutani came over and said they were going to the Waseda University pool. I got Mother's permission to go, and she made three *onigiri* [rice balls] for us and we left. The round trip was forty sen, and we could stay in the pool all day. We got off at Higashi Fushimi Station and waited until the pool opened. When we dived at the adults' end of the pool, where we didn't know how deep the water was, the pressure made our ears ring. Swimming on our backs in the middle of the pool, we got completely sunburned. The farthest I was able to swim was forty-one meters. We let ourselves into the school pool. The water was dirty, and our eyes got bloodshot. The circular distributed today was about a general summons on the seventeenth. The inn probably will be . . .[18]

August 16, Wednesday, clear
No. 2 Typhoid Shot

We got our second typhoid shots at 1:00 p.m. We went with our transfer card and handed it to Kōnaka-sensei. They stuck an approximately six-centimeter-long needle into my arm, so only about one-and-a-half centimeters showed. Because I rubbed it hard right away, it didn't hurt at the time but slowly began to hurt that evening. Volume 8 of the sixth-grade Japanese-language textbook arrived, so I returned the book I had borrowed and bought the new one. We prepared for the collective evacuation by carefully writing our names on our things. That evening we cut in half the chestnut squash we bought on the tenth and had it as a food substitute, and it was sweet and really good.

August 17, Thursday, clear

According to the circular sent around on the fifteenth, there was going to be a meeting of those participating in the collective evacuation at 9:00 a.m., so we left at 8:30. The Shōhakukan, where we'll be staying, is said to be one of the best inns in the area. Apparently, they have agreed to lend us rooms and had bathrooms built just for those of us coming from Tokyo. There was a distribu-

---

17. Manabe did not add the second character of this name.
18. This sentence does not make any sense.

tion of shoes. A lot of shoes were brought, and they circulated until just before my turn. There was a distribution of clogs but because shoes had just been given out, they started with the person just after those who had received shoes. I didn't buy any. They were really nice clogs, but I hadn't been able to get a pair of shoes. There was a distribution of notebooks, and I got one math notebook and one Japanese-language one. Pencils also were distributed, two per person, but they were strange looking.

August 18, Friday
To Saginomiya to Buy Vegetables

We went to Saginomiya to shop at about 10:00 a.m. Because it was late, we thought they probably wouldn't have anything, but we went anyway. Because the children left today for collective evacuation, the owner had gone to see them off at Nerima Station and wasn't home. Since no one was there, we didn't know what to do, but the grandmother appeared. When we asked her for vegetables, she said to wait a bit, and so we waited until the owner returned. When she returned, we gave her a fourth-grade girl's kimono, and although it wasn't a harvest day, she sold us one *kanme* worth of tomatoes, one *kanme* worth of eggplant, two chestnut squashes, and one egg.

August 19, Saturday, clear
A Circular from School

I went to school at 8:00 a.m. and took along a mosquito net. We were able to gather mosquito nets for only one four-and-a-half-mat room and one three-mat room.[19] Seven of us — Isotani, Ishishi, Makoto Nakamura, Noda, Matsumoto, Mikami, and I — contributed the nets. Maruyama brought a washbasin, Nakano a washboard, and Izumi a thermometer. We had take-cover drills from 1:00 to 3:00 p.m. In the evening, Kawachi brought a circular right in the middle of the drills. Apparently, school will start on the twenty-first.

August 20, Sunday, clear
A Distribution of *Nattō*

At around 10:00 a.m. we used a public telephone to call the Water Department. This was my first experience with a public telephone, and my heart was pounding. I took the receiver off the hook, brought it to my ear, and then waited a long time until a voice asked, "What number?" I shouted, "Nakano 2971, please!"

---

19. The area of Japanese rooms is measured in tatami mats. The smallest room is three mats, the next smallest is four and a half mats, and so forth.

Then the voice said, "Insert ten sen," which we did, but because this was enough for just half a minute, I had my uncle, who was waiting, take over. When he asked, "Is this the Water Department?" the party on the other side said, "Yes," and he started dialing and gave the phone back to me. When I heard the other party say, "Hello, hello," I couldn't say why I was calling and said only, "Yes, yes." There was a distribution of *nattō* at Sanya City.

August 21, Monday, clear then cloudy
Visiting Graves

School started today. The starting time was 9:30 a.m. but because of a teachers' meeting, the morning assembly wasn't until 10:00. Yanagisawa-sensei was not present. The miso soup at lunch had *wakame* in it. The main course was the usual. I had my number recorded and stood in line for rice gruel. Beginning today, we had *tane udon*, and it was eighteen sen a serving. It had winter melon in it — winter melon that we were able to buy only one at a time. At about 3:30 p.m. I visited Tama Cemetery to let my ancestors know I was going to be evacuated. I passed farmhouses along the way. When I gave a farmer an old undershirt, I received seven ears of corn, nineteen potatoes at one for five hundred sen, and beans. I was even treated to watermelon. He cut up a red one and a white one and gave me some. The white one was like white sugar. I didn't think I would eat any watermelon this summer.

August 22, Tuesday, clear

Sensei had been there, but the story was that he went off to negotiate at Nakano Station on behalf of the school and was still negotiating. We sang songs, and it was lots of fun. Pumpkin squash was the main course at lunch. We each had two slices. The rice was dry. In the evening Majima's uncle lent me a beat-up old bicycle that had been left outside and whose tires were flat, and I practiced riding it. At first, I kept falling over and didn't make any forward progress. I sat on the upper bar and it really hurt, so I put a blanket over the bar. By practicing a lot, I finally got to the point where I was able to stay on the bike for a long time.

August 23, Wednesday, foggy then clear
The Parents Association and Packing for the Collective Evacuation

Although school started at 7:00 a.m., something else was going on, and we had quite a long break. The morning assembly started at about 10:00 a.m. Lunch was miso bread, and the teachers said to take it home to eat it, so I did. At 1:30 p.m. there was a meeting of the people in the Parents Association who had family members going off in the collective evacuation. In his remarks the principal said, "I will not say who will be taking care of the children or which dorm mothers will go along. If I did, what would happen is that parents would give gifts to the dorm mothers and ask them to take care of their children." Mother was impressed. I sent my traveling kit to school. That evening the son of the owner of Kanemaru Shipping came over and wrapped small packages. He said everything came to about fifty pounds. Rice was brought. There were no soybeans and just some ugly ears of corn.

August 24, Thursday, clear then rainy
Loading Luggage at School

They said to come to school at 6:30 a.m. if it rains and because it was drizzling, I went to school. Because there were some really big bundles wrapped in straw, there was one big bamboo basket. The fathers carried and handled the heaviest ones. I thought that Konma and I might carry one of these, but Masashi-chan's uncle ended up carrying it for us. Our group—the no. 1 group of sixth graders going to the Shōhakukan—put our luggage in the classroom of the no. 1 group of second graders. We had pumpkin squash for lunch, and there was just one double portion of rice. Because I had practiced on the bicycle, I was able to take a fourth grader for a ride.

August 25, Friday, rain
Transporting Luggage for the Collective
Evacuation and a Circular from School

Somehow Kazuko arranged to have two days off in a row—today and yesterday. A circular arrived from school at about 8:00 a.m. It said there would not be enough people to transport the luggage for the collective evacuation to Nakano Station, so those who were free, please come to help. Fifteen people, including me, helped, but there was a downpour while we were carrying the luggage to the station, and we got completely soaked. We had pumpkin squash for lunch, and there was more rice than yesterday. There was a distribution of three lunch boxes, three teacups, and one canteen. We drew lots, and Nagano, Ishizawa, and Nakamura got the lunch boxes; Saitō, Nakano, and Yasukawa got the teacups; and Konma got the canteen. Today, when the *tsukudani* was distributed, mother put out a parasol and completely forgot. Horii.[20]

---

20. This sentence is incomplete in the original.

August 26, Saturday, rain then cloudy
Manhood Group Meeting and a Circular from School

At 8:00 a.m. there was a Manhood Group meeting for those going on the collective evacuation. Ironically, it was rainy and only a representative from the group made the pilgrimage to the Hachiman Shrine. The Manhood Group meeting started at 9:00 a.m. Miyoshi read the farewell addresses on behalf of those staying behind, and Sugiyama read the response. It's hard but I will try to persevere! We had bread for lunch. It was a pretty big piece. Their part-time jobs helped Noda, Hasegawa, and Nakamura Masa. They paid a one-yen luggage fee, gave a four-yen contribution, and had ten yen for spending money. Crackers were passed out. The no. 1 group of sixth graders had a commemorative evacuation photograph taken. After lunch we were told we should bring lunch money tomorrow. The community council sponsored a special gathering of the Manhood Group at 7:00 p.m. After the ceremony, there were skits, musical parodies, and a magic show.

August 27, Sunday, cloudy
A Circular from School

At 9:00 a.m. I collected sixty sen, the August lunch fee. The fee for the photograph, which was collected by each group, came to twenty-five yen, sixty sen, and since Yanagisawa-sensei wasn't there, we had Saitō Kiemon-sensei take the money. Mother was busy making a stomach warmer for me and writing my name on my things. I took croquettes to Masashi-chan's house, and they gave me red bean rice. We ate sweet potatoes, tempura, fish, and other things at the Manhood Group meeting. Because we're evacuating to Kikuyo-chan's place, we went to say good-bye. When I went to get the picture taken yesterday for the teachers, it was ready.

August 28, Monday, cloudy
Evacuating to Yumoto

Because we are finally leaving for Yumoto, I got up this morning while it was still dark. Before breakfast, I went to the Hachiman Shrine. We assembled at school at 5:00 a.m. The fathers and mothers performed a comic skit as a send-off, and we marched out of the school gate toward Nakano Station. Mother trotted along on the way to the station and gave me two apples. The trolley made creaking sounds. We boarded special Jōban Line cars that were going to leave Ueno Station at 8:24 a.m. Once aboard the train, we ate crackers and box lunches while looking out at the scenery. We arrived at Yumoto at 1:20 p.m. There was a band, and the local children were there to greet us and lined both sides of the road leading up to the inn. We visited the hot spring shrine, drank a delicious soba dipping sauce, and settled in at the inn.[21] That evening I went into a hot spring for the first time in my life, and it warmed me to my bones.

August 29, clear, 30 degrees

In the morning when I began to wake up, everyone was horsing around.[22] In the middle of the day we went out for the first time. We had only been inside up to now, and it felt good. We went to Echigoya and the other inns and met the sensei in charge of each. Tani no Yu and the other places look like temples.[23] There are vegetable plots and groves in the gardens, and they are pretty big. Ninomiya-sensei came along. We climbed the mountains, and they were split right down the middle, with steep cliffs on both sides. We went from there along the road that led downward to the school. Then we climbed along a mountain road, and Yumoto's observation post was on the summit. Everyone got to the top, and we looked in all directions with a pair of borrowed binoculars. We could see the mountains, forests, and the town of Yumoto all at once. We even could see the ocean at Onahama in the distance. The scenery was beautiful.

August 30, 29 degrees, clear

We took seriously what we had been warned about yesterday and slept a long time.[24] At about 10:00 a.m. Ninomiya-sensei took us to the Yumoto National Citizens School where we'll study for half a year. There were buildings on both sides of the school yard, and the southern building was for one group of fifth graders and the Yumoto Girls High School. The school yard was ten times as big as the Keimei School's. We were told to rest in the school yard, but instead we climbed the mountain path and steep cliffs from the Inner Mountain and went where we had gone yesterday. We climbed up to the observation post. We didn't see or hear the observation post personnel and were very surprised when they shouted, "You ruffians! Quiet down in the southeast!" When we got back, no matter where we looked, the teachers were nowhere to be found. When we got back to the inn,

---

21. Manabe is referring to the dipping sauce for cold soba noodles, which, after the noodles have been eaten, is diluted with the water in which the soba has been boiled, and drunk.

22. *Obarehajimeta* should be *abarehajimeta*.

23. The Echigoya is located about a third of a mile south of the Shōhakukan. The Tani no Yu also was an inn, but it no longer exists.

24. Manabe and his classmates must have been scolded for horsing around early in the morning.

Ninomiya-sensei appeared and lectured us in the Big Room.[25] After lunch, we climbed 140 steps and went to Onezudai and back.[26]

August 31, clear, 28 degrees

I couldn't sleep very well last night. We were permitted to go outside from 9:00 to 10:00 a.m. Eighteen of us climbed the 141 [sic] steps and went along the mountain road from Kannon Mountain to Onezudai. There were two separate roads.

September[27]

First: the admissions ceremony.
Second: meeting with Uncle and Aunt Sugiyama.
Third: a visit by his eminence, the division commander.
Eleventh: received red and white crackers from a woman
　in the Housewives' Association.

November 20, clear
Meeting with Mother and the Calisthenics Study Group

Because the Calisthenics Study Group was meeting, wake-up was at 5:30 a.m. It was still pitch black outside. The fourth-grade girls were going to be doing a number of things in the morning, so the boys quickly ate their breakfast. I waited eagerly for 11:02 a.m. and could hardly stand it. After breakfast the teachers went to school right away. In the morning we finished the sketches we started on the seventeenth. After I ate my lunch, I went in a great rush together with Takejima, Saitō, and Ishizawa to meet people at the station. Everyone went to school without their schoolbags. The visitors came with trunks, knapsacks, and packages. They settled in room 1. Mother went to the hot springs twice and said how grateful she was. Toshiko-chan was called, and she got an umbrella.

---

25. No doubt they were lectured about their unsupervised hike to the observation post. The "Big Room" was occupied by students in Manabe's group.

26. The path leading up to Kannon Mountain consists of 140 steps, and Manabe's group was probably made to climb them and then to hike to Onezudai as a punishment.

27. Manabe's diary entries suddenly stop. Given the faithfulness with which he wrote in his diary through the end of August and all the things he might have written about Yumoto, it is unlikely that he stopped writing. His September and October diary entries were probably submitted to his teachers and never returned, or simply were confiscated. It was common for the teachers to use the diaries to monitor the morale of the evacuated children.

The Shōhakukan in Yumoto. Author's collection.

November 21, cloudy, rain from time to time, 13 degrees
Teachers Went to Tokyo

Last night Mother and I slept together in the interview room on a futon with a cover. Because we talked late into the night about various things, I couldn't get to sleep afterward. We got up when the morning bell rang. There were three layers covering us, and they were heavy and hot and not comfortable at all. Mother went to our morning assembly. Because she would be upset if we didn't eat the things she brought, we gave our rice and miso soup to people sitting nearby. We went into the bath seven times. At 8:00 a.m. everyone went to the hot springs shrine and then practiced songs about marching to the mines, and Mother and the others arrived, too, at about 9:00 a.m.[28] We went to pay our respects at the school and the town offices. Before lunch, each one of us got New Year's decorations that the mothers had made at home for all of us. Saitō's and Ishizawa's aunts left on the 3:00 p.m. train, and because she was taking a piece of a "friend of the country," Mother left on the 5:00 p.m. train.[29] The teachers have a Parents

---

28. The Jōban coalfield is located in the southeastern corner of Fukushima Prefecture, not far from Yumoto.

29. A piece of a "friend of the country" may refer to the remains of a child who died after being evacuated.

Association meeting tomorrow at 2:00 p.m. at the Keimei School, so they left on the 2:00 p.m. train.

November 22, Wednesday, 17 degrees, clear

Mother returned to Tokyo, and I felt truly refreshed. I now have nothing at all to look forward to. Because the teachers were not at the morning assembly or roll call, Otogao-sensei took over. We did our math homework in the morning from 9:30 to 10:30 a.m. and had three rice crackers as a snack at 10:00 a.m. I was in the afternoon group, so I went to school at noon. Because Yanagisawa-sensei was not present, Higuchi-sensei studied in the classroom of Arakawa-sensei from the no. 1 group. For three hours we practiced reading "The Course of the Floating Chrysanthemum." In the afternoon we had salted kelp and a handful of popped beans for a snack. That evening a soldier who had returned from Sumatra told stories about the place and talked about different types of enemy aircraft.

November 23, Thursday, crystal clear
Rousing Words of a Mine Fighter

Today was the Harvest Festival, so we didn't have any school. Kuga-sensei called roll. At 8:30 a.m. the second-section students got together and we practiced songs about marching to the mines. We did it over and over, many times. We made a bonfire in the middle of the garden with a lot of trash from a box. Kuga-sensei put the eight sweet potatoes he had brought into the bonfire and roasted them. Just before lunch he cut them into slices and served them. They were crunchy and delicious. Before noon I went to Tani no Yu to pick up a message from Toshiko's aunt, but she wasn't there. The students from the second section gathered in the self-government hall and formed two units and saw off the miners until noon. We went to five mines. I read an inspiring book in the waiting areas. We saw off three groups that left by *jinrikisha*.

November 24, clear
Enemy Planes Bomb the Imperial Palace

At about 8:00 a.m. we asked the person in charge to make a bonfire. The acorn wood we had gathered earlier came in very handy. The fire was very hot. Before lunch there was a distribution of wooden clogs. We went to pick up our clogs at the dorm mother's room and lined up by size. There were two groups — the big and the small — and I got big ones. The wood was of poor quality, and the clogs looked as though they would break, and there was no strap attached. At school we studied again together with group no. 2 in Munakata-sensei's classroom. Higuchi-sensei told us that Tokyo had been bombed.[30] After we got back, a siren suddenly sounded, and there was an air-raid warning and announcement. We put on our air-raid clothes, but it turned out to be a mistake. For dinner we had tempura that the aunt who came to see a fourth grader had brought. We had one serving of *kintoki*, burdock, and carrot as well as miso stew.[31] It was delicious. And there was a lot of rice.

November 25, clear then cloudy

Today we made a bonfire again. We collected wood and used charcoal. After the bonfire was put out, we asked Otogao-sensei to let us search for firewood, and off we went. We went to Kuriyama and spent two hours climbing pine trees and breaking off dead branches from cedar trees. What we collected looked like a mountain. We had tempura for lunch. There was fried *kōnago* and sweet potatoes, in addition to pumpkin-squash leaves. It was very ungreasy. At school, we joined the second-section students in the same classroom as yesterday. In the second period we practiced memorizing one part of "The Course of the Floating Chrysanthemum," and those in the no. 1 group had to stand until the end if they couldn't do it. We did it for two hours and then returned. We had two tangerines for snacks. Students from the no. 1 group came, and five went to a family called the Okadas, where they were treated to sweet potatoes and popped beans and got quite full, and Takejima and Mikami fell asleep. That night we had tempura for dinner, which was delicious.

November 26, Sunday, 15 degrees, clear

Satō returned during our work period this morning. He apparently qualified. We left the dorm so we would arrive at school at 7:40 a.m. The classroom was the one we shared with the no. 2 group on Sunday, and this time we had Shimizu-sensei. We did not have a morning assembly but gathered in the lecture hall, and students from the second section already were there. When we had lined up single file and then sat down, twenty or so soldiers from the Toyama Army School Band, under the direction of a Major Yamaguchi, the band leader, played for us. They also did a sword-unsheathing demonstration and matched warships

---

30. From their base in the Mariana Islands, 111 B-29s bombed Tokyo for the first time. See Carter and Mueller, *Combat Chronology*, 505.

31. *Kintoki* probably refers to *kintokimame*, large red beans cooked in sugar, and the "burdock and carrot" is likely to have been a dish called *kimpira gobo*, julienned burdock and carrot sautéed in soy sauce, saké, and sugar.

for us. It was very manly and wonderful. Sergeant Genshirō Nagata did a solo and sang "The Katō Falcon" song.[32] Before lunch, for some reason or another, we just had self-study. Our box lunch consisted of steamed and fried sweet potatoes. After lunch, we put luggage away at the dorm, gathered at Tani no Yu, and had class outside. We went back between 2:30 to 3:30 p.m., and everyone was present and everything was in order.[33] We sunbathed at the shrine and had a bowl of popped rice as a snack.

November 27, cloudy
Sensei's Return and a Meeting with Kinoshita's Uncle

Sensei returned last night, and he appeared today during roll call. He said that all things considered, coming back is best. After breakfast, we borrowed matches from the front desk and made a bonfire. We put in all the firewood brought the day before yesterday, and the fire really flared up and was dangerous. Sensei told us to stop it, and we put it out. At 9:00 a.m. we put on our headbands and raced up to the top of the Hachiman Shrine together with Sensei and went out on the observation platform. The front and back of the line separated, and we played war games. We got really sweaty, but it was fun. Today we studied in our classroom. Kinoshita's uncle came for a meeting. That evening, in the Octagonal Room, he talked about the situation in Tokyo after the bombing.[34] While Sensei spoke, he gave us, as a snack, the roasted soybeans he brought back.

November 28, Tuesday, 13 degrees, cloudy
Kinoshita Returns to Tokyo

There was no school because today was Tuesday. Before morning assembly, at about 8:30 a.m., the second section gathered at the hot springs shrine, and they were going to talk about the speech that Aiba-sensei, the principal, gave, but the shrine grounds were filled with water, so the discussion was canceled. We tidied up our personal belongings after breakfast. Just before lunch, popped rice and beans were served as a snack. After lunch we had a compulsory outing, and fifteen of us wandered about town from 2:30 to 4:30 p.m. After the outing, we had a personal belongings inspection—Yasumi in room 76 was given a nine.

---

32. The "Katō Falcon song" refers to a war song released in 1943, "The Katō Falcon Squadron," which praised the exploits of Wing Commander Katō Takeo and his Sixty-fourth Squadron in Indochina early in the war.

33. Manabe leaves out the character for *i*, or "difference," in the phrase *zenmin . . . jō nashi*, which means literally "everyone present and no irregularities."

34. The Hakkaku Room, or "Octagonal Room," is the name of Manabe's "dormitory" and was probably a wing of the Shōhakukan.

Because of a chronic digestive problem, Kinoshita was taken away by his uncle and left the dorm.[35] The Octagonal Room was reduced to six people, and Sensei ordered Okutani to leave. The Big Room now had seventeen people. Two sweet potatoes and five rice crackers were served as a snack. They gave out the snacks that Kinoshita's uncle had carried on his back. Mine had seven slices of fried sweet potato and two tangerines. Mikami-sensei . . .[36]

November 29, Wednesday, clear, 11 degrees

I'll be on morning duty from today. The morning assembly was held in a classroom. In the second period, students in each school building lined up like we do for morning assembly and performed the farewell ceremony. Apparently a teacher named Yoshida Seitoku is enlisting in the navy, and he is the seventh faculty member from the Yumoto School to answer the "call of the clear sky." At lunch, boys served as the food attendants. Saitō, Nagata, Maruyama, and Adachi did it. From now on, for a week, male students will do the men's work at lunchtime. We had dumplings and half a bowl of rice for lunch.[37] After lunch we ate what we received yesterday and what was brought or passed on to us. For dinner, we had a slice of cod. That evening we practiced the play we'll perform on December 1. We gathered in the Octagonal Room, and each of us was given one of the walnuts the teachers brought back for us.

November 30, rain
An Air-Raid Warning and Alert Issued and Then Canceled

Last night the air-raid warning and alert sirens suddenly went off at about midnight.[38] I jumped up, got out my air-raid clothes and slept in them. The volunteer militia shouted that the Shōhakukan was too bright, and so all the lights were turned off, and it was pitch black. I wanted to go to the bathroom and was very upset. When things seemed to quiet down, the sirens started up again at about three o'clock. The military commander's reports were broadcast on the radio, and apparently Tokyo had been bombed indiscriminately.[39] The air-raid alert was called off at about five o' clock. It was raining and was very cold. During

---

35. Manabe miswrites the Chinese characters for "chronic digestion," using the wrong Chinese character for *man*.

36. Manabe did not finish the sentence.

37. These are probably *suiton*, a type of flour dumpling.

38. Late on the evening of November 29 and early on the morning of November 30, twenty-four B-29s attacked Tokyo. See Carter and Mueller, *Combat Chronology*, 509.

39. In the November 29–30 raid, American bombers dropped incendiary bombs on targets in the Japanese home islands for the first time.

first period, we saw off Yoshida-sensei and went to the front of the station. Our *tabi* were solid mud. We had one tangerine, three fried dough cakes, and one candied persimmon as snacks. After lunch, we wrote letters of sympathy for the miners, and the Big Room sent them to the coal-washing and -exporting desk. After dinner, the fifth graders and above gathered at the Yamagataya, and Aiba-sensei, the principal, came too, and we had the first combined school arts meeting.[40] The no. 1 group of sixth graders did "Fellow Boat Passengers" and the "Quack." Our interpretation of "Fellow Boat Passengers" was a little crazy and failed. We performed various skits, and it was fun. We took a bath after lunch and then before we went to bed.

December 1, cloudy then rain
Air-Raid Drill

At dawn I was still asleep but woke at five and got my air-raid clothes ready and then went back to sleep. The bells signaling an air-raid drill and calling for the volunteer militia to assemble began to ring, and the electricity was turned off.[41] We groped in the dark and got our footwear out of the clog box and went out into the garden — the Octagonal Room, Big Room, and number 12 in that order. The sensei and the old man from the inn guided us to the waiting places. We left the road in front of Mr. Kujiraoka's and went around the back to the place where dynamite was set and not the waiting bunker. We were in there for an hour and a half, and it was suffocating. Maruyama, Masuda, Nagata, Nakamura, and Saitō stayed in their rooms because they were sick. At about seven o'clock, we went back to the dorms. We had breakfast without a morning assembly and were late to school. In the fourth period we measured our chests. Mine was sixty-five and a half centimeters, which was half a centimeter less than the last time. For snacks, we had one bowl of garlic popped rice and, like yesterday, candied persimmons. A strange fish was served for dinner. It was cut up lengthwise and smelled.

December 2, cloudy

It stopped raining and was cloudy. In the second period Sensei brought a phonograph and played a record. It was something called "A Record of Victory" and brought back memories of what we felt on December 8.[42] We also heard about

---

40. The Yamagataya is another inn that housed evacuated children. It no longer exists.
41. In many communities, bells were used to signal air-raid alerts and warnings.
42. I have not been able to identify this song.

the meeting of Yamashita and Percival.[43] During the third period, we did a general cleaning of the hall. The floors really shone. After lunch, Sensei suggested that we go out into the garden, and we did. Then we went to gather firewood on Mount Urayama. We climbed quickly along the side of the pig huts and ended up on the summit, and then we went down to the middle part of the mountain where we gathered firewood. On the way back, we got completely confused and took a roundabout way to get back. Afterward, the last candied persimmons were served — we got one apiece. At dinner time, inspectors — about six of them — came and asked about the meals. At six o' clock we went to the Yamagataya and saw a movie. It was a consolation visit at the Jōban School for the fifth and sixth graders.[44] It was not a "talkie" and was boring. I took a bath before I went to bed.

December 3, crystal clear, fire in the braziers, 11 degrees

Today is perfectly clear and beautiful weather. At lunch yesterday, the sweet potatoes disappeared from our rice bowls, and potatoes have replaced them. It appears this was done to keep us from getting tired of sweet potatoes. Because it was Sunday, there were six hours of class, but for some reason we went without box lunches until just before noon — for four hours. Our morning assembly was held in the no. 4 school building. Principal Aiba gave a talk. In the third period a substitute, Shimazu-sensei, taught us. The sixth graders spent an hour saying many different complimentary things like "your manners are very good." At lunch, Iizasa, Yamada, Mikami, and Itoga were on food duty. It was curry. After lunch we learned from a general staff report that the enemy had come to attack Tokyo again.[45] For snacks, we had two sweet potatoes. After lunch we did . . . on a grand scale.[46] At night they made fires in the braziers. Yasumi started using leg warmers.

December 4, Monday, 12 degrees, clear
Gathering Scraps

Today it was extremely cold at dawn. This morning's temperature was six degrees, and ice had formed. I expected that it was going to be cold on the street. After breakfast we went to the dorm mother's room, and two sweet potatoes were

---

43. The famous meeting of Lieutenant General Arthur Percival and General Yamashita Tomoyuki took place when Singapore fell to the Japanese on February 15, 1942, with Percival surrendering to Yamashita.

44. Manabe does not say why the fifth and sixth graders needed to be consoled.

45. Nearly seventy B-29s attacked Tokyo early on December 3. See Carter and Mueller, *Combat Chronology*, 513.

46. Manabe never completed this sentence.

passed out as a food supplement. The wooden clackers sounded, and we went to school. On the way, my feet got cold, and I could hardly stand it. It seemed to be the boundary of Tamakawa Village and Onahama-chō, where we had gone to catch grasshoppers.[47] I went together with Mikami, Itoga, Izumi, and Den. We caught grasshoppers for about two hours, and my paint bag filled up.[48] Higuchi-sensei used hand flags to signal "assemble," and we ate our box lunches on the riverbank.[49] Right after that, the second-section students jogged the six kilometers back.[50] At the ward office a leader of the Kamitōno Village Housewives Group, who had come to see how we were doing, spoke to us and gave us popped beans.[51] She went to each dorm, and we had one cup of tea as a snack.

December 5, clear, 12 degrees

We slept a little later because it's Tuesday and a holiday. Sensei had a slight fever and did not appear at morning roll call. We were divided up and sent to different rooms. Last night my stomach rumbled terribly, and sure enough, I had the runs this morning. We studied after breakfast. We assembled in the Big Room for reading, arithmetic, geography, and Japanese history and collected desks from each room. We did Japanese first, then arithmetic. After that, we went to Sensei's room to talk about our plans for high school. I said I hoped to go to a municipal middle school. In the afternoon we sharpened our pocketknives on the veranda. At one o'clock we were taken by Kuga-sensei to see Nagakura Cave. When we entered the mountainous area, it was filthy. We had two tangerines for snacks. A letter arrived from my older sister.[52] In the evening there were fires in the braziers and leg warmers. We had grated radish for dinner.

December 6, 11 degrees

Last night Satō returned. It's the afternoon group from today. The sensei did not come to the morning assembly, and instead they carried out a general cleaning of their rooms. At breakfast, sensei said that we'd put on our headbands and go

---

47. This area is just about a mile southeast of the Shōhakukan.

48. The grasshoppers might have been collected to be eaten. In some poor farming communities, grasshoppers were cooked with soy sauce and sugar to produce *tsukudani*, a kind of preserve that was eaten with rice.

49. The river is the Fujiwara River, which runs into Onahama Bay.

50. What Manabe calls "six kilometers" is actually about three kilometers, or nearly two miles.

51. Kamitōno is a large area whose eastern edge is about three and a half miles west of Yumoto.

52. This is Kazuko, who remained in Tokyo with Manabe's mother.

out into the back garden only thirty minutes after we had eaten, but it appears that he forgot, and it was canceled. In the morning Kuga-sensei brought embers in a fire shovel and started a fire in the brazier. Everyone gathered in the Octagonal Room, and each of us got two fried balls as snacks. When I was on my way to school, I dropped the tall clogs that Mother had brought at the time of our meeting. We have a drill inspection the day after tomorrow, so we spent quite a little time outside and practiced quick marching. Because we did this barefoot, we got really cold. After we went back inside, dumplings were served as a snack. Sweet potato paste was smeared on them, and they were delicious. In the evening they started fires in our braziers but didn't do the same with the leg warmers.

December 7, clear, 10 degrees
National History Quiz and Cancellation
of the Air-Raid Warning and Alert

Last night I was asleep when an air-raid warning and alert were issued. I quickly got my air-raid clothes ready, put on seven layers, and went back to sleep. The air-raid warning was called off, then reissued again, and an all-clear sounded at about five o'clock. There didn't seem to be much damage. Before the morning assembly, we went out into the middle garden and did calisthenics with all our strength until we got warm. Some time after breakfast, everyone gathered in the Big Room, and we practiced countermarching. After that we went out into the garden, divided into four units and practiced quick marching, marching double time, and turning right. Then we double-timed to the hot springs shrine to pay our respects. At ten we had two dried potatoes. At noon we had *suiton* for lunch. At school we had a national history quiz in the first and second periods. After we got back, we had a gift from Satō. We separated ourselves up by room and then divided it up into seventeen equal parts, and we ate one little portion each. I couldn't eat what Mother gave me, and it was a lousy way of dividing things up. The bath was not running.

December 8, 7 degrees, clear
A Drill Inspection and Air-Raid Alert Issued, Then Canceled

Last night after dinner, Sensei went into a room, and when he turned on a switch, it went *jiji-*, and warnings and alerts were issued in the Tōhoku, Shinetsu, and Kantō areas.[53] Saying that evening was a dangerous time, Sensei put us to bed at 6:30 p.m. Enemy planes, a few of them, invaded from Bōsō and escaped to the

---

53. There is no record of an attack on Japan.

southeast without entering the imperial capital.[54] During the night the warning was lifted once, then reissued, and canceled at dawn. Today is Imperial Rescript Observance Day, and it is the third full year of the Greater East Asia War. Before the morning assembly we went out into the middle garden and did calisthenics. Then we marched in step to the hot springs shrine and then had a meal right after that. We went to school and stayed until 8:30 a.m. and then had our drill inspection after a morning meeting. We performed in order, beginning with the first grades. While quick-marching and double-timing, the sixth graders did mock cavalry battles and peeled off. The drill ended at one o'clock. At noon, we left school, and the boys served as food monitors. We had two sweet potatoes as snacks. At about two o'clock we took a bath. Izumi's aunt came and talked to us and said Izumi was going to move to a relative's house. We divided up the leftover baggage by lots, and I got a paulownia box, which I traded with Yamada for a notebook.

December 9, cloudy, 6 degrees
Izumi Moves to Relatives

Last night, too, an air-raid warning and alert were issued for the Kantō, Tōhoku, and Shinetsu areas at about 3:00 a.m.[55] Sensei, too, got tired of the warnings and alerts and said it was OK as long as we kept our air-raid gear next to our pillows. About fifteen minutes after we fell asleep, the air-raid warning was canceled. We went out into the back garden before morning assembly and did calisthenics. We paid a visit to the hot springs shrine and apparently will be doing this every day. In the morning they lit fires in the braziers and leg warmers. We assembled in the Octagonal Room, and each one of us received one chestnut from Sensei. We played Hyakunin isshu and other games, and in no time it was lunch.[56] This morning a little of something that looks like snow fell. Today Izumi gathered up her luggage and left with her aunt on the 9:02 train to Ueno. With that, the Big Room's sixteen people shrank to thirteen. We had Fueki-sensei at school. In the third period Sensei read to us about the "Monkey King."[57] We composed haiku. Otogao-sensei gave each of us a piece of salted kelp as a snack.

---

54. These may have been reconnaissance aircraft dispatched before the bombing raids on Nagoya that were carried out on December 13, 18, and 22.

55. More than sixty B-29s attacked Iwo Jima early on the morning of December 8. See Carter and Mueller, *Combat Chronology*, 517.

56. Manabe and his classmates were playing a traditional card game that was usually played with a classical collection of poems, *The Single Poems by a Hundred Poets* (*Ogura hyakunin isshu*), but they were probably using *The Patriotic Collection of Single Poems by a Hundred Poets* (*Aikoku hyakunin isshu*), a wartime version that featured "patriotic" poems.

57. The "monkey king" is the main character in the Chinese epic *Journey to the West*.

December 10, Sunday, 8 degrees, crystal clear
Picking Eulalia Spikes and an Air-Raid Alert Issued and Canceled

It was very nice weather, but the dry winds were horrible. In the morning, we did calisthenics before morning assembly and went to the hot springs shrine. We formed four perfect lines and double-timed it to the shrine. We passed under the torii and stopped and worshiped silently without moving for a minute. It felt really good. Perhaps because it was Sunday, we spent the morning picking eulalia spikes with students from the first section. Apparently one puts the eulalia into floats. We turned on the road just before the Onahama Highway crossing and walked for a long way. We came to what looked liked a basin and split up and picked eulalia, but it wasn't much fun. Along the way we passed an exhaust vent. Foul air (steam) was really pouring out of a fat smokestack. At 1:00 p.m. we went, together with the first-section students, to the Nyūzan Self-Government Auditorium and saw a moving Tōei film — *The Consoling of Eight Evacuated Children* — and the Hinawashida Cultural Movie News of Japan.

December 11, Monday, clear, 7 degrees
Sardine Labor Service and an Air-Raid Alert Issued and Canceled

Last night, too, an air-raid warning was issued, but it was canceled immediately. They said tomorrow we'll have an early start, so we went to bed at seven. The wooden clackers sounded at six while it was still dark. After we were properly dressed and ready to go, roll was called, and we immediately began our day. We had morning assembly, ate quickly, put on our boots, and left the dorm at 7:30 a.m. We took the 7:51 a.m. train to Izumi, and Higuchi, Kuga, and one other sensei led us along the road in front of the station to the sardine plant.[58] The sardine heads were piled up like a mountain in front of the plant. This was where they crammed sardines into boxes and pressed them for oil, and there were a lot of fresh sardines. We were introduced to the owner and then quickly got to work. For the first half of our time there, we moved sardines into bamboo steamers. After we put them into the steamers, we arranged them so the sun would hit them. There were about two hundred boxes. I really wanted to have my mother in Tokyo eat some of these fresh sardines with their heads pulled off and dried. I worked together with Takejima. (The steamer basket was a box with a bamboo net for a bottom.) Next, we brought out nests of boxes from the warehouse and filled them with the dried sardines that the no. 2 group of sixth graders had dried yesterday. We laid the sardines in the boxes with their heads facing outward and alternated them. Each box weighed about four *kanme*. We nailed each one shut

---

58. Izumi is the station just before Yumoto on the Jōban Line.

and took it outside. There was an awful lot of oil on our hands from handling the sardines. They gave us four sardines cooked in miso and pickles for lunch. It was really delicious. We rested for twenty-five minutes, then got to work again. Those who put on boots and did the water jobs in the morning were pitiful, so we switched jobs, and I was added to the special-attack force.[59] Eight people on a side. We pulled two metal blades over the raw sardines in the steamer and cut off their tails, then lined them up. It was unbearably cold. No matter how many we did, there was no end. What had been lined up was moved by a winch to the oven, where it was cooked and pressed for oil. Once the sardines had been flattened, they had no oil or flavor. The leftover sardines were then stuffed into boxes and sent to a food-processing company, where they will be made into food for soldiers. They gave us four sugared sweet potatoes at 3:00 p.m. After that we worked for about twenty minutes and then stopped. We left the old men at the factory and headed back to Izumi Station. The 4:00 p.m. train was thirty minutes late, and we reached the inn in total darkness at about 5:30 p.m. Dinner was canned salmon, and we took a bath an hour later.

December 12, Tuesday, 9 degrees, clear
Raking Fallen Leaves and an Air-Raid Alert Issued and Canceled

Again, last night, after we were asleep, an air-raid warning was issued. It was canceled, then reissued, and quickly canceled again. Somehow because the enemy planes don't really come, everyone sleeps through the night without getting ready for an air raid. Today was Tuesday and a holiday for the second-section students, and we went to rake fallen leaves. After one area was completed, we took off our overcoats and did calisthenics and then visited the hot springs shrine. It was very cold, but because a lot of oil was smeared on our hands yesterday, we didn't feel it much at all. After breakfast, we went to school and then left to gather up fallen leaves, singing war songs along the way. The no. 2 group did not go to the sardine factory. The no. 1 group of sixth graders left their share of fallen leaves at a farmhouse on the road in front of Kinpira Shrine. They brought seven big baskets of leaves. Each of us got three sweet potatoes at the farmhouse. We've had a radio in the Big Room up to now, but Nakano-sensei, who lent it to us, returned to Tokyo, and since he needed it, we gave it back to him. It was very lonely without it.

---

59. The children's teachers called the group of students doing the dirtiest and hardest work the "special-attack force," a reference to the newly formed kamikaze units.

December 13, Wednesday, 8 degrees; after rain and snow, clear
Air-Raid Alert Issued and Canceled

Last night the old man at the inn had the boys gather in the Big Room and gave us a picture card show. Takejima, Noda, and I were made to take part. The old man did "This Stomach, This Heart" and "Mom Was a Comic"; Takejima did the "Banana Train"; Noda did "The Seven Stones"; and I did "Chocolate and the Soldiers." When I finished my skit, the sirens began to wail — uu, uu — and then stopped. The air-raid warnings were issued and canceled many times through the night, and later I was told this happened four times. In the morning when I got up, it was raining. Apparently we had bought tickets, and they were wasted. After we washed up, snow began to fall, and by the time we finished breakfast, the flakes were large, but it stopped and the sun shone in the afternoon. We assembled in the Octagonal Room before noon and were warned about the braziers and took a bath afterward. Those who wanted to go to the barber got money from the sensei, and after lunch eleven of us went to a barber called Sekine. Boiled dumplings were served as a snack. (Because we went to school yesterday, today was a holiday.)

December 14, 7 degrees, clear
Transporting Daikon Leaves and an Air-Raid Alert Issued and Canceled

Yesterday was a bundling holiday, and today we cultivated our heroic spirit and transported radishes. Today, it was us and the no. 3 group of sixth graders, and apparently also the no. 2 and no. 4 groups. I slept soundly last night and thus was unaware that an air-raid warning and alert had been issued. When I got up and asked everyone, I was told there had been one after all. Because our departure was on the 9:20 train, we were late. Kuga-sensei came along. Saitō-sensei, Satō Shigeru-sensei, and a female sensei and the dorm mother came along too.

December 15, cloudy, 5 degrees
Air-Raid Alert Issued and Canceled

Today was really cold, and we really shivered. Our labor service work ended, and we'll finally get back to our studies. Because it was . . . we went to school right after we ate. This morning we had our morning assembly outside. Suzuki-sensei had us sing military songs and the no. 1 group students were full of pep. Because our feet were frozen and cold, we played push-and-shove during recess at school and got really warm.[60] In the third period, they measured our height at

---

60. Manabe calls the game they play *oshikura-gonbe*, which sounds like a variant of a game called *oshikura manjū*, which involved pushing and shoving in close quarters as a way of getting warm in winter.

the infirmary. They measured us in our socks, and most of us had shrunk. I was 136.6 centimeters and had shrunk four centimeters. After we got back, the boys helped with the meal preparations. Masuda, Yajima, Yasukawa, and I carried out *gomoku* rice. Then after a long time after lunch, we took a bath. There was hot water up to our ankles, and we all used it. After that, we had half a *manjū* each as a snack. We assembled in the Octagonal Room, and Sensei talked about his visit to see the air exercises at Tsuchiura Air Base,[61] and everyone wrote letters, which he will carry for us. Before we went to bed, we took a bath.

---

61. Tsuchiura was a naval air base where navy pilots received their basic flight training.

The Diary of an Evacuated Schoolgirl

Nakane Mihōko was born in Tokyo in 1935. When the war started, she was a primary school student and was evacuated twice. In late August 1944, school authorities, following government orders, sent students from the third through the sixth grades to the safety of Kumekawa in the Kita-Tamagawa area south of Tokyo. When the bombing of Tokyo intensified early in 1945, the first evacuation site proved unsafe, so another, more distant site was found in Fukumitsu, a village in Toyama Prefecture. On April 10, 1945, Nakane and 124 of her classmates, together with nineteen staff members from her school, were evacuated to Fukumitsu. Because evacuated children from another Tokyo school already occupied the temples in the area, Nakane and her classmates stayed with prominent local families. They remained in Fukumitsu for just over eleven months, returning to Tokyo on March 8, 1946.[1]

After the war Nakane completed her middle and high school education. She entered Tokyo University of the Arts in 1956 but transferred to Tokyo Education University in 1958, graduating with a degree in art in 1961. She began teaching art to middle school students in 1960 and retired from teaching in 2001. She is married and the mother of two children.[2]

Nakane was a precocious diarist and had kept an illustrated diary since she was four years old, which partly explains her faithful diary keeping during the evacuation: she didn't miss a single day. Many years later she wrote, "Everything written in the diary is the truth. There isn't a single lie. When I wrote 'something

---

1. Nakane Mihōko, *Sokai gakudō no nikki* (Tokyo: Chūō kōronsha, 1965), i–ii, 225–226.

2. Maki Mihōko, personal communication, 8/30/2003.

was really, really delicious' or 'really, really interesting,' these were my honest and true feelings."[3] Upon her return to Tokyo, her parents recognized the value of her diary as a record of the evacuation and carefully preserved it. Nakane's diary, along with some of her sketches, was published in 1965 as *Sokai gakudō no nikki* (*The Diary of an Evacuated Schoolgirl*), and the portion translated here is from pages 14 to 86. The comments in italics following some of the entries are by Nakane's teachers.

April 9, 1945 (Mon.), rain then cloudy

Today, it was finally decided that we will go to Toyama Prefecture.[4] I am so happy I can't bear it. In the evening I ate dinner and then packed. I probably won't be able to see my younger sister and brothers. My kid brother said, "Hō-chan, come back quickly, OK?" I said, "I'm leaving. Good-bye. Take care of yourselves," and went with Father, Mother, and the baby to Ueno. A lot of people were already there. After some time we went into the station. I said, "*Itte kimasu.*"[5] Father and Mother waved to me. We'll board this train. After some time it was 10:51 p.m. Then the train began to leave. With a clang, clang. The train sped along. Saitō-sensei said, "Good night."[6] It seemed as though we were going to be squashed. We got off the train. At that point, Iwamaru-sensei and people from the Fuku-mitsu Citizens School greeted us and carried our luggage for us.[7] Because my luggage didn't arrive, I stayed at the Setō house.[8]

April 10, 1945 (Tues.), rain

I opened my eyes. It was light gray outside, and everyone was still sound asleep. After some time Maeno, Tanaka, and Kobayashi woke up. They had told us, "No talking. If you don't go to sleep quickly, you'll be tired tomorrow!" so I fell

---

3. Nakane, *Sokai gakudō no nikki*, iii–iv.

4. Toyama Prefecture is located in central Japan and faces the Asian mainland across the Japan Sea. Farming and fishing were the mainstays of the Toyama economy, but the abundance of hydroelectric power led to the development of manufacturing as well. Nakane's group was sent to the town of Fukumitsu, which is in the western part of Toyama Prefecture.

5. *Itte kimasu,* "I'm leaving and will return," is a set expression usually spoken as one leaves. Here Nakane uses it when she leaves her family at Ueno Station.

6. Saitō Yosuke was one of Nakane's teachers and was the head of her dormitory.

7. In April 1941 the national government designated all schools as "citizens' schools" (J. *kokumin gakkō*) and had the school authorities intensify their students' spiritual training. All this was for the war effort.

8. The Setō family was in the dry goods business. Yoshinami Sumiko, personal communication, June 4, 2004.

asleep again. When I opened my eyes, it already had gotten light, Kobayashi was still asleep and snoring loudly. After some time she woke up. At that point the fifth- and sixth-grade boys said they were hungry, and Hori-sensei said, "Those who are so hungry they could die should eat!"[9] After standing for a long time, he got down. Then we boarded the luggage train.

April 11, 1945 (Wed.), rain then cloudy

Today we washed our faces at the Setō house. Then we were fed. Together with delicious hot rice, we were given hot miso soup, pickles, and something else that had been boiled in grated radish. Then, with our eating utensils in hand, we went off to school. We had an admissions ceremony and afterward had lunch in the sewing room.[10] After lunch, the second, third, and fourth graders went off to see various things with Hori-sensei and others. The scenery was very nice. It looked like a picture. I thought how really nice the scenery was and how really happy I was to be in such a nice place.

April 12, 1945 (Thurs.)

Today we worked all morning. Our luggage arrived, and the fifth- and sixth-grade boys carried the bags from the station. We cleaned Yamashita Dorm.[11] We cleaned it twice. There was a lot of dirt. In the afternoon we unpacked our luggage and then went to Maeda Dorm.[12] Iwamaru-sensei, Ariga-sensei, and Motegi-sensei untied the knotted ropes.[13] Then we tidied up. There really was a lot of luggage.

April 13, 1945 (Fri.)

This morning, after we beat our futon, they gave us places for our luggage. Then I arranged everything neatly and washed my face. Washing one's face while breathing in the cold morning air felt really, really good. Then we went to school.

---

9. Hori Shichizō was a teacher at Nakane's school in Tokyo who accompanied the evacuated children to Fukumitsu.

10. Nakane writes *hairei* instead of *ukeire*.

11. The Yamashita family ran a clinic that was used to house second- and third-grade girls and boys and no. 2 group fifth graders. See Nakane, *Sokai gakudō no nikki*, 17.

12. The Maeda family owned a saké brewery that became home to the no. 1 group of fourth and fifth graders, which included Nakane. Yoshinami, personal communication, June 4, 2004.

13. Iwamaru Shigeo was a teacher from Nakane's school in Tokyo, and both Ariga Kazuko and Motegi Fusako were in charge of Maeda Dorm.

The Hachiman Shrine in Fukumitsu. Author's collection.

After breakfast, we went back to our dorms and tidied up. After a bit, I finished doing this and knitted. After some time the people of the house — the Maedas — gave us red bean rice. Apparently the younger brother of the head of the house is leaving for the front. It was very, very delicious. Then we returned to school.

April 14, 1945 (Sat.), clear

Today I got up at 5:00 a.m. — someone in the Maeda house was going to the front, and we saw him off. The tips of our feet and hands were very cold. After some time, we shouted, "Maeda banzai!" and did it three times. He boarded the train. When that happened, the band started playing. It was very merry. We clapped our hands in time with the music, and before we knew it, the train had disappeared in the distance. In the morning we went sightseeing and saw many different places. When we were walking along a narrow road, a boy said, "Look! There's a *dojō*" [a little eel] and went into a narrow ditch and caught it.

April 15, 1945 (Sun.), clear

Today there was a festival at the Usa Hachiman Shrine.[14] We went together with students from the Akamatsu and Fukumitsu Citizens Schools.[15] There were a lot of girls wearing cute kimonos. We had candy and crackers for snacks, and

---

14. The Usa Hachiman Shrine is down the street from the Maeda Dorm.
15. The Akamatsu School was in Ōta Ward in Tokyo and its students also were evacuated to Fukumitsu and housed in a temple.

they were really delicious. The portable shrine left the Usa Shrine at 12:30 a.m. We heard it was very merry. In the evening they set off fireworks, and the rat fireworks were very interesting.

April 16, 1945 (Mon.), clear

Today after the morning assembly, we were weighed. I was very happy. Why? Because I was once 23.7 kilograms, and my weight had increased to 24.5 kilograms. Then Iwamaru-sensei took us to the Ogawa River.[16] The water was transparent and beautiful. We tried putting our hands into the water. Boy, it was because it was so beautiful. I thought it felt good. When we asked Sensei if it would be all right to put our feet into the water, he said fine, and so we did. That felt really good too. We played for a long time.

April 17, 1945 (Tues.), clear

Today we had our pictures taken after the morning assembly. We all had our picture taken together. I'm wondering what my face looked like when the picture was taken and want to see it soon. Then we went back to the lodge and got our plates. After we had lunch, we went to the Maeda house and took a bath. It was a very big bath, and I was really surprised. It felt very good. Then we tidied up our belongings. Ten fifth graders carried saké to the girls' school. I did my best and finished knitting a stomach warmer. I was very happy. I think I'll give it to my younger sister.

April 18, 1945 (Wed.), clear

Today Maeda Dorm went alone to Tatenogahara with box lunches.[17] Iwamaru-sensei walked fast, so he wouldn't be last and ended up being last. We wondered whether he was running and walked steadily onward. After we had walked for some time, Ariga-sensei and a fifth-grader said, "Sensei, this is not the place!" We asked a man for directions and then started walking again. When we had walked for some time, we arrived in the vicinity of the Tatenogahara Training Area. We enjoyed our box lunches in a sunny field. Then we went to the training site.

April 19, 1945 (Thurs.), rain

Beginning today we had fun classes. First period was Japanese, and the sensei was Ishida-sensei.[18] Today we studied a song in "Chapter 1: The Beach in the

---

16. Nakane miswrites "Oyabegawa" as "Ogawa."

17. Tatenogahara is about five miles southeast of Fukumitsu and was the site of a glider-training facility.

18. Ishida Sakuma was attached to Yamashita Dorm.

Morning." It was a song that went like this. Blown by the morning sea breeze, my younger brother and I, the two of us, ran along the beach. We ran steadily along the beach kicking up wet sand. The bright beach! The horizon is golden as far as the eye can see, and the sky and the water have become one. The bright sea! The refrain "As far as the eye can see . . . " goes on for five verses. Today Ariga-sensei's father visited.

April 20, 1945 (Fri.), cloudy

Today first period was supposed to be a science class, but because Sensei wasn't here, we did Japanese at the Yamashita Dorm. Ishida-sensei taught us. Today we wrote in our notebooks on the meaning of "Chapter 1: The Beach in the Morning." We continued our Japanese lesson in the second period. After a long time Sensei spoke. "If we do just Japanese, it's boring, so let's do math next. In the meantime, let's take a five-minute break." When our math lesson started, Sensei said, "Get out your abacuses so we can use them." Ishida-sensei wasn't like Yamaguchi-sensei and called twenty-three sen two tens and three sen. It was very interesting. In the evening I wrote a lot of postcards and was happy about this.

April 21, 1945 (Sat.), clear

Today was Tanaka's birthday.[19] We fourth-grade girls congratulated her. Tanaka seemed embarrassed, as she always is. It was funny but couldn't be helped. Just before lunch, my older sister came with a letter: she said, "Listen, our house burned down."[20] I was shocked! Hateful, hateful Americans and English! How hateful the Americans and English are! That's what I thought.

April 22, 1945 (Sun.), clear

Today is Sunday. After the morning assembly ended, we went to gather mugwort. We went to the Oyabe River embankment. When we looked across the way, the first-section sixth graders were washing their clothes in the distance. We split up and began to search for mugwort. Everyone was saying, "I wonder if this is mugwort. If we make a mistake and pick poisonous grass, it'll be terrible!" After we searched for a long time, Sensei said, "Stop!" We all put the mugwort we had collected in our hats into his big *furoshiki*. In the afternoon when we were

---

19. Tanaka was a classmate.

20. Letters from Nakane's parents were sent to Yūmiko, her elder sister, but were addressed to both of them. The letter with the news that their house, which was in the Ōtsuka District in Tokyo, burned down on April 13 arrived eight days later. On April 12 and 13, 94 B-29s attacked Tokyo, dropping incendiary bombs. See Carter and Mueller, *Combat Chronology*, 626.

washing our clothes, someone from the Maeda house showed us how to make rice cakes. We made mugwort rice cakes. Iwamaru-sensei also pounded the rice, but he kept making mistakes. After some time the people of the house gave each of us two mugwort rice cakes, which were delicious. We were having dinner soon, so I ate just one. After we got back, Sensei spoke to us and then gave us the names of our rooms. The farthest room in was "Lily of the Valley," a name that means you'll be able to live happily. The next was "English Daisy," which means you'll become innocent. The next was "Easter Lily," a name that means you'll become pure. And the last was "Violet," a name that means you'll become clever. All were very nice names. After that we received another mugwort rice cake, which was really delicious. After some time, we slept. Then we heard the continuation of the story of the "Dumpling Corporal." Su-su, zzzzzzz.

April 23, 1945 (Mon.), clear

Today we marched to the training site at Tatenogahara. The weather was very nice. After the morning assembly, we went off with our box lunches, and it was hot enough for us to perspire. The rice in the fields swayed like green waves. After a long time we arrived at an open field but we rested at a better place. After we were there a while, the chief talked to us and showed us the gliders. After a while we ate our lunches, which were really, really delicious. A spring breeze, no, a summer breeze, blew softly right in front of me.

April 24, 1945 (Tues.), clear

Today in Japanese class we studied "Chapter 2: Gathering Shells." It described the way a beach looks in the morning and was about fourth-grade students whose sensei took them to gather shells. In exercise class we played dodgeball. We took off our *monpe* before we started playing. Today the red team won. I was very happy. We took a bath after we got back, and it felt very good. It felt more relaxing than when we were in Kumekawa.[21] Because it was hot, the water came right out of the tap. At dinner they gave us apples, and I got two. They were given to us after we returned to Maeda Dorm. *(April 28 Examination. Both your diary entries and pictures were nicely written and well done. The scarcity of Chinese characters was unfortunate. Use as many Chinese characters as much as you can.)*[22]

---

21. Kumekawa was the evacuation site that Nakane's group left to come to Fukumitsu.
22. Teachers checked the children's diaries once every ten days and commented on their orthography and conduct. See Nakane's 5/18/45 entry. During the war all schoolchildren's diaries were periodically checked not only to correct their grammatical and orthographic mistakes but also to monitor their morale and thoughts. The comments by Nakane's teachers are in italics.

April 25, 1945 (Wed.), clear

This morning we had only Japanese in first period, and after that I washed all my clothes. I washed my underwear and pants. I scrubbed them as hard as I could, and they got really clean. I was happy. After I finished, I wrote in my diary until Sensei said, "Get ready to leave!" In the afternoon we played bucket ball during exercise period, which I really liked. Abe-sensei sketched.[23] He is very good. After some time we went to the sewing room and were given apples. Then we practiced the ceremony for the emperor's birthday.

April 26, 1945 (Thurs.), clear

Today first period was on ethics. We learned the imperial rescript.[24] Ishida-sensei taught us to raise it to eye level when we read it. No matter how much I studied it, I couldn't do it. I thought I must practice this. In drawing class we sketched Yamashita Dorm. I've gotten quite bad. Third-section fourth grader Suzuki is very good at drawing. In the afternoon we went to the barbershop. I had my hair cut at the same place as Mizuno, Sakomizu, Takashima, Hiramatsu, Yamazaki, Kobayashi, and Nagino did. Our haircuts made us look really beautiful.

April 27, 1945 (Fri.), cloudy

Today we were having our Japanese class on the grounds of the shrine when the wind suddenly started to blow hard and it began to rain. Ishida-sensei said, "Well, let's have our class in Yamashita Dorm," and so we went there. We had our class in the room of the third-section of fourth graders. We did "Chapter 3: Japan's Takeru no mikoto."[25] Japan's Takeru no mikoto understood very great things. Then we understood very strong and noble things.

April 28, 1945 (Sat.), clear

Today we spent first period studying science with Iwamaru-sensei. We did research on the maple at Yamashita Dorm. We learned that no matter what, the tree called the maple has leaves that turn red. After that we practiced tomorrow's ceremony. Both the Akamatsu and Fukumitsu Citizens Schools practiced to-

---

23. Abe Hiroshi was from Nakane's school in Tokyo.

24. Nakane does not say which imperial rescript they learned.

25. Yamatotakeru no mikoto was a legendary Japanese hero whose exploits were first recorded in the earliest surviving histories, the *Kojiki* (*Record of Ancient Matters*) and *Nihon shoki* (*A Chronicle of Japan*). He is known as the subjugator of the indigenous peoples that the Japanese called the Kumaso and Ezo.

gether. In the afternoon we aired our futon. I was happy. After that Kobayashi, Tanaka, and I practiced for Class Day. We'll sing a cute lullaby. After dinner was over, we brought in the futon.

April 29, 1945 (Sun.), clear

Today was the emperor's birthday, and it was a happy day! In the morning we put on our school uniforms. Beautiful rising-sun flags were flying at every house.[26] They fluttered in the morning breeze and were beautiful. I thought I want to have a heart as beautiful as those beautiful flags. We arrived at school. From the back I could hear happy voices reciting the lines "The flowers bloom like a storm in Yoshino. If I am born a Yamato man . . ." The words seemed to sail on the wind. When I turned around, it was the third-section sixth graders, who were all smiling more than usual. We entered one after another. The sewing room was brighter than usual. After some time passed, it was lunchtime. Lots of different delicious foods were served: beans, lotus root, bog rhubarb, sweet potato stems, cold tofu, and red rice.[27] It was very delicious. We played for a long time. Then we could hear the emperor's birthday song being sung solemnly, and we bowed our heads. After some time it ended and we entered the lecture hall, which had been decorated beautifully. Then after some time we performed the emperor's birthday ceremony. It was a happy, happy emperor's birthday.

April 30, 1945 (Mon.), clear

Today in the first period Iwamaru-sensei taught us ethics. Today we studied "Chapter 2: Kimigayo."[28] The song "Kimigayo" has this meaning. It is that the era of the emperor's reign will go on for a thousand or ten thousand years and prosper. In return, we will work as hard as we can. In the afternoon we wrote comfort letters

26. Nakane's language echoes that of "The Rising Sun Flag" chapter in the third-grade ethics textbook, part of which reads: A blue, clear sky. / Flying just at the eaves, / The rising sun flag / is truly dignified. See Kaigo Muneomi, ed., *Nihon kyōkasho taikei: Kindaihen* (Tokyo: Kodansha, 1962), 3:403–404.

27. *Zuiki* is the local word for the stem of the sweet potato plant, which is dried before it is used in cooking. Yoshinami, personal communication, June 4, 2004.

28. "Kimigayo" (Our Majesty's Reign) is the Japanese national anthem. The lyrics are from a tenth-century poem that reads: Thousands of years of happy reign be thine; / Rule on, my lord, till what are pebbles now / By age united to mighty rocks shall grow / Whose vulnerable sides the moss doth line. It was set to music by Hayashi Hiromori and was first performed for Emperor Meiji on his birthday, November 3, 1880. In 1893, the Ministry of Education began having primary school students sing "Kimigayo" on national holidays.

to soldiers in the south.[29] I wrote as well as I could to make the soldiers happy and described yesterday's ceremony on the emperor's birthday. Then I tidied up my belongings.

May 1, 1945 (Tues.), rain, later cloudy

Starting today it's May. This month, too, I want to do my best to become a splendid citizen.[30] We moved firewood all morning. The little second graders moved firewood, too. We did this while it was raining, but when I thought of the soldiers, it was easy. I made three or four trips. It wasn't as far as it usually is, and the wood was very light. Then we went back to Maeda Dorm. After we spent some time there, we went to school for lunch. After the meal was over, the fourth graders and above moved firewood. We returned to our dorm and took a bath. It was a very good bath. In the evening Ishida-sensei and Saitō Yoshikado-sensei came, and we had them tell us funny and sad stories.[31]

May 2, 1945 (Wed.), cloudy then rain

Today in first period we studied the section on the grass-mowing sword of Japan's Yamatotakeru no mikoto. We did this at Yamashita Dorm, and because it was raining we did it inside. For lunch they served rice gruel. It was very delicious, and many different things were in it. In the afternoon we went to Yamashita Dorm and received eight sheets of Wara paper and studied local customs. I drew straw sandals. Then I painted a picture on the cover, a picture related to the local area.

May 3, 1945 (Thurs.), clear

Today Ishida-sensei returned home, so we had self-study in Japanese class. I was writing in my diary for a long time when Osawa, a fifth grader, came and said to our class, "The fourth graders are going to be weighed, so please come with us." The fourth-grade girls went first. Everyone has lost weight. Today, it was reported in the newspaper that at long last that man Hitler has died. Oh — that Hitler . . . that Hitler who was pro-Japan from his childhood.[32] In the afternoon we had a vaccination. I thought it would hurt, but it didn't hurt one bit.

---

29. "South" refers to the South Pacific and Southeast Asia.

30. Nakane's aspiration to become a "splendid citizen" is not surprising. Her ethics textbook presented detailed descriptions of a "good child" (J. *yoi kodomo*), and no doubt her teachers encouraged their students to realize this goal. Her frequent references to becoming a "good child" confirm this.

31. Saitō Yoshikado was attached to Funaoka Dorm. The Funaoka family was in the flax business. Yoshinami, personal communication, June 4, 2004.

32. During the war Japanese knew quite a lot about Adolf Hitler, and many actually admired him.

May 4, 1945 (Fri.), clear

Today, we had physical exams in the morning. They looked at our ears, eyes, and body. In the afternoon I went back to my dorm and washed my clothes. I washed my underwear and washcloth, which were dirty. The washcloth got pure white. I was very happy. Then I went to pick up my luggage at Yamashita Dorm. Later we went with someone from the Maeda house to pick mugwort. The wind was very strong. Then we had class day rehearsals. We . . . cute nursemaids (*What happened after this?*)

May 5, 1945 (Sat.), clear

Today was the May festival — the boys' festival. For breakfast there was red bean rice, bog rhubarb, *konnyaku*, potato, cod roe, cold and grilled tofu. It was really, really delicious. Today Shuji-sensei (the principal) returned. I was very happy. Then Akuzawa-sensei and Katō-sensei entered.[33] Katō-sensei will teach us arithmetic. Both seemed like very kind teachers. In the evening we had a Class Day meeting, which Shuji-sensei and Takada-sensei attended.[34] Townspeople also came. Afterward we all had mugwort rice cakes covered with bean jam and rolled in soybean flour. They were made by members of the Maeda family, and the people who made saké gave us red beans. I felt really grateful. It was all really delicious.

May 6, 1945 (Sun.), clear

Today was Sunday, and the playing field was open, so the whole school had spiritual training there. For the first time in a long time we took off our *monpe* and trained in white slips. It felt good to train while warm morning breezes were blowing. The first-, second-, and third-grade boys and the fourth- and fifth-grade girls. Our voices echoed clearly in the sky. There we were under the big sky — in undershirts, red sashes, and white skin. Strong voices, a breeze that felt good, a spring breeze. We perspired. Iwamaru-sensei's smiling face was glistening, and everyone's eyes glittered. After the calisthenics ended, we threw balls. The fourth graders were divided up into red and white teams. We tried throwing the balls under a very hot sun. Dear me! I hit someone — the strongest person on the white team, Hotta. We all raised a battle cry.

---

33. Both Akuzawa Eitarō and Katō Yasunori were attached to Funaoka Dorm.
34. Takada Sumiko was a teacher from Nakane's school in Tokyo and was attached to Yoshinami Dorm.

May 7, 1945 (Mon.), clear

Today we had a fun march. It was very good weather and felt good. The second and third graders went to Tatenogahara, which is pretty close by. The fourth graders and above, which was us, went to a place that was a little far away to pick bog rhubarb, bracken ferns, flowering ferns, and various other things. We also went to the house where Hori-sensei was born. We were completely surprised because it was so big. Then we picked various things. It was lots and lots of fun.

May 8, 1945 (Tues.)

Today was Imperial Rescript Observance Day.[35] When I went to school in the morning, the beautiful rising-sun flags on each house were fluttering in the morning breeze. There was a ceremony at school, which was held in Fukumitsu Lecture Hall. After we returned to our classroom, we wrote letters to sailors. I did as I always did. I tried as hard as I could to write letters that would make them happy. Today we even made envelopes, and we did all this together. In the afternoon I washed my hair, which felt really good. Then we took a bath. It was a very good bath, and it felt very, very good.

May 9, 1945 (Wed.)

Today it rained and was very cold. In sewing class we did needlework. I gradually got good at it and was very happy. I did my very best, but I sewed crookedly and made both big and small stitches, and so I thought I must work harder at sewing. In the afternoon we put on our school uniforms and went to greet the spirits of departed heroes. It was raining, so we went with open umbrellas. Today Iwamaru-sensei returned to his home province. This was very, very sad. We had Ariga-sensei's really delicious *omiyage*. Apparently Ariga-sensei's mother made it.

May 10, 1945 (Thurs.)

Today fourth graders and above moved firewood. When I had made my third trip to where Ishida-sensei was standing, he said, "Mmm. What shall I call you? Let's see. 'Lance Corporal Nakane!'" I thought I'll work even harder and ran to where the wood piles were. This time Nagino and I carried a big piece of firewood together. When we did this, Ishida-sensei asked, "Nakane, what were you?" When

---

35. Beginning in February 1942, Japanese were ordered to read aloud on the eighth day of every month the imperial rescript that announced the declaration of war against the Allies. Imperial Rescript Day (Taishō hōtaibi) replaced "Public Service Day for Asia," which had been observed on the first day of every month since 1939.

I said, "Lance Corporal," he said, "Well, you're now a Corporal!" I was so happy I couldn't stand it. In the end we rose to the rank of apprentice officers. I was very happy. In the afternoon we welcomed the spirits of departed heroes.

May 11, 1945 (Fri.), cloudy

Today we had a fun march. It rained a little in the morning, so everyone talked about how we were going to have good weather. But only Kuniyuki and Koba-yashi prayed for rain. Before long it was good weather. I was very happy. Because of this, we got ready and went to school. Then we went to pick various things. It was lots and lots of fun. We picked mugwort, field horsetail shoots, *yamaudo*, bog rhubarb, bracken ferns, flowering ferns, chives, and wild rocamble. It rained on the way home, and we got wet.

May 12, 1945 (Sat.)

Today there was an air-raid drill. As we were leaving our dorm, we were ordered to observe an air-raid warning drill, so we put on our air-defense clothes and then left. During science class, we went outside and were walking around searching for various things when Sakomizu and Toki came running over. They said, "Everyone's evacuating! Hurry!" So we got directions from Katō-sensei and ran, evacuating to the grounds of the shrine.

May 13, 1945 (Sun.), clear

Today I was about to return to Maeda Dorm when Nakagawa's aunt arrived. Today we did a general cleaning of Maeda Dorm. Then we changed the location of our rooms and our baggage. This time I have "White Lily Room." There are four of us in "White Lily" — Sakaguchi, Toki, Uehara, and me. Because Uehara and Sakaguchi will store their baggage with the fifth-graders, we'll [be able to] tidy up. After we tidied up, we had an apple, which was very, very delicious. In the afternoon only the fourth graders washed their clothes.

May 14, 1945 (Mon.)

Today ethics class met during the first period, and we studied "Chapter 3: Yasu-kuni Shrine." Suzuki's grandfather is worshiped at Yasukuni Shrine.[36] In Japa-nese class, we studied "Chapter 4: Kimigayo Youth." They were really splendid, smart, and admirable young people, and I admired them so much I couldn't stand it. In the evening we had an apple.

---

36. Suzuki's grandfather was a superintendent at Yasukuni Shrine.

May 15, 1945 (Tues.)

Today we took a bath in the afternoon. It felt very, very good. I washed off a week's worth of dirt and looked like a different person. Sakomizu was very sensitive to heat, and although the water was just right, she said, "Oh, it's hot! It's hot!" Sakomizu's sensitivity to heat surprised me. Tanaka's undershirt disappeared, and we searched for it, and in the evening when we had a rubdown with a towel, she put it on by herself.

May 16, 1945 (Wed.)

Today during science class, Katō-sensei gave each one of us a leaf that had an egg on its underside. Then Katō-sensei said, "I am giving each of you a leaf, and an egg is attached to its underside, so study it beginning today." After we went back to the dorm, I immediately put the leaf into a cup and studied it.

May 17, 1945 (Thurs.)

Today was a fun presentation assembly. In the morning I took only my morning things. In Japanese class we learned about the era of the "Six Rice Nurseries." We had our School Arts Assembly at 1:30 p.m. At the very beginning, Otoha Hiroko, a second-section sixth grader, gave the opening speech for the ceremony. Next, the second graders did a dialogue called "Ushiwakamaru." Motegi was Ushiwakamaru. It was very cute. There were lots of funny things in it. The "Pink Egg" was very funny.

May 18, 1945 (Fri.)

The School Arts Festival ended today. Well, I thought I would study as hard as I could beginning today. In Japanese class we wrote compositions. I wrote on the topic of "Rain." In the fifth period we had self-study, so we played outside on the swing, slide, and seesaw. It was lots of fun. (*The pictures for the eighteenth were well done, but your writing is a little rough and too simple.*)

May 19, 1945 (Sat.)

Today in sewing period we put patterns on our own piece of cloth, and I used black thread. Next time we'll make a bag for our leftover thread. I want to make mine quickly. Then we set needle-handling records. On my first try I did twenty centimeters in one minute: twenty stitches. On my second try I did twenty-one centimeters in one minute: twenty-one stitches. Today we presented our diaries to the sensei. Ariga-sensei said, "We've been doing plays and singing everywhere. Shall we do it inside today?" The fourth graders were first. We sang the songs we performed recently. We sang "Factory," "Lieutenant Hirose," and the "Silent

Return." The fifth graders performed a dialogue called "Making Rice Cakes," which was about the fun they had had making rice cakes. It was very interesting. Then each of us sang a song, one by one. As we sang, we ate the beans that Nomura's relatives gave us. They were very delicious. Both Ariga-sensei and Motegi-sensei sang for us, and they had very good voices. It was lots and lots of fun.

May 20, 1945 (Sun.)

Today we were supposed to have all-school spiritual training, but we couldn't do it because it was cloudy. After the morning assembly, we went back to Maeda Dorm and tidied up our belongings. When I finished tidying up my things, I felt refreshed. I washed my clothes in the afternoon. That evening when we went back to Maeda Dorm, we passed a very beautiful pine tree.

May 21, 1945 (Mon.)

Today was a fun climb up Mount Kuwayama.[37] We left after the morning assembly was over. As we walked, I thought to myself, "Today I'd like to draw enough pictures to fill my bag." A torii finally appeared. Tanaka said, "You can probably see the torii over there. We'll probably go to that spot and climb that mountain." After a while it got steeper and steeper, and the path got mushy. Little by little I got separated from the sensei, but I didn't know this and just clambered up the path as fast as I could. We enjoyed our box lunches at the top of Mount Ishikiri.

May 22, 1945 (Tues.)

Today a ceremony offering an imperial rescript to young soldiers was held in front of the shrine. Then we took a bath. It felt very, very good and also was empty. Then I washed my hair and felt very refreshed. Then Shinya-sensei gave me my first typhoid shot, which did not hurt in the least.[38] Today Iwamaru-sensei went home. I was very happy.

May 23, 1945 (Wed.), rain

Today it's raining, and it's very boring. It may be boring for us, but the farmers will be very happy. If rain doesn't fall, it'll mean trouble for them, and rice and other foods can't be grown. Rain is something to be very grateful for. After we

---

37. Mount Kuwayama (elev. 293 meters) is located several miles northeast of Fukumitsu.

38. Shinya-sensei was the guardian of an evacuated child and a practicing Tokyo doctor who came often to see his child.

went back to Maeda Dorm, we ate the candy that Iwamaru-sensei brought as *omiyage* and the candy that Nomura's visitor gave us.

May 24, 1945 (Thurs.), clear

Because the weather today was good, we went to pick bracken ferns at Tatenoga-hara. There were lots and lots of bracken ferns. Yet because we didn't bring box lunches, we could pick bracken ferns only in the morning. We had a lot, and in fact, we had so much we were a little worried about it. We found some right away and even when we sat down. When we returned, a delicious-looking pot of bamboo-shoot rice was waiting for us. It was really, really delicious. After we got back, we wiped off our bodies.

May 25, 1945 (Fri.)

Today we did rabbit jumping on the playing field. After the morning assembly, we had our second typhoid shots. This time they gave us more drugs than last time, so it hurt more. During physical education period in the afternoon we went into the Oyabe River. At first it was cold, but it was a lot of fun. Iwamaru-sensei threw in a big log and said, Let's throw rocks at it. The boys threw a lot of rocks.

May 26, 1945 (Sat.)

Today the people at Fukumitsu Citizens School put on their arts festival for us. It was very, very interesting. First there was a recitation, then they did a play and comic dance called "Where Did the Fishhook Go?" In the afternoon they showed a film at Ishiguro Dorm. There were lots of very interesting things. They did three things for us.

May 27, 1945 (Sun.)

Today was the bucket ball tournament we had been waiting for. First there was a game between the third- and fourth-grade girls, and we fourth graders won. We were very happy. Then we played the third-section fourth graders, and sadly, we lost. In the end the third-section fourth graders were the victors in the lower grades, and the third-section sixth graders were the victors in the upper grades. In the afternoon I napped for an hour. Then I washed my hair.

May 28, 1945 (Mon.)

Today we went to pick wild vegetables at Tatenogahara and took box lunches. The weather was very nice, and it felt good. Along the way we rested and saw gliders. After some time, Iwamaru-sensei, Abe-sensei, and Hachikuwa-sensei, rode the gliders.[39] Iwamaru-sensei rode first. When he got on the glider, we could hear him say, "Iwamaru Shigeo is about to glide above the ground. Over and out." Iwamaru-sensei was the best, Hachikuwa-sensei was next best, and Abe-sensei was next. We went farther in and picked lots and lots of bracken ferns. We had our box lunches and came back.

May 29, 1945 (Tues.)

We went to the barber this morning and went to the one we visited recently. Maeno was the very first, then I was next. It made me very beautiful, and I felt wonderful. After we went back to Maeda Dorm, I tidied up my belongings. It was already time for summer hats and summer clothes. In the afternoon we took a bath. The second-grade girls came and took a bath, too. In the evening Shuji-sensei returned. Apparently Hori-sensei's house burned down.[40] In the evening Hori-sensei came to Maeda Dorm and took a bath.

May 30, 1945 (Wed.)

In the afternoon we went to Tatenogahara for nighttime drills. We were going to leave at 1:30 p.m., but we were late and soon it was 2:30. We took firewood, rice paddles, ladles, pots, pans, and buckets as well as miso, dried tofu, onions, box dinners, canteens, and side cups.[41] We finally arrived at Tatenogahara. We rested for a short time, and then the fifth graders and below collected firewood, and the sixth graders and female and male teachers dug a hole and made a stove and cooked the meal. After a long while it was time for dinner. In addition to our box dinners and the pickled onions, there was a really, really delicious miso soup, which we heated with the firewood we collected. After the meal was finished, we practiced military songs. It was all really, really interesting. Then we played "Search for the Treasure."[42] In the end our group couldn't find even one "treasure." It was very disappointing but lots of fun. Then we had dried cuttlefish. The fifth graders

---

39. Hachikuwa Shigeo was a teacher from Nakane's school in Tokyo and the head of Funaoka Dorm.

40. Hori-sensei's house must have burned down on May 25, when 464 B-29s attacked Tokyo, dropping incendiary bombs on residential areas in central Tokyo. See Carter and Mueller, *Combat Chronology*, 655.

41. A Chinese character is missing from this sentence.

42. "Searching for the Treasure" (J. *takara sagashi*) appears to be a Japanese version of a scavenger hunt.

found two bags of *tororo konbu* and five *onigiri*. And then we practiced walking quickly and striking the enemy.[43] It was lots and lots of fun. (*"Treasure" is the same character as the hō in "Mihōko." Use Chinese characters.*)[44]

May 31, 1945 (Thurs.)

Today we were tired, so we had no schoolwork. In the morning we washed our clothes. I washed my underwear, slips, and socks, and they got very, very clean. Then I read a book about Laclos's expedition.[45] In the afternoon Iwamaru-sensei put out our futon to air, and they were very, very warm in the evening when we went to sleep.

June 1, 1945

Today we went toward Kanazawa to gather wild vegetables. There were very, very steep mountains. It was cloudy, but as we went farther and farther, the weather got much better. We had our box lunches in the mountains, and they were really, really delicious. Then we climbed a steep mountain and picked bracken ferns. There were some very long ones but not very many. Because it was June, there were lots of farmers planting rice. In the evening we had a party. Today was lots and lots of fun. Tomorrow we'll pound rice for rice cakes at Maeda Dorm. Just fun things.

June 2, 1945

Today we pounded rice, and it was fun. Because we were going to pound rice at Maeda Dorm, we carried the rice and other things there. After some time, the different sensei arrived, and the rice pounding began. All of them went down-stairs, and the rice pounding started. Everyone went downstairs to see the rice pounding. When I went to watch, it was just when Hachikuwa-sensei was pound-ing the rice, and Ishida-sensei was adding water. When you pound the rice, it often sticks and you then stretch it. Then you make it round, and delicious-looking dumplings are made with a bean jam coating. For dinner we had two delicious rice cakes each, which filled us up. The teachers played lots of records at Maeda Dorm. While listening, I gradually got sleepy. It was nice music.

---

43. "Striking the enemy" is a type of bamboo spear practice.
44. The teachers who read Nakane's diary began to underline words that should have been written with Chinese characters.
45. Pierre Choderlos de Laclos (1741–1803) was a French author and general.

June 3, 1945 (Sun.), clear

Today we had spiritual training at school. At first we played kickball baseball with the fifth-grade girls.[46] We divided ourselves into the reds and whites. The whites lost 20 to 11, and it was very sad. Next time we'll devise a strategy. Then we did a three-color battle. The girls' gold school — grades 2 through 6 — played. The whites won 4 to 2, and I was very happy. At the very end we marched, and it was over. In the afternoon when we got back to Maeda Dorm, Iwamaru-sensei said, "Shucks! I forgot my cigarettes!" and Ariga-sensei asked whether anyone would go to get them, and I said I would and ran off to the school. I got the cigarettes from inside Sensei's desk and ran back quickly. When I climbed to the top of the stairs and handed the cigarettes to Iwamaru-sensei, he smiled and said, "That was fast, wasn't it! Shall I give you a pat on the head?" He patted me on the head and turning to Ariga-sensei, he said, "Look at how big they've gotten," and Sensei laughed. I sneaked away. Then Maeno and I went to the post office to buy post-cards. (*Thanks for getting the cigarettes. You've done a good job with your diary. The pictures are good, too. From now on let's use an underlay, OK? Because if you don't, the crayon marks from the previous day's picture will be on the paper. There are marks where I think you could have written Chinese characters. Use Chinese characters as often as you can.*)

June 4, 1945 (Mon.)

Today we had fun evening drills. We left here this afternoon at 2:00 p.m. We put on sedge hats and went off. It was very hot and seemed like summer. After some time, I could see Ishida-sensei strip down and put on a headband. We went there and rested for a while. Then we went to gather firewood. The third-section fifth graders already were there. We gathered firewood for some time and then returned. After a while we had a meal. The miso soup had dried tofu, strips of dried gourd, and two rice cakes in it. It was really, really delicious. After the meal, we practiced singing war songs. Then we played "Searching for the Jewel." The "jewel" turned out to be Kobayashi's apple, but because she wrote to please make it Hori-sensei's *omiyage*, it wasn't much fun for the rest of us. I searched as hard as I could, but in the end we were ordered to assemble. In our group it was Kobayashi alone. Then we were divided into attack and defense units and made war with each other.

---

46. It is not clear what game was being played. Nakane calls it *shuruikyū*, literally "kick base ball."

June 5, 1945 (Tues.)

Today in the morning we wrote down our impressions of night drills. I wrote as well as I could. After some time, it was lunchtime, so we went to school. Although today was a bath day, we canceled that and had classes. In science period we thinned out radish seedlings. Then Katō-sensei talked about the importance of continuing to do research.

June 6, 1945 (Wed.), clear

Today during science class, which was first period, they showed us how rice was planted. In Japanese class we did the section on a famous person who played the round flute. The writing was so very good that I didn't know what to say. In the afternoon we studied local history and read the section on "Toyama Prefecture." It was really difficult, but I wrote as well as I could and received a triple circle.[47] Today Ariga-sensei and Iwamaru-sensei gave us new clogs. *(Since you began to use this notebook, your pictures have been well done!)*

June 7, 1945

Today it's drizzling again. In local history class we did the section on "The Rainy Hokuriku District," and it was very hard.[48] I understood that the rain came from the other side of the Yangtze River.[49] In the afternoon we took a bath. The second-grade girls came and took a bath with us. It really felt good. After our bath I made paper dolls and gave them to Fukuyama-sensei.[50] Today we had rice gruel for lunch, and it was really delicious.

June 8, 1945

Today is Imperial Rescript Observance Day. When I went to school, beautiful rising-sun flags fluttered at every house. Beginning today, our schedule has changed. From now on we will not say Monday, Tuesday, Wednesday, Thursday, Friday, and Saturday. It has been decided that we will say First-Day Classes, Second-Day Classes, and so forth.[51] Today we had First-Day classes. In the after-

---

47. "One circle" was good, and "three circles" was very good.
48. The Hokuriku District is on the western coast of Japan and consists of Toyama, Ishikawa, and Fukui prefectures.
49. The Yangtze River is a major Chinese river.
50. Fukuyama Akiko.
51. This was done because special events, weather, and work projects often interrupted academic work, and makeup classes had to be held. So instead of holding a "Monday" makeup class on Tuesday, a "First Day" makeup class was held.

noon we wrote letters to soldiers and sent them to those in North China. I did my best to write a letter that would make a soldier happy. On the back of the letter I drew a comic book picture riddle.

I drew two comic book pictures. One was called "The Badger's Stomach Drum" and the other was "The Sleepyheaded Piglet." I also wrote nine riddles. *(Use Chinese characters carefully.)*

June 9, 1945

It rained again today, but it cleared up after a while. In sewing class I finished my bag for leftover thread, which I made out of a piece of pink cloth. I did a better job than I expected and was very happy. When I showed it to Ariga-sensei, she wrote my name on it and gave it back to me. Before we went to bed, we had a self-reflection meeting. Here's what I thought: As for bad things, from now on, no, from this moment on, I will correct them and practice doing good things, and I believe I'll gradually become a good child.[52] *(This is a good goal.)*

June 10, 1945

Today it was National Time Day. Then we went to pick bracken ferns at Tatenogahara, and there was a lot. We had our box lunches at a very, very beautiful place, and they were really, really delicious. Iwamaru-sensei went right away to fly gliders with the pilot trainees. After we got back, we wiped ourselves off and napped. Kuniyuki's mother came for a visit. But I wasn't the least bit envious. Those who persevere until we win the war are Japanese. Curry on rice was served for dinner.

June 11, 1945

This morning we went back to the dorm and tidied up. Everything was made very neat. While I was rearranging my things, the person on meal duty said, "Please hold out your cups," and I held mine out. Iwamaru-sensei then lined up the cups and poured something into them that looked like red wine. The person on meal duty then arranged two rows of different kinds of candies, all of which looked delicious, on top of tissue paper. Sensei said, "Anywhere is fine, so just line them up in front of you," and we lined them up in front of ourselves. We had Sensei lead a silent prayer. We had various things — beans, dried cuttlefish, grapes, and tangerines. They were very delicious.

---

52. Nakane began to underline passages for emphasis.

June 12, 1945

Today we had Third-Day classes. During gym class we played catch. First we had a race, but I fell down and came in dead last. It was very humiliating. Then we played catch and did it by size. Maeno, Kobayashi, Tanaka, Koizumi, and Kuniyuki qualified, but Sakomizu, Sugamura, Tsuchimichi, Umetani, and I did not. It was very humiliating. On my second try, I qualified and was happy. It was really hard. When Iwamaru-sensei said to do it quickly, we did it quickly. Then we were paired off and made to sing together. I was paired with Maeno.

June 13, 1945

Today we studied at the library. We had self-study because Katō-sensei is away in the countryside. We read books and did some other things. During the sewing period we washed our clothes and then recorded the number of stitches we made. I really increased the numbers of stitches I did and was very happy. In the shop period I started making a box for my calligraphy brushes, but I wasn't able to finish.

June 14, 1945

Today we did "Chapter 10: Machines" in Japanese class. The "Machines" chapter became a 4-4-4-4 song (a four-syllable practice form). In calligraphy period we did the "The Colt of the Young Grasses on the Plain" chapter, and this time Motegi-sensei taught us. In the afternoon we practiced our presentations. We did the dialogue called the "Bear's Walk," and I ended up doing the explanation and the greeting.

June 15, 1945

Today we went to Tatenogahara to pick bracken ferns. It was very hot. In our box lunch were pickled onions and pickled radishes. Lots of big bracken ferns had sprouted in the shade of trees, and I intended to pick enough to fill up my bag. When I picked as many as I could, my bag was full. It was a beautiful place, and we enjoyed our box lunches, which were really delicious. I ate my lunch near Abe-sensei and Iwamaru-sensei and felt really shy.

June 16, 1945

Today in shop period we painted patterns on various things, including circles and triangles. I drew rose patterns on triangles. Sensei said, "The colors are very good." I was very happy!

June 17, 1945

Today we went over what we'll do at the presentation assembly, and this time we had Hachikuwa-sensei decide. Today was a spiritual training day for the whole school, and we did something different — we did hand-to-hand combat. Iwamaru-sensei told us many different stories. Then we piggybacked the person across from us and ran and did other things. The next station was Akuzawa-sensei's hand grenade–throwing class. We used small balls for hand grenades and imagined that the large ball we used for the intergrade meet was the enemy's head and threw the small balls at it. We threw the hand grenades with all our might, but they didn't hit their target. Then we moved to Hachikuwa-sensei's station, where we practiced striking and killing with a wooden sword. We faked to the left and faked to the right. Then after some time we went to Ishida-sensei's station. We took our clothes off and practiced spearing someone. We used our foreheads to butt the chest of the person in front of us, thrust our hands into their armpits, and pushed with our feet firmly planted on the ground. In the end, only one person was still thrusting. Then when that was done, we went to Yoshikado-sensei's station, where we practiced spearing. Yoshikado-sensei said, "They're still there. Spear them! Spear them!" and it was really fun. I was tired, but I realized that even one person can kill a lot of the enemy. *(You really persevered, didn't you?)*

June 18, 1945

Today we went to Mount Kuwayama to pick wild vegetables. The second and third graders picked wild vegetables at the base of Kuwayama, and the fourth graders and up climbed Kuwayama. It was very tiring. Ishida-sensei said, "There are ghosts on the top!" This made it really fun, and we completely forgot we were tired. The fourth graders did not go to the top and, for some time, collected bog rhubarb below us. We climbed until it was time for lunch, and everyone else already had had their box lunches. We had our box lunches together with Motegi-sensei. They were very, very delicious. Then we went down the mountain. Along the way the people in front of us were not visible, so we ran down the mountain. When we had gone a ways and were near a stone quarry, Maeno said not everyone is here and began to worry. I said, well, we're probably on the same path, so if we go ahead to look for them, and everyone said, yeah, let's do that. After saying this, we went ahead and saw someone's umbrella and thought "Hoorah!" and went down the mountain as fast as we could.

June 19, 1945

Today in the afternoon we went to see a show at a place called the Kotobukiza.[53] There were really lots of different things to see. At first women appeared who played different drums and instruments, and they played what looked like a brass band. Then a woman wearing a really thin dress danced for us and was really good. Then there were songs and something like a play. It was very, very interesting. We went back, and after some time we went to school for our dinner. It was a curry-on-rice feast, and it was really, really delicious. From today we had someone read a difficult volume of "Wonder Woman." It was very, very scary. When I went to the bathroom, fireflies were resting on the window sill. They were very beautiful and made a swishing sound as they flew about and seemed happy.

June 20, 1945

Today we went to pick wild vegetables. We were divided into two groups — the third and fourth graders formed one group, and the fifth and sixth graders the other — and we went to collect lots of stone parsley. Our squad leader was Kimon-sensei.[54] We walked along the embankment of the river just before Tatenogahara and picked parsley. There was a lot of parsley, but also a lot of buttercups, which were easy to mistake for parsley, so we had to pick carefully. Someone fell into the river and got soaking wet. When we followed the river for some time, we lost sight of the people ahead of us and worried. Because Motegi-sensei was there, we asked her what we should do, and she said follow this path. When we took that path, Maeno turned up, and we were really relieved. After going on for some time, we came to a forest and enjoyed our box lunches. We even had apples! After we ate our box lunches, we picked trefoil, and although it was poisonous, I picked something that looked like it.

June 21, 1945

Today we prepared for our presentations assembly at the library. Although I was only doing a reading, Sensei told everyone to pick the form of a picture, and so I nervously took one. Umetani and I painted colors on only one. Then I made a clean copy of my diary and then practiced seriously. As I was doing this, a siren sounded *u- u -*. It was an air-raid warning. We sat for a long time at the library, but then Iwamaru-sensei said cheerfully, "Air-defense clothing!" and

53. The Kotobukiza was Fukumitsu's movie theater.
54. Kimon-sensei is not identified.

we stopped what we were doing and ran with him back to Maeda Dorm. We put on our air-defense clothes and hurried to school. In the afternoon a small package arrived for my older sister, and something for me was in it, too. I was very happy. When I showed it to Iwamaru-sensei, he put a handkerchief on my head. Then he said it was fine.

June 22, 1945

Today was the day the young students were honored with an imperial rescript. Because of this, we had a ceremony on the grounds of the shrine after the morning assembly. Afterward the fourth-grade girls practiced their presentations at the library. After doing that once, I practiced the piano in the music room. Yamaguchi-sensei praised me, saying, "You can play really well, can't you? The third-grade girls went fishing. You play really well." In the afternoon I practiced some more. Hachikuwa-sensei said, "You've gotten very good," and I was very happy. Today a big package came to me. Lots of different things were in the package. What I usually wear was in the package.

June 23, 1945

Today was the Sonouchi training assembly. It was held in the spiritual cultivation room at the girls' school. We were going to perform after the opening speeches of the assembly. I was going to be the first one of the whole group. Because I was first, I thought I'd have to do a first-class job, and so I calmed down and read my diary. When I finished, everyone clapped loudly. The third-section sixth graders did Morse code signals. Mukokasa put ink on his hand and made the signals. I thought he's really concentrating, and I tried to be interested. At that time everyone said, "Wow!" and laughed. The third-section fifth graders did "The Shadow of the Crescent Moon" and were really good. They did a picture card show, and their pictures were really, really good, which surprised me. The third-section fifth graders' picture card show was excellent! It was a picture card show about normal times.

June 24, 1945

This morning was a rest period, and so the fourth graders were the only ones in Maeda Dorm. We played Morse code signaling. I did this while looking at the paper I was given recently at Kumekawa. The following is all I could fully remember.

* * * *	nu
——	re
*	he
— *	ta

Morse code. *Nuhetare*—only this message. I understood *he*, which was really easy. It was just *. *Nu* was four * * * *. *Re* was three –. *Ta* was – *. Just two things: – and *.

In the afternoon we practiced in the lecture hall, and later the second-section sixth graders watched.

June 25, 1945

Today is, at long last, the day of the presentations assembly. I was really upset because all morning I couldn't calm down. I was number 1. It started. Everybody was quiet. At last it was our turn. The sound of clapping hands affected me. I climbed on to the platform. Everyone's heads were moving up and down as though they were a swarm. I calmed down and read out loud. It was a lecture hall. My strong voice reached every corner of the lecture hall. Everyone was quiet. After a long time our presentations were over. Everyone clapped for us. Everyone was really good. Hachikuwa-sensei praised us, saying, "You did a nice job, didn't you?"

June 26, 1945

Today everyone from the fourth graders and up went with box lunches to move firewood at Nishifutomiyama.[55] The second and third graders went to pick bracken ferns at Tatenogahara. We arrived at Futomiyama, where there was lots of lumber and firewood on both sides of the road. After resting for an hour, we carried firewood from the forest to the side of the road. Iwamaru-sensei and Hachikuwa-sensei neatly piled the firewood we brought to them. After we finished, we washed our hands in a stream with clear water. Then we really enjoyed our box lunches, which were really, really delicious. Then we returned, together with Sugamura, carrying firewood.

June 27, 1945

Today the second and third graders went to Futomiyama to move firewood. Today the firewood was at the side of the road, so we were able to move it right away.

---

55. Nakane left out the "yama" in the name of Nishifutomiyama, which is just west of Fukumitsu.

After resting, we went right away to move the firewood. I held one piece of wood shaped like a bomb. After some time Kushimoto came running from the back, holding firewood. When I glanced behind me, Hijiki was there. I imagined that the person in front of me was the enemy and that if I passed that person, I would kill one enemy soldier. If I was passed by someone, I would die, and I decided that if I passed someone within ten steps, I was OK. *(You found an interesting way to persevere.)*

June 28, 1945

Today we had Third-Day classes, but we also had a huge cleaning of Maeda Dorm. We aired the tatami. The tatami were very heavy, but when we concentrated as we held them, they weren't heavy at all. After we aired the tatami, we were given very delicious gelatin water. The red and the blue were really good, and we received a full cup of each color. In the afternoon we moved the tatami. Today we also hung miscanthus grass. I was very, very happy.

June 29, 1945

Today we moved firewood. The second and third graders picked bracken ferns. Today the people from the Fukumitsu School brought firewood. When we went where the firewood was, the Fukumitsu school people were already there. We rested. In an instant, the logs were piled as high as a mountain, and there was firewood only at the bottom. We took our firewood and rested at a spot just in front of the shrine. The Fukumitsu School people carried lots of firewood on their backs, and what they carried looked heavy. Here's what I thought: "I was really grateful. They helped move our firewood, and they carried more than we did. If it had just been us, we would have had to make many more trips. I am truly grateful. How happy I am!" After a time I plodded along, carrying firewood. We had a huge lunch. Today I may have been a "good child." In the afternoon I took a nap.

June 30, 1945

Today was the end of June. Was I able to be a "good child" in June? When I thought about that, I was embarrassed by the bad things I did. I thought I'll be a "good child" for sure in July. Today we had Fourth-Day classes. During calligraphy class we copied something called "The Colt of the Young Grasses on the Plain." It was very hard, but I wrote as well as I could. Today there was an awards ceremony for Ibata-sensei of Fukumitsu National Citizens School. In the afternoon I changed rooms in Maeda Dorm. I'm now in the "Orchid Room." There are seven of us—Umetani, Koizumi, Tanaka, Takashima, Nagino, Hiramatsu, and me. I think I'll tidy up my belongings. *(Good self-reflections. In July, please become a better "good child.")*

July 1, 1945

Starting today it's July. I think I'll try to study as hard as I can in July and become a wonderful little Japanese citizen. When I left the house, my dad and mom said, "If we win, as we are sure to, Mihō-chan must become a pure and good child and an honest and wonderful little citizen," and I could see their words as clearly as day. I thought I must do as Father and Mother said. In the afternoon I took a nap. When I got up, I was really sleepy. In July, Maeno will be the squad leader.

July 2, 1945

Today was a rest day. After the morning assembly we went back to the dorm right away. Then I wrote in my diary. Kobayashi saw me drawing pictures, and I was really embarrassed. Because I was drawing on the floor, Kobayashi lent me a trunk. I was grateful and borrowed it. Then I made a thong for my clogs. After I finished it, I washed my clothes. I washed my slip and underwear, and they got very clean. In the afternoon I tied the thong to my clogs. I was so happy I had done such a good job, and I tried the clogs on that evening. Maeno and I played post office.

July 3, 1945

Today, in the morning, we had First-Day classes. During Japanese class our last exams were returned. I had an eighty-four. I thought I must study as hard as I can and get a hundred. In science class we thinned out the radish seedlings, which had gotten really, really big. In the afternoon we went back to the dorm and took a bath. It felt really, really good. After that I washed my hair. I felt refreshed, and this also felt good. And I washed my clothes today. I washed my pajamas, my wiping cloth, and socks. They all got very clean. *(You can write very well. Your pictures are well done, too. You used a lot of Chinese characters, didn't you? Your characters are not well formed. Be careful. The places that are underlined are where I'd like you to write a Chinese character.)*

July 4, 1945

During our morning assembly, I didn't feel very good, but I thought it can't be helped and said to myself, "I'm not feeling very good. Just forget about it!" But I wasn't in very good shape, so when I went to Ariga-sensei and Motegi-sensei,

Mori-sensei and Motegi-sensei carried me to the music classroom.[56] After an hour, I finally got better and went to class.

July 5, 1945 (Thurs.), rain

Today we did spelling during our Japanese class. For some time it has been as Father said: I'm still not much of a speller. During exercise period, Sensei borrowed the playing field, and we did sumo in the sumo ring. Because I wrestled with a boy, I lost, unfortunately. Just before dinner Ishida-sensei came back. I was very happy! Apparently he just took a bride. I thought she must be tall if she is Ishida-sensei's bride. Then at dinner we had really delicious food. We had red rice, pickled radish, rice cakes, grated yam with seaweed, miso soup, and cabbage. Because of my upset stomach, I couldn't have the pickled radish and grated yam with seaweed. Won't my stomach get better more quickly? Today was really fun.

July 6, 1945

Today it rained. Maeno didn't feel well, so she slept late. I thought she was probably bored, so Kobayashi and I made clothes for her paper dolls. Maeno was very pleased. In the afternoon we went to the barbershop we always visited. When we go to the barber, we always feel so refreshed, and it felt really good. I don't like it when it rains, but rain is a very good thing for farmers. And not just for farmers. If it doesn't rain, the rice won't grow, so rain is truly something to be thankful for.

July 7, 1945

Today during science class we went to the field in front of Yamashita Dorm and planted *subena* and weeded. When we weeded around the radish plants, they seemed happy. Then I wrote in my diary. Dinner was really early. Then we greeted the spirits of the war dead. I really feel grateful to them.

July 8, 1945

Today was Imperial Rescript Observance Day. In the morning, when I went to school, beautiful rising-sun flags were waving at every house. The flags were so beautiful, and I want my heart to be as beautiful as those flags! In the morning we wrote comfort essays.[57] Today we sent them to soldiers in Central China. In

---

56. Mori Haru was the head of the Ishiguro Dorm.
57. These were written for Japanese servicemen overseas.

the afternoon Iwamaru-sensei returned to his home province, and although it was very petty to think this, I bet Yō-chan is happy.[58]

July 9, 1945

Today we had First-Day studies in the morning. We sketched the scenery around Mount Iōyama in drawing class.[59] It felt good to sketch in the warm sun. Mount Iōyama seemed really high, and smoke spewed from its summit. Sensei said, "This is very well done!" and showed it to everyone, which was embarrassing. Today we stopped after third period and had lunch. After we finished eating, the sixth graders cleaned. Then we greeted the spirits of the war dead. As I greeted them, I thought, "I am truly grateful to you."

July 10, 1945

Today we had fun making rice cakes. We had self-study at the girls school in the morning. In the afternoon we took a bath. Today the second squad went in first, and the third squad immediately washed their hair.[60] It felt really good! Since my hair gets dirty easily, the water turned dark black. I was impressed by how black it got, even though it all came from me. Then we went into the bath, and it felt really good! When I scrubbed hard, lots of dirt came off. Ariga-sensei scrubbed our backs! In the evening we each received two rice cakes and enjoyed them. They were really, really delicious, and my cheeks were about to fall off, so I held them with my hands and kept them on.[61]

July 11, 1945

Today we had Third-Day classes. Ishida-sensei didn't come today because he had an upset stomach, so we had self-study. A boy said, "Ishida-sensei's house is right near the Takamiya Bridge, so we can go there." I was surprised and asked, "Is that true?" and he said, "It's true!" I was really surprised. I took a nap in the afternoon.

July 12, 1945

It happened right during lunch today. Saitō-sensei made an announcement. "During lunch a conscription notice came for Ishida-sensei. He'll leave on

58. Yō-chan was Iwamaru-sensei's oldest daughter.
59. Mount Iōyama (elev. 939 meters) is southeast of Fukumitsu.
60. Nakane and her classmates were now formed into "squads" (J. *han*).
61. Japanese believe that when one eats something delicious, one's cheeks feel as though they are about to fall off.

August 11 and join the 136th Infantry Regiment." When we heard this announcement, no one said a word. I thought to myself, "Well, so Sensei is going off. Please be strong and go off in good spirits." I took a nap that afternoon, and when I got up, I was really sleepy.

July 13, 1945

Today the morning assembly started late, so classes began in the second period. We had Fourth-Day classes. During calligraphy class we did the section called "Visiting Yasukuni Shrine." It was very difficult, but when I did the best I could do, it wasn't that bad. When we were taking naps in the afternoon, Koizumi's mother came for a visit. Then we received postcards and glucose.[62] It was really delicious.

July 14, 1945

Today it rained again. We had Fifth-Day classes. When the morning assembly ended, all of us from Maeda Dorm went immediately to Yamashita Dorm to weigh ourselves. Unfortunately, I've lost weight. I thought, I'll make it up. I went back to the dorm and tidied up. Everything got really neat, and I felt good. I napped in the afternoon. The nap felt good. In the evening there was one rice cake in each of our rice bowls, and it was really, really delicious. With just a bit more, my cheeks would have fallen off. Today was really fun! Beginning today they read "The Hero Next Door" to us.

July 15, 1945

Today was a day off. Kobayashi's foot was sore, so she stayed in the dorm. In the morning I spent all my time tidying up and writing in my diary. Lunch was spotted kidney beans mixed with rice. It was really, really delicious.

July 16, 1945

First period today was Japanese, and it was Ishida-sensei. After we did "The Imperial Standard," we moved to "A Barracks Letter." Ishida-sensei had been in the army, so he really understood these subjects. We learned that life in the army is very busy. Because there was a teachers' meeting in the afternoon, we stayed at the girls' school. I had nothing to do, so I arranged my crayons and borrowed a deck of playing cards and played. In the evening after we went back to Maeda Dorm, I asked Motegi-sensei to trim my nails.

---

62. The children were given glucose (J. *budōtō*) as a dietary supplement.

July 17, 1945

Today was the day to send off Maeda-sensei. In the morning we had the send-off ceremony in the No. 2 classroom. We prayed for his success in war and shouted banzai three times. After that, we opened our umbrellas and accompanied him to the station. While we waited for the train, we sang war songs with great enthusiasm. Miyaji-sensei imitated university students and clapped his hands "Ta-ta-ta."[63] Then the train carrying Maeda-sensei disappeared from sight, leaving puffs of smoke floating in the air.

July 18, 1945

Today during local history class Ishida-sensei took the fourth graders to his house, which is right next to the Takamiya Bridge. I was really embarrassed when we went into his house, but because everyone else was doing it, I went in together with the group. It was a really big and beautiful house. We played "Riddle, riddle" for some time. Then after a little while, Ishida-sensei told us three scary stories. After a little while longer, Ishida-sensei's wife appeared, and we each got two thin rice crackers and some soybean flour poured onto our palms. The rice crackers were red and green. When we ate the soybean flour, a lot of it ended up around our mouths. Ishida-sensei's wife was shorter than I thought she would be, but she was really, really pretty. After we got back, we thought that lunch would be starting soon, so we hurried and had our dishes put out. Today our stomachs really got full.

July 19, 1945

Today we made rice cakes for Ishida-sensei's celebration and had self-study in the morning. Tanaka and I together made things to give to Ishida-sensei. We'll give him a charm, two dolls, and a little of the "Ishida-sensei Diary" that I wrote. In the afternoon we had a send-off ceremony. Tokorozawa represented us and read things that were written on a piece of paper. I felt that today was far sadder than the send-offs I went to when I was in school in Tokyo, but I had happy feelings when I thought about Ishida-sensei's going to war for the sake of the country. Then we had a prayer service in front of the shrine just before dinner. We had dinner right away after that. When we went to the classroom, there were two delicious rice cakes, fish, rice, and a banana sword on everyone's plates. Today we had meals with different guests, and they were all really, really delicious. Ishida-sensei came at about 8:30 p.m. and told us stories about his boyhood. (A very interesting diary ["Ishida-sensei's Diary"]).

---

63. Miyaji-sensei mimicked the rhythmic hand and arm movements of college cheerleaders, who were always male. He is the head of Yamashita Dorm.

July 20, 1945

Today's Japanese class with Ishida-sensei was the last one! We spent a lot of time exploring in detail "A Barracks Letter." Sensei knew this was the last class and taught with lots of enthusiasm. We also knew this was the last one, and we studied as hard as we could. In the afternoon we had free time, so Koizumi, Tanaka, and I took naps in the dorm. When it was time to get up, Umetani woke us, but I was really sleepy and had a hard time getting up.

July 21, 1945

Today we were seeing off Ishida-sensei, so we got up early. We gathered at school and then went right away to the train station. It was drizzling, but we didn't open our umbrellas and went on to the station singing war songs we had learned from Ishida-sensei. There was still time until the train came, so we sang war songs while we waited. When we finished a song, we shouted, "Ishida-sensei banzai! Banzai! Banzai!" Those voices! Strong voices! Everyone sang as loudly as they could. After a short time the train arrived. Sensei boarded it, and we shouted banzai and kept clapping hard until he disappeared from sight. It felt as though the train Ishida-sensei boarded left faster than most.

July 22, 1945

Today Ishida-sensei wasn't there, so it felt lonely. Another sensei will come. In the morning the weather was good, so we marched for about two hours. It was really hot. We went along the road where we moved wood, and it turned along the way, and we passed the Higashihiro Bridge and came back. Because we haven't marched recently, even this short hike somehow seemed long. For lunch we had miso soup with herring in it. It was really delicious.

July 23, 1945

Today for breakfast we had rice gruel with one rice cake in it. It was really delicious. We were going to have First-Day studies with Motegi-sensei. Ariga-sensei was sick and sleeping in Maeda Dorm. I felt so sorry for her. Now Japanese class will be with Motegi-sensei, and local history with Katō-sensei. Even though it was a special Japanese class, Motegi-sensei did not show up, so we quietly studied by ourselves. In the afternoon we welcomed the spirits of the dead, and people from both the Fukumitsu and Akamatsu schools joined in. It was a truly sad affair. Uehara's mother came for a visit, and she seemed really happy.

July 24, 1945

Today we had Second-Day classes. Then we studied Japanese with Motegi-sensei for the first time. We did "Chapter 15: Summer." "Summer" was a poem, and I copied it neatly into my notebook. I copied it as carefully as I could and showed it to Sensei. In the evening I went for medical treatment with Hagino, Kuniyuki, Sakomizu, Sugamura, Kobayashi, and Yaotani. When we came back, it was pitch black, and I had the feeling a ghost might appear. Then each of us had two of the white cakes that Uehara's mother brought, and they were really, really sweet and delicious.

July 25, 1945

This morning we went to the Oyabe River to gather grass for burning. The girls cut grass on the other side of the bridge and the boys on this side. Today we cut cranesbill grass. After we had been cutting for a while, Hori-sensei said, "Girls, it's OK to eat the strawberries," and I had a really delicious-looking strawberry that Tanaka gave me. It was really, really delicious. When we had gone a ways, there was no road, so we went along the lower part until we arrived at the Higashihiro Bridge where the boys were. Then we left them and walked a little more, then rested. Then we cut *hohozuki*. I wasn't able to cut any, so I got some from Tanaka. We went back and had a meal right away. Because my stomach was empty, everything was delicious. In the afternoon we rested in our respective dorms.

July 26, 1945 (Thurs.)

Today Princess Kaya visited Fukumitsu Girls High School.[64] Because of her visit, we tried not to leave the classrooms. We didn't go back to the dorm in the afternoon but stayed at school. We had popped rice at about 3:00 p.m., and it was really, really delicious. Was I able to be a "good child" all day today? Did I do anything bad? I must become an even better "good child." When it was time to go to bed in the evening, it was unbearably hot, and I couldn't get to sleep until 10:00 p.m.

July 27, 1945 (Fri.)

Today we sketched people in the drawing period. I sketched Maeno, and she sketched me. I drew as well as I could, but my sketch didn't look at all like Maeno.

---

64. At this time there was a training exercise for the Kanazawa Ninth Division at Tatenogahara, and Princess Kaya had come to the area to review the troops.

When the third period was over, I went right back to the dorm and washed my hair. My hair really gets dirty easily, so the water turned black! Afterward I really felt refreshed, and it felt good. In the afternoon we took a bath. We started with the fifth graders and entered the bath in order of smallness. I went in with Motegi-sensei, and it really felt good.

July 29, 1945 (Sun.)

Today the entire school went outside and had a kind of spiritual training. At first we did calisthenics and then played with balls. We divided into fifth- and sixth-grade girls, fifth- and sixth-grade boys, and second-, third-, and fourth-grade girls and boys. At first we were divided into the reds and whites, and the reds won twice. Because I was on the whites, it was really a shame. Then the girls played alone but still were divided into reds and whites. This time, I thought, let's win, and when we played, my team won twice. I was very, very happy! Then we did the kind of sumo wrestling we did the other day. While we were doing this, a siren began to wail "u-u-u-," sounding an air-raid warning, and so we quickly went into our classrooms and put on our air-raid clothing. Then we had class from the third period. In the fourth period we went to see an exhibition.

July 30, 1945 (Mon.)

Today was a rest day, and it was a perfectly clear Japanese day. In the morning we washed our clothes, and I washed my underwear, my wiping cloth, and socks. Everything got really clean, and I felt refreshed. Then we aired our futons. Because I went first, I stood at the top of the stairs and was given the futons, which I passed down to the teachers. At the time I felt I was going to drop them. For lunch we had miso soup with sardines in it. In the afternoon we brought in the futons, and I wrote in my diary. In the evening when we went to bed our futons were warm and really fluffy. It seemed a shame to be sleeping on top of warm and fluffy futon.

July 31, 1945

Today is the end of July. I wondered whether I was able to be a "good child" in July. In August I want to be a better, better child and make Sensei happy.[65] We had First-Day classes. In Japanese class, we studied "Chapter 17: The Brown Cicada." Somehow it seemed like science and was really interesting. In the afternoon we took a bath and went in with the no. 3 squad. Because I was the first one in, the

---

65. Nakane's teacher crossed out "sensei" and wrote in "father and mother."

water was really clean. Usually Sakomizu and Kobayashi say, "It's hot! it's hot!" but today they said it was perfect. Ariga-sensei said, "Today I made it lukewarm for Sakomizu and Kobayashi," and laughed.

August 1, 1945

Starting today it's August. This month I'll be more of a "good child" than I was last month. During the morning assembly we had a ceremony to appoint squad leaders. This time I'm becoming a squad leader. Because of this, I want all the more to be a "good child" and to act like a squad leader. Today we just had first-period classes and then carried firewood from Yamashita Dorm to the girls' school. It was really hot, but when I thought, "It's for us," I completely forgot it was hot, and my feet moved quickly. In the afternoon we had a snack of popped rice. It was really delicious.

August 2, 1945

Today we had Third-Day classes. In the morning the teachers had something to do, so we had self-study. In the afternoon Maeda Dorm went swimming in the Oyabe River. When we got there, the third-section sixth graders were already swimming. We swam with one layer of pants on. Before we went into the water, we did calisthenics and then went in. I was sorry, but I couldn't swim. Motegi-sensei taught me how to swim, but I just couldn't do it. All the fifth-grade girls could swim. Among the fourth-grade girls, only Tayaka and Koizumi could swim. I don't want to be beaten by everyone else, so I'll soon learn to swim.

August 3, 1945

Today we had Fourth-Day classes in the morning. In sewing class I sewed a desk cloth, but I didn't have a piece of cloth, so Ariga-sensei gave me one. First I sewed an edge, and then I sewed on a pattern I liked. In the afternoon everyone swam in the Oyabe River in front of Yoshinami Dorm.[66] I was finally able to swim with a face mask. I was very happy, and I could feel my heart beating. We went back to the dorm and had really, really delicious popped rice. Today was really fun.

August 4, 1945

Beginning today and through the tenth, there will be a week of special drills, and we'll have to take part in different drills. Today we spent the morning swim-

66. Yoshinami Dorm was the residence of Yoshinami Hikosaku, the principal of To-nami Middle School, and where the no. 2 group of sixth graders lived.

ming in the same place as yesterday. I've gotten really good at wearing a face mask and was very happy. Then after a while we watched students from the third section — Nie, Miki, and the Mukigasa siblings — swim the breaststroke. They swam smoothly in a circle in the middle of the river. I was completely surprised at how much I was able to swim. The Mukigasas can really swim. We took a nap in the afternoon. Today my shoulder got really sunburned and hurt.

August 5, 1945

This morning we got up at 4:00 a.m. and met at the shrine before going off on a march. We went to the bridge on the way to Ango Temple.[67] It felt really good to breathe in chestfuls of morning air that was so fresh. The rice plants in the paddy fields were being blown about by the wind and looked like green waves. As we marched, there were mountains on each side, tall peaks in the distance, and clouds that looked like cotton floating in the sky. The wind was cool, and the river made a murmuring sound as it passed through the silent mountains. In no time, we reached the bridge. We rested for ten minutes and then marched back.

August 6, 1945

Today we swam in the morning. We swam upstream from the Fukumitsu Bridge, which was a really neat place to swim. The bottom there was sand, and it was really easy to swim. After we swam for some time, students from the Yoshie Citizens School arrived, and we went back.[68] Then we had popped rice, which was really delicious. In the afternoon we took a nap. When I got up, I found I was drenched in perspiration and had drooled, so Tanaka laughed at me. In the evening someone from the train station came to the Maeda house and told us interesting stories. We listened, holding our fans in front of us and looking up. Then we were given three biscuits.

August 7, 1945

Today was a wonderful Seventh-Night Festival. Because here we're one month behind, it was held today.[69] We expected to swim in the morning, but the fourth and fifth graders from Yamashita Dorm were moving to Nishio Dorm, so I wrote

---

67. The Angoji is a temple of the Shingon sect located east of Fukumitsu.

68. Yoshie Citizens' School was a local school located on the southeastern edge of Fukumitsu.

69. Rural folk still used the old lunar calendar in which everything occurred approximately one month later than the Gregorian calendar adopted on January 1, 1873.

in my diary and played cards at school.[70] We had really delicious food for lunch. We had eggplant fried with miso and sugar, mashed cucumbers, miso soup with eggplant in it, and sweet potato rice. When we were about to leave, our principal came along with a knapsack on his back.[71] He said, "You're all well, aren't you?" Then we tidied up our belongings in the dorm. We went to the girls' school at about 2:30 p.m. and had a delicious snack. We had sweet tea and potatoes — five potatoes. After some time we heard a talk by the principal and had dinner. Today was lots and lots of fun. *(You were able to write a lot, weren't you? Keep this up. Your pictures were very good. I liked them.)*

August 8, 1945

Today was Imperial Rescript Observance Day. When the morning assembly was over, we had an imperial rescript reading ceremony at the shrine. Saitō-sensei read the rescript. Then we wrote comfort letters in the classrooms and sent today's letters to soldiers in hospitals. I thought soldiers in hospitals must surely be bored, so I tried to write letters that would make them happy and wrote with all my might. I took a nap in the afternoon. It was really hot during nap time, and I couldn't get to sleep. Then we had popped rice at 3:00 p.m., and it was really delicious.

August 9, 1945

Today in the morning we helped a section of Yamashita Dorm move to Honda Dorm.[72] We moved the luggage of the second and third graders first. We carried Kawai's cloth bundle, which was very heavy, but because it was for our younger sisters and brothers, we used all our strength to carry it to Honda Dorm. We carried a lot and then rested. My throat was so dry, I drank hot tea, which was more delicious than I can say. After some time we had lunch. I was hungry, so it was really delicious. In the afternoon we took a bath and washed our hair, and it felt wonderful.

---

70. The owner of the hospital that served as Yamashita Dorm had gone off to war, but later he returned to the village and the hospital was reopening, so two new "dorms" had to be found. The "new" Nishio and Honda dorms were named for the Nishio and Honda families, who were in the dry goods business. Yoshinami, personal communication, June 4, 2004.

71. Fujimoto Manji was the principal of Tokyo Girls High School.

72. Honda Dorm housed the no. 2 group of fifth graders and second- and third-grade boys and girls. Yoshinami, personal communication, June 4, 2004.

August 10, 1945

Today I spent the morning writing in my diary at school because Makoto at the Maeda house was sick. Because I was able to write entries in my diary up through yesterday, I got tired, and when I put my head down on the desk, I fell asleep before I knew it and entered a dream country. The dream went like this: I was standing in the middle of a very, very wide field. There was a god with a white beard who said, "Hello! Mihō-chan, how old are you?" When I answered, "I'm eleven," he asked, "Have you ever told a lie?" "Yes," I answered. Then the god said, "From now on if you tell a lie, you'll fall into a huge hole deep in the forest," and then he disappeared. Right at that moment, Tanaka said, "It's lunchtime!" and waked me, and I opened my eyes. I thought about the dream I had just had, and from now on I must not tell lies. If I do, I thought, it'll turn out just like my dream. In the afternoon the fourth graders went to the barbershop. We went in order of smallness, but not to the one we usually go to but one near Funaoka Dormitory.[73] Then in the evening we had popped rice, which was really delicious. In the evening before we went to sleep the Maedas gave us ice, and it was served together with strawberry-red gelatin water. It was really, really delicious.

August 11, 1945

Today we worked in the morning. The second-section sixth graders worked with the fourth and fifth graders in preparing the potatoes. The fourth graders sorted potatoes in classroom No. 2. Lots of potatoes were infested with maggots. At first I found it disgusting, but when I thought, "If I can't do this, I'm not a Japanese," there was nothing to it. After we finished, I wrote yesterday's diary entry. In the afternoon, we swam, which we had not done for a long time. We swam near Fukumitsu Bridge. At 3:00 p.m. we had a potato snack at school which was really, really delicious.

August 12, 1945

Today we had First-Day classes. In second period we went back to drawing people in our class. I finally finished mine, but the background color had become completely strange. I thought that rather than purple, the color of the walls would be good. In Japanese class we continued "Chapter 17: Cockroaches" and explored the subject in detail. The chapter described how it takes cockroaches two or three weeks after they are born to become parent bugs. We spent the afternoon

---

73. The Funaoka family had a dry goods business. Yoshinami, personal communication, June 4, 2004.

at school. Because I didn't have anything else to do, I drew pictures and played. In the evening Ariga-sensei related how she roasted popped rice and made it so delicious. It was very good.

August 13, 1945

Today we had Second-Day classes in the morning. We had a test in Japanese class. I got a ten for dictation, a six for short composition, and a six for my use of *kana*.[74] I completely forgot the characters for "hard" and "skin," and there were others I was unsure of. In the afternoon we went swimming. At first we swam at a place near the Fukumitsu Bridge, and then, in front of Yoshinami Dorm. The water was really, really warm. Thinking that it'll be fall soon, we swam to our heart's content. While doing that, I slipped off some rocks.

August 14, 1945

This morning we had Third-Day classes. We had a test in math class — division and multiplication. We also heard about Katō-sensei's hometown for the first time. He asked where we had explored and then told us about the remains of a castle on the road we had taken when we moved firewood.[75] It was really, really interesting. I spent the whole afternoon at school. Because I had nothing to do, I went to the playing field and watched soldiers training. They are brave people. I watched them practice holding their guns, shouting and thrusting.

August 15, 1945

Today was the All Souls Festival. It was held today because everything is one month late here. This morning they weighed us. They borrowed the National Citizens School's scales. Unfortunately I've lost weight. Then we had self-study, and I wrote in my diary and did other things, and then because I was sleepy, I slept. A cool breeze blew through the classroom window, and it felt really good. For lunch we had broiled eggplant and cucumbers and tomatoes. It was really, really delicious. In the afternoon we had popped rice for a snack. Then we didn't go back to the dorm but went to school. At dinnertime we had three bean-covered rice cakes and potatoes. It was very, very delicious, and my stomach got full. *("Got full" means your stomach filled up.)*

---

74. The Japanese language has two phonetic syllabaries — *hiragana* and *katakana* — and here *kana* refers to the latter.
75. This must be Fukumitsu Castle, which warriors occupied in the twelfth century.

August 16, 1945

Today at breakfast we heard very sad news from Miyaji-sensei. At long last, Japan was forced to surrender unconditionally to the Soviet–American–British alliance. It was because of the atomic bomb. On August 15, His Majesty said, "We have endured hardships and sadness, but we have been defeated by that atomic bomb, and all Japanese could be injured and killed. It is too pitiful for even one of my dear subjects to be killed. I do not care what happens to me." We heard that he then took off the white gloves he was wearing and began to cry out loud. We cried out loud too. Watch out, you terrible Americans and British! I will be sure to seek revenge. I thought to myself, I must be more responsible than I have been.

August 17, 1945

Today we had the day off. In the morning I went back to my dormitory to do my laundry, tidy up my belongings, and write in my diary. I tidied up, did my laundry, and wrote in my diary. When I was going through my belongings, I found the crayons I had lost. I was so happy. Then I did my laundry. My heart feels so clean when there are no dirty clothes piled up. I took a nap this afternoon. It felt wonderful! When I woke up, the Maedas had gotten some ice from their family. I ate it with some blue water. I also had one and a half cookies that Hakusui's family sent. I had some glucose, too. It was all very delicious.

Glossary

The items in this glossary appear as they are presented in the translation. Those that are well known and appear in *Webster's Collegiate Dictionary*, 11th ed., such as futon, or are untranslatable (*furoshiki*, for example, would make no sense as "wrapping kerchief") remain in Japanese.

All Souls Festival: Obon or Urabon in Japanese, a festival that takes place in mid-July or August and welcomes the souls of ancestors back to their home villages.

Amida Buddha: The major deity of the Pure Land sect of Buddhism.

ayu: A kind of sweetfish (*Plecoglossus altivelis*) found in Japanese rivers and streams that is a summer delicacy and usually grilled and eaten whole.

bamboo shoot rice: A literal translation of *takenoko gohan*, a spring dish in which sliced bamboo shoots and diced chicken are cooked together with rice.

bancha: The green tea that Japanese customarily drink during the day. It is made from older, coarser tea leaves.

banzai: "Ten thousand years," the Japanese equivalent of "hurrah," which is shouted on celebratory occasions.

barley rice: A literal translation of *mugihan*, rice mixed and cooked with barley.

barn swallow: *Tsubame* (*Hirundo rustica*).

body-crashing: A literal translation of *tai-atari*, the tactic used by Japanese aircraft during World War II on what were called "special-attack" missions.

bog rhubarb: *Fuki* (*Petasites japonicus*), Japanese butterbur, usually translated as "bog rhubarb." It is fried, pickled, or candied.

Boys' Festival: A festival of ancient origins and one of the five major national festivals. It is held on May 5.

bracken fern: *Warabi* (*Pteridium aquilium*, var. *latiusculum*).

brown cicada: *Aburazemi* (*Graptopsaltria nigrofuscata*).

bucket ball: The wartime version of *tamaire*, a game still played by Japanese youngsters in which small balls are thrown into an elevated container.

candied persimmons: *Tarugaki*, persimmons that have been soaked in saké.

-chan: A suffix indicating familiarity and endearment. Children, for example, often are called by shortened versions of their given names plus *chan*. Thus "Mihōko" becomes "Hō-chan."

chestnut squash: *Kurikabocha* (*Cucurbita maxima*).

Chinese lantern plant: *Hōzuki* (*Physalis alkekengi*).

chive: *Asatsuki* (*Allium schoenoprasum*, var. *foliosum*).

comfort women: Women and girls forced into sexual slavery by the Japanese military. They were called "comfort women" (J. *ianfu*), and most were Korean.

cranesbill grass: *Gennoshōko* (*Geranium nepalense*, var. *thunbergii*).

cuckoo: *Hototogisu* (*Cuculus poliocephalus*).

dojō: A freshwater loach (*Misgurnus anguillicaudata*), or small eel.

dough cake: *Karintō,* a kind of cookie made of dough and deep-fried.

dropwort: A type of parsley (*Oenanthe javanica*) that is used in salads and casseroles.

Ebisu: The Japanese god of wealth.

eulalia: A type of grass (*Miscanthus sinensis*), called *susuki* in Japanese, which produces beautiful long spikes.

fiddlehead fern: *Zenmai* (*Osmunda regalis*).

field horsetail: *Sugima,* field horsetail shoots, which are blanched and used in salads.

flowering fern: *Zenmai* (*Osmunda regalis*).

furoshiki: A type of kerchief that is used to carry things. After the object being wrapped is placed in the center of the kerchief, its four corners are brought together and knotted.

futon: A Japanese-style comforter. There are two types: a *shikibuton* is spread on the floor like a mattress, and a *kakebuton* is used as a blanket.

geta: Wooden clogs.

gomoku rice: Literally, "five-things rice," a dish consisting of rice, diced chicken, julienned vegetables, and soy sauce.

gyokusai: "Shattered jewel," a word taken from a sixth-century Chinese classic that the wartime government used to describe the collective deaths of Japanese servicemen.

habu: A poisonous snake found in Okinawa.

Hachiman: A Shinto deity commonly regarded as the god of war and the protector of local communities. Nearly every neighborhood has a shrine dedicated to this god.

Harvest Festival: Niinamesai, a festival of some antiquity that offers the bounty of the new harvest to the gods. It takes place on November 23.

herring roe: *Kazunoko,* a delicacy and staple in the food prepared for New Year's. It is either salted or dried and has to be soaked in water for several days before it is eaten, usually with a dipping sauce made from broth and soy sauce.

hibachi: A charcoal-burning brazier used in Japanese houses during the winter.

inkan: A seal or chop used in lieu of a signature.

janken: A game in which players simulate with one hand a scissors, rock, or paper: scissors cut paper, paper covers a rock, and a rock resists scissors, and so forth.

jinrikisha: A single-seat pedicab-like vehicle pulled by one man.

kamaboko: A type of steamed fishcake that often is shaped like a long half cylinder.

kan (kanme): A unit of weight, approximately 8.3 pounds.

kanpan: A biscuit that was widely distributed on the home front and in war zones.

kendo: "The way of the sword," a modern form of fencing that was taught in Japanese primary schools from 1939 to 1945.

kintoki: A dish in which vegetables—beans or sweet potatoes—are cooked in sugar.

Kitano Shrine: Built in Kyoto in 947 to placate the spirit of Sugawara Michizane (845–903).

konbu: A kind of kelp (*Laminariaceae*) that is a staple in the Japanese diet. It is used to make stocks, added to soups and stews, or salted.

kōnago: A type of fish.

konnyaku: A tuber (*Amorphophallus rivieri,* var. *konjac*) that is used to make a gelatinous substance with the consistency of tofu but more translucent. It is sliced into noodle-thin pieces and added to one-pot dishes like sukiyaki and *oden.*

leg warmer: *Kotatsu*, a leg warmer consisting of a table over which a thin comforter is draped. One sits with one's legs under the table and the comforter.

lotus root: *Renkon*, a vegetable (*Nelumbo nucifera*) that is used in salads, simmered dishes, and tempura.

mamemeshi: Literally, "beans rice," a dish in which soybeans or green peas are cooked together with rice.

manjū: A steamed bun made with either wheat or rice flour and filled with sweet bean paste or pork.

matsutake: A wild mushroom (*Armillaria matsudake*) gathered in the fall that has a subtle, woodsy taste and is used in rice dishes and clear soups.

matsutake rice: A rice dish in which slices of *matsutake* mushroom are added to the rice in the last stage of cooking.

mazetakimi rice: Literally, "mixed and cooked with rice," a dish in which cooked ingredients are added to the rice as it is steaming.

meisen: A durable and inexpensive silk fabric used to make kimono for everyday wear. *Meisen* kimono were popular before the war.

miscanthus grass: *Kaya*, a grass used to thatch roofs.

miso: A thick paste made by mixing cooked and mashed soybeans, rice or barley, salt, and water and letting the mixture ferment. It is used to make miso soup, to flavor sauces, and to dress seafood and vegetables.

miso soup: A soup made with miso and stock that is a fixture in the Japanese diet and is traditionally served at breakfast, lunch, and dinner.

misosazai: Winter wren (*Troglodytes troglodytes*).

mizuhiki: Ceremonial cords, usually red but also black and white, used to wrap gifts.

mō: One-tenth of one *rin*.

monme: A unit of weight, approximately 0.132 ounces.

monpe: A type of cotton trousers traditionally worn by farm women. During the war, the government encouraged all women to wear them.

mugwort: *Yomogi* (*Artemisia princeps*), which is prepared in several different ways: blanched, served in soups, or added to rice cakes.

mugwort rice cake: A rice cake made with mugwort for special occasions, usually in the spring. It is called *kusamochi* in Japanese.

Namu amida butsu: A famous chant of the Pure Land sect of Buddhism, imploring the Amida Buddha to grant salvation to the chanter.

Namu myōhō rengekyō: "Glory to the Sutra of the Supreme Law," the most famous chant of the Nichiren sect of Buddhism.

nattō: Fermented soybeans, a staple in eastern Japan and typically eaten for breakfast.

nori: Several types of seaweed belonging to the *Porphyra* genus of marine algae. It is cultivated in inlets and estuaries, harvested in December and January, and then dried. After being toasted slightly, it is used to make sushi and *onigiri* or dipped in soy sauce and eaten with rice.

obi: The sash worn with a kimono.

okara: The residue left after soybeans are cooked, strained, and pressed into blocks of tofu. It is combined with julienned green onions and carrots to make a delicious and nutritious side dish.

omiyage: Gifts that travelers bring back for those who stay behind or for their hosts.

onigiri: Cooked rice shaped into triangles or balls and lightly salted. It is a staple in homemade box lunches.

pomelo: A type of citrus fruit (*zamboa*) known as *zabon* in Japanese and native to Asia.

popped beans: *Irimame*, or "popped beans," peas, or soybeans that have been fried and lightly salted. They are served as a snack.

popped rice: *Irigome*, or "popped rice," rice prepared in the same way as popped beans.

pumpkin squash: *Kabocha* (*Cucurbita moschata*), which is often fried or added to stews.

red bean: Azuki (*Vigna angularis*) bean, a staple in Japanese cooking.

red bean rice: *Sekihan*, literally, "red rice," a dish made of rice and red beans that is served on special occasions.

rice cake: A rice cake, *mochi* in Japanese, made from glutinous rice that has been steamed, pounded to the consistency of a sticky paste, and formed into little cakes, which usually are circular or flat.

rice gruel: *Zōsui*, a hearty gruel made from cooked rice and stock, to which meat, fowl, or vegetables are added.

rice porridge: *Okayu*, or *kayu*, a porridge made by simmering uncooked rice in an uncovered pot for several hours.

rin: One-thousandth of one yen.

ryokan: A traditional Japanese inn.

samisen: A three-stringed lute that reached Japan from China via the Ryukyu Islands in the early modern period and quickly became the musical instrument of choice in the pleasure quarters.

sanma: A Pacific saury (*Cololabis saira*), a long thin fish that appears in Japanese markets in the fall.

sen: One-hundredth of one yen.

senbei: Light, waferlike crackers made from either rice or wheat flour.

sencha: A high-quality green tea that is typically served to guests.

sensei: A title meaning "teacher," used to refer to anyone in a position of authority, such as a school principal, doctor, or dentist, or any older person worthy of respect.

Seventh Night Festival: Tanabata matsuri, one of the five major Japanese festivals. Although it originated in a Chinese folk legend about two stars—the Weaver and the Cowherd—that were lovers but could meet only once a year, this myth was thoroughly naturalized, as the festival's associations with Shinto purification rites reveals. It is held on either July 7 or August 7, depending on whether the Gregorian or lunar calendar is followed.

shakuhachi: A bamboo flute with five finger holes that is important to both traditional and modern Japanese music and classical as well as folk music.

shō: A unit of volume equivalent to two quarts or a half gallon.

short-necked clam: A type of clam (J. *asari* [*Tapes* (*Amygdalum*) *philippinarum*]) harvested in Tokyo Bay and typically used in soups.

soba: A thin, spaghetti-like noodle made from buckwheat flour that is eaten cold with a dipping sauce in the summer and hot in a soup with various garnishes during the rest of the year.

stomach warmer: A knitted scarf, usually wool, for covering one's midsection and called a *haramaki* in Japanese.

stone parsley: A type of parsley (*Crytotaenia japonica*), also known as home wort.

subena: A cabbage-like green vegetable.

suiton: A type of flour dumpling that is a staple in wheat-producing areas in Japan and typically served in a soup.

sumo: A traditional form of Japanese wrestling that dates from ancient times and is a popular spectator sport.

sweet potato: *Satsumaimo* (*Ipomoea batatas* [*Convolvulaceae*]), a type of sweet potato brought to Japan by either the Spanish in the 1500s or the Chinese through the Ryukyu Islands in the 1800s. It has become a staple in the Japanese diet and was especially important as a substitute for rice during World War II.

sweet potato paste: A type of paste (J. *an*) made from sweet potatoes that is used to coat or fill rice cakes.

sweet saké: *Amazake*, translated here as "sweet saké," is made by mixing with cooked rice the mold used to make saké and simmering it from twelve to twenty-four hours. Sugar and ginger are added before it is served.

tabi: Japanese cotton fabric socks, with a separate space for the big toe to enable them to be worn with thonged sandals.

taro: *Satoimo* (*Colocasia antiquorum*), a kind of sweet potato.

tatami: Mats made of straw and rush and edged with a cloth border that are used in traditional Japanese rooms. Tatami vary in size from region to region but are generally three feet wide and six feet long. They are turned periodically and are replaced at longer intervals. When new or freshly turned, tatami have a fresh, grassy smell that Japanese associate with cleanliness.

tempura: A dish using a method of frying introduced by the Portuguese in the sixteenth century. Typically, seafood and vegetables are dipped in a batter, fried, and served with either just salt or a dipping broth to which grated radish is added.

tenmangaki: Calligraphic inscriptions that Japanese children write on New Year's Day and offer at Tenmangu shrines, where the god of calligraphy, Sugawara Michizane, is enshrined.

to: A unit of volume, just short of five gallons.

tofu: A protein-rich food made from soybeans. There are several varieties, among which are "silken tofu," which has the consistency of custard, and "cotton tofu," which is stiffer.

tonkatsu: A breaded and fried cutlet, usually pork but sometimes chicken.

torii: The gate or archway that marks the entrance to Shinto shrines.

tororo konbu: A type of *konbu* (*Kjellmaniella aniella*), or sea tangle.

trefoil: *Mitsuba* (*Crytotaenia*), a member of the parsley family. It has a delicate flavor and is used in soups, Japanese egg custard, and one-pot casseroles.

tsukudani: A type of preserve made by slowly simmering fish, meat, or any other edible creature in soy sauce, sugar, and *mirin*, a sweet saké used in cooking. *Tsukudani* is eaten as a condiment, usually with hot rice.

udon: A soft, white, linguine-like noodle made with wheat flour and usually served in a soup.

unagi: A freshwater eel (*Anguilla japonica*) that is typically basted with a sweet sauce and grilled. Japanese believe that one should eat protein-rich foods like eel when the summer heat is at its height.

unfiltered soy sauce: *Moromi*, which is used exclusively in cooking.

wakame: A kind of seaweed (*Undaria pinnitifida*) that is often added to soups or salads.

warahanshi: Literally, "wara paper," a local, handmade paper.

wheat gluten: *Fu,* which has the lightness and texture of very old and dry bread and is added to soups, cold noodle dishes, and one-pot casseroles.

wild rocamble: *Nobiru* (*Allium nipponicum*), a wild vegetable gathered and eaten in the spring.

wild vegetables: My translation of *sansai,* literally "mountain vegetables," the omnibus term for bog rhubarb (*fuki*), bracken (*warabi*), mugwort (*yomogi*), and fiddlehead ferns (*zenmai*) that are gathered and eaten in the spring.

yamaudo: A vegetable (*Aralia cordata*) that grows wild and is picked in the spring, boiled, and served with other wild vegetables such as bracken and flowering ferns.

yellowtail: *Buri,* Japanese amberjack (*Seriola quinqueradiata*), which appears in fish markets in the fall and winter and is usually eaten raw or grilled.

yen: The basic unit of modern Japanese currency.

zabuton: A thin cushion, typically about a square foot in size, used to kneel on. During the war it was used as a head covering during air raids.

zenzai: A thick soup made from red beans to which toasted rice cakes are sometimes added.

Bibliography

Akimoto Ritsuo. *Sensō to minshū: Taiheiyō sensōka no toshi seikatsu*. Tokyo: Gakuyō shobō, 1974.

Baerwald, Hans H. *The Purge of Japanese Leaders under the Occupation*. University of California Publications in Political Science 8. Berkeley: University of California Press, 1959.

Bix, Herbert P. *Hirohito and the Making of Modern Japan*. New York: HarperCollins, 2000.

Borton, Hugh. Review of *The Rising Sun: The Decline and Fall of the Japanese Empire, 1936–1945*, by John Toland. *American Historical Review* 77 (1972): 193.

Bunkers, Suzanne L., ed. *Diaries of Girls and Women: A Midwestern American Sampler*. Madison: University of Wisconsin Press, 2001.

Buruma, Ian. *Wages of Guilt: Memories of War in Germany and Japan*. New York: Farrar, Straus & Giroux, 1994.

Butler, Judith. "Performative Acts and Gender Constitution: An Essay in Phenomenology and Feminist Theory." In *Performing Theory and Theater*, edited by Ellen Case. Baltimore: Johns Hopkins University Press, 1990.

Butow, Robert. *Tojo and the Coming of War*. Princeton, NJ: Princeton University Press, 1961.

Carter, Cathryn. *Voix Feminists, Feminist Voices: Diaries in English by Women in Canada, 1753–1995, an Annotated Bibliography*. Ottawa: CRIAW/ICREF, 1997.

Carter, Kit C., and Robert Mueller, comps. *U.S. Army Air Forces in World War II: Combat Chronology, 1941–1945*. Washington, D.C.: Center for Air Force History, 1991.

Chang, Iris. *The Rape of Nanking: The Forgotten Holocaust of World War II*. New York: Basic Books, 1997.

Choi, Chungmoo. "women: colonization, war, and sex." A special issue of *positions* 5 (Spring 1997).

Coffman, Edward M. "The New American Military History." *Military Affairs* (January 1984): 1–5.

Cook, Haruko Taya, and Theodore F. Cook, comps. *Japan at War: An Oral History*. New York: New Press, 1992.

Coox, Alvin C. *The Anatomy of a Small War: The Soviet-Japan Struggle for Changkufeng/Khasa*, Contributions in Military History 13. Westport, CT: Greenwood Press, 1977.

———. *Nomonhan: Japan against Russia, 1939*. Stanford, CA: Stanford University Press, 1985.

———. Alvin C. "The Pacific War." In *The Twentieth Century*, vol. 6 of *The Cambridge History of Japan*, edited by Peter Duus. Cambridge: Cambridge University Press, 1988.

——. Alvin C. Review of *Japan's Imperial Conspiracy*, by David Bergamini, *American Historical Review* 77 (1972): 1169–1170.

——. *Year of the Tiger*. Philadelphia: Orient/West, 1964.

Culley, Margo, ed. *A Day at a Time: The Diary Literature of American Women from 1764 to the Present*. New York: Feminist Press at the City University of New York, 1985.

Daniels, Gordon. "The Great Tokyo Air Raid, 9–10 March 1945." In *Modern Japan: Aspects of History, Literature and Society*, edited by W. G. Beasley. Berkeley: University of California Press, 1975.

Daws, Gavin. *Prisoners of the Japanese: POWs of World War II in the Pacific*. New York: Morrow, 1994.

Dingman, Roger. *The Sinking of the Awa Maru and Japanese-American Relations, 1945–1995*. Annapolis, MD: Naval Institute Press, 1997.

Dower, John. *Embracing Defeat: Japan in the Wake of World War II*. New York: Norton/New Press, 1999.

——. *War without Mercy: Race and Power in the Pacific War*. New York: Pantheon Books, 1986.

Drea, Edward J. *In the Service of the Emperor: Essays on the Imperial Japanese Army*. Lincoln: University of Nebraska Press, 1998.

Dull, Paul S. *A Battle History of the Imperial Japanese Navy (1941–1945)*. Annapolis, MD: Naval Institute Press, 1978.

Duus, Peter. *The Abacus and the Sword: The Japanese Penetration of Korea, 1895–1910*. Berkeley: University of California Press, 1995.

Duus, Peter, Ramon Myers, and Mark Peattie, eds. *The Japanese Informal Empire in China, 1895–1937*. Princeton, NJ: Princeton University Press, 1995.

——, eds. *Japan's Wartime Empire, 1931–1945*. Princeton, NJ: Princeton University Press, 1996.

Eley, Geoffrey. Foreword to *The History of Everyday Life: Reconstructing Historical Experiences and Ways of Life*, edited by Alf Lüdtke and translated by William Templer. Princeton, NJ: Princeton University Press, 1995.

Fogel, Joshua, ed. *The Nanjing Massacre in History and Historiography*. Berkeley: University of California Press, 2000.

Foucault, Michel. "The Subject and Power," *Critical Inquiry* 8 (Summer 1982): 777–795.

Friend, Theodore. *The Blue-Eyed Enemy: Japan against the West in Java and Luzon, 1942–1945*. Princeton, NJ: Princeton University Press, 1988.

Gibney, Frank. *Five Gentlemen of Japan*. New York: Farrar, Straus & Young, 1953.

Gibney, Frank, ed., and Beth Carey, trans. *Sensō: The Japanese Remember the Pacific War*. Armonk, NY: Sharpe, 1995.

Gluck, Carol. "The Idea of Showa." *Daedalus* 119 (3): 1–26.

Goodman, Grant. "24 in '44: Filipino Students in Wartime Japan." Occasional Papers, Series 2, no. 4 (1985): 1–21.

Hakuō izokukai, comp. *Kumo nagaruru hate ni*. Tokyo: Nihon shuppan kyōdō kabushiki kaisha, 1953.

Harries, Meirion, and Susie Harries. *Soldiers of the Sun: The Rise and Fall of the Imperial Japanese Army*. New York: Random House, 1991.

Harris, Sheldon H. *Factories of Death: Japanese Biological Warfare, 1932–1945.* Rev. ed. New York: Routledge, 1994.

Hatano, Isoko, comp. *Mother and Son: The Wartime Correspondence of Isoko and Ichiro Hatano.* Boston: Houghton Mifflin, 1962.

Havens, Thomas. *Valley of Darkness: The Japanese People and World War Two.* New York: Norton, 1978.

———. "Women and War in Japan, 1937–1945." *American Historical Review* 80 (1975): 913–934.

Hynes, Samuel. "Personal Narratives and Commentaries." In *War and Remembrance in the Twentieth Century,* edited by Jay Winter and Emmanuel Sivan. Cambridge: Cambridge University Press, 1999.

Ienaga, Saburō. *The Pacific War: World War II and the Japanese.* Translated by Frank Baldwin. New York: Pantheon Books, 1978.

Iriye, Akira. *Power and Culture: The Japanese American War, 1941–1945.* Cambridge, MA: Harvard University Press, 1980.

Ishikawa, Tatsuzō. *Soldiers Alive.* Translated by Zeljko Cipris. Honolulu: University of Hawai'i Press, 2003.

Itabashi Yasuo. "Itabashi Yasuo nikki." In *Ware tokkō ni shisu: Yokaren no ikō,* compiled by Orihara Noboru. Tokyo: Keizai ōraisha, 1973.

Johnson, B. F., with Mosaburo Hosoda and Yoshio Kusumi. *Japanese Food Management in World War II.* Stanford, CA: Stanford University Press, 1953.

Kaigo Muneomi, ed. *Nihon kyōkasho taikei.* Vol. 3. Tokyo: Kōdansha, 1962.

Karsten, Peter. "The 'New' American Military History: A Map of the Territory, Explored and Unexplored." *American Quarterly* 36 (1984): 389–418.

Kasza, Gregory J. *The State and the Mass Media in Japan 1918–1945.* Berkeley: University of California Press, 1988.

Keegan, John. *The Face of Battle.* New York: Penguin Books, 1978.

Kerr, E. Bartlett. *Flames over Tokyo: The U.S. Army Air Forces' Incendiary Campaign against Japan, 1944–1945.* New York: Donald I. Fine, 1999.

Kohn, Richard H. "The Social History of the American Soldier: A Review and Prospectus for Research." *American Historical Review* 86 (June 1981): 553–567.

Kratoska, Paul H. *The Japanese Occupation of Malaya, 1941–1945: A Social and Economic History.* Honolulu: University of Hawai'i Press, 1997.

Langford, Rachel, and Russell West. "Introduction: Diaries and Margins." In *Marginal Voices, Marginal Forms,* edited by Rachel Langford and Russell West. Atlanta: Rodopi B.V., 1999.

Lebra, Joyce. *Japanese-Trained Armies in Southeast Asia: Independence and Volunteer Forces in World War II.* New York: Columbia University Press, 1977.

———. *Jungle Alliance: Japan and the Indian National Army.* Singapore: Asia Pacific Press, 1970.

Linderman, Gerald F. *Embattled Courage: The Experience of Combat in the American Civil War.* New York: Free Press, 1989.

———. *The Mirror of War: American Society and the Spanish-American War.* Ann Arbor: University of Michigan Press, 1974.

———. *The World within War: America's Combat Experience in World War II.* New York: Free Press, 1997.

Lüdtke, Alf, ed. *The History of Everyday Life: Reconstructing Historical Experiences and Ways of Life*. Translated by William Templer. Princeton, NJ: Princeton University Press, 1995.

Mabuchi Fujio, comp. *Kaigun tokubetsu kōgekitai no isho*. Tokyo: KK Bestu serazu, 1971.

Maeda Shōko. "Joshi kinrō hōshi taiin no kiroku." In *Chiran tokubetsu kōgekitai*, compiled by Muranaga Tsutomu. Kagoshima: Yugensha japurau, 1998.

Manabe Ichirō. "Manabe Ichirō nikki." In *Shiryō de kataru gakudō sokai*, vol. 3. Vol. 5 of *Gakudō sokai no kiroku*, compiled by Zenkoku sokai gakudō renraku kyōgikai. Tokyo: Ōzorasha, 1994.

Matsumura, Janice. *More Than a Momentary Nightmare: The Yokohama Incident and Wartime Japan*. Ithaca, NY: Cornell East Asia Series, 1998.

Monbushō. *Kuni no ayumi*. Vol. 3. Tokyo: Monbushō, 1946.

Morley, James William. "Introduction: Choice and Consequence." In *Dilemmas of Growth in Prewar Japan*, edited by James William Morley. Princeton, NJ: Princeton University Press, 1971.

Naemura Shichirō, comp. *Mansei tokkōtaiin no isho*. Tokyo: Gendai hyōronsha, 1976.

Nakane Mihōko. *Sokai gakudō no nikki: Kyūsai no shojo ga toraeta shūsen zengo*. Tokyo: Chūō kōronsha, 1965.

Nomura Seiki. *Okinawa haihei nikki: Gyokusaisen ittōhei no shuki*. Tokyo: Taihei shuppansha, 1974.

Nornes, Abe Mark, and Yukio Fukushima, eds. *The Japan–America Film Wars: WWII Propaganda and Its Cultural Contexts*. Camberwell: Harwood Academic Publishers, 1994.

Norris, Margot, ed. *Writing War in the Twentieth Century*. Charlottesville: University of Virginia Press, 2000.

Ōda Makoto. *The Breaking Jewel*. Translated by Donald Keene. New York: Columbia University Press, 2003.

Ohnuki-Tierney, Emiko. *Kamikaze, Cherry Blossoms and Nationalisms: The Militarization of Aesthetics in Japanese History*. Chicago: University of Chicago Press, 2002.

Okamoto, Shumpei. Review of *Japan's Imperial Conspiracy*, by David Bergamini. *Journal of Asian Studies* 31 (1972): 416.

Peattie, Mark R. *Nanyō: The Rise and Fall of the Japanese in Micronesia, 1885–1945*. Honolulu: University of Hawai'i Press, 1988.

———. *Sunburst: The Rise of Japanese Naval Air Power, 1909–1941*. Annapolis, MD: Naval Institute Press, 2001.

Peattie, Mark R., and David Evans. *Kaigun: Strategy, Tactics, and Technology in the Imperial Japanese Navy, 1887–1941*. Annapolis, MD.: Naval Institute Press, 1997.

Peukert, Detlev. *Inside Nazi Germany: Conformity, Opposition, and Racism in Everyday Life*. Translated by Richard Deveson. New Haven, CT: Yale University Press, 1987.

Reischauer, Edwin O. "What Went Wrong?" In *Dilemmas of Growth in Prewar Japan*, edited by James William Morley. Princeton, NJ: Princeton University Press, 1971.

Rekishigaku kenkyūkai, comp. *Taiheiyō sensō-shi*. Vols. 4 and 5. Tokyo: Aoki shoten, 1971.

Sano, Peter. *A Thousand Days in Siberia: The Odyssey of a Japanese-American POW.* Lincoln: University of Nebraska Press, 1997.

Shillony, Ben-Ami. *Politics and Culture in Wartime Japan.* New York: Oxford University Press, 1981.

Soviak, Eugene, and Kamiyama Tamie, trans. *Diary of Darkness: The Wartime Diary of Kiyosawa Kiyoshi.* Princeton, NJ: Princeton University Press, 1999.

Steinberg, David Joel. *Philippine Collaboration in World War Two.* Manila: Solidaridad Publishing House, 1970.

Stephan, John. *Hawaii under the Rising Sun: Japan's Plans for Conquest after Pearl Harbor.* Honolulu: University of Hawai'i Press, 1984.

Storry, Richard. Review of *Japan's Imperial Conspiracy,* by David Bergamini. *Pacific Affairs* 45 (1972): 276.

Sugihara Kinryū. "Diary of First Lieutenant Sugihara Kinryū: Iwo Jima, January–February 1945." *Journal of Military History* 59 (1995): 97–133.

Takahashi Aiko. "Kaisen kara no nikki." In *Shōwa sensō bungaku zenshū,* edited by Agawa Hiroyuki et al. Tokyo: Shūeisha, 1972.

Tamura Tsunejirō. *Shinsan: Senchū sengo kyō no ichi shōmin nikki.* In *Sōsho-dōjidai ni ikiru,* vol. 4, compiled by Oka Mitsuo. Kyoto: Mineruva, 1980.

Tanaka, Yuki. *Hidden Horrors: Japanese War Crimes in World War II.* Boulder, CO: Westview Press, 1998.

Toland, John. *The Rising Sun: The Decline and Fall of the Japanese Empire, 1936–1945.* New York: Random House, 1970.

Truman, Harry S. *Years of Decisions.* Vol. 1 of *Memoirs.* Garden City, NY: Doubleday, 1955.

Tsurumi Shunsuke. *Senjiki Nihon no seishinshi.* Translated as *An Intellectual History of Wartime Japan, 1931–1945.* London: KPI Limited, 1986.

Victoria, Brian A. Daizen. *Zen at War.* New York: Weatherhill, 1997.

———. *Zen War Stories.* London: Routledge Curzon, 2003.

Wetzler, Peter. *Hirohito and War: Imperial Tradition and Military Decision Making in Prewar Japan.* Honolulu: University of Hawai'i Press, 1998.

White, Hayden. *Tropics of Discourse: Essays in Cultural Criticism.* Baltimore: Johns Hopkins University Press, 1978.

Yamanouchi, Midori, and Joseph L. Quinn, trans. *Listen to the Voices from the Sea: Kike Wadatsumi no Koe.* Scranton, PA: Scranton University Press, 2000.

Yang, Daqing. "Convergence or Divergence? Recent Historical Writings on the Rape of Nanking." *American Historical Review* 104 (June 1999): 842–865.

———. "A Sino-Japanese Controversy: The Nanjing Massacre in History." *Sino-Japanese Studies* 3 (November 1990): 14–35.

Yoneyama, Lisa. *Hiroshima Traces: Time, Space and the Dialectics of Memory.* Berkeley: University of California Press, 1999.

Yoshimi, Yoshiaki. *Comfort Women: Sexual Slavery in the Japanese Military during World War II.* Translated by Suzanne O'Brien. New York: Columbia University Press, 2000.

Yoshizawa Hisako. "Shūsen made." In *Shōwa sensō bungaku zenshū,* edited by Agawa Hiroyuki et al. Tokyo: Shūeisha, 1972.

Index

About the Author

Samuel Hideo Yamashita is the Henry E. Sheffield Professor of History at Pomona College. He received his Ph.D in Japanese history at the University of Michigan in 1981 and was a postdoctoral fellow at the Reischauer Institute of Japanese Studies at Harvard University and senior tutor in East Asian Studies there before he moved to Pomona in 1983. Among his publications is *Master Sorai's Responsals: An Annotated Translation of* Sorai sensei tōmonsho (University of Hawai'i Press, 1994). He has been collecting and translating wartime letters and diaries written by ordinary Japanese for more than a decade.

Production Notes for Yamashita | LEAVES FROM AN AUTUMN OF EMERGENCIES
Cover and interior design by April Leidig-Higgins
Text in Adobe Electra and display type in FontFont Seria Sans
Printing and binding by The Maple-Vail Book Manufacturing Group
Printed on 60# Sebago Eggshell, 420 ppi